SOME RISE
BY SIN

A FIVE DIRECTIONS PRESS BOOK

Some Rise by Sin

a novel

Courtney J. Hall

ISBN-13 978-0692371190
ISBN-10 0692371192

Published in the United States of America.

Cover photographs: Red-haired girl ©novelexpressions.com
Hampton Court © Anthony Baggett/Photos.com.

A Five Directions Press book

Book and cover design by Five Directions Press
Five Directions Press logo designed by Colleen Kelley

FIVE DIRECTIONS PRESS

CONTENTS

Chapter One

THE DARK STONE WALLS OF RIVERVIEW HOUSE, SIR CADE Badgley's family residence on the Strand, rose in front of his eyes. He lifted his face to the cool sting of rain that sputtered from the iron-gray sky. The months spent in prison at Castel Sant'Angelo seemed as if they'd happened to someone else, a long time ago.

He was home at last.

Three years and three months had passed since he'd set off for Rome at Her Majesty's command. The hours had gone quickly now and then. At other times, they dragged to the point where Cade was afraid to look at himself in the glass for fear he would see a white-haired old man looking back at him.

But after five days of bouncing from bow to stern and back again—thanks to a thunderstorm-ravaged journey across the Channel from Le Havre-de-Grâce—and another three atop the borrowed horse that took him from Brighton to London, Cade found the vile stench of the refuse-strewn streets as welcome to his nose as a bouquet of fresh-picked Michaelmas daisies to that of a farmer's daughter courted for the first time.

Cade allowed the exhausted horse to trudge into the courtyard. He slid from the saddle before tossing the reins to a young groom he'd never seen before.

"Welcome home, Lord Lunsford!" the groom exclaimed. Cade smiled a greeting, amused that the boy in his newness had mistaken him for Stephen, then entered the house and stopped inside the hall where he inhaled air fragrant with the sweet scent of familiarity.

Let Stephen have the earldom, the estates, and the responsibility that came with it all. Let him worry about keeping Easton's people fed, its walls strong. Cade thanked God almost every day for making him the younger son and giving him the sense that had sent him running from the misery of his father's home—without it, he never would have realized that he belonged in the city, serving Queen Mary and her court. His brother had done one wise thing in his entire life, and that was giving Cade free rein over Riverview House. Stephen rarely had need of it. He visited London only when duty forced him; he didn't have a sophisticated bone in his pudding-soft body. But Cade couldn't imagine life anywhere else.

"Welcome home, Lord Lunsford," someone repeated as Cade moved in the direction of his library.

Lord Lunsford again? How many new servants had Jefferson hired in his absence? And why did they all seem to think he was Stephen? He'd sent word ahead. They should know it was he.

But when he turned to the source of the voice and saw that Jefferson himself had addressed him, he stopped short. Jefferson would not mistake him for Stephen. Cade's belly twisted; his heart lurched in his chest.

No. I don't want to hear it.

He swallowed hard and forced a grin, trying to pretend that his steward hadn't addressed him by his brother's title.

"Jefferson, you old dog, 'tis good to see you!" he said with false joviality. "Your hair's gone gray and you've developed a squint, but other than that you haven't changed a bit! You have no idea what a comfort that is. Thank you for keeping the house standing while I was away. I trust the man I sent ahead reached you a few days ago? I would sell my soul for a hot meal. I've had naught but stale oat cakes and dried meat for nearly ten days now. And please tell me my chamber is prepared! I long to sleep in a bed that doesn't sway or smell of mildew. I must meet with Her Majesty tomorrow, and I would be refreshed."

The easy tumble of words did nothing to relax the strangely pinched expression on Jefferson's face. Of course, it wouldn't, not if what Cade suspected was true. "I apologize for the poor reception, my lord, but we expected you last week." The steward cleared his throat.

"Of course, Jefferson." Cade breathed with purpose, forcing the air into his nose before allowing it to pass slowly through his lips. He'd learned in Rome that this technique could calm even the most anxious man. *It worked in prison. Why isn't it working now?* "The weather was poor. Our departure was delayed several times," he added.

Jefferson nodded, his gaze fixed on a point over Cade's left shoulder.

Cade clenched his fists. The pain as his nails dug into the flesh of his palms cleared his mind. "Let's stop pretending, shall we, Jefferson? I'm not a stupid man. I'm not Viscount Lunsford unless my brother no longer holds the title. And the only way my brother loses the title is if he dies." One more deep breath, in then out. "How did Stephen die?"

Jefferson twisted his hands in front of him. He appeared almost as terrified as Cade felt—if that were possible.

"An epidemic, my lord," he confessed. "Not the sweat, but not unlike it." Jefferson crossed himself. "It spread through the entire country but hit Worcestershire particularly hard in the late winter. Viscount Lunsford succumbed. Your father the earl took ill but has survived. Not knowing you were on the Continent, he sent a messenger here a few weeks ago to inform you of the viscount's death. That's how we learned."

Cade struggled to absorb the words. *Epidemic. Viscount Lunsford succumbed.* In late winter? So Stephen had been dead for nearly three months, and his father had thought to inform him only a few weeks ago. Typical. He wondered why the old man had bothered to send word at all. He hadn't wanted Cade to be earl any more than Cade had wanted it himself.

I will be earl. The world in front of him grew hazy-edged. Blood roared in his ears. He reached out to support himself on the first thing he could find, which happened to be Jefferson.

"My lord. My lord!" The steward, who was several inches shorter and of much slighter build, barely remained upright as Cade gripped him for support. He shouted to someone passing by. "Wine for his lordship!"

Something stronger, Cade shouted from inside his head. *I'm my father's heir.* There wasn't enough wine in England to dull the brutal impact of *that* ugly truth.

A servant returned with a goblet of wine, and Cade tossed it back in one gulp.

His racing heart began to slow, his sight cleared, and the roar in his ears settled to a hum. He took a deep breath before a thought occurred to him that turned his blood to ice water.

"My cousin, Sir Hayden?" he asked Jefferson in a horrified whisper.

"Fine, my lord," Jefferson assured him. "He was not affected, thank God. However…"

The steward looked at the ground. "Lady Welles took ill and died. She was one of the first."

"Jesu." Cade let out a breath he didn't know he'd been holding. "The baby?" Though she wasn't a baby anymore, was she?

"Mistress Margaret survived as well."

"Well, thank God for that." Cade tugged at the collar of the linen shirt beneath his jerkin. It was too tight; he couldn't breathe.

Could it have been only a few moments ago that he'd been reveling in how wonderful it felt to be home again, where he was happy and could count on the delights that life would bring him? Things like the queen's favor, which had earned him a knighthood, a small but profitable estate that brought in gold to line his pockets, and pretty females eager for a discreet liaison. How had his entire world turned upside down so quickly?

Nausea knotted his stomach. "I've got to go to Easton, don't I?"

"Get a night's rest first, my lord," Jefferson advised. "You have had a long journey. And please excuse me for being blunt, but Lord Lunsford, your brother will still be dead tomorrow." Jefferson's usually impassive face flushed.

"That is the unfortunate truth," Cade agreed. "Thank you for the concern, Jefferson, but I have to go now. Today. If I put it off, I'll find reasons not to, believe me. I'll send a quick message to Her Majesty. She'll understand."

Jefferson nodded. "As you will, my lord."

"I'll be gone a few weeks at most. See that Riverview is kept ready for my return." Cade forced a smile that felt more like a grimace and went back out to the courtyard.

❀

The soft drizzle that had welcomed him home just five days before became a relentless, driving rain as Cade drew closer to his childhood home than he'd been in twelve years. He could barely make out Whitehawk's head just a few inches in front of his face. At least he was on his own horse. Any bit of familiarity was a comfort right now. Through vision blurred by the downpour he saw Easton Manor, a dank gray blob that loomed over the crest of land upon which it perched like a huge crow.

He cursed the sense of responsibility that had forced him to come.

He loved the city. In London, far from the rolling hills of Worcestershire and the ancestral home he'd tried so hard to forget, he was the queen's loyal servant and not the hated son of the third Earl of Easton, the ungrateful wretch who had deserted his widowed father and older brother to seek a new life for himself.

Well, what had his father expected? Cade was a second son. Even if his father had cared, it was still up to Cade to find his own way.

And he had, supporting Her Majesty through the turbulent early years of her reign. He'd been awarded a knighthood and given the duties of a diplomat—such was her trust in him. He was proud of what he'd accomplished in the years since leaving his father's house. And though being imprisoned by the pope on trumped-up charges of espionage had dampened his enthusiasm for diplomacy, he was still a creature of the court. A self-made man with the queen's favor, and he'd planned to stay that way—until he'd been unceremoniously dumped right back where he'd started, this time with the black cloud of the earldom stubbornly occupying the space over his head.

What would he say to his father when he saw him for the first time in nearly half his life? Had the old man changed at all? Though the lack of initiated contact over time suggested not, Cade couldn't help wondering. Stephen, in addition to being their father's heir, had also been the favored child. Could his death have left a hole in his father's heart that might be filled by his other son? Was there any possibility, no matter how remote, that the old man wanted to set things right?

Ha. Unlikely.

Every fiber of Cade's being screamed at him to turn tail and flee back to the sanctity of his life in London, the predictability of it. But he wouldn't give in. His father could say what he wanted—he always had anyway—but he would not be able to say that his son had ignored his familial obligations.

Cade dug his heels into Whitehawk's sides, and the horse broke into a gallop.

Needles of rain stung his eyes. Each slap of the horse's hooves against the ground egged him on. *Go-back. Go-back. Go-back.* But he pushed onward.

The portcullis was open, and no one stopped him at the gate, which only served to increase his sense of foreboding. Even if they'd been expecting his arrival, someone should have been there to keep watch over the entrance to the manor.

When he guided his horse into the courtyard, there was no one in sight to take Whitehawk to the stables. He was quite alone.

Gooseflesh rippled over his arms. Once, as a child, he had broken free from his mother and ended up stumbling into the churchyard. He remembered the eerie feeling that had settled over him as he realized that living souls did not belong there. In the courtyard of the manor house in which he'd been born and raised, the same sensation sent a chill racing through his veins.

"I'll wait a few more moments," he said out loud. He patted the tuft of wiry hair between Whitehawk's ears. "Someone will see us."

But no one did.

Cade himself took Whitehawk to the stables, where he was comforted to find two other animals. At least *something* still lived here. He brushed the stallion down and filled a battered bucket with oats he considered a lucky find, no matter how wretched they looked. Whitehawk nudged the bucket with his nose and whinnied. He looked at Cade as if to question his sanity. Cade chuckled.

"I know." He stroked the horse's velvet muzzle. "I'll see if I can't dig up something better for you."

Whitehawk's presence was comforting, and Cade lingered in the stable as long as he could. Soft snorts from the horses and the shriek of an outraged bird were the only sounds. For one foolish moment he considered leaping onto Whitehawk's back and tearing out before anyone even knew he'd been there. He could pretend he'd never received the summons. His Riverview staff, paid handsomely enough, would deny ever seeing him. He could return to the Continent—not France, and he never wanted to see Rome again, but surely there was a country that would harbor him! The Low Countries perhaps? Belgium, maybe Holland?

But he shook the thought away and squared his shoulders. He was here; he would do this. He was not a frightened boy any longer. He was a man of twenty-eight, a man who had faced down an army of rebels to keep his queen on her throne, a man who had spent months in prison at Pope Paul's behest and lived to tell the tale. He could certainly face his own father without fear. He would be the earl someday. His life was here now, no matter how much he hated the idea.

He patted Whitehawk; whether his intent was to reassure the horse or himself he didn't know. He turned up the hood of his sodden cloak to shield his already wet hair from the lashing rain.

Easton Manor's hall was as silent as the courtyard had been. It stank. The musty air, damp and cold as early spring despite the fact that it was nearly the middle of May, penetrated his wet clothes and he shivered. *My inheritance.* Even his own voice in his head was bitter. When had a human being last ventured here? Where were the servants?

It amazed him that after so many years away, anything would feel habitual. But without a thought Cade mounted the spiral stone staircase behind the dais that led to the first floor and his father's rooms. It was dark, but the faint, nauseating stench of tallow lingered in the air. Candles had recently burned here. But who had lit them?

Trepidation pressed harder against him with each echo his foot made against the narrow stone steps. When he reached the summit and entered the small chamber, he stepped into a puddle of faint light that spilled from the larger room beyond. Someone was in there.

A few more steps brought him to the entrance of his father's bedchamber. Cade peeked in with one eye. A fire blazed in the corner, so large he could feel the heat from where he stood and was grateful when it began to seep into his bones. With the warmth came courage, and he entered the room.

He saw an old man, dwarfed by the large bed, with lank gray hair that grazed his bent shoulders and twisted, knotted hands. One hand pressed against the old man's mouth as he coughed, sending a spray of dark blood over his dingy gown and the tattered velvet coverlet that concealed him from the waist down. The other stretched for the bedside table, toward a pewter goblet that had seen better days.

Cade gripped the door frame.

Father.

Cade's memories had been of a man who was tall and strong, with an arrogant tilt to his head and a cruel, mocking laugh of which Cade had been the target more times than he could remember. The man in this bed was a stranger. A wave of nausea swept over him, and he swallowed hard to fight it back.

"My God," he said, without meaning to speak.

His father's head jerked toward him. The old man's watery eyes, once a darker blue than Cade's own, were now a milky gray. He stared until his face split into a toothless grin made all the worse by the smears of blood around his mouth.

"Ha! The prodigal son has returned!" he crowed in a wet wheeze as he put the goblet down and settled against the pillows. "To what do I owe this honor? Come to pay your respects to your dying father, have you?"

Cade had gone numb. "You're dying," he echoed.

"Yes, I am," the old man gasped. "You'll be the Earl of Easton. Does that make you happy? For all you tried to run, it did little good. You're tied to Easton for life." His expression twisted. "It should have been Stephen!" He spat the words with as much contempt as his fading voice could muster. "Stephen was capable. He took the time to learn rather than running around London and the Continent, full of his own importance."

In an instant the years slipped away, as if someone had ripped a warm and comfortable cloak from Cade's shoulders. He was a boy again, wondering what he could have done to make his father hate him so much.

After twelve years this was all the old man had to say? He'd expected references to Stephen—the only time his father had really ever spoken to him was to tell him how he paled in comparison to his older brother. But the old bastard had wasted no time, had he?

Cade took a deep breath in an attempt to crush the instinct to retaliate. Her Majesty hadn't trusted him in Rome because he was heedless and rash. His father's blood might flow in him, but he would not be like his father.

He could be gracious. He *wanted* to be. A dying man deserved that much, no matter what kind of a person he had once been. But nothing had changed. His father was still spiteful and vindictive. Only when the feeling vanished did Cade realize he'd been harboring a small hope of reconciliation. He was disgusted with himself. He'd been a fool to imagine, even for a fleeting second, that the old man would recognize his past wrongdoings, let alone make the effort to atone for them.

I'm not a boy any longer. I don't have to take it from him now.

Cade dug his nails into the palm of his hand. As always, the familiar needles of pain quelled his anger and helped him focus.

"Perhaps you're right, my lord father." He shrugged. "No doubt Stephen would have been a splendidly successful earl. Why, I saw the fruits of his labor the moment I crossed onto the land. Tell me, did he manage to destroy the entire estate, or did he harbor a special hatred for the manor itself? I ask only because I'd like to know exactly how much work I have cut out for me. I have a life to get back to, you know."

Perhaps he was more like his father than he thought. He regretted the words the instant he spoke them—he hadn't meant to be cruel. *You fool. He is dying. You're better than that.*

The old man opened his mouth, and Cade braced himself. But instead of releasing the barrage of insults Cade expected, his father began to cough. His body stiffened as one of his knotted hands grasped at the coverlet and blood trickled from the corner of his parted lips. He stretched his other hand out to grab at the goblet. His fingers scrabbled at nothing. He couldn't reach it.

Should Cade hand the old man the goblet and risk him knocking it from Cade's grip? Or should he watch his father choke on the blood filling his lungs? Neither option was particularly attractive. He took a hesitant step toward the bedside table, but he was too late. Before his fingers could make contact with the goblet, someone pushed him from behind. He crashed to the floor, his hip making painful impact. For a long second his view was of nothing but grubby wood planks desperately in need of sweeping, while the impression of movement told him that whoever had shoved him had fled to the bed where his father lay.

Cade got to his feet, brushed the dust from his breeches, and prepared to rebuke the woman who'd had the audacity to shove him out of the way. But words escaped him when he realized who it was. God's foot, but the old bat looked as if she was on death's doorstep herself! He should have known that Goodwife Hawke wouldn't leave while the old man still had breath in him. She'd always been strangely devoted to his father.

"Here you are, my lord," she soothed as she pressed the battered goblet to the old man's cracked and bloody lips. Cade's father gulped from the cup until he seemed able to breathe again. Goodwife Hawke smoothed his greasy hair, produced a cloth which she used to wipe away the blood, and nudged him back against the pillows before she turned bitter, rheumy eyes on Cade.

"Come to claim your inheritance, eh?" she asked with the boldness even a longtime servant should not dare.

Cade kept his gaze leveled on her as he considered his response. If time had not been kind to his father, it had been downright pitiless to the old housekeeper. If he thought hard enough about memories he had tried to suppress, he could remember a time when Goodwife Hawke, though never a nice woman, had nonetheless been lovely. Now her once lustrous golden hair was white and sparse. Her creamy skin had become powdery and paper-thin. Yet she still held herself far above her station.

If he was going to be earl, she must go. He would not have her undermining his authority.

"Look at him, Goodwife," Cade finally said. "You have eyes in your head. Do you honestly think he will live to see many more dawns?" He tried, unsuccessfully, to ignore the spasm of pain that crossed her face. A bitch she might be, but she had feelings. Somewhere in there. "Does your daughter Joan still live in the village?"

"Yes," the woman muttered.

"Good. Once my father no longer needs you, you will retire. If your daughter cannot accommodate you, I shall see that a cottage is built for you."

The housekeeper's mouth, with its smattering of blackened teeth, gaped at him.

"You would turn out an old woman?" she asked in a voice that had gone from arrogant to querulous. Cade gritted his teeth. He knew what she was about, and it wouldn't work. He pitied her, really. But she would not make a fool of him. If he allowed it, he would never be respected.

"Not at all." He softened his tone, adopting the cajoling quality he'd perfected, the one that never failed to make a woman cave to his demands. "You are fortunate, Goodwife. Most domestic servants fully expect to work up until the moment of their death. Instead, you can spend your twilight years warming yourself at your daughter's hearth with your grandchildren around you."

Goodwife Hawke remained infuriatingly silent, her eyes flickering toward his father, who observed the exchange with an expression Cade could not fathom.

"Tell me honestly, Goodwife. You've never borne any love for me. Do you really want to work for me? I plan to manage this estate quite differently from the way you're used to."

"Manage the estate? Hah!" his father burst out before the housekeeper could respond. "What do you know of managing an estate, I ask? What have you learned from those useless popinjays at the queen's court?"

"Far more than you would think." He ignored the feeling that his father was probably right. He'd learned plenty, but nothing that would keep Easton's people warm and fed.

"You certainly seem sure of yourself," the old man spat. "You should not even be standing here." He clutched at his hair with talon-like fingers and closed his eyes. "Damned accident."

"Accident?" Cade raised an eyebrow. The heat from the fire was quickly becoming stifling rather than cozy. Beads of sweat blossomed along his hairline. "What are you talking about? Stephen died of an illness. There was no accident." He forced patience into his voice. Had his father's illness addled his brain?

"*You* were the accident," his father moaned. "You shouldn't have happened. I never wanted you."

The old man could have thrown a brick into his stomach and he wouldn't have been as shocked. Cade's muscles went tight, and he stood rigid. His stomach churned.

I never wanted you.

Of course, he'd always known it. He'd have been a fool not to realize. But to hear the truth spoken aloud hurt far worse than deducing it from his father's actions. He didn't know what upset him more: the fact that he'd been right, or that the confirmation had managed to wound him.

"You don't deserve any of this," the old man continued. "You're worthless! Easton doesn't need its *rightful* earl." His father's voice, even in its weakness, was taunting. "There are others. It doesn't have to be you. I have cousins who would gladly slice off your head for the title and a piece of my fortune."

Cade swallowed hard, forcing the ache in his throat down so he could speak.

"Empty threats, Father." His father's dying wish might be to break him, but it was a wish Cade wouldn't grant. The old man would never be aware of the blow his words had struck. "Even if you legally could, you wouldn't. Your pride has ever been all-consuming. And what fortune? I see no evidence of a fortune here. Only selfishness and stupidity."

His father's face contorted.

"Get out!" he howled. The old man's bony fingers clawed at the bedside table, where they wrapped around the stem of the goblet. He picked it up and hurled it toward Cade. But his father's arm was weak. The goblet landed on the floor several inches short of Cade's feet. Cade bent and retrieved it, placing it back on the bedside table next to the dumbfounded Goodwife Hawke.

"Try and get some sleep, Father." Cade heard the tremble in his own voice. He had to get out of there. "If I'm still here tomorrow, I'll come back to see you. Perhaps."

Chapter Two

Damp, chilly air greeted Cade as he escaped his father's bedchamber and made his way to the dimly lit gallery, added to the manor by his grandfather fifty years prior, that connected the wings of the manor. The cold calmed his frantic heartbeat and dried the sweat that threatened to trickle into his eyes. He was furious, though whether at his father or himself he wasn't sure.

You shouldn't have reacted like that, he railed at himself. *It's what he would have done. You try to be better than that!* Once he'd seen that his father was dying, he could have swallowed the hurt and faced the old man with the decency and composure an honored member of the queen's court should possess. *Did* possess. But it hadn't taken much to bring all the long-suppressed memories rushing back. After the inevitable comparison to Stephen, Cade wouldn't have been able to stop himself if he'd tried. Even in death Stephen's worth surpassed Cade's own.

He gulped the air down eagerly, as if it could rinse his blood free of the fury and hurt that boiled within it. He'd known this wasn't going to be a pleasant trip but wished he'd been given at least some idea of his father's condition. Now not only did he have to get used to being his father's heir, he had to accept that he would be the earl much sooner than he'd anticipated—and even if he'd known how to manage the estate, could he save it from total destruction?

At least he would be spared the trouble of returning to London only to have to come back once his father had passed—an event that was obviously imminent. And nobody would be able to say that he had ignored the old man as he lay dying. Not that he had any reason to wonder about what people would say. Thanks to his father, he was aware that everyone from here to Edinburgh probably already thought the worst of him. Would he even be able to command their respect, once he was lord?

Too many questions. His muscles moaned their fatigue, and he supposed he should at least try to get some sleep. But as he wondered where to begin what he assumed would be a futile search for a servant who would bring him some water for washing, another chilly burst of air ruffled the hair that clung limply to his forehead. Air? Where had it come from?

"What in hell," he said aloud. He glanced around. The stone walls were dotted with sconces that provided scarcely enough light to see his hand in front of his face. The sickening stench of tallow was stronger here, and Cade fought the urge to retch. His years with the royal court had given him a preference for some of the finer things in life, and candles made from rendered animal fat were not one of them.

Cade swallowed his nausea and silently vowed that his first task as earl would be to procure a large supply of beeswax candles. He moved to the wall and trailed his fingers against it as he hunted for the source of the cold air. The unadorned stone was damp and almost slimy to his touch, bringing back memories of the walls at which he'd stared for months at Castel Sant'Angelo. They should be paneled with sturdy wood, not left bare! He walked carefully, but not carefully enough, for after only a few steps he found himself sloshing through a puddle of icy water.

"God's foot!" he swore. Then he groaned in dismay. The window beside him was broken, the rare glass gone except for a few jagged shards that poked like broken teeth from the frame. Cade rested his hands carefully on the ledge and leaned his head out into the dark, wet night.

"Perfect," he muttered. The window would need to be replaced— and if one was broken, it was almost certain that more were too. Glass was expensive. He wondered if Stephen had managed to destroy the family fortune as completely as he had everything else.

Cade's head swam with exhaustion. It suddenly seemed ten years since he had boarded the ship in France that was destined to take him home. He needed to sleep. But where would he lay his head? Surely his old rooms, like the rest of Easton Manor, had been completely forgotten.

Sure enough, Cade gagged on a swirl of dust as he entered his childhood bedchamber and surveyed the room. It was almost as if he had stepped back in time. To his amazement the chamber was exactly as he had left it twelve years before, only filthy. The tables, chairs, and wardrobe rested beneath a thick film of grime. The bed, encased in a dingy, moth-eaten coverlet, was child-sized; as he remembered how his feet had dangled over the edge when he was sixteen, Cade wondered if it wouldn't be a better idea to sleep in the loft in the barn. The manor had guest chambers, of course, but if his rooms and the parts of the manor he had seen were any indication, it would take days for the servants to prepare them for visitors—assuming he could even find any servants. He doubted that Goodwife Hawke would do it for him, and although he could force her, he was too tired for another battle of wills. He wanted only to sleep.

Stephen's rooms might be clean.

As soon as the thought materialized, he shook his head, as if he could shake it right out of his mind. The last place he wanted to be was the room in which his brother had grown up. Stephen's ghost would probably haunt him if he dared to lay his head on the sacred pillow. But then a rat the size of a well-fed barn cat scurried over the toes of his boot. Cade kicked it away and grimaced when the rodent landed across the room with a dull thud and a squeak. He sighed in resignation; there was little other choice. He would try Stephen's rooms. If they proved too filthy for human habitation, he would spend the night in the stables with Whitehawk as a bed mate. It wouldn't be so bad. He'd slept beside worse.

He returned to the hall and was startled to discover a maid by the dais, her back to him. What on earth was she doing there? If the cobwebs that fluttered in the ceiling corners and the stench wafting from the moldy rushes below the high board were any sign, Easton Manor's main room had not seen a servant in months. Goodwife

Hawke's priorities obviously lay elsewhere, and he wondered how long it had been since she ordered the silver polished and a fire lit.

"You, there," he said, and winced. He hadn't meant to speak so loudly, but his voice boomed off the bare walls, walls that should have been hung with tapestries to keep out the cold and the damp. He knew they had some—his mother had been a genius with her embroidery needle.

The maid gasped and whirled to face him, a cloth in her hand. She'd been wiping down the high board. Her clothing was tattered and threadbare.

"Yes, milord?" she squeaked, dropping into a quick curtsy.

So she knew who he was. From the looks of her, she'd still been in nappies when he took off for London. He wondered what else she knew about him, and who had told her.

"What is your name?" he asked her.

"Margery, milord." She came to stand in front of him.

"Margery. Where are all the other servants?" he demanded. "*Are* there any?"

"Well, there's Goodwife Hawke." As if he wasn't well aware of that. "There's Wat, who is a pot boy and also works with the horses. His brother Ned was Lord Lunsford's personal attendant, but now he helps Goodwife Hawke with taking care of his lordship the earl. Robin was the butler, but now he is also the head groom—it's Robin who went searching for you, milord. Goodwife Crosby is the cook. And then there's me." Her freckled face flushed.

Cade was aghast. "That's it? Six servants?" Even the bailiff had disappeared? No wonder the manor was falling down around them.

She nodded. "Yes, milord." She bit her lip.

"Well." He looked around. "That explains a few things."

Margery nodded as she stared at her feet, clad in boots so small he could see the outline of her toes. A wave of pity for her washed over him. He wondered about her family, and how desperately they must need money. Even more than Easton did.

"Margery," he said, and she raised her head. "I want you to gather all the household staff in the Great Hall at nine o'clock the morning after tomorrow. I would speak with everyone and learn more about what has happened here. Do you understand?"

"Aye, milord." She nodded, the fuzzy red-blond hair that had escaped from her cap glinting in the dim light.

"I would like some food," he continued. Uncertainty flitted over her freckled face. He groaned inwardly. They had to have food, didn't they? "And have Wat bring a basin of water to my brother's rooms," he continued, deciding not to ask. "If they are clean, I will be staying in them, and I'd like to wash."

"I will have him bring everything right up to you. Will you need anything else?"

He needed a great deal, but little the maid could give him. "Were my brother's clothes packed away after he died?"

"Oh, no, milord," the maid said. "The earl wouldn't let anyone pack up his lordship's things."

"That will be all, then."

Margery curtsied again and scurried away. Cade went back upstairs.

He shouldn't have been surprised when he entered Stephen's chambers and found that the rooms bore evidence of daily sweeping and changing of the bed linens. They were cleaner than he could remember his own rooms ever being, even when he lived in them. It was as if his father expected Stephen home at any moment.

Cade drifted through the bedchamber, loath to touch anything lest Stephen's ghost appear to berate him. But his attention was caught by a portrait of his late half-brother, which hung above the fireplace across from the large velvet-clad bed. Cade remembered it well. His father had commissioned it from a visiting Dutch artist, who had painted it while Cade's mother lay dying. In the portrait Stephen was clad in jewels and finery that would have made old King Henry envious. His chest puffed out like a robin's, and a fringe of yellow hair framed his pale, round face. Stephen was thin-lipped and weak-chinned but somehow still managed to convey the inflated sense of importance that had made him so unbearable—a result of a lifetime of being pampered, spoiled, and allowed to get away with anything and everything he did, Cade supposed.

Uneasiness rolled over him in waves. He would order his own rooms cleaned immediately. He wouldn't last long sleeping before a shrine.

Wat arrived, struggling beneath a basin of steaming water and shattering Cade's reverie. Margery followed, in her hands a tray holding a mug of ale and a bowl of something that looked so unappealing Cade promptly lost his appetite. He stripped off his garments, dusty and stained from several days' hard riding from London, and handed them to Wat with instructions to brush the mud from them before dismissing both servants. He gulped down the ale and attempted a spoonful of the potage, which tasted as vile as it looked. After he washed, he hesitated for just a moment before he dug an old dressing gown of Stephen's from the chest at the foot of the bed and yanked it over his head. He pulled back the coverlet and climbed beneath it. Cade shivered until the heat of his body warmed the mattress enough for him to get comfortable and drift off to sleep.

❋

Despite the unpleasant familiarity of his brother's bed and his mountain of problems, Cade slept through the night. He woke to brilliant sunshine pouring through the windows.

He felt groggy. It took him a moment upon waking to remember exactly where he was, but once he did, he leapt from the bed as if the coverlet were on fire.

In fact, he almost wished it was. The room was freezing. From the position of the sun in the sky it was far past time for a chambermaid to have come in and lit a fire in the room. So why hadn't it been done?

"Of course," Cade muttered when he remembered. There was only one chambermaid in the entire household. Margery probably hadn't even made it to his side of the manor yet.

At least Wat had returned his clothes. Cade ignored his screaming muscles, sore after so many days on horseback and only one proper night's rest, as he dressed, washed his face and hands in the icy remnants of last night's water, and left the room with no particular destination in mind.

Before long, he found himself standing at the top of the stairs leading to his father's apartments.

From the sound of it, the old man had lived through the night after all. He bellowed as well as he could in between gasps for breath, shouting that he didn't need anyone to pray for him and banishing his poor victim from his sight. Before Cade could enter the bedchamber, a short, black-clad figure rushed out, its head bowed, and plowed into Cade's chest.

"Oh!" the figure huffed, and looked up. Recognition dawned in the man's eyes at the same time it flooded Cade.

"Father Vincent," he said. The priest's familiar face was a welcome sight, though it was now more lined and jowly than Cade remembered. A liberal amount of silver threaded the priest's once dark hair. Like his uncle before him, Father Vincent had been Easton's priest since the moment he took his vows.

"Viscount Lunsford," the priest replied with a small smile. "It's good to see you again."

"Please, Father." Cade's laugh sounded wry even to his ears. "There's no need for formalities. Besides, I'll never grow used to that title, not that it seems I'll have time to anyway. How is the earl today?"

The priest lost his smile and fingered the crucifix around his neck.

"Worse," he admitted. "It pains me to say it, but it is almost as if he's willing himself into death."

"It doesn't surprise me. With Stephen gone, I imagine he feels he has very little left to live for." Father Vincent's mouth opened but Cade stopped him before he could speak. "Come now, Father. You've been with this family since before I was born—please don't pretend. You know as well as I do that my brother was the old man's pride and joy. Not I."

The priest sighed. "God has a plan for everyone. He knew what He was doing when He made you the heir."

"I hope so," Cade muttered. He looked at the priest. "I assume that in time I will forgive God for this appalling shift in circumstance. But please excuse me if I'm not feeling particularly magnanimous at the moment."

Father Vincent nodded solemnly, but his eyes sparkled with humor.

"Well, I've been forbidden from setting foot here for the time being," he said. "But I will return at nightfall. The earl is no longer able to hear Mass in the chapel, so I say it at his bedside."

"I'll see that a meal is prepared and waiting for you," Cade promised before he remembered the unappetizing gruel he'd been served the night before.

The priest nodded again and moved toward the stairs, no doubt in a hurry to pray for the lost soul that inhabited these rooms—and for his own soul, if he were forced to eat Easton's food that night. Cade moved toward the door but stopped before he entered the chamber. His father's gasps for breath reached him even beyond the doorway, and Goodwife Hawke murmured words his ears could not decipher. No. It was too soon—he couldn't face them again yet. There were other things he could do while he formulated calm and respectful replies to the insults his father would no doubt fling at him when they did speak again.

Cade turned and went down the stairs, into the deserted and dusty hall, out into the courtyard and down to the stables.

Whitehawk whinnied softly when he entered. The poor beast looked terribly uncomfortable in the little stall. He nudged the empty bucket and looked at Cade, who imagined he saw accusation in the horse's shining black eyes.

"I'm sorry," Cade said. He opened the door to the stall and drew Whitehawk out. "What do you say we get some exercise? Would you like that?" He saddled the stallion and mounted him, kicked him lightly in the sides and set off at a canter.

What he saw as he rode turned his stomach.

He'd heard the stories many times during his childhood. Easton had once been a successful estate, with flourishing apple and pear orchards that produced exceptional cider and wine that were valued all over the land. The drought that had ravaged the county in 1528 had killed many of the trees, forcing his father to pour the majority of his fortune into starting over. When the following year proved to be just as dry, killing the new trees as well, his father had been forced to wed his mother, who was the precious only daughter of a local minor but incredibly wealthy baron. Her dowry included enough gold to replenish the orchards for a third time and to purchase a healthy flock of sheep which produced excellent wool and nicely supplemented the estate's income. His mother even had her own property that she passed to Cade when she died, and which had kept him independent after he'd left Worcestershire. Thanks to little Mary Cade, Easton's prosperity hardly skipped a beat, and Cade hadn't had to rely on his father or brother for anything.

But as Cade rode over the hills he found nothing that reminded him of the thriving land his family had once held. The fruit trees were broken and bent, without a green leaf to be seen even though it was spring and they should be in bright, fragrant bloom. The few sheep he saw were skinny and ragged. Fury at his father and brother and lack of confidence in his own ability to fix their mistakes mingled and grew into a lump in his throat so large it threatened to cut off his air supply.

He yanked on the reins, perhaps a bit too hard, and Whitehawk skittered to a stop with a whinnied protest. How quickly Cade's life had turned on its head! He had been home less than a full day, and already he felt like he was drowning. He needed a break—just a bit of time to remember that while he would soon be Earl of Easton and had a certain reputation to build and maintain, he was also still Cade Badgley and not above indulging in things that gave him pleasure. He was starving for a bit of normalcy.

He nudged Whitehawk in the ribs again, gently, to make up for the rough stop of a moment before. The horse took off, and Cade guided him to the edge of the forest that separated Easton land from the Earl of Brentford's. A stream meandered through the trees and emptied into a small clear lake that was half on Easton land and half on Brentford's. Whitehawk had to be thirsty, and beneath his linen shirt Cade's skin was covered with a thin film of sweat. The thought of diving into the cool water for a few moments of uninterrupted peace was overwhelmingly tempting. The path through the trees was narrow and strewn with rocks and roots, so he slid off of Whitehawk's back and grabbed the bridle, carefully leading the animal through the trees to the water.

Cade had never, in all the times he had escaped to this place as he was growing up, seen another human soul in this spot. Fishermen preferred the Severn for its salmon and pike. The solitude he was able to find at this tiny, little-known lake had always been its most attractive quality. So as he approached the familiar spot where he knew the trees would give way to a grassy bank, he was surprised—and a bit dismayed—to hear a splash.

He tethered Whitehawk to the nearest tree and shifted, silent, to a spot where he could watch without being seen. He peered through the bright green leaves, and his eyes widened in surprise.

Was it a nymph? He squinted and observed a slender female in the water. She swam about as if she hadn't a care in the world, her hair dark and plastered to her head and shoulders. He couldn't quite make out her facial features, or whether she had any clothing on. A pile of blue that could have been a gown lay on the grassy bank.

As he watched, she flipped herself onto her back and floated, her eyes either staring at the sky or closed. He was too far away to tell.

Cade swallowed laughter. It wasn't every day a man stumbled upon a female splashing about in a hidden lake. Who was she? Only a certain kind of girl would indulge in such pleasure without worrying if she would be caught. But did she belong to him, or to Brentford?

He didn't care. He'd wanted to feel like his old self for a few minutes—here was his chance. He might not know where to purchase apple tree saplings or how to shear a sheep, but by God, he knew how to seduce a woman.

He parted the branches, strode onto the grassy bank, and paused at the water's edge.

"Hello," he said.

The girl in the water shrieked and righted herself, her arms thrashing in the water as she struggled to stay upright.

"Who are you?" she gasped. Though the water came to her shoulders and by now he was close enough to see that she wore a chemise, she wrapped her arms around herself in a futile attempt at modesty.

"Who are *you?*" he countered. He gifted her with his most disarming grin.

"That is none of your concern," she snapped.

He laughed. A spitfire! Very well, then. Too easy a conquest would bore him.

"Should you be here?" he asked her, and laughed again when a blush stained her cheeks. "No, I didn't think so."

He sat down on the bank and pulled off his boots. The girl eyed him warily.

"What are you doing?" she asked.

He stood. "Joining you." He pulled his linen shirt over his head and tossed it to the ground next to what he assumed was her gown.

"You most certainly are not!"

"No?" He paused with his hand at the waistband of his breeches. "No!"

"This is my property." He gazed at her, daring her to argue.

She opened her mouth as if to speak but seemed to think better of it and clamped her lips shut. Her eyes darted to the piles their clothing made, and her cheeks burned a most becoming shade of crimson.

"Then we are agreed? I'll leave my breeches on if it makes you feel better." It would be harder to remove them if they were wet, but so be it. He didn't wait for her to answer. He took a step toward the lake, toward her.

"Please, my lord." Her voice was not so haughty anymore. In fact, she sounded close to tears. "Turn away for a moment. I'll come out and dress. Then you may have the lake all to yourself."

"I'm not a selfish man. I'm willing to share it with you." With a grin, he took a running leap into the lake. The rain had made the water deliciously cold, and it shocked his skin as he plunged beneath the surface. His arms and legs cut through the water until he emerged, mere inches from her face. She shrieked again.

"Isn't it more fun to swim with a friend?" he asked the girl.

"You are not my friend, my lord." She had removed her hand from her eyes but still wouldn't look at him.

"Perhaps not yet," he agreed. He drank in her profile. Up close, the girl's beauty was staggering. Her face was a perfect heart, with delicate features. He'd never seen a peasant so lovely, though they often had their own, earthy appeal. This girl was different. Not a peasant at all, it would seem. A by-blow of Brentford's, perhaps? To his recollection, Brentford's countess had died shortly after his own mother's passing. But the girl was definitely older than eleven or twelve. He would put her closer to sixteen. Not that it mattered; many noble men had mistresses of some sort. She could very well have been born on the wrong side of the blanket while the countess was alive.

Then a horrifying thought crossed his mind. *Maybe* his *father had sired her!* But he shoved the idea away. His father had never been one for dipping his wick where it didn't belong. He could barely bring himself to touch his own nobly bred wives, let alone romp with peasant women.

Such thoughts threatened to dampen his ardor, so he turned his attention back to the girl in front of him. She had finally deigned to look at him and gazed with eyes dark green and flecked with gold, wide with what he assumed was terror and filled with a mixture of desperation and curiosity.

He ignored the desperation. Indulging one's curiosity always proved to have a much more satisfying outcome.

"Who are you?" he asked again. The wet fabric of her chemise clung to the smooth curve of her shoulder.

"That is none of your business," she retorted. The tremble in her voice was barely discernible, but it was there.

"I think it is," he replied. "You are trespassing."

"Only half of this land is Easton's," she said. "The other half belongs to my—the Earl of Brentford." Her cheeks were red again.

He raised an eyebrow. "*Your* Earl of Brentford?" he asked. "You are his, then?"

She lifted her narrow chin proudly. "You could say that."

Something like a memory tugged at him. He almost felt like he should know this girl. But he knew he had never seen her before. He certainly would have remembered her.

Cade pushed the feeling aside and winked at her. "Are you his mistress?"

Her cheeks flamed, and her eyes snapped so angrily he expected to see sparks burst from them.

"How dare you ask me such a thing?" she demanded. "Just who do you think you are?"

"Viscount Lunsford, darling," he drawled. "Earl of Easton before the week is out, I imagine." Her fine skin was ivory with a golden tint.

She even had a smattering of freckles across her high cheekbones. He liked them. Court ladies bleached their skin to the lightest shade they could attain or smeared white paint on their faces. It made them look dead. He far preferred the life in this girl's sun-kissed cheeks.

She worried a full lower lip between unusually straight, white teeth. He took advantage of the momentary silence to graze a fingertip along her collarbone, which peeked invitingly above the neckline of her sodden chemise. But to his utter shock, she slapped his hand away with vehemence.

"Do not touch me," she hissed. "My—Brentford would be furious if he found out that you were here with me. You must go."

"He would only be furious to find you with a man?" Cade inquired. "Not that you—whoever you are—are here swimming alone and nearly naked?"

"All of it." Her voice was more desperate than ever. "Please, my lord, you must not say a word. To anyone." She glanced at the shore. "*I* will leave. Then you can swim to your heart's content. But please, turn away until I am dressed."

He pretended to think a moment, then sighed. "Very well. If that's what you want." He turned himself around so his back was to her. The chilly water lapped at his bare shoulders, and he made a show of putting his hands over his eyes. "All right. I'm not looking."

He heard splashing and imagined her rushing for the shore. Again he had to fight the urge to laugh. She certainly was modest for a peasant wench, for all he'd found her swimming like a mermaid in his lake. He wondered if she was playing a game—if her modesty was just for show, an act to entice him. He'd never met a village girl who was above a quick tumble in a well-hidden spot.

And nothing would make him feel more like himself.

He tossed aside his promise not to look as the girl dressed—it had been half-hearted anyway—turned toward shore and began to swim. She had lifted the blue pile from the grass. It was a strange, one-pieced concoction of fabric the likes of which he'd only ever seen on portraits of fifteenth-century noblewomen. She struggled to pull it over her wet undergarment, but the sleeve was inside-out. She didn't notice him coming out of the lake and toward her. When he reached her on the shore, she had righted the sleeve and was working on the other.

"Don't," he said, and reached out to take the stubborn sleeve in his hand. The girl went still.

"What?" she asked. Her voice was soft.

Cade grasped the other sleeve and pulled at it. He lifted the dress over her head and dropped it back to the grass. She gaped at him, and he could see her trying to process what he had just done. Then she flung her slender arms about herself in what he supposed was an effort to shield her body, the shape of which was blissfully evident through the saturated lawn of her chemise, from his eyes.

"Don't," he said again. "You don't know how lovely you are, do you?" He stepped toward her, close enough to cup her smooth golden cheeks in his hands. The hem of his breeches dripped water on his bare feet.

He saw too late the danger in her green eyes. Before he could react, her hand reached out and administered a stinging slap to his cheek.

Astounded, he could only drop his hands and stare at her.

"You say you will be Earl of Easton in a few days, my lord?" Her voice dripped venom. "Then your father is dying, and I am sorry. However, you would do well to take a page from his book. I've met your father, and from what I recall, he was a true *gentleman*." She spat the word like it tasted bad.

While Cade could only stare at the girl in shock, she thrust her arms into the dress, successfully this time, and pulled it back down to cover her. She squeezed the water from her dripping curls—he could see now that they were a blazing shade of red—stepped into a pair of boots he hadn't noticed until then, and without another word took off running away from him and through the trees in the direction of Brentford's lands—like Artemis, only equipped with sharp words instead of silver arrows. He stared after her until the last branches closed over her fleeing figure.

Cade shook his head. Had he dreamed what had just happened? Certainly he had exchanged barbs with females before—to some of the women at court, it was akin to foreplay—but that peasant wench had put him in his spot quite neatly. He might have felt admiration for her, or at least amusement, if she hadn't angered him so damnably well. His father a gentleman indeed! What did she even know of his father? As if he believed for a moment she'd ever laid eyes on the old man. Not only was she prudish and prideful when she had no right to be, but she was a liar as well.

He glanced at the ground before him, where the tall lake grass still struggled to rise from the weight her feet put on them. Something brown caught his eye. He knelt and picked it up. It was a small portfolio, made of leather, and when he opened it he was astounded to see black-and-white sketches.

"What on earth?" he mumbled to himself as he flipped through them. Did the drawings belong to the girl? But what female—peasant or otherwise—had the time or the inclination to be interested in art? It was a man's pursuit. Women didn't, or shouldn't, engage in such activities.

Unless Brentford had taken it upon himself to educate the girl alongside his legitimate daughters, which would be strange enough in itself.

He scanned a drawing of a horse in mid-leap, followed by an older woman embroidering. A bowl of brambleberries sat upon a wooden table and a rosebush bent in the breeze.

She might be prideful. She might be prudish and dishonest. But she was very, very talented.

And one of the most beautiful females he'd ever seen.

Christ's bones. He never should have come back here.

Chapter Three

THOMAS HAUGHTON, EARL OF BRENTFORD, SAT AT THE HIGH board in his hall and observed the unusual flurry of activity around him. Servants bustled from the kitchen and back, bringing trays laden with sliced rare beef dripping in juices, spiced perry from his wine cellar, loaves of bread, and bowls of water in which his daughters and his guests dipped their fingers between courses.

He glanced around the table. Jane Norris, the Marchioness of Wexley, was a pale, mousy woman who had yet to speak a word despite Thomas's efforts to make her feel comfortable since the beginning of the meal. She sat to his right, her head bowed as she fed herself. To his left was Henry, the marquess, who was probably the reason the marchioness never spoke—because Hal never *stopped*, and his every word was loud enough to rattle the glass in the windows. To Hal's left sat Katherine, Brentford's middle daughter; his youngest, Cecily, faced them from the opposite side of the high board. Wexley's son Peter, Viscount Waltham, slouched over the bench to Katherine's left. At the far end of the table, in the seat belonging to the lady of the house, was Samara, Thomas's eldest daughter and the most confusing thing in his life.

As he watched her, Thomas swallowed his disappointment. He had placed Samara next to Waltham for one simple reason. Hal had casually suggested the possibility of a match between the two, and Thomas wanted to see if they suited each other. He'd seen the boy flirting with Samara on several occasions since the family had arrived for their visit. Waltham liked her, and that was good. But Thomas wasn't certain how Samara felt about Waltham and hoped that if he put the boy next to her, she would make an effort to get to know him. Perhaps she would take a liking to him as well, and while she would never be the kind of girl who used her wit to allure and entice, she might be distracted enough to refrain from the peculiar things she normally did and might actually engage in what could pass for ordinary, if not sparkling, conversation.

Thomas's plan had failed.

Waltham hunched over his plate and barely looked up, except to ogle the servant girls who refilled his goblet. As usual, it was Katherine who directed the servants while Samara absentmindedly nibbled on her supper and ignored their guests, tilting her head this way and that as she looked at—hell, he had no idea *what* she looked at. The bowl of strawberries? One of the lopsided, half-melted candles? He didn't have a clue, and that was one of the things that frustrated him most about her. She was odd. She was seventeen years old, and if he couldn't match her with Waltham, Thomas had no idea *what* he was going to do with her.

But he had no one but himself to blame for the current state of affairs in his household. As Samara's father he had every right to tell her to give up her strange fancies and learn what was necessary for the noble wife she would be one day, to accept no argument from her. He should have chosen for her the first suitable husband he could find and seen her married a year ago. But he hadn't, and while he tried to console himself with the fact that it might not be too late, the truth was that he just didn't know.

If he was *very* honest with himself, he had let far too much time go by without giving serious thought to the futures of his three daughters. Samara and Katherine had been so young when Cecily was born and their mother had died—just five and three. He had vowed to Anne, in her few lucid moments after Cecily's birth and before the childbed fever stole her away from him, that he would do whatever it took to protect their girls as long as he could. And he had. He had kept them physically close, safe from the dangers of the outside world where politics and unscrupulous men lurked, waiting to ruin their lives and reputations and break their tender hearts. He had kept himself safe, too, by keeping his own heart distant. His girls were all he had left of his wife, and if he didn't love them *too* much, it would hurt less if he lost them as he'd lost Anne.

He had indeed stumbled blindly through the past twelve years without his beloved wife. The last time he'd really looked at his daughters, they'd been but children. When had they grown into women? Where had the years gone?

The brutal reality was that his attempt to keep his promise to Anne had caused him to fail in his duties as a father. His daughters faced a life he couldn't even imagine for girls of their status—a life alone except for each other, with no household to manage except his own, and no one to love them after he was gone.

Somehow, he knew that wasn't what Anne had meant when she made him swear to protect them.

He had made some grave mistakes. But perhaps there was still something he could do.

A match with young Waltham hadn't occurred to him. He hadn't even noticed the boy's interest in Samara until Wexley began to drop hints—actually, subtlety was not Hal's style, and it was safe to say that the hints were hurled at Thomas's head more than they were dropped—that perhaps his son and Samara could be matched. It was then that Thomas noted Waltham trying to engage Samara in conversation on several occasions.

Now why hadn't Thomas ever thought of that? The Norris family could trace its ancestry back as far as the Norman invasion, perhaps even farther, and its coffers were as rich as its history. Thomas himself had no need of extra coin, although it was always helpful—and though others of his station might consider it odd, he did not seek to profit, at least monetarily, from any marriages his daughters might make—but it would be comforting to know that Samara would be well supported and cared for. If she married Waltham, it would unite two families who already shared decades of friendship and cement that friendship for the future. And though Her Majesty had done her best to bring the true faith back to England, she had no children and there was a good chance her sister—Lady Elizabeth, rumored to be a heretic—would end up as queen. God only knew what would happen to England then. The Haughton family was still Catholic, and if Thomas married his daughter to a fellow Catholic like Waltham, the alliance could only help if Elizabeth reinstated the heresy of her father and brother.

But something made Thomas hesitate.

The idea itself made perfect sense. He should be relieved at the prospect of being rid of Samara and shifting the responsibility of her to someone else—someone who would know how to break her of her strange habits rather than indulging them by supplying her with charcoal sticks and paper the way he did whenever she made her pretty pleas.

Was it the thought of his beautiful, radiant daughter wasted on someone as unappealing as Waltham that made him balk? Though the boy was the son of his old friend—wealthy and titled and, on paper, more than worthy of her—he had the charisma of a lump of suet and was only slightly more attractive. Lord Waltham was a grown man but acted like a spoiled boy. Look at him slumped in his seat, pouting because the cook hadn't made enough custard tarts to allow him a third! Nor did rumors that he tried to take liberties with Brentford Hall's female staff sit well with the earl. Thomas took good care of those who served him and did not appreciate having them manhandled by his guest. If Waltham acted that way in his own home, he would be fortunate to survive a year of marriage to Samara with his hands—or other precious appendages—intact.

Thomas sighed. If there were any other options, he hoped they would present themselves before he watched his eldest daughter, the mirror image of his beloved wife, ride off to a new life in the cold and snowy Yorkshire moors.

❋

Later, when Cade had finally managed to push the memory of the red-haired girl to the back of his mind, he sat at the high board with Father Vincent as they ate the evening meal together. Although it was not as distasteful as the slop he'd been served the night before, it was still not an elegant spread—potage that was more vegetable than meat and a paltry loaf of brown bread that the men shared between them. Even his meals in prison had been more appetizing. Cade made a mental note to arrange a trip to the closest market town where he could purchase livestock and grain, something else that had not occurred to him. At court, he sat at a banquet table and food appeared in front of him. Such was not the case here at Easton.

"I explored the lands today," Cade said as he tore off the end of his half of the bread and scanned the high board for butter. There was none. "They are in abysmal condition."

"Yes," Father Vincent agreed in his soft voice. "Much of that is due to the rains we've had over the last few years. There have been some very wet summers. But—and forgive me for saying so, my lord—your father and brother must shoulder much of the blame. Lord Lunsford was not as capable as your father thought. While his lordship the earl was away, he thought it would be a good opportunity for your brother to get a taste of what running Easton would be like. It was a grave error."

"Is *that* what happened?" Cade demanded. "The earl up and left without making sure my brother knew what he was doing? He just let him ruin everything?"

"There is more to it than that, my lord." The priest sipped at his ale and winced. Cade sympathized. The ale was so bitter he would have served water if he didn't believe it would kill them both. "The earl first began to show signs of the consumption illness about eight years ago. Once he could no longer deny the symptoms, he decided to go on pilgrimage to Santiago de Compostela in hopes of cleansing his soul and curing the disease."

Cade raised an eyebrow. His father had gone to Spain? He must have been worried about his soul, indeed. At least for a while.

"He was gone nearly two years," Father Vincent continued. "Unfortunately, while he was gone, he left your brother completely in charge, with only the help of the bailiff. I don't know how much you recall, but the manor house already suffered from neglect. It is old, and much of the necessary upkeep has not been done since your family received the earldom. Stephen had no sense of the land, no idea how to make use of it or how to direct the servants or care for his people. He failed to replace glass that had broken or stones that had begun to crumble. Rather than correct him, the bailiff simply ignored it, as he was too busy stealing the dwindling amount of gold that was coming in." Father Vincent gave a sad smile. "At least, that's what we assumed. When word of your father's impending return reached Easton, the bailiff disappeared. His body was found two weeks later, halfway to the Scots border, his throat slit and everything of importance robbed from his person."

Cade closed his eyes and inhaled, forcing back the anger that burned his throat.

The priest went on. "We expected the earl to be angry with Stephen, but he was not. He was angrier with the murdered bailiff. The earl said only that your brother still had plenty of time to learn, as the earl had been cured of his disease while on pilgrimage. And indeed, his symptoms did seem to ease. But his mind was never the same. He claimed to be helping your brother learn his duties, but we never saw any evidence of it. Basic maintenance chores in the castle continued to go undone. The trees in the orchards withered, and corn crops were planted only sporadically and provided just enough food to keep the household from starving. The servants were paid even less frequently. After last Michaelmas, when seven quarter-days had passed in a row with no wages paid, the servants realized that they were not likely to see any more coin for their services—and how could they with none coming in? Some stayed out of loyalty to the family, but most began to disappear from the manor. Some turned to poaching to feed themselves and their families. Others went to the Earl of Brentford to beg for work. That man paid your father several visits to appeal to him to guide Stephen, but the earl was stubborn. Brentford is a good man. When he saw that your father was holding his ground, he made spots for those who were so desperately begging him for employment."

So not only am I responsible for bringing this godforsaken estate back to life, I am in debt to Brentford as well. The hole he was in was getting so deep, he wondered if it would be much longer before he was buried alive.

"When the epidemic struck, Stephen died almost immediately. The earl took ill as well, although his case was mild and he recovered quickly. Unfortunately, it weakened him and his consumption symptoms returned tenfold."

"Why did my father ignore everything that went wrong?" Cade asked. "Surely he knew the manor could not maintain itself. It was already crumbling when I left. And why let the servants starve? My father has never been a kind man, but as far as I can recall, he always took his responsibilities seriously."

Father Vincent was silent for a moment, looking as though he wanted to say something but thought better of it. "The illness weakened the earl's mind," was all he said. "He may have been serious about letting Stephen learn on his own, but he would not scold him when things were done improperly or not at all. Once Stephen was gone, he no longer cared about any of it." The priest looked at Cade, his eyes brimming with genuine sympathy. "For all intents and purposes, you must start over here."

"God give me strength," Cade muttered, and dropped his face into his hands.

"He already has," the priest said. "If He had not, you would not be here."

❇

Cade thought on the priest's words as he climbed the stairs to his father's chambers after the meal and hoped that his God-given strength included the willpower to not strangle a mad, dying man, no matter how sorely he was tempted.

He entered the bedchamber without knocking, startling his father and nearly causing Goodwife Hawke to drop the spoon with which she fed broth between the old man's shriveled lips.

"The estate is in ruins," Cade announced without preamble. "There is nothing to eat, nothing to sell for profit, and the very walls are crumbling around us. What were you thinking, my lord, allowing Stephen to take control when he had no idea what he was doing? Did you not see the damage he was causing? It will cost a fortune to make this estate habitable again, let alone profitable! A fortune we have no way of making!"

The old man glowered at him. "Stephen was learning," he growled.

"By letting the manor collapse and the people go hungry?" Cade demanded. "Where *are* the servants, I ask you? Do you even know?" He went on before his father had a chance to answer. "They are either in our woods poaching just to keep themselves from starving to death, or they are serving the Earl of Brentford. The very man who begged you to *really* teach Stephen how to run an estate. He was kind enough to make work for the people who needed it, and I don't assume I can convince them to come back. So I will have to search among the people who remain to see if any of them are willing to serve me."

Goodwife Hawke scowled at him, but he barely registered that fact, for he had thought of something even more horrifying than the tasks that lay ahead of him.

"Do we have *any* gold, my lord?" Cade asked his father.

His father looked at him, and his watery gray eyes narrowed. "You have evidently already taken over the earldom despite the fact that I cling to life. You figure it out." He barked a sharp cough, and Goodwife Hawke was upon him in an instant, brushing hair from his eyes and whispering words Cade couldn't hear.

She glanced at Cade, and her expression was frosty.

"Your father needs his rest," she said. The implication in her words was clear. *Leave.*

She could be punished for her presumption, but he wouldn't do it. Not now. There was a bond between his father and the housekeeper that Cade didn't—and wasn't sure he wanted to—understand. That was fine. He was content to let them spend these last moments together. If she was busy caring for his father, she wouldn't have time to sow discontent in his household, and he would be able to pin his attention to everything else that had to be done. Besides—and he was loath to admit it, even to himself—he didn't have it in him to deny the woman any time by his father's side. She loved him. Only God knew why, but she did. Had someone tried to remove him from his mother's bedside as she lay dying, he would have killed them. He wouldn't do that to another human being, no matter how wretched the person.

So Cade nodded to them, then turned and left the room.

❀

On his second morning at Easton Cade found himself standing in the Great Hall as the church bells in the distance chimed nine o'clock.

Margery had followed his orders and gathered the pitiful excuse for a staff in the Great Hall. She was there, of course, as were Wat and an older boy Cade assumed was Ned. A nondescript gray-haired man who had to be Robin stood on Ned's other side. A plump woman—Goodwife Crosby, the cook?—stood beside Margery.

The only one not there was Goodwife Hawke.

"Where is the housekeeper?" Cade asked.

Margery's face blushed crimson.

"I tried, milord, honest I did," she pleaded. "She just wouldn't come."

It didn't matter. She'd be gone as soon as the earl breathed his last. No sense upsetting Margery over it. But it rankled that she would openly defy his authority in front of the rest of them.

He hoped none of them thought they could do the same.

"Thank you," he said uncertainly to the five people that stood in front of him. *This is ridiculous.* He was days from becoming earl, and he'd had his own household in London for years: what was he so nervous about? He tried to stand up straighter.

"On behalf of the earl and my late brother"—his voice was hoarse, and he coughed to clear his throat—"I apologize for the situation, and thank you sincerely for staying on to serve the estate despite the unfortunate circumstances. Your loyalty will not go unrewarded." He was discomfited by the way they looked at him. Was that derision in their eyes, or did he just imagine it?

"I am fully aware that you have not been regularly paid for your services in the last few years," he continued. "I intend to rectify that as soon as possible and ask you to stay on even after the earl has departed this world." He forced himself to make contact with the five pairs of eyes before him, one at a time, and hoped they didn't realize the dire state of Easton's finances. The income from his mother's estate would let him support these five, but it would never suffice for an entire staff.

Nevertheless, the castle *needed* a staff. It was a conundrum, and one he needed to solve right away. Somehow.

"For now, I will have you continue in your duties as you have been," he told them. "If you have any questions, or if there is a dire need for any supplies, please inform me immediately. I know you haven't had an easy time of it for the last several years. I promise you that as soon as I am able to change that, I will."

They murmured their consent, and he was slightly cheered to see that the derision had been replaced by a grudging admiration.

As the small group shuffled from the Great Hall and, presumably, back to their duties, Cade called Margery back to him.

"How old are you, Margery?" he asked her.

"Eighteen, milord."

Older than he'd thought, then. "And how long have you been in service here?"

"Since I was ten, milord. My mother was head laundress before she died last winter." Her hazel eyes were glossy. With tears?

Cade shifted his weight from one leg to the other and avoided her gaze. If there was one thing that made him more uncomfortable than his newfound position of authority, it was a sobbing female.

"I'm sorry to hear that," he muttered. He cleared his throat. "I'd like you to take over as housekeeper, Margery."

"Me?" she squeaked. "What of Goodwife Hawke, milord?"

"Her duties now lie entirely with caring for the earl. As soon as his suffering is over, she will retire to her daughter's home in the village," he told her. "She is aware of my plans for her, and nothing will change my mind. I've seen what's become of this place with her in charge, and it will no longer be that way."

"Thank you, milord," Margery breathed. "If I may be so bold … no, never mind."

"What is it, Margery?"

"Well," she began. "I have a little sister, and it would help us greatly if she were given a spot in the household. She's thirteen, and she's strong and a good worker. There's just the two of us, you see, since both of my parents are dead. I see her when I can, but she gets lonely in that little house all by herself."

"Bring her to me tomorrow," he said. "We have more than enough spots to fill."

"Oh, thank you!" Margery's plain, freckled face was wreathed in smiles. "She will prove worthy, milord, I promise!"

"We shall see," he told her. He fought his own smile. He'd finally done something right. "Now go back to work. Tell Goodwife Crosby that Father Vincent will again share the evening meal with me."

"Yes, milord." She scurried off.

The days slipped by. His father's health worsened, and Father Vincent lingered like a ghost in and around the old earl's chambers. Cade checked in on the old man every day but devoted the rest of his time, from dawn until twilight, to trying to rectify the damage done by his brother's ignorance, his father's stubbornness, and the passage of time. He sent for Jefferson in London with the intent to make him Easton's steward.

He had the marvelous good fortune to find a man in the village named Harry Stanton who could, by some miracle, read, write, and do numbers. After hearing several others testify to his honesty, Cade hired him as bailiff. Some sturdy village girls, including Margery's sister, Nell, were hired to work as scullery maids, chambermaids, and laundresses. He also had them replant the vegetable and herb garden along the castle's south wall. It was a bit late in the season for that, but he hoped that the garden would at least produce a small bounty to keep them fed through the winter.

He took a two-day trip to the market in Bewdley with a pouch containing a generous amount of his own gold. He returned with cattle, three dozen live chickens and a few roosters, some healthy sheep and a ram that he hoped to introduce to his current flock, bags of corn both for planting and feeding the horses—and an empty pouch. He arranged to have stone brought from a nearby quarry, though with only women and weak older men in the vicinity, he wondered how they were going to haul the stone to repair the castle's walls.

Harry Stanton told him, after inspecting the trees in the orchards, that they weren't in the hopeless condition Cade had initially thought. With some careful pruning, extra attention, and the blessing of cooperative weather, they would again produce fruit—not this year, but certainly the next.

Occasionally Cade's thoughts drifted to the red-haired girl in the lake. Where had she gone? He wondered if the girl had given *him* another thought after she'd fled and left him fuming on the shore of the lake, clad only in his wet breeches.

One night, after a particularly grueling day helping to plough the fields, Cade collapsed into bed without even taking the evening meal. The weather had been strange all day, and the sky was an ominous shade of violet. A summer thunderstorm was certainly on its way. Cade burrowed down in Stephen's bed, which was easier now that he'd taken that damned portrait down, and attempted to block out the howl of the wind as it tore through the branches of the oak tree by the window. He yanked the coverlet up around his ears to drown it out. But it was useless. It grew louder and more intense and took on an irritating whine.

Something gnawed at him. A flicker of memory—that ridiculous Irish myth about banshees—*Oh.*

He sat up.

That horrific keening was not coming from outside. It was not the wind.

Cade leapt from beneath the coverlet and took a cedar-scented nightshirt from the chest at the foot of the bed. He pulled it over his head, left the chamber, and fled to his father's rooms where the house servants had gathered, wrenched from sleep by Goodwife Hawke's noisy grief.

Cade's father lay against his pillows, his sightless eyes staring blankly at the ceiling, his face twisted into an expression so grotesque it might have been comical if a dead man hadn't worn it. Goodwife Hawke sprawled across the corpse and wailed. She was not wearing her cap, and tufts of sparse white hair fluttered like tattered moth wings as her bent body heaved with sobs. Cade shifted his weight from one leg to the other. His father was dead. What was the next step?

Then he realized the servants were staring at him.

"Someone see to it that Goodwife Hawke is taken to the servants' quarters," he said at last. "And give her a sleeping draught to calm her."

"We will, my lord." Ned stepped from the small horde, yanking Wat by the wrist.

"And someone else will need to prepare the body for burial." After a moment, Goodwife Crosby took a tentative step forward.

"I will, my lord earl," she mumbled.

His gaze whipped toward her. *My lord earl.* How strange it sounded.

Cade was numb as Ned and Wat gently detached Goodwife Hawke from the old earl's remains. They half-carried, half-dragged her resisting form away, murmuring gently to her the entire time. Her wails faded as they descended with her to the servants' quarters. When Cade turned his attention back to the bed, Goodwife Crosby and Robin, who had been returned to his status as butler, struggled to lift the body from the bed. Goodwife Crosby was at the head, Robin at the feet, and together they moved to shift the earl's body into the air.

The next morning Goodwife Hawke was gone. He sent Robin to scour the grounds for her, and she was eventually located in her daughter's cottage, the very cottage to which he'd wanted to send her once his father died. Cade had planned to have her keep watch over his father's body at night and send her away after the funeral, but he decided to let her stay where she was. He didn't wish to be cruel by asking her to spend all that time with his father's body, only to dismiss her once the old earl was buried. And now that Cade had a funeral to plan, he didn't need any distractions.

The last, and only, funeral he'd planned was his mother's. He wondered what she'd say if she had survived the old man instead of the other way around. Before he could stop it as he usually did, an image of her flashed through his mind—his mother on her funeral bier, her pale, still face framed in the golden hair he himself had carefully brushed into glossy ringlets, as he sat alone with her body in the Great Hall and sobbed while his father and Stephen were out on a hunt. A spasm of pain seized Cade and he tried to shake off the memories. God, he hated this place.

❁

Thomas, Wexley, and young Waltham sat around the big oak desk in Thomas's great chamber. Though the June afternoon was warm, one of the chambermaids had lit a fire and the heat in the room was oppressive. Or perhaps it was Thomas's nerves that caused beads of sweat to roll from his hairline and over his temple before snaking behind his ears. He wasn't at all sure that what he was about to do was the right thing.

"What's this about, Tom?" Henry boomed.

Thomas's eyes flickered to Peter, whose gangly frame slouched against the carved wooden chair. He must have been warm too—a mustache of sweat glistened over his thin upper lip.

No, he wasn't sure at all.

"I wanted to talk to you about the matter you mentioned the other day," Thomas said.

Henry's fleshy face scrunched. "What matter?"

How could he have forgotten? "About a marriage. Between Peter and my Samara." Best get the words out before he changed his mind.

Waltham arched a carroty eyebrow and cast a glance at his father, whose eyes had widened.

"Ah. Of course." Henry shifted in the chair, which was almost comically dwarfed by his massive frame.

"I'm prepared to give my consent," Thomas said, though he wasn't. "Under certain conditions."

Henry reached for the tray on Thomas's desk, grabbed at the bread that sat there, and tore off a hunk. He stuffed it into his mouth and chewed. "What think you, boy?" He addressed his son with his mouth still full, damp crumbs of bread flying with each word.

Waltham shrugged.

"She's pretty," he said. "But I don't know. She's rather prudish."

"She has been gently raised," Thomas said. Hot anger swept up his neck and into his cheeks. How dare this boy act as if chastity were a fault instead of a virtue? He fought to keep his temper in check. Losing it would not help his cause. He had to have a plan for Samara.

Henry reached out and cuffed his son on the side of his head. Waltham yelped as he tried to deflect his father's open hand.

"What kind of son have I raised that would attempt to have his way with a nobly bred virgin without the benefit of marriage?" Henry roared. "Servant girls are one thing, boy. Ladies are quite another. I will hear no more talk of that sort from you."

Waltham scowled and rubbed at his temple.

"And she's strange," he went on, eyeing his father warily. "Always staring at things no one else can see and disappearing for hours on end. Lady Katherine's the one who takes care of the household. Anyone can see that. I don't know that I'd want a wife who spent most of her time in some imaginary world while the manor got dirty and the servants lax."

Thomas looked down at the goblet in his hands and twirled it in his fingers. In this case the impudent fool was right. Wasn't Samara's oddness one of the things that had kept him from seeking a husband for her to begin with?

Still, it hurt to know that others saw it as well. Anne's eccentricity had been one of the qualities that had drawn him to her. He hated that the same qualities in their daughter had the power to push potential suitors away.

"She has an independent spirit," Thomas replied, but the defense sounded weak even to his ears. "Surely a strong husband will be able to break her of those habits." Even though he wasn't sure if he *wanted* them broken. Who would she be without them?

"I don't know," Waltham whined.

"What don't you know?" Henry demanded. "The girl's a beauty. She may be odd, but as Tom says, a good husband can cure her of bad habits. She's your equal in rank. I fail to see the difficulty." He glowered at his son. "You should be satisfied with the wife you get. I won't deny that. But remember it's still my duty as your father to help you choose."

Waltham's face flushed.

"I want a wife who will enjoy the marriage bed," he said. "Not a cold fish." He shrugged again. "I don't believe that's too much to ask."

Thomas looked to Henry, hoping his friend would cuff the boy again, but Henry laughed instead. "It's too much to ask of a *wife*, son." He chuckled. "That's when a houseful of pretty chambermaids comes in handy. Besides, I don't doubt that you'll succeed in proving to her that joy can be found in the marriage bed. Women are nervous fillies, my boy. They need breaking in."

Thomas struggled with his fury. God's toenail, this was his *daughter* they talked about!

"I understand your concerns," he said before he let his anger get the better of him. "Waltham, if it eases your mind at all, I'm actually of the opinion that Samara should make her own choice."

"Her own choice?" Henry boomed. "Tom, what nonsense is that? Since when can a girl be trusted to make a wise choice about something like marriage? She should marry where it best benefits *you*. Your way, she's more likely to make a foolish mistake and lie with the first handsome face to pay her a pretty compliment."

"Her mother was my choice," Thomas said quietly. "And we were happy together until the childbed fever took her. I want no less for my daughters, Hal. If your son isn't yet enamored of the idea of marriage to Samara, I will send her to London this autumn, to Mary's court. She'll have until Christmas to find a man who suits not only her but me. I will have final say." Now where the hell had *that* idea come from? He'd never once thought to send her to court. Rumors of the queen's poor health flitted through Worcestershire with some regularity. Was there even a court to which he could send her?

Well, he couldn't take it back now. "Samara is not unintelligent. She knows her worth. She will choose wisely. However, if for some reason she's unable to find someone suitable, then I propose a match between our children."

"I don't know," Henry hedged. He glanced at his son. "What do you say about all this, Peter?"

Waltham fidgeted in the wooden chair.

"I suppose," he finally said. "I can't deny she'll make a pretty ornament on my arm when I take her to court myself. Going there now will help her make some useful connections. And if she has her fun first, she will be more likely to settle down and be a proper wife when the time comes. My mother can teach her what she'll need to know."

Thomas seethed. A pretty ornament? His Samara was so much more than that. He was right—she would be wasted on this young idiot. How could he gracefully retract his offer?

"Then it's settled? Aye, Tom. It's a deal. She only has until Christmas, though. Barring bad weather, if we don't receive word from you by Twelfth Night, I will look elsewhere for a wife for Peter. I've been compiling a list since Jane Rowling died last winter and have come up with a decent selection. "

"Fair enough. Thank you for understanding." Thomas managed a smile for his guests, but was sick in the pit of his stomach.

What have I just done?

Chapter Four

SINCE HE WAS A YOUNG MAN, CADE HAD ANTICIPATED THE BLESSED relief that would surely come when his father died. Not joy—he wasn't callous enough, even after everything his father had put him through, to be actually *happy* that the old man was dead. But he'd always imagined he would feel a bit lighter, as if the weight his father's cruel words piled upon his shoulders had finally fallen off.

The reality was different.

If anything, he felt worse. He had *not* magically forgotten every spiteful word the old man had ever hurled his way. They met him at every turn. *Was* he useless and a failure? Would he ever be able to turn the crumbling ruin that was Easton into even a semblance of what it once had been?

He wondered.

Another day was almost at an end. On the old oak desk in the library, a candle burned—beeswax, thankfully, discovered in a coffer that for some reason had been stashed out of sight high on a shelf in the pantry—and cast a dim, flickering light over the pages of the ancient account book Cade had found.

"My lord earl?" The voice floated from the doorway.

Cade glanced up. "Yes, Jefferson. What is it?" He was grateful for the interruption. He had never liked mathematics, and after a few hours of staring at the tiny, faded, handwritten numbers they had begun to flit before his eyes like a swarm of particularly irritating gnats.

"Sir Hayden has arrived, my lord."

Cade nearly knocked over the stool upon which he'd been perched. "Where is he?"

"He awaits you in the Great Hall."

Cade was already halfway out the door. "Bring some refreshments." He rushed from the library before the steward could even acknowledge the command.

The man who stood by the hearth swept into a theatrical bow when Cade entered the hall.

"My lord of Easton," he said with exaggerated deference. "I apologize for the inconvenience of my unexpected arrival—"

"Don't torment me with that, Hayden." Cade laughed. "What in hell are you doing here?" He went to his cousin and hugged him. It felt good. He'd been back in Worcestershire for weeks but so wrapped up in his own problems that he had not written to his cousin—a man who was mourning the loss of his own wife. *What a selfish monster I am.*

When Cade stepped back, Hayden nodded his head toward the corpse on its bier, which still awaited burial after three days.

"I thought you might need me," he said simply.

A warmth Cade hadn't felt in some time spread through him. No wonder Hayden was not just his cousin but his best friend. He always had been, ever since a sixteen-year-old Cade had arrived unannounced at Hayden's father's home with no place to stay, very little coin, and only the clothes on his back.

It had been a graceless introduction to the side of his family he'd known only from stories, despite their close proximity to each other, the family that would go on to unofficially foster him since his father had seen no need to make other arrangements. So Cade had no reservations when it came to telling his cousin exactly how overwhelmed he felt.

"Thank you," Cade said. "As usual, you're right. I do need you. I have no idea what I'm doing here. The funeral is in two more days, and I imagine everyone within fifty miles will be here expecting a feast. I don't know what I'll feed them and where I'll put them. I hope to God the deer in our park didn't run off in search of greener pastures as the servants did. Otherwise I will be serving boiled carrots, black bread, and not much else."

Hayden laughed. He'd always had a hearty, easy laugh, which was just one of the reasons Cade had felt an immediate and effortless kinship with him even when they were strangers. But the laughter was different now. Hollow. Cade looked closely at his cousin for the first time and noted the dark circles beneath Hayden's eyes, his sunken cheeks, his joyless smile.

"I'm sorry about Penelope," Cade said at last. "And sorrier still that I was too concerned with my own troubles even to send a message. If I were you, I would not give me a passing thought."

Hayden sighed, and his face twisted into a poor attempt at a smile.

"Thank you," he said. Jefferson appeared and offered his master and his guest each a goblet of wine.

They took them, and Hayden tossed his back in what seemed like one gulp before he put the goblet back on the tray in Jefferson's outstretched hand. "Please don't feel guilty. We're more than even. I was so devastated over losing Penelope that I couldn't muster the sense to send a message to you in Paris about Stephen." He gave a little laugh. "I can but imagine the look you must have had on your face when Jefferson told you that you were the new heir to Easton!"

Jefferson emitted a cough that sounded suspiciously like a laugh. Cade laughed too, and with that, the mantle of sorrow that had hung over the room slipped away.

"It was a shock unlike any I'd ever had," he agreed. He sipped from his goblet. "How are you, Hayden? Honestly?"

Hayden shrugged.

"It was God's will," he said. "The epidemic claimed much of the country, but luckily it was a small outbreak in our part of the county. You were fortunate to be in Rome, and safe."

Fortunate? Safe? Cade wondered what his cousin would say if he knew how close he'd come to losing his life.

Later. Now was not the time to burden Hayden with the news, or himself with the memories.

Hayden gave a bleak smile. "So I am a widower at twenty-six, and with a motherless daughter to boot."

Cade gestured helplessly. "I don't know that this place is any happier, Hayden," he said. "Not that I don't want you to stay. Quite the opposite, in fact. You can stay as long as you like. But I don't want to make you feel worse."

"I'm not looking for something to make me happy. It would be impossible right now anyway." The desolate words were so unlike his cousin that Cade's heart lurched. "I'm just looking for something to keep me busy. And from what I saw of your estate, I've found it." He gave a lopsided grin then, and though it didn't quite reach his eyes, a wave of relief washed over Cade. At least Hayden had it in him to try.

"It's the truth," Cade admitted. "The place is a mess. I've been lucky to get so much as an hour's sleep each night, I'm so much on my mind. Things that need to be fixed, servants that need to be hired—I've combed the village and still haven't managed to find enough men strong enough to lift a single plate of glass for a window. How will I ever make this place habitable? I may as well just knock it down and sell off the stone."

Hayden frowned. He took the second goblet of wine Jefferson offered him, sipping it this time, and then looked at Cade.

"Who is your nearest neighbor?" he asked.

Cade thought for a second. "I suppose the Earl of Brentford, to the east," he replied. "Why do you ask?"

"Have you considered asking him for help?"

"I barely know the man," Cade said. "He and my father were friends of sorts, but I haven't seen him in twelve years. I can hardly show up at his door and ask that he part with half of his staff for a few months so that I can restore my own castle."

"If he was your father's friend, he might do it out of sentiment," Hayden suggested.

"Hmm." Cade bit into a biscuit and chewed as he thought. "I can't pay them," he said after swallowing. "The bailiff that was here in my father's time ran off with the gold while my father was on pilgrimage. The monies from my own property will keep us afloat for several months, but I can't squander them. And if my father managed to save any gold, he didn't tell me, and I've yet to find it."

"It can't hurt to ask."

Perhaps Hayden was right. What was the worst that could happen? *Brentford could say no and humiliate me in front of the entire county.*

Or he could say yes, and all my problems will be solved.

"Nell," Cade said to the maid as she passed. She stopped short and curtsied quickly to him.

"Yes, my lord," she said.

"Prepare a room for Sir Hayden. He will be my guest indefinitely."

"Yes, my lord." She curtsied again and scurried off.

Cade turned back to his cousin.

"Well, Hayden, I can't promise that it will be exactly like old times, but I daresay it's about to get a bit better for both of us."

Hayden raised his goblet before tipping his head back and downing the rest of his wine.

❋

For the first time since he'd returned, Cade was able to sit and enjoy a meal. He and Hayden dined in Stephen's chamber before the fire, gorging themselves on the food Goodwife Crosby sent up—the star being a capon, roasted golden and stuffed with bread and dried apples. Cade wondered where the gorgeous bird had come from, but he didn't think long on it, for it looked and smelled too appetizing to waste time on minor details when he could be eating it. They had been too busy earlier in the day to sit down for supper, but now it was past sunset, and Cade's stomach rumbled with hunger.

Goodwife Crosby had prepared boiled asparagus and tiny carrots and loaves of fresh white bread along with the capon, and they ate hungrily, stopping only for occasional conversation and the opportunity to gulp from their tankards of ale between bites. When Cade felt stuffed to bursting, Goodwife Crosby sent up a bowl of ripe wild strawberries with sweet cream to drizzle over them. Cade groaned in delight and fell onto the fruits, barely hearing Hayden's demand to leave a few for him.

It was by far the best evening Cade had spent since coming home. His cousin was with him, his belly was full of good food and not vegetable potage, and though he still found hard to believe the amount of work that needed to be done to make the manor habitable, he felt as though finishing it lay within the realm of possibility.

"More ale?" he asked Hayden. "Or some wine? There is plenty stored in the cellar. At least Stephen had the sense to see to that."

His cousin shook his head and yawned.

"Much as I'd love to stay up and drink myself into oblivion, I'm exhausted," he replied. "I hope you don't mind if I just seek my bed."

"Of course not!" Cade answered, though he was a bit disappointed. But perhaps Hayden had the right idea. Maybe he would attempt a full night's sleep tonight himself. "I'll have a maid show you to your rooms."

When the door closed behind his cousin, however, Cade wasn't yet ready to seek his own bed. He drank another mug of ale, then wandered into the kitchen, where a few of the new scullery maids scrubbed down the pots and Goodwife Crosby kneaded dough for bread. *White dough? Where on earth did she get the flour?*

"Goodwife Crosby," Cade asked. "Where did the food for tonight's meal come from? I know our larders don't have anything as delicious as the capon Hayden and I ate."

"'It was sent over, my lord," she answered.

"Sent over? From where?"

"From the Earl of Brentford, my lord." She punched the bread dough with a plump, floured fist. "He sent this flour, too. You were out in the fields all day, and one of Brentford's men showed up in the courtyard. He gave Wat a basket and said to bring it to the cook for supper."

"I see." So Brentford *was* the sentimental sort. Was there actually a chance he would be willing to lend Cade a few strong men to do things like install the windows and lay new stone? It was something to think about. The man had already tried to help once. Perhaps he was kind enough to do it again.

"Thank you, Goodwife Crosby."

"Yes, my lord." She tore the mass of dough into smaller chunks and began to shape them into loaves.

Cade returned to the library. He lit the candle, now barely more than a stump, on his desk and sat, flipping the battered account book open to the page at which he'd last looked. But it was pointless. The numbers swirled in front of his eyes, and after just a few moments of staring at them he was unable to make heads or tails of the information—not that it would have mattered, really, since the book was more than five years old. It would have nothing with which he could settle current accounts. He sighed and shut the thing.

The tiny red-gold flame from the candle caught his eye and retrieved the girl he'd met at the lake from the back of his mind. The flame was the same shade as her hair and burned as hot as her temper. He wondered again what had become of her since she'd run off. Did she have a protector in Brentford? Had she told him what had happened?

Not that it mattered. He'd probably never see her again. Once the manor was restored and generating a steady income, he wouldn't have to spend much time there at all. The memories that haunted Easton were not the kind with which he wanted to surround himself. But if the rumors were true and the queen would be forced to name Lady Elizabeth as her successor, Cade's future in London and his place among the royal circle were at serious risk. He was fortunate to have Glenwood on which to fall back. The property his mother had bequeathed him was in Shropshire, and the black-faced sheep it raised generated enough money for him to repair Easton and support himself. Could he build a life for himself there if London became dangerous?

Too, now that he was earl he'd have to marry and sire a few children. He could leave his wife at Easton while he settled himself at Glenwood. He would have to visit Easton several times a year, if only to show his people that he cared, but there was no reason to set up a permanent residence. Was there?

He sighed again. He didn't know. Despite the smattering of knowledge he'd picked up from his short time with Hayden's family, there was so much he had to learn about his new position, his new life. Had he been a coward to run off when he had, confident that things would stay the same and that Stephen would inherit everything? Why hadn't it crossed his mind, just once, that something might occur that would leave Cade heir? Accidents happened all the time, and epidemics were not discerning of who they killed—he knew that now. He'd been so stupid not to consider that his world could be yanked out from beneath him.

Maybe—he shuddered at the thought—his father had been right. Maybe it *had* been foolish to run off to London when anything could happen, as it eventually did. He'd found his own way, certainly, as second sons were expected to do. He'd even survived Rome and a trip to Paris at a time when France was the last country in which an Englishman should have found himself. But his was a way that had cut him off entirely from his past. It was what he'd wanted, what he'd set out to do. But had it been a mistake?

It was too late for speculation. He was here for the time being, doing all he could until his estate and his people could take care of themselves. Or until he found a wife who could do that for him.

He glanced at the candle, cheerful with its dancing orange flame, and blew it out.

❋

Cade's wrists felt like they would crack beneath the weight of the wooden bier that bore his father's corpse as they made their way to Easton's small church. He hadn't thought that the body, as emaciated as his father had been at the time of his death, would weigh so damn much. He held his breath, shifted his hands just a few centimeters, and reveled in the minor wave of relief that washed up his burning arms. On the other side of the bier, Hayden's face contorted into a pained expression. Cade grimaced in sympathy. Although his knees also ached, he longed to come upon the next cross in the road for a chance to put the bier down and rest while he prayed yet again for his father's soul.

The church bells pealed a sorrowful reprise that grew deafening as Cade, Hayden, and the other two pallbearers—Ned, who had been promoted to head groom of the stable thanks to his facility with horses, and the Earl of Brentford—led the procession into the churchyard.

Father Vincent met them at the church stile.

"He will be with God soon, my lord earl," the priest said piously.

"Thank you, Father," Cade murmured. His arm muscles screamed.

The four pallbearers followed the priest into the church and set the bier at the front by the altar. The stink of incense was strong. Cade's eyes watered, and he swallowed his cough.

The mourners that made up the funeral procession shuffled into the church. Their black robes swirled about their feet, and their sobs were muffled. Cade wanted to laugh at the implausibility of it. Of course, mourning was to be expected whenever someone passed—indeed, it was a social requirement. But he wondered about their sincerity. Given the harsh life they'd lived under his father and brother, they couldn't be sad. Could they?

Cade was not, and for that he felt guilty. Well, perhaps he was mourning a bit, but not for his dead father. If he was sad about losing anything, it was the life he had once known, the life he would never live again. If that made him the idiot his father had always accused him of being, so be it. He would make no apologies for the man he'd become.

He *would* do his duty. He would see that his people were secure, warm, and fed. He would see that his servants were paid fairly and on time. Hell, he'd marry and sire children to carry on his line.

Even if that particular thought made him want to flee to the safety of Bedlam.

One of the saving graces of being the younger, mostly ignored son was that there had been no familial pressure on him to marry. He'd been free to waste his time on discreet dalliances with noble wives and widows at court, and he'd always found that lifestyle quite satisfying. He knew Her Majesty might take it upon herself to choose a wife for him as she had for Hayden, but she had never mentioned it, and he had never brought it up. After witnessing the disastrous union between his parents, marriage was something he'd hoped to avoid entirely.

But now it was inevitable. If anything was going to bring him to tears today, it was the thought of having to marry and beget an heir for an earldom he didn't even want.

Cade shifted in the pew and attempted to focus his attention to the altar, where Father Vincent spoke the familiar words of the funeral Mass and sprinkled holy water around the bier.

"Earth to earth, ashes to ashes, dust to dust, in sure and certain hope of resurrection to eternal life," he droned, and cast a handful of dirt onto the coffin.

The late earl was to be interred inside the church, as his father and grandfather, the first earl, had been before him. Stephen, his mother, and Cade's mother were there as well. Cade had never given much thought to the place where he would spend his own eternal rest, but now he realized that he too would lie here someday. The thought was not a disturbing one, so long as he was nearer to his own mother than to the men of his family. He would have to be sure to put that in writing at some point, just in case. Though he wondered who would take the responsibility of burying *him* if the time came anytime soon.

"Godspeed," Father Vincent said at last, and the funeral was over. Cade could barely stifle a sigh of relief. Now he could feed his guests and his people, hand out the alms, and untangle the mess he had inherited.

❀

Cade surveyed the scene in the hall of Easton Manor. The room teemed with people, both local gentry and members of the aristocracy who happened to be in the area when word of the Earl of Easton's death spread through the countryside. Wealthy or not, they wouldn't pass up the opportunity to indulge in a free meal. Cade tried to count heads but could not. He guessed that there were at least fifty people in the Great Hall alone—not taking into account the people in the courtyard feasting on whatever their hands could grab. Thanks to a hunting trip he and Hayden had taken the day before, the high board inside the castle groaned beneath the weight of twenty roe deer, eight wild boar, dishes of meat pies stuffed with pheasant, loaves of fine white bread, and even some fresh-churned butter. Salads of herbs dressed with vinegar broke up the heaviness of the meat dishes. Ale and perry from the cellar flowed freely, and had he allowed any dogs into the hall, they surely would have eaten a king's feast from the scraps his guests dropped to the newly polished floor.

"My lord earl," said a man's voice, yanking Cade from his thoughts.

Cade turned his head. A portly man stood beside him. Gentry no doubt, perhaps even nobility, for the clothing the man wore might once have been elegant and fashionable and still could have appeared so from a distance, but up close the wear was evident around the edges of his faded, slightly dingy doublet. The man's round face was red above his yellowed lace ruff, and sweat beaded beneath the fringe of thin black hair that framed his forehead.

"Good day," Cade responded, inclining his head slightly and hoping the man would mention his own name, since Cade had no idea what it might be.

"I thought I might introduce you to my daughter, Mistress Agnes," the man said. He gestured to the female beside him.

Let us cut to the chase, shall we? Cade thought with a mix of annoyance and amusement. The man was daft if he thought he'd been the first to approach Cade that day with a marriageable daughter at his side. Most had been slightly more subtle about it, but it was obvious that whatever his reputation might have been, he was now regarded as a very eligible bachelor. Would all these men want him for their daughters if they knew he'd yet to find any trace of his family's money?

Cade glanced at the girl. She was not large like her father but thin to the point of boniness, which Cade thought was less attractive. Her face was long and narrow, with deep-set, mud-colored eyes that briefly met his before dropping to stare at the floor. Her complexion was ghost-pale—due not to artifice but to a lack of life. She wore an old-fashioned gable hood, which did nothing for her face, and a gown of drab greenish-brown fabric.

The poor thing had to realize she hadn't a prayer.

"It's a pleasure to meet you, Mistress Agnes," he forced himself to say.

"Thank you, milord," she mumbled in a voice so low he would have had to lean closer to hear what she said if he'd had any interest.

"So, Easton," the man—whoever he was—said. "What say you to the possibility of a match between you and my daughter?"

Cade gritted his teeth to keep his jaw from dropping. He sneaked a glance at poor Mistress Agnes. Oh, she wasn't so ghost-pale anymore. Her skin had turned a blotchy crimson.

He had to get away. The way Cade saw it, only two things could come of such a conversation: he could refuse the match then and there, thus embarrassing the poor girl even more than she obviously already was; or he could confess that his father had left him no money whatsoever and risk the entire country learning that he was, for all intents and purposes, a pauper.

Neither prospect was particularly appealing.

Cade glanced across the hall, toward the hearth, where Brentford stood and chatted with another man Cade didn't know but who at least looked vaguely familiar. Brentford's three daughters had accompanied him to the funeral, but Cade had yet to see their faces except from a distance. He had been putting off approaching the man. He still worried that a request for further help might be met with derision or worse, a flat-out refusal. Cade wouldn't blame him. Brentford had already done far more than he should have, just out of kindness.

But he had to get away from Mistress Agnes and her tactless father.

"If you'll excuse me," Cade said, "I see someone I must speak with."

"But—" the man said.

"It was a pleasure to meet you, Mistress Agnes." Cade smiled at her but was gone before she could lift her head to see it.

He hurried toward Brentford and reached him just as his companion—*the Marquess of Wexley! There, I am not completely ignorant*—turned away. Cade could see two of the earl's daughters clearly as he approached. One was prettily plump, with pink cheeks, a sweet smile, and a bit of golden brown hair visible at the edge of her French hood. The other was a tiny, elfin blonde with bright blue eyes. Both lovely. Their faces wreathed in shy smiles, they curtsied as he approached. Only the third daughter still had her back to him, but as he drew up next to her, she turned, and—

God's nightshirt, it couldn't be!

The gold-flecked green eyes were familiar, certainly. As were the burnished curls that threatened to spill from the French hood that struggled to contain them. Her mouth fell open, and her face took on an expression he knew he had seen before. Hadn't it been haunting his memory these past few weeks?

The saucy redheaded wench from the lake—Brentford's daughter—they were one and the same.

He gaped at her like an idiot, while she had the presence of mind to close her own mouth after a second. Her eyes were wide enough to allow a white circle around her irises. The bitter-tasting knowledge that she had made a fool of him rose in the back of his throat like bile. He'd tried to seduce his neighbor's daughter—the neighbor he needed to ask for help—as if she were no more than a common tavern wench! Of course, he reasoned with himself, a girl who cavorted half-naked in a lake should expect to be treated as such, but still!

He forced his horror aside and turned to her father. "Lord Brentford," he began at the same moment the girl flung her cup of wine to the floor, where it pooled at the edge of her skirt.

"Samara!" the darker-haired daughter gasped. "What are you doing?"

"Oh," the girl exclaimed. "How clumsy of me! It slipped right from my hand!"

"Jefferson!" Cade called. "We've a spill that must be cleaned up." He looked down at the girl and gripped her elbow, drawing her away from the spreading puddle. She stared up at him, eyes wide.

"You don't want to stain your skirt, do you?" he asked pointedly. How stupid did she think he was? If he told her father what she'd done, he would have to confess what he'd done as well. Then he'd be known as not only a pauper but a lecher. And Brentford would never help him.

Still, he had to admire her bravado.

"No, my lord. Thank you." She was polite, but there was no mistaking the fear in her voice.

He released her elbow. The little blonde giggled.

"Well, Lord Easton, allow me to introduce you to my daughters," the other man said with a sigh. "Lady Cecily." The blonde curtsied. "Lady Katherine," he said, and the other girl did the same. "And Lady Samara," he finished.

The redhead bit her lip and curtsied quickly. "I swear to you that they are not ill-bred," the earl added. "Just unused to spending time among people other than themselves and our household."

"It could have happened to anyone," Cade assured the man. The unexpected urge to laugh came over him. He choked it back. "Lord Brentford, if I may have a moment alone with you?"

"Certainly." The other earl's expression was mildly curious.

He turned, hoping Brentford would follow for he had no desire to look back. He was terrified that he would burst into laughter.

Cade led Brentford into his library, where he lit a new candle and picked up a flagon of Malmsey from the desk. He filled two goblets and slid one to his guest; they tapped them together.

"To Easton," Brentford said.

"Yes," Cade said after a second's hesitation. They both drank deeply before speaking.

"I'm afraid there's really no graceful way to go about this," Cade said at last. "My lord, I've been told that you know how in the last years of their lives my father and brother neglected their people terribly, to the point where most of the servants deserted and many of them, and their families, died of illness and starvation."

Brentford nodded, his gray eyes serious. "I was aware," he said. "I took in those that I could, but I only had so many positions to fill. A few scullery maids and a groom or two, that's all."

"You have my gratitude," Cade assured him. "I can't thank you enough for helping the people you did, and for trying to help my family. I really have no right to ask another boon of you, but, my lord, I can't think of any other place to turn."

Brentford sipped his wine. "Go on," he said.

"You see Easton's condition," Cade said. "It's crumbling before our eyes. And because my father and Stephen cared so little for our people, I have no one strong enough to do the work required to make it habitable again. We need stone hauled, glass windows replaced, fields tilled, and crops planted."

Cade sighed. "I'm afraid I have no choice but to presume on your long friendship with my father and ask if you have any able-bodied men that you can spare for a time to help me rebuild my home."

The other man was silent. Cade held his breath.

"When do you plan to start the work?" he asked at last.

"As soon as possible. I've already placed orders with the glass maker and the quarry in Staffordshire. And it may be too late in the season to sow new corn crops, but I am going to attempt it anyway. I have no choice. My people need to see that I am trying to build a new life for them. They need to feel safe and taken care of."

"How long do you think the work will take?"

"Two months, perhaps three at the most."

"And their pay?"

"I have my own property that generates an income," Cade admitted. "I will match the wages they would earn from you, plus a fifth more." He tried not to wince. He could do it, but the remaining income would be stretched paper-thin.

Brentford considered this for a moment before he put his goblet on the desk and met Cade's eyes.

"I have another idea," he said.

"My lord?" Cade frowned.

"My men will work for you for free if you will sell me your other estate. You can use the monies from the purchase to keep Easton going until it can sustain itself again."

Cade blinked. His shock would allow no other reaction. Brentford would take Glenwood from him? The only part of his mother he had left?

"Where is the property located?" Brentford asked politely.

"Shropshire, my lord," Cade choked out. "I raise sheep there. But it's small." *Don't do this to me.*

"Any extra income helps, Lord Easton. I have three daughters to dower, and soon."

Cade was aware of that. And intellectually he knew that what Brentford proposed was indeed the most sensible plan. He would be able to continue living comfortably while Easton recovered. But could he part with the estate? He'd not spent much time there at all, but it was a gift from his mother. Could he let it go to save the land his father and brother had nearly succeeded in destroying?

No. He couldn't. But he would have to. People relied on him.

"Yes." He swallowed hard to dislodge the lump that had suddenly sprung into his throat. "I will sell you the estate. Thank you." He forced a smile. "I truly am grateful. If I'm ever able to do anything for you, don't hesitate to ask." Of course, Brentford would have no idea what Cade *had* just done for him by preserving Lady Samara's secret.

"We shall speak on that at some point," Brentford murmured. He raised the goblet to his lips and drained it before placing it back on the desk. "I will contact my lawyer in London about the transfer of the property. And come and see me sometime in the next few days. You can choose the men you think will best suit your purposes."

"I will," Cade replied. He set down his own goblet and stretched out his trembling hand to the other earl. They shook, and Cade led the way back to the hall.

The crowd had thinned but Brentford's daughters stood where their father had left them. Hayden had joined their tiny circle and the looks on their faces revealed they'd been taken in by his charm. The little one—Cecily?—wore an especially rapt expression as she gazed at him.

"I think it's time we took our leave," Brentford said.

"Won't you stay?" Cade asked, more out of politeness than any real desire to have them as overnight guests. He wanted to be alone to mourn this latest loss. But Brentford *did* have those daughters, although Lady Samara, he'd wager, could hold her own against highwayman or beast alike. "It is already dark, and you have a bit of a journey ahead of you."

"No, no," Brentford said, "though I thank you. Girls, say your goodbyes."

"Goodbye, Sir Hayden," Lady Cecily said, her high, childlike voice dripping sweetness. Her sisters stifled their giggles, and Hayden flushed.

Lady Katherine curtsied to both of them. "Thank you for your hospitality, my lord," she said to Cade. "I'm very sorry for your loss."

Lady Samara raised her eyes to his boldly, but her expression was unreadable. Then she dipped into a curtsey.

"Thank you, my lord," she murmured. Her voice sent a chill over him.

"Thank you for coming," he replied. Was that *his* voice? It sounded hoarse. He hoped he wasn't coming down with an ague. It was likely just the damn lump that refused to be dislodged from his throat no matter how hard he swallowed.

Brentford led the girls away. When Cade turned back to Hayden, his cousin wore a grin.

"Well, I may have been the so-called eligible bachelor here today, but none of the fathers that approached me made their intentions as clear as Lady Cecily did," Cade remarked.

"A valiant effort, Cade, but do you mean to tell me that Lady Samara *wasn't* vying for your attention when she threw her wine to the floor?"

Cade shrugged. "It appeared to me that she just dropped it."

"I'm sure." Hayden raised his eyebrow in the conciliatory way he sometimes had.

"What?" Cade demanded.

"For some reason, I just don't believe we've seen the last of those girls." Hayden's grin finally bore a hint of his old self.

Chapter Five

LADY SAMARA HAUGHTON LONGED TO SLOUCH AGAINST THE UP-holstered seat of the bouncing carriage, close her eyes, and pretend that the last few weeks—this day in particular—had been a nightmare from which she would awaken at any second. Unfortunately, the stiff bodice of her gown prevented her from doing so, so she was instead forced to sit upright and alert, doing everything she could to avoid the suspicious gaze of her sister Katherine.

Samara scowled at Kat but didn't speak. Her sister was too observant for her own good.

"What is wrong with you?" Katherine asked, not the least bit intimidated by Samara's frown.

"Nothing," Samara replied, hoping she sounded as innocent as possible under the circumstances. Innocent, however, was a bit of a stretch. A man—and not just any man, but the infuriatingly gorgeous Earl of Easton—had caught her swimming in nothing but her chemise. Why, he might as well have seen her naked as the day her mother had borne her! And as if that hadn't been embarrassment enough, he had *flirted* with her. He'd thought her some peasant girl, running away from her duties under the hot May sun for a quick refresher in the cool water. Which, if she was honest with herself, was really the only conclusion he *could* have drawn. But she was in no mood to be honest, with herself or anyone else.

Panic at discovery and fear that word of her activities would reach her father had made her bold—and *stupid*, she thought. She had no idea if Lord Easton's father had been a gentleman or not.

She had met the old earl but twice, on visits with her father, and he had never spoken a word to her. How she had known a compliment to his father would touch a nerve and shut him up, she didn't know. But it had. She'd seen the stricken look on his face before realizing her legs felt steady enough to carry her back home.

She had not wanted to come to the funeral today, but custom— and her father—had insisted. Even Betty, her faithful nurse-turned-maidservant, had seen through her complaints of an ache in her head and like a traitor informed Lord Brentford. Betty thought the problem was that Samara hadn't been to a funeral since her own mother's and concluded that Samara was concerned about the memories it would dredge up. Samara wished that were true, but personally she had little recollection of her own mother's funeral. She had been only five at the time, and her memories were limited to dodging the feet of the dozens of strangers that crowded her father's Great Hall to avoid being crushed and wondering what she had done to make her lady mother go away from her.

But this morning she played along with Betty, hoping against hope that her father would tell her to stay home and rest until she felt better, futile as that wish proved to be. Her father the earl had chosen a very inconvenient time to exercise his parental authority over her. For all the times in the last twelve years she had wished he would come out of the fields or his study and act like the father she remembered— the one that would take her up on his horse and bring her down to the village, teach her about the different wildflowers that grew in the meadow, or even scold her for something she'd done wrong—his wielding of power had been sporadic at best, which was how she was able to get away with slipping down to the lake and swimming for hours in nothing but her undergarments, among other things. The one time she *wanted* him to dismiss her, though, he had instead forced her to dress, bid farewell to a man she barely knew and hadn't particularly liked, and spend the rest of the day quivering in fear that the new Earl of Easton would inform Samara's father of how she spent her free time—a building terror which had culminated in her flinging a glass of wine to the ground to distract him and staining the hem of her best gown. Her father the earl would have been angry enough at that. She couldn't imagine his fury if the Earl of Easton had informed on her.

"Nothing is wrong," she told Katherine.

Katherine narrowed her eyes, an act that rendered her normally lovely, deceptively gentle face rather unattractive, Samara thought. Samara widened her own eyes in another attempt at conveying innocence.

Cecily, oblivious to the tension between her older sisters, suddenly giggled.

"What's so funny?" Samara asked, pouncing on an opportunity to shift Katherine's attention from her.

"I was imagining what Papa would say if I told him I wished to marry Sir Hayden," Cecily replied.

"He would likely—" Katherine began, but Samara cut her off. Poor Cecily; she was still so young and naive.

"Marry!" she exclaimed. "Oh, Cecily, darling, marriage is not for us."

Katherine's eyes were so narrowed, Samara wondered how she could see.

"What are you talking about, Samara?" she said with a note of warning in her voice.

"Marriage, Katherine," Samara replied patiently. "Look at us. Beautiful, all three of us—yes, even you, Kat, if you stop squinting like that. We are the daughters of an earl and heiresses. Yet has Papa even mentioned the possibility of a betrothal for any of us? I am seventeen. If he had any plans to see us married off, I think he would have at least stated his intentions by now."

"Papa will arrange matches for us," Katherine said. But the steel in her voice had given way to doubt. "He has simply let time get away from him."

"Oh, no. I'm afraid we are doomed to spinsterhood, Kat. Frankly, I prefer it that way. I rather like the idea of answering only to myself."

"What do you mean, Samara?" Cecily asked. "We answer to our lord father."

"Samara does not," Katherine pointed out, poison in her tone.

Samara ignored it. "Do you think a husband would let me do half of the things Papa does?" she asked. She meant drawing and exploring, of course. She didn't mention the most daring of her secret habits. Katherine would have been apoplectic, and Samara would have to worry about another person knowing of her penchant for swimming in her underclothes. "A husband would be more likely to pack me into the dogcart for a ride and consider it entertainment enough, and that's if he let me out at all. He wouldn't want anything from me but a horde of screaming babies to carry on his precious name, and I wouldn't be allowed out of his house until I produced them. Not for me, Kat." She had no interest in the duties of a wife. "I would much rather be a man's mistress than his wife."

Katherine shrieked, as Samara had expected. "Samara! Papa would lock you up and throw away the key if he heard you speaking like that!"

"It's the truth," Samara insisted. "I've grown up doing exactly as I please, and I've no desire to stop now. A husband would try to control me. As a mistress, however, I would be able to live my life without suffocating under anyone's thumb, and if I were lucky I would have a house and jewels on top of it and no one to answer to but myself."

"Mistresses can die in childbirth." Katherine *would* latch on to what she knew was Samara's greatest fear. Even worse was the fact that she was correct.

Samara shifted uncomfortably. "Oh, what does it even matter?" she demanded. Cecily was silent against the cushion beside her, and Samara had the unsettling feeling she'd gone too far, but she wanted Kat to see her point. "Nobody even knows we exist. Our father may be an earl, but he is not important in the grand scheme of things. Who would think of him and his three daughters alone out here in the country? If he were so inclined, he could have betrothed one of us to Viscount Lunsford, though I thank the Lord he did not think to match one of us with that pudding-head."

"Samara, you know our father has never recovered from our lady mother's death." Katherine spoke in a hiss now—to avoid upsetting Cecily further, Samara guessed. Cecily twirled the ends of her pale hair in her fingers, as she did whenever she was distressed about something. "He could not bring himself to remarry even to sire a son," Kat went on. "We are all he has left of her. He doesn't want to let us go, for if he does, she will be gone."

"Our mother *is* gone." The words flew out heedlessly. "And I do wish you wouldn't persist in bringing her up at every opportunity."

Katherine opened her mouth to issue what Samara knew would be a tearful rebuke. Guilt flooded her, hot and prickly. Katherine, being only three when their mother died, had even less memory of her than Samara did. Their father would not speak of her. Kat, for all her steely-voiced statements and bossy façade, was only trying to fill in the blanks, and Samara shouldn't begrudge her a few memories. But the constant mention of their mother grew tiresome. In Samara's opinion, it was best to leave the past in the past. Incessant talk wouldn't bring their mother back.

Still, Samara knew she should apologize. She hated to upset her sisters, though Kat *had* asked for it.

"Kat," she began, but was interrupted by a groom, who opened the door to the carriage and poked his head inside.

"We are home." Katherine's voice was toneless, and she allowed the groom to take her hand and help her out of the carriage. Samara was next, and then she waited for Cecily. Once her littlest sister had her feet firmly planted on the ground, Samara took her hand and squeezed it, giving her a reassuring smile. Cecily was a different creature from herself and Katherine, and the idea that she might have dashed the girl's hopes made her feel awful. They were young, beautiful, and noble—why shouldn't they be able to dream of their futures, no matter how different those dreams might be, and how unlike the reality they would most probably face?

"Kat," Samara called, hurrying after her other sister. But Katherine stormed ahead, skirts flouncing indignantly, and ignored Samara's voice.

"You've angered her," Cecily observed.

"It's not a difficult thing to do," Samara agreed. "I will allow her the pleasure of stewing in her anger overnight, and tomorrow I will grovel at her feet. Will she forgive me, do you think?" Samara glanced at Cecily. "Will *you* forgive me?"

"I forgive you," Cecily replied. "Our futures are not set in stone, I don't think. I will make Sir Hayden fall in love with me, and Papa will not say no to such a match. He is the younger son of an earl, and my equal."

Samara was surprised to hear an adult's voice come from the childish, elfin face of her youngest sister. She sighed. She would not disillusion her little sister again, but she did wonder what would happen when Cecily realized someday that their father had no interest in them or their futures. Samara didn't resent him for it. It was the way things were.

"Come along then, Mistress Determination," Samara said instead, giving Cecily's hand a little tug. "It has been a long day, and I must get some sleep if I'm to beg Katherine's forgiveness in the morning."

❋

The next day rain came to the Malvern Hills. From her vantage point at the window of her bedchamber, Samara glared first at the sky, a thick mantle of angry gray, then at the early-summer roses in the courtyard that had just started to bloom into delicious bursts of deep red, palest gold, and soft pink. If it kept raining, they would drown, she thought irritably. The grounds keeper employed by her father knew nothing of roses, and they flourished only under *her* care. She had raised those particular bushes from cuttings, and they were dear to her.

Katherine, who had grudgingly forgiven her after what Samara considered to be an obscene amount of pleading for absolution, sat on a cushion on the floor in the adjoining chamber, in her lap a book of poetry from their father's study. Cecily sprawled beside her and played with their spaniel puppy, Lady.

"I am dying of boredom," Samara announced, and dropped to the floor beside Cecily.

Katherine raised her head from the tome in her lap and arched one feathery eyebrow at Samara. "Why don't you work on the altar cloth for the church that you've been embroidering since you were twelve?"

Samara made a face and reached out to tickle the puppy's round belly. "Very amusing, Kat. You know I detest embroidery."

"I shudder to think of how disappointed your husband will be when he learns that you possess none of the skills a wife should have," Katherine said with a disapproving shake of her chestnut curls.

❋ *67* ❋

Again? Kat might be only baiting her, but Samara's instinct overrode her good sense, as it too often did.

"God's nightshirt, Kat, I swear—"

"You're sure you must leave today?" Their father's voice floated from the hall below. "The rain is fierce and shows no sign of letting up."

"Aye, we must," a voice boomed in return. "It's been grand visiting, and I daresay old Easton's funeral was a jolly time, but we must start back."

Suddenly the day seemed brighter, despite the clouds in the sky that grew thicker by the minute.

"Thank God!" Samara couldn't help exclaiming, instead of finishing her sentence.

"What is it?" Katherine asked.

"Wexley is leaving today," she replied. "And taking his horrible son with him."

The marquess, an old friend of their father's, lived in Yorkshire. He had family in Wales, and on his return journey from a visit with them he had decided to stop and visit Samara's father, who was a childhood friend of his in some way or another—Samara had not cared enough to remember what she had been told. She knew only that the marquess was a noisy, overblown bull of a man whose mousy wife cowered at the mere sound of his voice. His son Peter was the most odious boy Samara had ever met—which was not difficult, considering that the only boys and young men she knew were the ones from the village and those who worked for her father—but she had loathed him on sight. He had an irritating leer, which he had sent her way every chance he'd had during his two-week stay at Brentford Hall. When he wasn't leering, he was waiting until her father's back was turned and groping at her with sweaty hands.

"Oh, good," Katherine said with venom.

Betty bustled into the chamber and threw up her hands at the sight of them.

"What are you doing still sitting here? Go and bid farewell to the marquess and his family," she ordered.

"Yes, let's," Samara said as she dodged Betty's swat and left the chamber, her sisters following. "And if I am very lucky, perhaps

Lord Waltham will finally succeed at grabbing my person before he departs."

Wexley and his family stood in the Great Hall.

"Ah, here they are. Girls, say goodbye. The marquess and his family are leaving," their father instructed.

Samara and her sisters lowered their eyes and curtsied.

"Farewell, my lords, my lady," they chorused.

To her dismay, Samara felt an all-too-familiar, clammy hand touch her beneath the chin and draw her up. She looked at Lord Waltham's smirk, noting the sparse orange hairs that dotted his upper lip and competed with the red pimples on his otherwise pale forehead and cheeks for dominion over his face. She tried not to cringe.

"Farewell, Lady Samara," he said in a voice she guessed was supposed to be alluring. It had very much the opposite effect. She swallowed hard and forced herself to make a gracious reply.

"It has been a pleasure to host you, Lord Waltham," she murmured.

"The pleasure has been all mine." His voice was heavy with innuendo. Samara's temper flared. Why, he had never touched her— never *succeeded* at touching her, she corrected herself. Suddenly she longed to raise her knee so that it made direct, hard contact with that disgusting, oversized codpiece he wore.

"Enough flirting, boy," the marquess huffed with a laugh that sounded more like a gasp for breath—which was not surprising, considering the amount of fat that was wrapped around the upper portion of his body and no doubt squeezing his lungs. "If you're lucky you'll see Lady Samara again soon enough. Come along, it's already later than I planned. We must depart." He turned and lumbered down the staircase. The marchioness gave Samara and her sisters a watery smile before following him, and Lord Waltham threw a final leer in Samara's direction before he did the same. Then the three of them were gone.

"Samara," her father said, waving a hand at her. "Stay with me a moment. I must speak with you. Katherine and Cecily, excuse us."

Curiosity blatant on both their faces, the younger girls left the hall without argument. They would demand answers later.

"My lord father?" Samara asked, puzzled and not a little nervous. She couldn't remember the last time she had spoken with her father, alone, at any great length. Was she in trouble? But what had she done?

Suddenly her heart plummeted into her gut. *He knows.* Lord Easton had taken him into his library last night, hadn't he? What else could Easton have to say to her father other than the fact that he had caught her—on his property—*swimming in her chemise?*

That had to be it. Samara's stomach twisted. What would he do to her? Her father could be stern, though he had never beaten her. But what she had done deserved a whipping. She lowered her head to avoid eye contact.

"Samara, I owe you an apology," her father said. Samara's head snapped up.

Wait. What?

"An apology? For what, my lord father?"

"For neglecting you these past twelve years and failing to see to your future. You're seventeen years old, Samara. You should be wed with at least one child and another one started by now."

She was thoroughly confused. Had Easton informed on her, and marriage was her punishment? Or had her father simply gone mad? *Marriage?* He had never mentioned it before. Why now? Had Katherine said something to him?

"It's all right," Samara said carefully. "I am happy here. I don't mind if I never marry."

Her father smiled a bit sadly, and the expression cragged his face. Samara saw for the first time the deep lines around his mouth, the sagging around his jaw and beneath his eyes. His hair was more gray than brown. When had he turned into an old man?

"I mind," he told her. "I wouldn't be doing my duty as a father if I did not see you settled and safe. A woman's life is marriage and family, Samara. There is no way around it. Twenty-five years ago, you could go to the Church. Unfortunately, that's not much of an option anymore."

Samara shuddered. "I don't believe I'd make a very good nun, anyway." Not that she would make a good wife, for that matter. Or mother. Assuming she survived the birthing.

"I didn't think so." Her father smiled again. "Listen to me, Samara. You must wed. It is what girls are born for. But I don't think you should be unhappy. That's why I'm giving you the choice. I've decided to send you to the royal court in the autumn."

Samara's heart leapt from the pit of her stomach to the back of her throat. "Court?" she squeaked. *What is going on?*

"Yes. I believe it's your best option. You'll meet many eligible suitors there—and many not so eligible, I'm sure. You're a bright young woman, and I trust you'll be able to tell the difference. But you will only have a few months, Samara. If you can't find a suitable husband in that time, you will return and marry Lord Waltham. The marquess and I have discussed it."

Samara tried to hide the shudder of revulsion that ripped through her.

Her father went on, "That way, if you don't find anyone at court, you will still have a prospective husband. Waltham is no longer contracted, as the girl to whom his father betrothed him as a child died late in the winter, in the epidemic that killed Lord Lunsford. But first and foremost, if it is possible, I want you to find the love your mother and I had, Samara."

Love? No, I do not want love. Her father had loved, loved deeply. But when she looked at him, all she saw was a man who had given so much of himself to another person that when that person died, he had nothing left. Why would she want that for herself?

"Or at least a husband with whom you can get along," he continued. Yes, that sounded better. If she absolutely had to marry, she'd marry a man who was a friend and nothing more. She could make a friend. "Only if you do not meet someone by the end of December will I insist on a match with Waltham. The marquess and his son are aware of my desire to let you have a choice, although I can't say either think me wise for it." The earl chuckled, a strange sound to Samara's ears.

Was this what a person meant when he said his head spun? Samara didn't know what to do. She had no want of a husband and really no desire to change things. She would much rather see her life continue on its current path. She was happy with the future she envisioned for herself—continuing to draw, ride, and grow flowers while Kat ran the household—and had never expected her father to take notice of the fact that she was of marriageable age. Until now, things had worked out mostly in her favor. Would she even survive in a marriage, as used to freedom as she was? Had she not said just as much to Katherine only twelve hours earlier?

"Are my sisters coming too?" Samara asked.

"No," her father replied. "You are the oldest, and should be contracted first. If you make a good match, it will open doors for Katherine and Cecily to make better matches than they would otherwise. So choose wisely, my daughter. Not just for yourself, but for your sisters as well. If you don't succeed, I may not be able to match them at all."

Damn. He was heaping much upon her shoulders. Would it even be possible to find a man she liked, who liked her, who let her be who she was, and who could help her sisters find good prospects for themselves? In three months?

Failure was unthinkable. Her father could be bluffing about Waltham, but calling the bluff wasn't worth the risk. She could end up married to that disgusting creature. Waltham would be a marquess someday, so a union with him would be good for her sisters, but she couldn't live with him. She could not allow him to touch her.

Samara bit down hard on her lower lip. And her father *cared.* That was the most bewildering part of this whole exchange. He'd apologized for the years of indifference. He wanted her safe for the future. He loved her enough not to saddle her with the first man to offer but to give her a chance at happiness.

He cared.

Affection for her father welled inside her, warming her and making her do something she hadn't done in so long she almost forgot how to do it—she threw her arms around him.

He stiffened in her embrace, but after a moment he relaxed and tentatively put his arms around her too. Samara inhaled the familiar scent of him—the sweet soap he used to wash his face and shave, mingled with the underlying tang of sweat from his morning ride around the fields—and felt comforted, like a little girl again.

The feeling was short-lived. After only a moment her father let go and gently disengaged her arms from his torso.

"You will need certain things," he informed her. He cleared his throat. "New gowns. Lessons to brush up on your French and Latin, and perhaps we should call on your old dancing master to see if there are new dances you should learn. The royal court is a world unlike any you've ever known, and you must look like you belong if you're to have success."

"Yes, my lord father," Samara answered, the spell broken. Lessons—ugh! But the thought of new dresses was appealing, and she had always loved to dance, though she had all the grace of a pregnant cow. If only her mother were there to see—but no, she wouldn't think of that. She would be perfectly all right with Betty and her sisters helping her prepare. She had managed twelve years without a mother; she didn't need one now. She would do just fine.

Wouldn't she?

Doubt suffused her. All of Kat's taunting came back to her. She knew nothing of being a wife. She had no time to learn. She was beautiful and wealthy, but would that be enough to attract a man with whom she could live?

And she would be expected to bear children. Childbirth killed. Was a random man's baby something she was willing to die for?

Can I do this? Or am I already doomed to fail?

Time would tell, and soon.

Chapter Six

THE COLD STONE FLOOR PRESSED AGAINST SAMARA'S KNEES AS she knelt before the carved oak chest at the foot of her bed. She flung fine lawn chemises and clean bed linens over her head as she dug for what must have been the fifth time that week without finding what she was looking for.

Hot frustration flooded her as she sat back on her heels and flipped an errant curl from her eyes, wondering what she could have done with the leather case that contained her drawing paper and pencils. It was a beautiful day, her rose bushes had not been drowned by the rain after all and were in full, glorious bloom, and she was anxious to get outside and breathe some fresh air. The rainbow of blossoms visible from her bedroom window stirred her, and though her father would not allow her to paint—painting was for men only, but if she wanted to work with color, the hall could benefit from tapestries of her favorite biblical scenes; how utterly boring!—she longed to put charcoal to paper and try to capture the shape of their bold petals as they yawned toward the sun.

Samara sighed and began to gather the garments and linens surrounding her, giving no thought to how she folded them before she stuffed them back into the chest. Her arms were elbow-deep in chemises when the horror of realization struck her.

You left your things at the lake.

That was where they *had* to be—she had sneaked down to the lake to draw that day. A gorgeous, snow-white swan had taken to nesting near the water and she wanted to sketch it before one of her father's men shot it and it ended up on the high board for her supper. But the bird had not been there, the reeds and trees were common and uninspiring, and the sun was hot, so she'd decided to swim instead. When Lord Easton appeared, she'd left in such a hurry that she had forgotten her materials.

"No," she whispered, dismayed. Even if her things were still there, they would have been destroyed by the rain. And after she had had to beg her father for so long just for the paper and charcoal sticks, he wouldn't allow her more simply because she had been careless with them.

Perhaps she would have to begin weaving tapestries after all.

What a terrible day it was turning out to be.

Samara gathered up the remainder of the clothing on the floor, not bothering to fold anything, and shoved it all into the chest. Betty burst into the room as she closed the lid.

"The Earl of Easton is here," she exclaimed. "You must go down and receive him and his party. Quickly!"

"Me?" Samara squeaked. "Why me? Where's Kat?"

"Lady Katherine is overseeing the soap making today. Besides, 'tis you who are lady of the house, not your sister. Lord Easton would expect to see *you*."

Samara scowled. Ever since she had informed her maid that they would be going to court to find a husband for Samara, Betty had been peppering her with her "lady of the house" nonsense every chance she got. True, Samara was the oldest, but Kat was a natural—and even seemed to enjoy it. Samara wouldn't deny her sister that pleasure, especially if it left her free to pursue her own.

"Fine," she grumbled. She stood and brushed halfheartedly at her skirt, which was wrinkled from being crushed between the floor and her knees. She pushed back the curls that had dropped over her forehead, only to have them tumble right back down. She must look an absolute mess! What was Betty thinking, insisting she greet the earl like this?

"No time for primping. Mustn't keep his lordship waiting." Betty gave her a little shove. "Now go!"

Samara stumbled from her room and descended the staircase into the hall. She'd taken only a few steps when her heart started to thud against her rib cage. She stopped and glanced down. From her vantage point at the final curve of the staircase, she could see him—the top of his head, glossy as the underside of a raven's wing, and the broad shoulders beneath his plain black jerkin and doublet. He stood with another man, a man whose bald pate shone like he'd polished it with wax as he rifled through something—a bag?—in his hands. Samara hesitated before she took the next step. Why was the earl here? What business could he have with them?

As if the earl could hear her thoughts, he lifted his head and caught her hovering on the staircase. The corner of his mouth twitched, and he acknowledged her with a slight dip of his chin. Even from several feet below, the earl's startlingly blue eyes sent gooseflesh rippling over her arms, and her heart hammered in an even more staccato rhythm. She'd forgotten how *attractive* he was. She was suddenly very, very aware of her hopelessly wrinkled skirt and messy hair.

Samara took a deep breath and squared her shoulders. She wouldn't show him that he made her nervous. He'd already seen enough vulnerability from her. She could handle this! She stomped—*no, no, don't stomp. Be graceful!*—down the remainder of the steps and came to rest in front of him.

"Welcome to Brentford Hall, my lord." She injected as much formality into her voice as possible. She avoided his gaze by focusing on the smooth, square ivory plane of his left cheek. "I apologize for keeping you waiting. To what do we owe the honor of your unexpected visit?"

"Good morning, Lady Samara. This is my lawyer, Master Hawthorne. Master Hawthorne, Lady Samara Haughton." The lawyer looked up from the leather satchel in his hands, nodded and smiled absentmindedly, then returned to whatever papers he had in his bag.

"We've business with your father," the earl added in a tone that matched hers in formality. But her attention wasn't so focused on the side of his face that she didn't notice as his eyes swept over her, taking her in from head to toe. She tried to shake out her skirt to keep him from noticing the creased silk. She had to fight to keep her hands from her hair.

"Is that so?" Why did her voice sound so breathless? He was—oh! She should call for refreshments. She turned to look for a maid and spotted Howell, the steward, by the hearth trying hard not to look as if he was listening.

"Wine and biscuits for Lord Easton and Master Hawthorne, Howell," Samara ordered. The command felt unfamiliar on her tongue. "And—um, inform my father that he has guests. Please."

"Yes, my lady, of course. Right away." Howell scurried back toward the kitchens, but not before Samara noticed the excitement in his small brown eyes. Howell leapt on any piece of gossip he could like a starving mutt on a scrap of meat. He was worse than any old woman.

Master Hawthorne thumbed through a sheaf of papers while Samara and the earl fell into awkward silence. Samara shifted from one foot to the other and wondered if she should ask Lord Easton if he had indeed been discreet regarding their first encounter. Her father hadn't mentioned it, and it didn't seem like something he would ignore, but the timing of his decision to see her wed was eerily coincidental. She bit her lip, wondering how to put her question into words—acutely aware of the lawyer's presence and not certain if she wanted yet another stranger to know her secret—when her father entered the room, effectively shattering the uncomfortable atmosphere. Howell scurried behind him with a heavily laden tray.

"Lord Easton," her father said, and the men clapped their hands together and embraced. Samara felt herself shifted off to the side as her unimportance in whatever matter had brought the earl and his lawyer to her home became evident.

"Please excuse me," she said. "There are household matters that require my attention." Which matters, she didn't know, but surely she could find *something* to keep her busy until the earl was gone. He saw too much. He made her uncomfortable.

Her father waved her off, but Lord Easton surprised her by again tilting his head toward her. "You have made me feel most welcome, and I appreciate it, Lady Samara." When he straightened, she was astounded as he winked at her.

He must be making fun of her. Of course, she hadn't made him feel welcome, standing there in silence as she had! How dare he come into *her* home and mock her? But instead of being angry, she was overcome by the most furious urge to burst into laughter. This stranger—and if this kept up, soon she would not even be able to call him that—was an enigma. She rather liked the way he treated her, as if she was not the sheltered, pampered daughter of a nobleman but a girl with her own sense of who she was, a girl who was capable of living her own life. Waltham would never see her that way. And, most likely, neither would the man she ended up marrying, even if she *could* choose him herself. It just wasn't how a man would be.

Was it possible that Lord Easton was not nearly as awful as her first impression led her to believe?

Would he be a good choice for a husband?

The suddenness of the thought almost stopped her dead in her tracks as she turned for the stairs. She sneaked a glance at the earl, whose eyes were on the lawyer as the other men spoke words that floated past her without being heard. Easton was certainly physically appealing—but though that was a point in his favor, especially compared to Waltham, it wasn't enough. He did live close by, so she wouldn't miss her father and sisters nearly as much as she would if she lived in York—or even London. Another advantage.

But he had spent the last days of his father's life on his horse, seeking out village girls for a tumble. Hadn't he? Well, perhaps not. Maybe he'd just wanted to cool off, as she had, and had only taken advantage of the opportunity he believed she presented. He hadn't known who she was, after all. And while an affinity for peasant girls wasn't a quality she would seek in a husband, surely that would change once he was married.

The seed of a plan sprouted in her mind, and the more she thought about it, the more alluring it seemed. She might not even have to go to court, which was disappointing, but perhaps the earl would take her there once they were wed.

Samara started to climb the steps more gracefully than she'd descended moments ago, in case one of the men looked up, but once she was safely out of their view she hurled herself into her chamber.

"Betty!" she called out. "I would like to bathe before supper, and lay out my best gown!"

❋

It was done.

As of this day, the sixteenth of June in the year of our Lord fifteen hundred and fifty-eight, Thomas Haughton, fourth Earl of Brentford, became sole owner of a small but profitable sheep-breeding estate in Shropshire.

It was easier if Cade thought of the arrangement in straightforward legal terms, rather than what it really meant to him.

He *should* be grateful, and he knew it. Brentford remembered him only as a child, then as the young man who'd abandoned his family, yet was spending thousands of his own pounds to help Cade rebuild his home. It was the kindest thing anyone outside of Hayden's family had ever done for him. But Cade couldn't help feeling that, along with his mother's property, he was selling a bit of his soul to the man. His father's death should have freed him from obligations to other, more powerful men, he thought. Not sent him running straight into the keeping of another.

"Thank you," Cade said again, hoping that if he said it enough, he might actually feel it.

"If it helps the son of my old friend, then it is my pleasure," the other earl said as he glanced out the window at the darkening sky. "Now. It's past suppertime, and I'm hoping at least one of my daughters had the foresight to inform the cook that we'll have guests for the meal."

"Oh, I appreciate it, but that's not necessary. Master Hawthorne and I won't be any further trouble today." Cade's traitorous stomach growled.

"Nonsense." Brentford's tone was firm. "You will stay the night as well. I'd hate to force you to make a second trip out here in just a few days. In the morning you can take my men with you."

Cade bit back a sigh at seeing his hope for a quick departure dashed. As much as he wanted to get away, after all the man was doing for him it would be rude to refuse. And really, taking another trip over here *would* waste a full day when he had so few to spare. But would he spend the rest of his life at the mercy of this man's whims?

"Thank you, Brentford." There was nothing else he could say.

The fact that the meal was a masterpiece eased his irritation. Those at the high board feasted on a side of rare beef, a large salmon caught that day from the icy waters of the Severn, loaves of fine white bread, and a supply of delicate white wine to which there seemed to be no end.

Despite himself Cade enjoyed the food immensely. How long had it been since he'd tasted good country fare? Too long. In prison he'd had only watery broth and stale bread to sustain him. Even at court the palace chefs too often made their dishes excessively rich, heavily spiced and over-sauced. One had to struggle to push himself back from the board after only a few bites.

"So tell me, Easton. How often did you visit Glenwood?" Brentford's normally solemn face was alight, probably with ideas for his new property, and Cade felt a sharp twinge in the area of his heart.

"Not enough," he admitted. "My duties at court kept me away more often than not, and for the last three years I was in Rome serving as the queen's … ambassador."

Brentford raised thin gray eyebrows. Was he impressed, or merely surprised that old Easton's wastrel of a son could accomplish something so prestigious? What would he think if he knew Cade had really been a sort of spy, a spy who'd been imprisoned and could have been executed?

"I see." Brentford lifted his tankard of ale to his lips.

Cade was glad for the silence it brought, however momentary. He didn't want to talk about his time in Rome, and he certainly didn't want to talk about Glenwood. Didn't want to think about it. It wasn't his any longer, and the sooner he accepted that fact, the sooner he could get on with life.

With the hope of conveying that particular message to Brentford without being blatantly rude, he allowed his attention to wander to the man's daughters.

Here was something odd.

Though Lady Samara sat beside her father at the long board, where the lady of the household normally sat, he wondered why Lady Katherine was the one directing the servants, nodding when it was time for the next course and asking that empty dishes be cleared away. Why would Samara relegate her duties to her younger sibling? And why would her father allow it? Didn't he care?

And he'd thought *his* family was strange.

Pity for the three girls washed over him. With their mother dead and their father withdrawn, they'd clearly grown up with little parental attention. That was something with which he could certainly sympathize.

Did that have something to do with why the older girls weren't married? Especially Samara. She was what—sixteen? Seventeen? Certainly she had habits a husband would find less than desirable. Even now her hand, clutching her goblet, stilled in midair halfway to her lips as she gazed at something apparently only she could see. Her forest-green, gold-flecked gaze was distant, and the adorable smattering of sunny freckles faded as her high ivory cheekbones flushed with some kind of unseen pleasure—he couldn't imagine what. She'd changed her dress into some tawny confection that was pretty but too subdued—it looked like a costume on her. The messy halo of curls that had framed her face earlier had been somewhat tamed by an old-fashioned golden snood attached to a ribbon that circled her head, and he mourned that only the first few inches of her hair could be seen. A few curls managed to escape, however, and hung in tempting disarray, framing her heart-shaped face.

He imagined untying that ribbon, removing the net and letting her curls swirl down around the two of them like a thick silk curtain, enveloping them in their own private world. He wondered what her hair would smell like. Sunshine, perhaps.

"And the animals, Lord Easton?" Brentford's voice came at him, wandering over the edges of his awareness until it penetrated his ears. "They are healthy?"

"Yes, yes," Cade replied, forcing his eyes away from Lady Samara and back to her father. "They are beautiful."

Brentford looked at him oddly, and from the other end of the table he thought he heard a giggle. What? He had answered the question, had he not? He glanced back at the girls and noticed that Lady Cecily had a small hand over her mouth. Lady Katherine appeared to be fighting a smile as well, while Lady Samara simply looked at him from behind the goblet of wine she held to her lips.

God's foot, he thought, resisting the urge to smack his hand against his forehead. *Beautiful.* He'd said the damned sheep were beautiful. What in hell was wrong with him, to be so distracted by a temperamental chit of a girl that he could say something so stupid? He'd been at court for more than ten years, for God's sake. He was a *seasoned courtier.* He was far too sophisticated to make such a ridiculous mistake.

But he was still a man, and Lady Samara a pretty young woman. Of course, he'd notice. As for his slip of the tongue, well, he was just consumed with losing Glenwood.

Really, that was all.

❋

After supper the small group congregated before the fireplace in the Great Chamber. Samara's father must have been feeling particularly generous, for he'd opened up some of his best Malmsey and ordered Howell to keep the goblets full. The men's voices—even that of the so far taciturn Master Hawthorne—got louder as they shared stories about life in London and the people they knew in common. Samara knew she should pay attention. If she was unable to make the earl want to marry her before her father sent her to court, she would have to be familiar with that of which they spoke so she wouldn't be lost when she got there. But she was too nervous.

It was the perfect time to put her quickly developed plan into action, but she wondered how to go about getting the earl's attention—and, if necessary, to mend his opinion of her. Really, based on what he knew of her there was only one opinion he *could* have, and it wouldn't help her cause. No real gentleman would want a wife who took off her clothes and jumped into a lake! She glanced down at her dress. At least she looked beautiful. Betty hadn't understood why Samara wanted to wear her very best gown, and Samara hadn't been ready to confide in her maid, so at Betty's urging she dressed in a pretty, but demure, gown of embroidered tawny silk. It had turned out to be a wise choice, as it flattered her coloring. Betty had wrestled with her hair, containing it at last in one of her mother's old snoods, and she felt that she looked the very picture of a respectable—and marriageable—young woman.

"Lord Easton," she said, hoping she wasn't about to ask a question that had already been answered when she wasn't listening. "Are there many unmarried girls at court looking for husbands?"

He regarded her thoughtfully, sipping his wine before answering.

"At times, yes," he said after a pause. "It's been three years since I've been in attendance on the queen, so I'm not sure who might be there now. But it is a common thing for parents to send their daughters to court. Not only to make matches but for polishing."

Was it her imagination, or did he say that last line pointedly?

Her cheeks warmed. "I see." Maybe it would take more than a pretty dress and neat hair to entice him.

"And surely they learn the things a *proper* wife must know," Katherine added before Samara could speak again. As Samara swung her incredulous gaze to her sister, Kat favored Lord Easton with a smile that dripped with sweetness. "Samara cannot be bothered learning household tasks. She is too busy being an *artist.*"

What on earth is she doing? Samara couldn't look at her father. Master Hawthorne was suddenly busy looking for something he seemed to have lost in his wine goblet. But Lord Easton merely raised a thick black eyebrow.

And as Samara saw it, she had two options. She could either deny Kat's words, or she could fling them right back at her.

The first option was undoubtedly the wiser. Alas, prudence was not one of Samara's strong suits.

"It's true, I'm afraid," she said with a sigh. "I'm far too caught up in trying to capture the beauty of the world to be excited by linens and soap like my dear sister." She smiled at Katherine. "After all, *anyone* can learn to perform those tasks. Although I will say that Katherine wears the scent of beef tallow better than anyone I know."

Katherine emitted an unladylike splutter while Cecily clapped a hand over her mouth. Both Master Hawthorne, still gazing into the depths of his cup as if he expected the dregs to tell him his future, and the earl had pressed their lips together, though the corners of their mouths twitched in a telltale manner. Samara was satisfied. If Kat thought she was going to land the Earl of Easton for herself, she was in for a rude awakening.

"Samara," her father said, and she glanced at him. His eyes were closed, but he opened them and fixed her with a steely gaze. "We have guests."

"Yes, my lord father." She waited for him to admonish Kat, but he didn't. Of course not—Katherine was the perfect chatelaine, while he disapproved wholeheartedly, if usually silently, of Samara's drawing. Well, so be it. She would just work that much harder to gain the earl's approval.

First, though, she had to let him know she wasn't useless.

But how?

Her father's cooperation would be nice, but she could do it without him if she had to.

She just had to figure out a way.

"It is getting late, my lord father, and I would beg your leave to be excused," Samara said. She would never convince the earl she was a good choice for his wife as long as Katherine was near.

"Go ahead," her father replied. Thinly veiled relief passed over his face. "All three of you may seek your beds. Lord Easton and Master Hawthorne, there is another bottle of Malmsey in my study. Won't you join me?"

The girls curtsied to their father and his guests and made their way to their apartments. Samara shook her head as Katherine stomped in the direction of her rooms and slammed the door.

"Tell me she did not deserve that," Samara said to Cecily.

"She did," Cecily agreed. "She would discredit you in the Earl of Easton's eyes because she has set her sights on him."

"Well, so have I," Samara confided. "Do you think it is hopeless?" *It must be, if I am asking a twelve-year-old!*

"No," Cecily replied. "He does not know you, but he thinks you're pretty. He never once looked at Kat. But I saw him looking at you." She laughed. "Just before he said the sheep were beautiful."

"Really?" Samara wanted to gloat, but that was not Christian, so she tried a serene smile instead. "Well, it will work out as God has planned." *No one ever said I could not help His plan along!* She hugged Cecily goodnight and shooed her sister to her own rooms, anxious to be alone.

She found Betty in the daychamber, dozing before the fire.

"Betty," Samara whispered. She shook the maid by her plump shoulder.

Betty leapt from her chair, her eyes wide. "Oh, Lady Samara! I'm sorry—it was so warm and close in here, and before I knew it, I was drifting off."

"It's all right," Samara assured her. "Help me undress, and then you can go off to bed."

Betty got to work unlacing Samara's bodice, undid the ribbons that held on her sleeves and the tapes holding up her skirt, drew off her petticoats, slippers, and stockings, and set everything aside for the laundress.

Clad only in her chemise, Samara untied the ribbon holding her snood to her head and removed it. Her hair tumbled free over her shoulders, and she shook it out, loving the feeling of the air in her curls. She went to the basin by the window and splashed her face. The cold water felt good against her heated cheeks.

She supposed there was nothing left to do but climb into bed. Betty had pulled back the coverlet, but Samara shoved it down to the end of the bed—the heat of the day lingered despite the late hour, and she hated to wake up in a pool of sweat beneath the heavy velvet. She rearranged the pillows, plump and heavy with goose feathers, and climbed atop the mattress. She lay back, pulled the sheet up to her chin, and closed her eyes.

Within seconds they popped open again. Now that she was alone, and it was quiet, her mind shouted. Should she have reacted to Kat's barbs, or should she have let them go? She had wanted to show Lord Easton that she was not a milksop of a girl who would not stand up for herself, but perhaps he *wanted* a milksop?

She hoped not. She could try to be many things, but weak and docile were probably not possible. Still, Kat had told him about her drawing. She knew enough to realize that a man would probably find that odd at best, intolerable at worst. She could not marry a man who would force her to give up what she loved most.

Oh, why even bother? Easton would never want to marry her. He might flirt with her, because she was a pretty girl and that's what men like him did, but he knew too much about her, and what he knew did not paint her in the favorable light in which she hoped her future husband would regard her. Now she felt stupid for not paying more attention to all the talk of London tonight. The knowledge she might have gleaned from the conversation could have helped.

What if her father brought her to court and everyone saw her for the green maid she was? It would be only too easy to make a total fool of herself. Her father knew the queen! He would never forgive her if she did something to embarrass him in front of Her Majesty. He might even take her right back home and wed her to Waltham. Oh, she could not let that happen! She either had to make Lord Easton want her before she left—and how would she do that without following him home?—or she would have to do her best to at least appear marriageable and not completely bizarre once she got to court. *Someone* worthwhile would want her!

Nerves thrust her heart against her ribs. She squeezed her eyes shut and forced her mind to more innocuous details. The palace gardens, which of course she'd never seen but which were famous for their splendor. The beautiful gowns she would wear, the people she would meet. The man who would eventually court her if Lord Easton decided—as he would, of course—that Kat was a better choice for his wife. Ah, there was a subject she could dwell on: not the earl marrying Kat but someone wanting to marry *her*. Even though she didn't want love, she wouldn't mind a gorgeous man falling all over her. A man with too-long, wavy black hair, icy blue eyes framed by ridiculous thick brows, square cheekbones, and chiseled chin—yes. He was close enough that she could reach out and touch him if she wanted—just one brush of her hand against his cheek…

"Ugh!" she gasped when she realized what she was doing, and her eyes flew open. She sat up, clutching the sheet to her chest as if he were actually in the room with her. She shook her head. She was being ridiculous. Kat had annoyed her, and her nerves were overwrought, that was all. Her life was about to turn on its head. She was permitted to be anxious, wasn't she?

As if to prove her point, a soft knock at her bedchamber door made her yelp.

Once her heart returned to beating at its normal speed, Samara slipped from the bed and went to the door. Poor Cecily had probably had another bad dream and was standing out there, terrified and alone, wanting nothing more than to climb into Samara's bed—her usual safe haven.

Samara reached the door, lifted the latch, and pulled it open. "Cecily, you poor dear—"

Her words were cut off by a sudden, choking intake of breath.

Unless her little sister had suddenly grown a foot taller, cut her hair short, and dyed it black, it was the Earl of Easton at her door, not Cecily.

Samara's hands flew up to clutch the ribbon at her collarbone— it was closed—and cover her chest.

"What do you think you're doing?" she hissed, all thoughts of *proper* and *demure* fleeing as she noted how he filled up her doorway. His right hip was angled inward, practically in her room, and his hands were behind his back.

He smiled at her but didn't look totally comfortable. He seemed to be trying very hard to keep his eyes on her face.

"I have something that I think belongs to you," he said.

"And it cannot wait until tomorrow?" she demanded. What could he have of hers?

"I thought you might want it immediately," the earl answered. "I imagine it's very important to you."

She bit her lip and clenched the ruffle of fabric at her neck in her fingers. Was he drunk? Did he think that just because he'd already seen her once in her undergarments that she wouldn't mind him appearing at her door to see her in them again? What if someone caught them?

"Well, what is it?" she asked after a pause. "And if you are trying to trick me, know that the fireplace poker is well within reach." Yes, because beating him with a long piece of iron was precisely the way to win him over.

He grinned. "I don't think that'll be necessary." He drew his hand from behind his back and held an item out to her. Her eyes not leaving his—she wasn't sure if she trusted him to keep them on her face—she extended one hand and took the item from him.

Her fingers touched the soft, smooth, *familiar* leather, and at once she forgot he was there.

It was her case. Her leather case of paper and pencils, which only that day she'd imagined she would never see again. The earl had found it and brought it back.

"My drawings!" She flung the case open.

Everything was intact and undamaged. The blank paper was smooth and dry, her sticks neatly arranged, and her drawings—little bits of her innermost thoughts and feelings—were there and untouched.

"Thank you," she breathed, bringing the case to her face and inhaling the sweet, familiar fragrance of paper and leather.

"You left them at ... at the lake," he said.

Heat flooded her face.

"They're very good," he added.

Her eyes flew up to meet his. "You looked at them?"

"I didn't know what it was when I found it," he said quickly. "I wasn't even sure it was yours. But since I'd never seen anyone else there, I thought it was safe to assume that it might be."

"Oh." She thumbed lovingly through the pages, a little unnerved that he had been privy to things she considered personal. Kat kept a written diary, but she had seen it and it was boring—just a log of her daily activities, with a complaint, usually about Samara, thrown in here and there. Samara's drawings, in effect, were *her* diary—they captured the things she found most beautiful in the world.

She closed the case and hugged it to her.

"Thank you for returning it," she said as she felt the thin lawn of her chemise beneath her arms and reality came crashing back down.

"You're welcome," he said.

"Well, goodnight," she said, and attempted to shut her door. But he put his hand out and stopped her, taking her wrist in his hand.

"Wait," he said. "I have something to say."

The speed of her heartbeat picked up.

"Oh?" she said, the word a squeak.

"I know we didn't have the most promising first meeting," he said. "Or second meeting, for that matter. But I want you to know that I never said a word to your father about how we met. He believes we were strangers at my father's funeral. I thought it would be better that way. For both of us." He smiled, and she felt as if someone had drizzled warm honey over her heart.

"Samara?"

Oh no. Oh, this was too much.

Katherine, a candle in her hand and Howell at her side, stood at the top of the staircase. Her eyes took in Lord Easton, his large hand encasing Samara's wrist, and Samara in her nightclothes. Kat opened her mouth, then closed it, and her cheeks grew red even in the dim light cast by the candle in her hand.

"What is this?" she demanded.

Samara glanced at Howell, who almost panted in his delight at coming across a scandal in progress. Rodent-like little man. Well, they were caught. Try as she might she couldn't think of a way to lie herself out of the situation, so she opted for the truth. Hopefully that would carry weight with her father, and he would be easier on her once word of this reached him.

But before she could speak, the earl dropped her wrist and spoke instead.

"I realize what this must look like, and I assure you that I'm not trying to compromise Lady Samara in any way," he said. "I found her drawing materials by the stables, and thought I would bring them to her. I didn't want to wait until morning and risk forgetting, since I'm sure they mean much to her."

He smiled. "You were right, Lady Katherine. Your sister is indeed an artist. A very talented one."

Samara thrilled from her fingertips to her toes, and she was almost positive that it was due to the earl's words and not the look on Kat's face—as if she'd swallowed a lizard.

"Well, she wastes enough time on it," Kat said after a pause. "If you'll excuse me, it is late. I would seek my bed. Thank you, Howell."

"Yes, Lady Katherine." The steward scurried away, not without a backwards look at Samara and the earl. Samara wondered how long it would be before the lowliest kitchen maid knew of this midnight meeting.

Katherine swept past the earl, through the room to her own apartments. Once she was out of sight, Cade turned to Samara with a sheepish expression.

"We seem to keep finding ourselves in awkward situations," he said. "Perhaps it would be best if we steered clear of each other from this point on."

Samara was almost certain she did *not* want that at all. How could she make herself appealing to him if they stayed away from each other?

But could she argue with him? They were barely acquainted. What reason could she have for wanting to be near him without making him think his first impression of her had been correct?

A thought occurred to her. Men were known to want what they couldn't have, weren't they?

"Perhaps you're right," she said. "After all, my father is sending me to London soon to find a husband. It would be hard to do that if my reputation were in any way sullied." She hugged her drawings to herself and waited for his reaction. It came, rather disappointingly, in the form of an awkward smile and nothing more. She deflated. "Goodnight, Lord Easton."

"Goodnight, Lady Samara." He nodded to her and stepped back, this time allowing her to shut the door.

Samara took a deep breath and thanked God that Betty had not woken up. She didn't even want to think about how Kat and Howell would spread the story; she would worry about that in the morning. Samara fled to her bed and climbed beneath the coverlet, but once there she remained sitting and took out a fresh sheet of paper and a charcoal stick. She touched the stick to the paper. As usual, she didn't have to wait long before instinct took over. Her fingers performed an intricate galliard over the paper—how she had missed that feeling these last few days!—sweeping into straight lines and curves, details and shading. She blended with her fingertips, darkened areas that were too light, lost herself in the sheer joy that came with creating an image. She had to remind herself to breathe.

There was nothing quite like the exhilaration she felt when she put her imagination to paper.

When she had finished, her fingers were black as night, and her head felt strangely empty, as if her very being had gone into her sketch. She picked the paper up and regarded her creation. She rarely thought about *what* she was drawing while she was drawing it, and one of her favorite parts was the surprise she felt when she looked at her final product.

A fish on a hook?

Well, that was odd. They had had salmon for supper, and it had been delicious, but had fish really been on her mind enough to have drawn a picture of one? How strange. Maybe she had been inspired by Kat—her mouth popping open and shut like a gasping fish out of water? Samara giggled at that. And the way the angle was embedded so deep into the salmon's mouth—as if it couldn't be removed without tearing away a chunk of the poor creature. Where had such an image come from?

Still, it was good. Its silvery scales looked as if they would rub off on her finger if she touched them, and the fish's eye, staring out at her, seemed to beg her help as it struggled in the angle's cruel grasp. Shrugging, Samara tucked the drawing into her pouch, folded it shut, and went to the basin of water by her bedside where she dipped her hands to rinse the charcoal smudges from her fingers before touching her bedclothes and risking a stain. She climbed into bed, pulled the sheet up to cover her, and without any further thought to strange imaginary fish, horrible sisters, and handsome but puzzling earls who slept just a short distance away, she drifted off to sleep.

Chapter Seven

BRENTFORD STARED AT HIS STEWARD. THE LITTLE MAN STOOD IN front of him, his face flushed and his eyes lowered, but not before Brentford had caught the sparkle of delight in his eyes as he relayed his information.

"Let me see if I understand, Howell," Brentford said. "You and Lady Katherine observed the Earl of Easton and Lady Samara together last night after we had all retired? Alone?"

"Yes, my lord," the steward confirmed. "Lady Katherine and I were checking to make sure all the candles had been extinguished when we came upon the earl and Lady Samara together in her doorway. The earl was fully clothed, but the lady was wearing naught but her shift. And they appeared to be clasping each other's hands."

Howell injected the proper amount of righteous indignation into his words, as if he couldn't believe that their guest would be so ill-bred as to approach his host's daughter right under his roof. And indeed, Brentford was certain that Howell's take on the situation was nothing close to what had actually happened. He was an excellent judge of character and while young Easton might have an affinity for women—really, what healthy young man didn't?—he was sure that the boy wouldn't have dared approach Samara. Even if he had wanted to, which Brentford considered a distinct possibility. What actually *had* happened, Brentford didn't know, but he intended to find out.

"Thank you, Howell. Send Lady Katherine to me and resume whatever it is you were doing."

Howell departed, and within moments Katherine appeared in the doorway to the Great Chamber.

"Yes, my lord father?" she asked.

He looked at her—his lovely daughter, with hair like molten gold, roses in her cheeks, and one of the sweetest smiles he had ever seen. It was difficult to believe that such an angelic-looking creature could have any malice in her, but he had seen it last night.

He smiled.

"Good morning, Katherine. I hope I'm not taking you away from anything too important, but I wanted to speak with you about something Howell brought to my attention."

Katherine nodded. "Lord Easton and Samara."

"Yes," Brentford replied. "Why don't you tell me exactly what you saw?"

"I will never forget it," Katherine exclaimed. "I wanted to be sure that we had not left any candles burning. I met Howell in the Great Hall, and he helped me check."

Brentford nodded. So far, so good. "Continue."

"When we came up the stairs, we heard voices. It wasn't until we got closer that we realized it was Samara and Lord Easton. Papa, she was in her shift! She was clinging to his arm, and it was quite obvious that she had been—" Katherine gulped and lowered her voice. "Trying to *kiss* him.*"

Brentford swallowed the urge to laugh. Samara, trying to kiss the earl? Now that was a sight he wished he could see, if only for the amusement it would provide. His eldest might be odd, but she was definitely no wanton. He'd seen her slap the sense out of village boys and servants alike when they'd gotten a little too close for her comfort. Easton was a handsome chap, but his daughter was proud. She wouldn't ruin her chances for a good marriage by letting herself get caught in a compromising situation.

So why was Katherine so insistent that she *had?*

"Thank you, Katherine. That will be all."

"My lord father?" she said. "I've been thinking…"

"What is it, Katherine?"

"I know that it is up to you to decide who and when I marry," she said in a rush. "And I will accept any decision you make with gratitude. But if I may make a suggestion, Papa? I think Lord Easton and I would suit each other very well."

And there it was.

So Katherine wanted the earl for herself, did she? And she had noticed, as had he, that the earl's eyes instead strayed to Samara.

"Lord Easton, you say?" His daughter nodded. "We don't know his situation, Katherine. He may already be contracted." He paused as her face fell. "I make no promises. But I will think on it."

Her expression brightened, and a smile lit her face.

"Thank you, Papa," she said. She flew to him and pressed a kiss to his cheek before departing.

He would indeed find out Easton's situation, and if it was agreeable, think on a marriage arrangement with him. But not for Katherine.

No, he wanted the earl for Samara.

❁

Cade, his solicitor, his host, and ten of Brentford's burliest male servants gathered in the courtyard, squinting in the brilliant morning sunshine as they prepared for their journey to Easton. Sweat beaded along Cade's forehead where his black velvet cap met his skin.

"Thank you again for all you've done," he said to the other earl. "I owe you more than I can repay." *Please, do not make me try.*

"Nonsense," Brentford replied. "It's one friend helping out another. Just promise that I'll have them back in time for the harvest. My old arms can't do much, and girls are useless when it comes to scything." He chuckled.

"I promise I'll return them as soon as I can." He made a motion to mount Whitehawk, but Brentford put a hand on his arm and stopped him.

"I know you're anxious to be on your way, and I promise I'll be brief. But I have a few questions for you."

Cade stifled a sigh and forced himself to smile. "Of course, my lord."

"Are you contracted to marry?"

Well, that wasn't what Cade was expecting. Worse, he didn't know how to answer. Of course, he wasn't contracted. His father hadn't cared enough to see to it. He realized that Her Majesty might have had plans for him once his duty in Rome ended, but since he hadn't seen her since setting foot back on English soil, he didn't know what, if anything, she was thinking. An even bigger question: what was *Brentford* thinking?

"No, I'm not," Cade answered after a while. "I know it's something I need to think about, but I'd rather ensure Easton's sustainability before I go searching for a wife. I would need something to offer her, after all." As he spoke, he realized how true the words really were.

"Very sensible." Brentford smiled. "You have a good head on your shoulders. Now, just one other thing. I'd like to send Samara to court. Do you know of anyone who can sponsor her? I can't go. I need to be here for the harvest, and I do not think Katherine and Cecily are ready for a stint at the royal court. But I promised Samara the chance to go and choose her own husband, and I can't renege on that promise."

Cade paused. Did he know anyone? He hadn't been to court in three years; he didn't know which, if any, of his old cronies might still be there. Not that he would trust any of them with Lady Samara anyway. He would be mad to send an innocent girl, raised in the country, to the viper's nest that London could be and leave her at the mercy of experienced courtiers. However—

"There is my aunt, Lady Morley," Cade said slowly. She was another he hadn't seen since before Rome, and she was elderly now—at least fifty—but he had always been fond of her. Even with no children of her own, she was like a mother hen, clucking around the children and grandchildren of her brothers. She might enjoy being with Samara in London. Aunt Madge was a bit of a spitfire herself, if his memory was accurate. The two of them would get along fabulously.

"Madge Howard? I remember her well." Brentford wore a fond smile. "I imagine she'd be a very suitable chaperone. Assuming, that is, that together they can manage to stay out of trouble."

Cade laughed.

"I will write her at once," he promised. "I'm sure she'll be happy for the opportunity. They can stay at my house, Riverview."

"Samara will love Riverview," the other earl replied. "I remember well how stately it is. But Lady Morley must be getting up there in years. Do you think she'll be able to keep up with Samara? She is just seventeen, after all, and has never been away from home. A girl that naïve and, shall we say, *lively* could easily find herself in trouble."

Cade found himself nodding. Brentford was right, of course. Had a similar thought not just occurred to him? He would hate to see Lady Samara ruined and married in haste to the first man her father could find.

"I suppose I should go as well," he heard himself say. "I have things to take care of in the city anyway and should do so as soon as possible. Will a mid-September departure give you enough time to prepare your daughter for the trip? With luck and God's grace, Easton should be well on its way to recovery by then. And London is safer once summer's past. Less chance of contracting the plague."

"That will certainly be enough time," Brentford answered. "Thank you, Easton. You have eased my mind. Now I know that my daughter will enjoy her trip. I've heard that the two of you have become rather friendly."

Cade's face grew warm, but it wasn't from the sun.

"I don't know what you were told, Brentford, but I swear that there was nothing improper about what happened last night." The words spilled from his lips. "I was merely returning Lady Samara's drawing supplies to her. I had found them by the stables and didn't even know they were hers until Lady Katherine mentioned her art. I wanted to return them before I forgot I had them."

Brentford waved his hand.

"I know," he said. "Though it might have been more prudent of you to give them to me rather than directly to my daughter, I understand. Over the years I've learned to take Howell with a grain of salt. He sees what he wants and reports it as truth. He should have been a woman. He enjoys gossip far too much for a man."

Cade's laughter was born more out of relief than amusement. He could have cheerfully strangled the meddlesome steward.

"I thought to have him accompany Samara," Brentford continued. "Along with her maid, Betty. It's not that I don't trust you, Easton. But for propriety's sake, I must send some of my own people with her. However, Howell might stir up trouble where there is none. I can't have that when she's looking for a husband."

"I understand." Cade glanced at the sky. The sun was already almost directly overhead. "If that is all…"

"Oh, of course," Brentford said. "I'm sorry to have kept you. Be on your way. I'll be in contact regarding the trip."

The men embraced, and Cade finally managed to mount his horse without Brentford stopping him. With a wave, he wheeled the horse around and trotted out of the courtyard, Master Hawthorne and Brentford's men on his heels.

In the near distance Cade spotted a row of rose bushes, plump and bright with their different-colored blooms dancing in the gentle breeze. They were beautiful—some a radiant, sunshiny yellow, some creamy white, others deep red and blush pink.

He squinted in the blinding sunlight. His mother had loved roses, though his father had refused to grant her a single bush to nurture. But she had talked of them to Cade, telling him of the beautiful flowers her merchant father had imported from countries all over the world. He wondered if she had ever seen roses like the ones he looked at now, with their unusual reddish-gold color. He nudged Whitehawk closer, wanting a better look, and then burst out laughing.

The sunlight played tricks on his eyes. Reddish-gold roses, indeed!

Lady Samara lay on her back in the grass, her hair spread out like a flame around her. Her eyes were closed, and her face tilted toward the sun. She wore a green dress, which matched almost perfectly the vibrant green of Brentford's well-maintained lawn—and the leaves of the rose bushes. Her case of drawing materials lay next to her, apparently forgotten in her delight with the beautiful summer day. Cade fought the urge to slide from Whitehawk's back and join her. It really was gorgeous.

Someone cleared his throat. Cade turned.

His borrowed men sat atop their horses, watching him.

"Sorry," Cade said. "I was looking at the roses. I think I'd like some for my own garden. Do any of you happen to know if these particular varieties are native to England?"

Replies came in the form of mumbled choruses of "Don't know, my lord" and "Ask his lordship the earl."

"I will," Cade answered. As Whitehawk began to trot, Cade turned back one more time. He was too far away to be certain, but he thought he saw a smile on Lady Samara's face.

❀

It was early afternoon when Samara wandered back into the cool darkness of the hall, her drawing materials in hand and her skirt a damp, rumpled mess from spending the morning lying on the dewy grass. It had been a wonderful morning. But the warm sun had made her sleepy, and as she moved toward the steps, she almost walked into Katherine, who was coming out of the kitchen.

"Honestly, Samara!" Katherine exclaimed. "It would do everyone a world of good if you could manage to join the rest of us here on the ground from time to time." She shook her head.

"Yes, Katherine," Samara said sweetly. She continued to the stairs, wanting nothing more than to take a nap, but she was stopped by her father.

"Samara, I'm glad you're here. I need to talk to you," he said.

Samara tried not to sigh. Thwarted again. "Yes, my lord father?" She noted Katherine's curious eyes darting between Samara and their father.

"You will be leaving for court in September," he told her.

Before Samara could reply, or even react, Katherine was whining.

"Court?" she demanded. "Why is Samara going to court?"

"That is none of your business," Samara started to say, but her father interrupted.

"I promised her the chance to choose a husband," he said.

"Choose a husband?" Katherine exclaimed. God's toenail, was she hard of hearing? "Are we all going?"

"No, and that is why I need to speak to Samara." Her father turned his attention toward her. "You will be staying with Margaret Howard, Lady Morley. She is the Earl of Easton's aunt."

"Oh," Samara said. Well, this was a surprise. She hadn't given much thought to who would be accompanying her to the city. She had assumed that her father would go with her, leaving her sisters at home. Kat was more than capable of running the household with Howell's help, a fact she was only too eager to share at every opportunity. But the news that Samara's father was *not* going with her didn't bring her much disappointment. She loved him, even more so now that he'd shown he cared, but the thought of constantly being under his nose while she searched for a husband was a bit daunting. This Lady Morley was a stranger, but perhaps she would be easygoing, content to leave Samara to her own devices. And she was the earl's aunt? Then she was elderly and wouldn't be able to keep up with Samara anyway.

"All right," she said, and smiled at her father.

"Why is Samara being sent to court, and Cecily and I must stay here?" Katherine persisted. "We are all of an age where marriage must be considered, my lord."

"Katherine, you try my patience," the earl snapped. "I am well aware of your ages. I am also well aware of the differences between you. Did you not tell me this very morning that you will accept with gratitude whatever decision I make on your marriage?"

"Yes," Katherine admitted, her eyes dropping to the floor.

"Then I demand you trust that I know what I'm doing," Samara's father said. "Now, Samara, we have not worked out the exact date, but sometime in September you will be leaving for London with Betty and the Earl of Easton. You will stay at Easton's residence there. You have until Epiphany to make your decision. If you cannot find someone who suits us both, you will, as we discussed, wed young Waltham."

Samara's head whirled. Christ's Mass and the New Year at court? It would be wonderful! And the earl was going with her? That was perfect! So much for his suggestion that they would be better off if they kept away from each other. She could certainly win him now!

"Whatever you think is right, my lord father," Samara said. She swallowed the joyous giggle that had worked its way up from her throat.

The tension flowed from his face. "Your lessons will begin sometime next week," he told her. "You need to perfect your French, and I have a dancing master coming up from the city to teach you the latest dances." He smiled sadly. "Enjoy these last few weeks of your childhood, my daughter. Once you leave this house, you'll be a child no longer."

He left them then, and Samara made a third attempt to climb the stairs to her rooms. Now she was not only tired and dirty but wanted a chance to absorb this new development. She would have three months, alone and virtually unsupervised, with the Earl of Easton. But she was stopped, again, by Katherine's fingers digging into her arm.

"Do not think that just because the earl is also going to London, you have some kind of claim on him," Katherine hissed. "It happens that I spoke to our father this morning and asked him to consider a match between Easton and me. Not that I think he would ever be interested in you—you are far too odd—but he is an honorable man. I'll not see him trapped if you decide to play a trick on him."

Samara shook Katherine's hand from her arm.

"Katherine, do be serious," she said. "Not all of us have to resort to underhanded tricks to get a man to pay attention to us. Why, it certainly didn't take a trick to get the earl to come to my door last night!"

Katherine stepped back, her mouth agape. Samara took the opportunity to flee up the stairs and into her rooms where she immediately regretted her hasty words but couldn't help giggling at the expression on Katherine's face.

Later that evening, Katherine made herself scarce while Samara and Cecily sat by the fireplace in Samara's bedchamber. Cecily embroidered while Samara pored over *The Third Book of Pantagruel*—a novel, and one that her father would be mightily displeased to find her reading, but at least it was in French. And it distracted her from the seedlings of new doubts that bloomed every time she thought about going away.

"Kat says our father is sending you to court," Cecily said, as if reading Samara's mind. She pushed her embroidery needle through the circle of cloth on her lap.

"He is," Samara said carefully. She laid the book on the floor beside her and tried to read Cecily's face for a hint of reaction. The youngest Haughton girl was very different from her sisters, and jealousy was not an emotion with which she was familiar. Still, Cecily *was* a young girl. A stint at court must seem like the stuff of which dreams were made. Would she resent being left behind?

Cecily looked up, and the sparkle in her dark eyes chased Samara's guilt away.

"I think it is very exciting," she said. "I never thought any of us would see London, let alone the queen's court. Imagine how many men you'll have to choose from!"

Samara laughed at that. "More than I have here, I would think. But remember, they'll have to like me too."

"Of course they will." She tugged on her thread. "You are wonderful. The best sister in the world."

Those guileless words warmed Samara's heart. "Thank you for that," she said softly. "But sometimes I wonder if I couldn't be a better sister."

"To Katherine, perhaps," Cecily replied. "Sometimes you don't give thought to her reaction before you say things to her, and you upset her. But then, she sometimes purposely says things to distress you."

"She does," Samara agreed. "But you're entirely correct. I don't always think before I speak. I don't mean to upset her. It's just so damned easy!"

"Samara!" Cecily gasped. Then she giggled.

"No, Ceci, you're right. I should be, and can be, a better sister to both of you." She thought of all the harsh words between herself and Kat, of the times she felt the need to dash Cecily's hopes if only to prepare her for the reality of life. She needed to make up for that. And she would.

"And if I can be a better sister, perhaps there is hope for me as a mother," Samara said slowly. "Assuming—of course—that the birth doesn't kill me."

A shadow crossed Cecily's face and she looked down at her embroidery. Shame immediately flooded Samara. She flew from her pillow to kneel on the floor at Cecily's feet, clasping her sister's thin hands in her own.

"You see! That is a perfect example," she cried. "Cecily, darling, I'm so sorry. I didn't mean to make you feel bad. If I had only thought on my words before speaking them!"

"It's all right," Cecily said softly. She gave Samara a little smile. "I know I'm not the only one ever to take her mother's life. But it's something I intend to make up for. Someday."

Samara squeezed her sister's hands. Cecily's wisdom came in unexpected bursts and left Samara reeling, but it always made her think.

She might miss that most of all.

❀

The next few months soared by so quickly that in later years Samara had to strain to remember the details. While she resented being cooped up in the house during the best time of the year, forced to regurgitate French words to the stuffy tutor her father had found, and tripping over her own feet to the dismay of the dancing master, she couldn't help but be excited about the new wardrobe her father was having made for her.

A seamstress from London arrived in mid-July, laden down with bolts of luxurious cloth and two wide-eyed assistants. From that moment on, Cecily could usually be found hovering near Samara's rooms, hoping to be allowed in to see the process. Even Katherine set her jealousy aside and joined them. All three girls, though daughters of an earl with plenty of gold, had never seen such an abundance of colors and fabrics. What need did they have in the country for such things? Samara fingered a bolt of silk the warm moss-green of the pond at dusk while Katherine and Cecily cried out with delight over rich scarlet and silver-blue taffetas. The seamstress produced miles of delicate ivory lace, buttons made of bone and brilliantly colored paste jewels, satin ribbons, and scented kid gloves. There were silk slippers in a rainbow of colors and silk stockings, both plain and embroidered, to be held up with fetching little garters.

Samara gazed at the sea of silk and satin around her, unable to speak for fear that it would all disappear before her eyes and she would find that her upcoming trip to court was naught but a dream. Katherine and Cecily, however, were not so careful.

"No one has ever rendered Samara speechless before," Cecily told the seamstress, and even Katherine laughed.

Samara stood in her chemise while the seamstress measured her, marking the numbers down as she worked. Her assistants busily selected fabrics for Samara's wardrobe. With her dark coppery hair, creamy pale gold skin, and green eyes, they decided she would look her best in both bold jewel tones and earthy shades. They set aside bolts of shimmering, supple fabrics in rich gold, copper and daffodil yellow. Samara rejoiced inwardly when she saw the beautiful moss-green silk go into the pile, followed by bolts of topaz, crimson, emerald, and sapphire. Finally, they selected ivory and brown silks to finish the pile—no black or white, for they claimed those shades would wash her out.

"I shall never have opportunities to wear so many gowns," Samara protested.

"Then I will wear them!" Cecily piped up, wrapping herself in a length of silk and twirling about the room.

"You will not," Katherine said. She took the silk from her sister. "You would drown in one of Samara's gowns. She towers over you."

"Hmph." Cecily pouted for a moment, then picked up her favorite ice-blue taffeta and skipped over to the glass.

Katherine shook her head and came over to stand next to Samara, who was trying on a gorgeous pair of silk-heeled slippers the color of a Mary's Gold blossom.

"I'm sorry I won't be there to see you in these," she said wistfully, touching her finger to the strand of pearls that would adorn one of Samara's French hoods.

Samara eyed her sister. "No, you're not."

"I am," Katherine insisted. "I know I am horrible to you sometimes. It is not easy being the middle child, responsible not only for myself but for everything you are supposed to do, and don't."

"Is this supposed to be an apology?" Samara demanded.

"I just want you to know that I'm happy for you, and I hope you find a wonderful husband at court," Kat said. She paused, and her lips curled up in a sad little smile. "Only, please, not Lord Easton."

"Why not Lord Easton?" Samara asked. She almost didn't want to know the answers to her next questions, but she asked them anyway. "Has he said anything to you? Or to Papa?"

"No," Katherine replied. "I just think I would suit him far better. Look at his situation, Samara. He has been away from home for years. He has no idea what he's doing. He needs a wife capable of running his household, and I can. He needs a wife who is content to birth and care for his children, not one who would spend all her time out of doors or off somewhere, *drawing*." Katherine's tone implied she thought it would be less shameful if Samara spent her free time dancing naked round a bonfire into which she tossed infants as sacrifices to a pagan god. "Face it, Samara. You are not the type of girl a man looks at and thinks *marriage*. He may think other things, but not that."

The room in Samara's view took on hazy red edges. The seamstress yelped and hopped out of the way as Samara lunged forward, put her hands firmly on Kat's shoulders, and shoved her to the floor.

Katherine landed on her backside in a pile of fabric with a *whomp!* and Cecily turned from the glass, startled. The seamstress and her assistants averted their eyes from the scene and began to pick up fabric and put it back down in what Samara assumed was an attempt to look busy rather than scandalized by what had just happened.

"Lord Easton can make his own decision about which of us *suits him better*, Katherine. It could be neither of us. But I will guarantee you one thing. While we are in London together, I will see to it that he does not even remember your name!"

The tasks at hand forgotten, Samara stormed from the chamber and into her bedroom, slamming the door behind her.

She trembled as she tried to still her heart. What if Katherine was right? Who was Samara fooling, thinking all she had to do was go to London, convince a man—any man—to want her, and live happily ever after? Even the past few months of half-hearted studying had left her with no real idea of how to be a wife. Soap and medicine bored her. She ate what was put in front of her but had no interest in how it got there. Her embroidery always looked as if someone had either bled or vomited onto the cloth. She was hopeless. She had no right to be anyone's wife, no reason to expect that anyone would want her for himself.

Over the next few weeks Katherine busied herself with things that kept her far from Samara. The seamstresses picked up where they left off as if nothing had happened, and no one said a word about the shameful incident. By the middle of August Samara's court wardrobe was completely done. She possessed more beautiful gowns than she had ever thought possible and more accessories than she could have hoped for. She had silk gowns and velvet capes, sheer stockings, and fetching little hoods. Her underclothes were either embroidered or trimmed lavishly with lace. She had embellished underskirts, ribbons for her hair, and delicate silk slippers. The only thing she didn't have was jewelry. Exhibiting unusual foresight, her father remedied that situation the night before her journey.

He knocked softly on her chamber door and entered after Samara called out for him to do so. He held a long, slender black velvet box in his hands, which he thrust at her.

"It belonged to your mother," he said almost shyly. "It's been a long time since I've been to court, but I remember that a lady needs jewelry."

Samara lifted the lid of the box to reveal a strand of perfectly matched, creamy white pearls and sparkling pink diamonds set in pale yellow gold.

"Papa," she gasped, using her babyhood name for him. She stood and ran to her looking glass. Her father followed, standing behind her as he took the necklace from her hands and fastened it around her neck.

"It is perfect, as I thought it would be," he said. Samara turned herself from side to side in the mirror, admiring the glittering stones that hugged her throat. Then she turned and flung her arms around her father's neck.

"Oh, thank you," she breathed. "They are beautiful, and to have something of Mama's will make me feel close to her when I am alone. Thank you."

"I will miss you, Samara," her father said. Holding her by her arms, he leaned forward and pressed a kiss to her forehead in a rare gesture of affection. "Go to bed now. You have a long day ahead of you tomorrow. I have told Betty to wake you shortly before sunrise."

"Yes, my lord father," Samara said, and her father left her.

She stared at her reflection just a few moments longer, willing herself into being the fashionable, mature young woman she wanted everyone to think she was. The necklace helped. She'd never had anything like it, and it was easier to see herself as a completely different person while she wore it.

She brushed her fingertip against one of the pink gems. A tear forced its way to the corner of her eye, and she wiped it away, annoyed at herself. What reason was there to cry? Some girls could only dream of the journey upon which Samara was about to embark. And she was crying like a child. Ridiculous.

She removed the necklace and laid it carefully in its velvet box, which she set into her trunk, where it would rest alongside everything else she'd need to start her new life.

Chapter Eight

SAMARA WOKE WHEN IT WAS STILL DARK, FLED TO THE WINDOW, and threw open the casement. She leaned out and inhaled the sweet, clean air, trying to suck as much into her lungs as she could. Who knew what the air in the city would be like? Her father had mentioned a thing or two in passing about how London was crowded and dirty and nothing like the pristine Worcestershire countryside in which she'd spent her whole life. It had alarmed her at first. She couldn't imagine a world without the rolling green hills, clear cool water perfect for swimming, and opportunity for artistic inspiration everywhere she looked. Why, in just a few days the trees would be ablaze in an autumnal glory of crimson, gold, and a deep red-purple the same shade as her father's favorite Burgundy.

But London will have its own beauty, something brand-new and untapped. And it's waiting for me.

When Betty finally stumbled from her own small chamber, the sun was just peeking over the distant Malvern Hills and Samara was surprised her pacing hadn't worn a path in the wood floor.

"I'll have water brought for your bath, for the Lord only knows when you'll get another one," Betty told her. "But you can't dally. The lord your father said that the Earl of Easton will be here an hour past sunrise, and 'twill take nearly that long to get you dressed."

"Put the tub by the window," Samara instructed the servants when they arrived with the heated water. "I want to look out while I bathe." She was excited to be going to the city—who wouldn't be? But she wanted to savor every last second of home before she departed.

Betty scoured her well, even taking a few extra moments to give Samara's hair a good hard scrub. She muttered about the conditions of the inns they would frequent along the way over Samara's yelps of pain.

"Stop that," Betty scolded. "This washing needs to last you the duration of the trip. Would you shame your good father by meeting Queen Mary with dirty hair?"

"There is no guarantee I will even meet Her Majesty."

"You're going to court, aren't you? What's a court without a queen?" Betty's strong fingers dug into her scalp, and Samara winced.

"True," she replied. "But over the summer we've heard tell that the queen has been ill. That her child was due in spring but never came and seems to have been another phantom pregnancy. Yet her belly still swells."

"Gossip," Betty declared. "Malicious gossip, no doubt spread by heretics that would see her sister on the throne. Now stand up."

Samara did, thinking on Betty's words as the water, cool now, sluiced down her bare skin. If the queen was ill, wouldn't the Earl of Easton know? He had just come from London. The court of a dying queen would hardly be the kind of court that would produce a husband for her. He would know that, and tell her father so.

Betty must be right.

When Samara was dry, she donned her chemise. It was one of her new ones, made of fine linen with a low neckline trimmed in ivory lace. She let Betty help her into her corset and farthingale, her bodice and petticoat, impatient to at last put on her embroidered ivory kirtle and the taffeta gown of shimmering bronze that would go over it. Her traveling outfit was so beautiful that it almost made up for the fact that her father was forcing her to ride in the coach like a child rather than riding, as she wanted. She had heeled silk slippers to match, into which she stepped before she went to the glass to observe her reflection.

Is that me?

It certainly looked like her, but the differences between this woman and the girl at whom she was used to looking were astonishing. The rich color of the gown made her hair and eyes brighter, and her skin clearer—although it *did* emphasize the freckles that dotted her nose and cheeks. She lifted her skirt an inch and pointed her foot to get the full effect of the beautiful silk slippers. Betty approached and fastened her mother's necklace about her throat, and it was the finishing touch on her transformation from a child to a woman.

"Look at you. You're all grown up," Betty said in a voice thick with tears. Samara heard it and her own eyes burned, but she blinked the emotion back as she leaned over and hugged her.

"Try to tell Katherine that. I very much doubt that she would agree," Samara teased.

"This is your day. Forget about your sister."

"Oh, gladly!"

Betty chuckled, swatted at Samara and pointed her toward a stool. She deftly braided Samara's mass of fiery hair and wrapped it in a thick coil at the nape of her neck. Atop her mistress's head Betty placed a little French hood embroidered with tiny pearls, with a silky black veil attached.

"If you can manage to keep yourself neat, Her Majesty will be very pleased with you," Betty finally said.

"If I meet her," Samara reminded Betty. "Even if she is so healthy she's leading a hunt when I get there, there is no guarantee I'll be able to obtain an introduction."

"Not if you don't get a move on, you won't," Betty told her. "I must finish packing the rest of your necessities and set myself in order, my fine lady. Your father is downstairs waiting. I imagine the earl is with him."

Samara's heart stuttered once, before it began to beat so hard she feared it would burst through her chest and bloody her new gown. This was it. There was no turning back. She wanted to sprint to the courtyard and fling herself into the coach, bypassing altogether the certain agony of goodbye.

But once at the top of the stairs, she stopped. She'd anticipated this moment ever since learning that Lord Easton was going to London with her, and not her father. If she was to win him for her husband, she had to be perfect from the start, or her entire future was in question. If she failed, the next time she stood in this spot it would be as Lord Waltham's betrothed.

Samara sucked air into her lungs, smoothed her hands over her stomacher, descended the stone staircase into the hall, and walked out to the shady courtyard, where her father and sisters waited. Katherine's expression was stony, but Cecily's face lit up.

"Oh, Samara!" she breathed. "You are so beautiful!" Her lips trembled.

"Thank you," Samara said, unable to help preening just a bit. "It doesn't make me look too old? Too stodgy?"

"No!' Cecily exclaimed. "It's perfect. I hope someday I'll have something like it."

Samara hid her smile. Cecily didn't know it yet, but she'd asked the seamstress to make a dress for her as well. And for Kat too, as a peace offering. Hers was of lovely ruby satin that would complement her golden-brown hair and rosy skin, and Cecily's a taffeta the same rich blue as her eyes. Each gown shimmered with beads, crystals, and metallic threads, and her sisters would love them.

"Ahem."

Samara lifted her gaze to meet the Earl of Easton's eyes, so light and so blue she shivered. His approach had escaped her notice. His lips curved up ever so slightly at the corners. A traitorous blush stole over her cheeks. She wondered what he thought of her gown.

"My lord," she said with a calm that belied the turmoil suddenly raging within her. Was it possible that he was even handsomer than he had been in June, the last time she'd seen him? And why did he always appear to be laughing at her?

"Lady Samara." His deep voice sent a tickle down her spine. "It's a pleasure to see you again."

"The pleasure is mine," she answered. Oh, *why* did the sight of him make her want to giggle like a ninny? She'd seen maids behave in such a fashion in the company of men, and it had always irritated her.

She forced herself to move from his gaze to face her father and sisters. Kat had tears in her eyes. Whether it was because she would miss Samara or because she saw her chance at marriage to the earl slipping away, Samara didn't know, but she could guess.

"I'll only be gone until Epiphany," Samara reminded her family. She tried to swallow the lump in her throat before it dissolved into a flood of tears. "Or as long as it takes to find a suitable husband. I will write, too. As often as I can. I promise."

"Will you tell us all about the queen and her court?" Cecily asked.

"Of course." Samara took one of Cecily's curls between her fingers and gave it an affectionate tug. "I will tell you everything."

And if there's nothing to tell, I'll make things up to keep you happy.

Cecily responded by throwing her arms around Samara's waist and clinging until Samara reluctantly disengaged her. She kissed Cecily's smooth, pale cheek and set her back next to their father. She could see Cecily fight to keep her face from crumpling.

No one moved then, until a nudge from their father pushed Katherine forward.

"Goodbye, Samara," she said. "I will miss you."

"I'll miss you too, Kat." Samara put her arms around her sister's stiff form.

After a moment's hesitation, Katherine returned the embrace. "Good luck," she said sweetly, but the tremble in her voice gave her away.

Samara's father was last, and his faded blue eyes were kind as he took her in his arms.

"I will do my best to make you proud, my lord father," Samara whispered. The lump in her throat expanded, and it hurt.

"You already do. Just be happy," he responded. He embraced her. "I look forward to your return."

Betty emerged and crossed the courtyard, dressed in her traveling garments and with a small trunk in her arms.

"Now, you two behave," she said, her voice gruff with emotion. "Don't let me hear from Clemence and Millicent that you ran roughshod over them in my absence." She hugged Samara's sisters, and Samara noted that Kat's embrace of Betty was far more sincere.

"I'm sorry," the Earl of Easton said when the hugs continued. "But we must be on our way if we're to make it to our first stop by nightfall." He gave an apologetic smile. "The baggage cart has gone on ahead, Lady Samara, but the coach awaits you."

"Yes, my lord." Samara let her gaze slide over her family and gave them a small wave. Then, before she could cry, she swept past the earl, out of the cool shade of the courtyard and into the warm September sun. Betty hurried in her wake.

A small group of her father's men, perched on horses, waited next to the coach—a shabbier rendition of the one her father kept. Samara recognized the earl's cousin, Sir Hayden, who greeted her with a grin and doffed his velvet cap. Too bad Cecily had not noticed him! His presence might have distracted her and made Samara's departure easier to bear.

At the coach Samara was greeted by one of her father's grooms, who opened the door and took her hand to help her inside. But her attention was stolen by the fact that Easton had not followed. Instead he lingered in the courtyard, his head bent toward Katherine, who had her hand on his arm and her lips against his ear.

"That brazen little hussy!" Samara exclaimed. "Just look at her pawing at him!" Her heart thumped in her chest, and her cheeks burned as her anger mounted. The groom's hand remained outstretched, waiting for her to place hers in it, but she ignored it.

Katherine pulled away, and she and the earl smiled at each other. Samara longed to run back and claw the satisfied grin from her sister's face. In fact, she took three steps before she got hold of herself again. She backtracked to the coach, where the groom still stood, his hand dangling awkwardly in the air. Samara cupped a hand around her mouth.

"My lord!" she called. "The day grows shorter, and you are the one who said we must be on our way, are you not?"

Betty sighed behind her.

"Of course, you're right, Lady Samara." The earl hurried to them and waved away the groom who still waited to help her into the coach. His patience was to be commended. Samara regarded the earl warily but took his offered hand and hoisted herself into the vehicle. He helped Betty next, and when the women were settled, Easton spoke.

"The men-at-arms, Hayden, and I will surround the coach at all times on the journey," he informed them. "The route we're taking is mostly safe, but it won't do to tempt the Fates. We've rooms booked at The Rose and Quail tonight and should reach it by dusk. Provided we're making good time we will stop once or twice to stretch our legs and take care of other necessities. Do you have everything you need?"

Samara's gaze drifted to a small basket of food by her feet. Her stomach emitted an embarrassing growl, for she had not broken her fast, and she hoped the rude noise had escaped the earl's notice. Kat would never do something so vulgar.

"We do, thank you," she said. "May we draw the curtains aside so we can look out as we travel?"

"Of course. I think you will enjoy seeing the countryside, Lady Samara. Did you pack your drawing materials?"

She fidgeted, embarrassed. Ladies who liked to draw were strange. He must have known that. And men didn't like strange ladies. How many times had Kat told her that?

I will curb the habit if it means I can win him, she vowed. Surely his positive reaction to her drawings had been born of politeness and not of an actual desire to compliment her. But could she stop? She'd already vowed she wouldn't give up her art for a husband. She loved drawing. Sometimes her desire to draw was as strong as her desire to breathe.

"Not that I think he would ever be interested in you—you are far too odd." Kat's voice mocked her from the recesses of her mind.

"I did not," Samara lied.

"Shame," the earl said. "There will be some beautiful sights on the way. Why don't we see if we can't find some supplies for you along the route, hmm?"

"As you wish, my lord." What kind of beautiful sights? Oh, if only she hadn't packed her supplies with the items that had gone ahead in the baggage cart!

He gave her a curious glance, then shrugged. "Off we go," he said, and closed the door to the coach.

Betty sank into the comfortable seat and reached down to lift the food basket.

"Oh, yes, Betty!" Samara leaned over to peer inside, anxious to think of something other than drawing and marriage and men. "My stomach is making the most awful noises."

Betty withdrew an apple, a loaf of warm bread wrapped in a linen napkin, and a piece of hard yellow cheese and handed them to Samara.

"There's wine too," she said.

Samara tore off one end of the bread, placed a chunk of cheese on it, and bit into it with enthusiasm. The warm, yeasty flavor of the bread went perfectly with the cheese's nutty bite. She wondered if the food at court would be half as good as Goodwife Howell's.

"Let's save some for later," Betty cautioned once the edges had been taken from their appetites. "We don't know the kind of inn we'll be staying at. The food might not be good, and then we'll wish we hadn't eaten it all."

"You're correct, as always, Betty," Samara agreed. Her hunger was sated for the moment anyway. She wrapped the remaining half of her food in the napkin and took a final sip of wine. The fruity bouquet exploded on her tongue, bringing with it a sense of homesickness. She didn't care how good the wine at court might be. She'd miss this.

She sat back, making herself as comfortable as possible against the cushioned seat, and waited.

Betty, while exhibiting the foresight for which she was known, needn't have worried. The Rose and Quail was shabby in appearance but clean, and the scents that wafted from the kitchen made Samara's mouth water. The fat, red-faced innkeeper greeted them when they arrived and thoughtfully provided their party with the entire ground floor, including the dining room, for their private use. Samara and Betty had their own bedchamber, and the earl and his cousin would share as well. The men at arms would be comfortable in the loft in the barn.

"You can use your rooms to wash and refresh, and supper will be ready when you are," the innkeeper told them.

Samara rinsed her face in the basin of blissfully cool water set up in her room. Even though she'd spent the better part of the day in the coach, she could have sworn the dust from the road had found a way to embed itself in her skin and coat her hair. The air inside the inn was warm and stuffy, and for a moment she entertained the idea of wearing just her shift to the meal. The earl had already seen her in it, twice—what was the harm?

She laughed to herself. If they'd known then the situation in which they would eventually find themselves!

The dining table was a long, polished oak board that stretched from one end of the hall to another, with room for the servants to move around with food. Weathered but comfortable benches lined the table's perimeter. Betty, being a servant, normally would have eaten after her betters, not with them. But since the men-at-arms were comfortable in the stables and the earl and his cousin had not brought any other people with them, there was no one with whom Betty could eat, save the innkeeper and his family, and Samara did not want to make her eat with strangers. Her motives were also partially selfish. Having Betty beside her would help her keep calm as she ate a meal with the two handsome men who'd accompanied her.

The servants milled about the dining table, put a bread trencher filled with some kind of stew in front of each of the guests, and poured ale into wooden mugs that had seen better days. Still, the stew was fragrant, the room clean, and the company enjoyable. The Earl of Easton laughed with his cousin and ensured that the serving girl, undoubtedly the innkeeper's daughter judging by her rotund form and rosy cheeks, filled Samara's cup with ale before she filled his.

"Is there anything else I can do for you, my lord?" she cooed when his cup was filled to nearly overflowing.

"No, thank you, sweetheart." Cade grinned up at her. The girl's round face creased into a self-satisfied smile, but despite a resurgence of the ferocity felt only once before—that very morning, toward Katherine—Samara forced herself to remain seated and watched as the girl and her generous hips sashayed back to the kitchen. Was *that* what men liked? Honestly?

If it was, then she was dead in the water. *She* couldn't sway like that.

"How are you enjoying your journey so far, Lady Samara?" Sir Hayden asked, jerking her attention back to the people that surrounded her. "I know we've only gone about ten miles, but I remember even that distance as quite overwhelming the first time."

Samara patted her mouth with her napkin before speaking. "It certainly is," she confessed once she was certain gravy did not dribble down her chin. "I have never been more than a few miles from my home and that when I was a child. I knew there was more to England than Worcestershire. I just never thought to experience it."

"Wait until you get to London," Hayden said with a grin. "It's like another world."

"I have to admit that I'm quite nervous at the prospect. My father tried his best to mold me, but though I don't mangle my French *too* badly and I can dance without falling down, I still have no idea how to conduct myself in such surroundings."

"The queen is the center of the universe, and the courtiers scramble for her favor and attention like little dogs," Hayden said. "That's all you need to know."

"It really is a shame you didn't pack your drawing supplies," the earl interrupted. "The gardens at St. James's Palace are legendary for their beauty."

"It doesn't matter much, does it?" Samara asked. She nudged a chunk of carrot with her wooden spoon. "My father has sent me to find a husband. A girl who draws is odd, and no man is going to want an odd lady to wife. My art is but a silly hobby, Lord Easton, and one I must put away if I'm to succeed at this goal my father's given me." Her eyes stung as frustrated tears forced their way out. She blinked furiously to keep them back. No man would want a wife who cried like a child denied her poppet, either.

"I see," the earl replied after a moment. He raised his cup to his lips and drank.

Desperate to change the subject, Samara seized upon the first thought that entered her head. "What did my sister Katherine say to you this morning, my lord?"

Damn, she hadn't wanted to talk about that either.

The earl swallowed, put his cup down, and arched an eyebrow at her. Thick and dark, his brows cast shadows over his piercing blue eyes.

"I'm sorry?" he asked.

Well, it was too late now. At least she would discover if there was any damage to his opinion of her that needed repair.

"I saw her speak to you before we left this morning. I am curious as to what she said."

"Oh." The earl paused, and small creases appeared in his forehead as he gave the impression of thinking hard. "She merely wished us a safe and successful trip. That's all, really."

"I see," she echoed. That's all, *really?* Was he lying? But why would he, unless Kat had said something so awful he didn't want to hurt her feelings?

Lord Easton grinned and shoved his trencher away.

"I don't know about all of you, but I'm ready for a sweet," he said.

"I believe your *sweet* is still in the kitchens with the other servants," Samara said, still stung at the idea of Kat disparaging her and the earl lying about it, and before she realized the words were that close to her lips. "But I'm sure if she knew your cup was only three-quarters full, she would waddle right out here and take care of you."

The earl stared at her. Betty put a tentative hand on Samara's arm, and Sir Hayden pressed his lips together.

Samara was horrified. Had she *said* that?

The long and uncomfortable silence that followed suggested she had indeed.

"I—" she began. "Betty, I'm tired. Will you help me prepare for bed?"

"Of course," Betty replied. They bid an awkward goodnight to the men, who, to their credit, rose as she left the table as if she were a lady who deserved such treatment, and Samara headed back to her room, trying not to run as Betty hurried in her wake.

"Whatever is bothering you, you can tell me," Betty said as she helped Samara divest herself of the pieces of her traveling gown. "I know it's more than what just happened. You've not quite been yourself these last months. And you lied to the earl this morning about not having packed your drawing supplies."

Samara sighed. "It's so ridiculous I don't even know where to start."

"At the beginning," Betty suggested.

"Very well. I told you my lord father has said that if I don't find a husband on this trip, he will marry me to Wexley's son, Waltham."

"You did. Forgive me, my lady, but…" Betty shuddered.

"I know." She stilled as Betty undid the hooks that held her skirt to her bodice. "So I've set my sights on the Earl of Easton." She paused, holding her breath, waiting to hear what Betty's reaction would be. As the woman who had been Samara's substitute mother nearly her entire life, Betty's opinion was important.

"I don't blame you," Betty said. A small half-smile made her lips quirk in one corner. "If I were as young as you and as comely, I would set more than my sights on him."

"Betty!" Samara gasped, and then she laughed.

Betty removed her hood and veil and sat down on the large bed. She patted the space next to her. "Sit, so I can take your hair down and comb it," she said. Samara obeyed. "Now tell me the bad part."

"There are several bad parts," she confessed, closing her eyes and relishing the feel of the comb running through her hair. "He knows too much about me to ever find me desirable as a wife."

"How is that?"

Samara sighed. "Betty, what I am about to tell you must never leave this room. Promise me." The comb paused for a second.

"I promise," Betty said at last, and resumed her work.

"Do you remember, in the spring, when I used to go down to the pond to draw the swan that nested there?" Betty's murmured agreement prompted Samara to continue. "Well, I went one day and the swan was not there. I decided to wait a bit to see if it arrived, but it was so hot. I took off my gown and got in the water."

Betty's gasp of horror was warranted, Samara knew. But it still made her hackles go up.

"I know it is not proper," she defended herself. "But it was hot. I left my chemise on. And I was alone."

"Not for long, I'm guessing," Betty said. She tugged the comb through Samara's hair.

"No, not for long. The earl arrived and caught me. I didn't tell him who I was, for fear he'd tell my father, and I did my best to get away from him without him seeing anything, but he must have assumed I was some peasant wench, for he lied about not looking as I got out of the water and proceeded to—well, he didn't *proposition* me, exactly, but his intent was clear."

Betty's voice, when it came, was strained.

"And what did you do?"

"I slapped him. Hard as I could."

The comb stopped again, and Betty emitted a strange noise. It took a moment for Samara to realize that Betty was *laughing*.

"Oh, my child," she said, mirth making her wheeze. "You are so like your mother it is almost like seeing her ghost at times. No wonder your father lets you do whatever you like."

The thought momentarily distracted her. Was that true? Samara knew she resembled her mother physically, but that was all. No one had ever said she *acted* like her. Interesting.

And he didn't *allow* her to do whatever she liked. He didn't care what she did. There was a difference.

She shook it off. She had enough to think about. "Lord Easton knows I draw. Have you heard him? He keeps bringing it up. I think he must be ridiculing me."

"I don't think he is ridiculing you, my lady," Betty said softly. "Have you noticed the way he speaks of it? As if he knows it's important to you. Not all men are like that. Most would try to quash your interest, not encourage it. It must mean something."

"It means he doesn't care if I'm suitable," Samara said. The admission saddened her, and her shoulders slumped. "Kat has her eye on him, too. She may be far more vinegar than honey, but she is perfectly suited to be his wife. He must see that. And I'm sure she did her best to get her claws into him before he went off to spend a few months with me. Only she, the earl, and God Himself know what she said to him. I'm sure he lied to spare my feelings."

"Does it matter?" Betty asked. "You are the one who will be with him for the next few months. Not Lady Katherine. And your father must have an idea or two in *his* head; else he would've forced you to wed that loathsome Waltham. Pardon my bluntness, my lady." She made a visible effort to look contrite, drawing another giggle from Samara.

"I suppose you're right," Samara said. "I had already planned to try my hardest to win him while I had the chance. I got disheartened when I saw Kat speaking with him. And I am not used to people encouraging me to draw. Quite the opposite. I wonder if you're right about the earl, Betty."

"I think he's worth it," Betty replied.

"How did you get to be so wise?" Samara asked, stretching out and laying her head in Betty's lap. "You have never married, and you have no brothers. How do you know so much about men?"

Even though Samara couldn't see her face, she felt Betty smile.

"It will be more fun if you find it out for yourself," the maid said.

Chapter Nine

CADE SAT ALONE IN THE DINING ROOM, NURSING A MUG OF ALE before seeking his bed. They planned to leave at sunrise, so he should already be asleep, but he wasn't quite there yet. His thoughts were too loud. It was September, and he'd been back in England for nearly half the year, but he still had occasional trouble reconciling the difference between the life he'd thought he would live and the life he *was* living.

His old existence seemed like another man's life, lived centuries ago. Cade couldn't recall his last thoughts before Jefferson told him of Stephen's death. His memories of the Paris wedding and three years in Rome were as hazy as secondhand, or even thirdhand, accounts. He supposed he was lucky to have had those experiences, even the imprisonment; the queen had assured him before he'd joined the envoy that it would give him much clout among her subjects. But did he even want such power? It had been appealing to his twenty-four-year-old self. He'd thought he could live his life free of encumbrance to anyone or anything.

Which was ridiculous, now that he thought about it. He'd done Her Majesty's bidding without question for years, hadn't he? But he'd been young then, and dazzled by the fact that the greatest queen in Christendom had not only noticed him but rewarded him for his devotion to her. Not that his sojourn in Rome had been a pleasure trip. Thanks to King Henry and his son, England's connection to Rome was tenuous at best, frayed even more by the pope's hatred of the Habsburgs, his alliance with France, his desire to rid Naples of Spaniards and the resulting war with King Philip—Cade's own king, though Cade was well aware of the mistake his queen had made when she'd married her cousin the emperor's son.

England backed Spain's war on France, making Mary Tudor and her closest Catholic ally, Cardinal Pole, enemies of Pope Paul IV. The pope would have taken any opportunity he could find to lash out at them. Cade would never believe that the heresy charges against Cardinal Morone hadn't been fabricated. Morone was a friend of Cardinal Pole, and therefore not to be trusted by the pope. Cade, as Morone's secretary, was suspicious as well.

He'd done nothing. It was pure dumb luck that the pope's investigators had discovered his communications with allies in France just days after word of France's defeat at Saint-Quentin had reached them in Rome. Cade had been accused of creating a network of English spies in France who could then report papal and French doings to England's king and queen. Nonsense, of course, but it had looked bad for a time. Very bad. He was damned fortunate that the pope and the Inquisition had failed to make any kind of case against Morone. Had they been able to, Cade knew for certain he would have been executed. But Morone's many allies spoke up for him, and the pope reluctantly released him. He must have realized by then that he would never win the war against the Habsburgs, and falsely imprisoning an innocent English subject would bring further wrath upon the papal states—wrath they could ill afford after so many years at war. The charges against Cade had been dropped. Poor Cardinal Morone, though the charges against him had been dropped as well, still languished in prison, awaiting an apology that would probably never come.

Well, it was over now. And while he'd escaped relatively unscathed, with barely even a fear of enclosed spaces like some former prisoners, nothing he'd learned there would help him with Easton. He would be better off if his father had sent him to some random nobleman's household as a child, rather than keeping him around to serve as Stephen's whipping boy.

Those lessons served only to haunt him, not help him.

At least Hayden was with him. Cade wasn't someone who always needed to be surrounded by people, but he enjoyed good company.

It remained to be seen if Brentford's daughter could provide it. She was beautiful, certainly, and sometimes he found himself feeling more friendly toward her than their relationship, such as it was, warranted. But she was also flighty, moody, and quick with a sharp word or even a slap. He would be fortunate to return to Easton without suffering permanent injury.

But Hayden had proven himself over the years to be good company. It was nice to have someone there who knew him, someone who understood him and to whom he could talk. Hayden had always been there when Cade needed him. The guilt Cade felt at being away while Hayden's life fell apart continued to gnaw at him. He would make it up to him, somehow.

Cade sighed, handed his empty mug to the innkeeper's hovering daughter, and wandered back to his room.

They departed soon after dawn the next morning. The innkeeper's wife had kindly packed them another basket of food, winning her a hearty buss on the cheek from Hayden; they would need it, for tonight they would not be stopping at an inn. Instead they would make camp beneath the stars. They traveled the entire day, breaking only once to stretch their legs and relieve themselves, and ground to a halt not long past dusk when they came upon a small clearing that bore the remnants of a fire.

"Clean up the animal bones," Cade ordered. "I don't want anything lying around that will attract any beast larger than a pheasant. I'll get a fire started."

"Don't think there's enough food here for all of us, my lord," one of the men called. He lifted the food basket.

"Do we have anything with which we can hunt?"

"Couple snares, not much else."

"Set them up then. Maybe we can catch a few rabbits."

"I'll help." Hayden and the man-at-arms disappeared into the trees.

An hour later, the air was fragrant with the scent of roasting rabbit as the unfortunate creatures turned on makeshift spits over the fire. Lady Samara's maid, Betty, had taken to setting up what looked like sleeping spaces. The lady herself was perched on a log in front of the fire, her face lit golden by the flames.

Though Cade thought he might be taking his life—or at least his pride—in his hands, he slid onto the log beside her. She didn't seem to notice him, and he wondered what she saw as she stared into the depths of the blaze. Certainly not what he saw: it was a fire; they all looked the same. But he suspected that was not true for her. What *did* she see? Colors? He squinted. Maybe. There did seem to be several shades of orange, and a few reds and yellows. Even blue-green, deep in the fire's heart.

Hmm. It was lovely, once you looked at it.

The heat licked the skin on his face, making it tight over his cheekbones. He turned from the fire, his gaze locked on the girl, and something about her prevented him from looking away. No doubt he'd been around beautiful women before. But her profile would make Titian drop everything and run for his paints. She had removed her hood and let her hair fall in a tangled, shimmering jumble down her slender back. He struggled with the overpowering desire to reach out and take a curl between his fingers, wondering if it would feel as silky as it looked.

Without warning she turned to him, caught his gaze, and looked startled. Her face softened, and she smiled tentatively at him, her small, even teeth glowing white-gold in the blaze from the fire.

"I'm sorry," she said. "Did you say something? I'm in a world of my own, I'm afraid."

"No." His voice was hoarse, and he coughed to clear it. "No, I didn't say anything. Just thinking about how glad I am to be settling down for the night. It feels like we've been on the road for ages, but it's been less than two days."

"I agree," Samara said. Her tone was subdued. "Given the time I spend—rather, *used* to spend—outdoors, one would think I would be better accustomed to the hardships of travel. But I find myself already looking forward to my next chance to fall asleep in a real bed."

A real bed sounded good to Cade as well. His own bed at Riverview, with its down pillows so soft his head sank into them like a stone dropped into mud. With the thick coverlet that always smelled of fresh lavender and kept him warm when a chill breeze sneaked in through the window he liked to keep open. With Samara beside him, her skin gilded by moonlight, her hair spread over the pillow just like the flames that danced in front of them…

Jesu! What was he thinking? Yes, the girl was beautiful and intriguing. But she was also in his charge and on the hunt for a husband. He couldn't allow himself these little fantasies. She wasn't for him, and if she had been, he didn't know if he would want her for longer than a night. What would he do with a wife who spent her time drawing among the roses, swimming when she should be seeing to her household, or accusing him of dallying with innkeepers' daughters?

Nothing. Easton would crumble to the ground all over again, and this time it would be his own fault for taking a girl to wife simply because he was unable to see past her beautiful hair and the faintly floral scent of her skin or forget the sight of her in a dripping wet chemise.

"My lord?" She stared at him, confusion evident in her furrowed brow.

"Sorry. I was lost in thought." He should flee to the opposite site of the fire, away from the temptress beside him. Instead, he offered her a grin. "I suppose you're not the only one wandering in your own world."

She favored him with a small smile. "The rabbits are ready to eat," she said, nodding toward the spits.

Grateful for a chance at escape, Cade got up and strode to Hayden's side to help him divide their rations.

A few moments later, they were too busy eating to speak.

❋

Though she had never before spent a night out of doors, Samara fell asleep quite easily. The fire had died down some but still burned, and she was surprisingly comfortable and drowsy after the satisfying meal.

It was still dark when her eyes flew open. She didn't know what had awakened her, exactly, but the low fire was surrounded by sleeping men-at-arms—including the one who was supposed to be watching for danger—and Betty snored contentedly in the space beside her. The sky was a fathomless black, broken only by whorls of gray smoke rising from the embers.

We are very exposed.

Indeed, the clearing was small and surrounded by only sparse copses. Anything could be lurking in those trees, from wild animals to highwaymen, attracted by the flames and waiting to attack. She closed her eyes again and tried hard to go back to sleep, but every cracking twig and rustle of leaves made her jump, and each time she felt brave enough to close her eyes they flew open again.

With a whimper Samara drew her blanket closer around her. Her imagination could be both a blessing and a curse, and right now each scene it invented was more horrifying than the last. Betty continued to snore. On the other side of the fire, one of the men rolled over with a grunt. A log crackled in the fire as it fell, and a shower of sparks fluttered into the air. Samara pulled the blanket over her face but could still see shadows. Every one of them was something or someone coming to rob them, rape her, maybe even kill her.

Then she heard footsteps.

They were obviously human and came from the trees to the left of her—or was it the right? She couldn't tell. Fear and open space had distorted her senses. She reached out, and her fingers scrabbled at the leaf-strewn ground around her sleeping space. They came into contact with a thick branch, which she dragged—haltingly, so as not to alert the intruder—toward her. She might not be able to kill the trespasser, but maybe she could stun him if she could make contact with his head. The men-at-arms could take care of him afterward.

Everyone around her continued to sleep soundly. It was up to her to save them all from certain death.

Samara crawled from her makeshift bed and crouched as she had once seen a mouse-stalking barn cat do. She gripped the branch with both hands and waited for the highwayman to attack.

He emerged from the trees, a menacing black shadow in the glow of the fire's flames. He skirted the circle their group made, never looking in her direction. That was good. He wouldn't see her. She crept toward him as he slunk forward, and when she felt she was close enough, she leapt, wildly swinging her branch.

"Jesu!" the intruder shouted. He reached up and, with incredible reflexes, grabbed the branch and stopped her blow in mid-air before it could make contact with his skull.

It wasn't a highwayman after all. It was Lord Easton.

The men around the fire jumped up, rubbing sleep from their eyes. Samara was mortified. There she was, before a group of men who were strangers to her, wearing nothing but a shift and a wool cloak and holding a branch to their lord, whom she had clearly intended to kill. The earl appeared confused as he gripped the other end of the branch. The men began to laugh. Even Betty, who had bolted from her own sleeping space at the earl's shout, let out a hearty chuckle.

"At least this time I was able to fend off the blow," the earl said with some humor as he yanked the branch from her hands and tossed it behind him into the brush. "You've shown the palm of your hand to be a formidable weapon already, Lady Samara. If you're of a mind to injure me, you don't need a club."

"I thought you were a highwayman, come to murder us and steal our things," she muttered as she stared at the ground, her cheeks burning with shame and more than a little humiliation.

She didn't see that the earl's expression had softened until he took her chin between his fingers and forced her face up so she could meet his eyes.

"You've never slept outside, have you." It was a statement, not a question.

She shook her head. "No, my lord."

He sighed and released her. "I should have realized, of course. I'm sorry. Nature called. What can I say?" He shrugged as she felt her face grow redder at his implication. "Lie back down, Lady Samara. With luck we can get a few more hours of sleep before we must be on the road again. We have only three more days of travel ahead of us. If you like, I'll pull my things closer to you so you feel safer. I promise not to rob or murder you. Or do anything else to you."

In her mortification she considered refusing but then realized that he was being kind. Especially considering she had attempted to kill him.

"Thank you," she said in a small voice.

"Geoffrey, get back to your post and try to stay awake this time. Hayden, move your things so that you're on Betty's other side. Between the two of us we should be able to keep the ladies safe from any evil that might be lurking in these woods." He smiled at her.

Oh, he wasn't being kind at all! He mocked her, and this time she couldn't deny she'd given him reason. She lifted her chin and turned away. He would not intimidate her!

As she busied herself rearranging her sleeping space before crawling back into it, she wondered what Katherine would have done in the same situation. Probably she would have cornered the highwayman and bored him away from them with a lecture on medicinal herbs.

Samara lay with her back to him, but when the earl dragged his blankets next to her and settled himself, she was very aware of his closeness. Her anger was already dissipating, but she refused to give in to the temptation to roll over and look at him. He was such a strange man—so friendly and warm one moment, teasing and horrible the next. Would she ever know exactly where she stood with him?

The grunts and sighs of settling men subsided over the next few moments, leaving Samara to ponder her most recent humiliation against a backdrop of crackling logs and, eventually, the Earl of Easton's soft, deep breathing. She focused on that. Eventually the rhythm of it lulled her into drowsiness.

At least he does not snore.

❁

They entered the city through Aldersgate. Samara had suspected for hours that they were almost there, for the tree-lined road had given way to clusters of narrow white-walled, black-framed houses. But when the gatekeeper lifted the creaking, ancient portcullis to let them through, she knew they had entered the city she'd only ever heard about, and only in her wildest dreams had she thought she'd visit.

The smell hit her first.

Hot, thick, and sour, it was worse than the foulest chamber pot her imagination could conjure as it assaulted nostrils that until then had known little but the fragrance of clean sweet air, delicious foods, and lavender-packed linens. Her fingers scrabbled for the new pomander ball at her waist as, next to her, Betty lifted her apron and covered the lower half of her face.

"What is it?" Betty demanded, her words muffled by the cloth at her lips.

Samara wondered the same thing. Surely *this* couldn't be London?

Their coach rumbled along, and Samara dared a glance outside the vehicle's window. They traversed an alarmingly narrow, dirt-paved street and fought people, cattle, and chickens for the right of way. The houses were three and four stories high and stuck out further over the street as they got higher. The top stories stuck out so far Samara would have liked to see if residents on either side of the street would be able to shake hands from their respective windows. It was quite strange. But fascinating.

And what was that in the distance? It rose over the houses like a needle-tipped moon, silvery even in the golden September sun. Even as she wondered if it was a church she realized it was the famed St. Paul's Cathedral. She would have loved to see the holy treasures once housed inside the grand building but knew from her studies that the previous two kings had seen them either confiscated or tragically destroyed.

After almost an hour of stubborn pushing through noisy, crowded streets, the carriage at last ground to a stop. A wave of fear crashed over Samara and pinned her to the safety of the seat.

The door to the coach opened, and the groom's head appeared.

"We've arrived, milady," he announced. Samara looked to Betty.

"Don't lose courage now," Betty scolded. "You've made it this far. Where has your sense of adventure gone? Or have you decided that you really do want to marry Waltham?"

"I should have you whipped," Samara grumbled, but forced her lips into a shaky smile. She would *not* make any more mistakes. Easton would think her the most ill-bred woman ever born if she let her tongue get away with her again or let her fear get so out of hand she tried to murder him. She would keep her mouth shut, her hands to herself, her fears buried deep. She was a different girl from the one who had left Brentford Hall less than a week ago. She would be a lady worthy of the Earl of Easton's hand.

She accepted the groom's hand and let him draw her out. Her feet, clad now in boots she'd days ago substituted for her slippers, touched the ground.

They had been traveling for five days, and everything ached. Her shoulders, her hips, her neck, even her knees. She felt permanently bent into a sitting position. But as she stretched her stubborn muscles, she looked up, and her soreness faded. "Oh!"

The earl's house was like a building from a dream. The street-facing façade glittered with glass windows, dressed in columns and decorative stone masonry. Some of the stones had designs carved into them—cherubs and lions, chariots and robed, bearded men. They were the most enchanting things she'd ever seen.

"This is considered the back of the house," the earl explained as a groom led his horse away. "Because the river is used for travel more often than the street, the front of the house faces the water. In fact, if the queen were staying at Whitehall or Greenwich, we would use my barge to travel. Riverview may not be the grandest house on the Strand, but I'm lucky enough to have my own quay." He laughed. "Actually, saying the house is not the grandest on the Strand is an understatement. It's comfortable though, and far better than taking up residence in the palace as some do."

"It's wonderful," Samara breathed. "The carvings are extraordinary!" She longed to run over and touch one. *Already, you forget yourself. Ladies are not supposed to be interested in such things.*

The earl smiled at her. He offered her his arm, which she accepted after only a moment's hesitation.

"Well, if it isn't his lordship! To what do we owe this honor, my lord earl?"

The reedy voice distracted her and Samara turned from the carvings to determine its source. But the earl laughed, released her arm, and started toward a small woman who had emerged from the open door. Easton swooped down and gathered the woman into his arms, swinging her around.

"Put me down, you big oaf!" The woman pummeled his back with scrawny fists as her skirts flew. The earl's laughter was a great, happy sound that came from his belly. It rang through the courtyard as he obliged and set the woman on her feet. She took a moment to straighten her brown skirts and pat her hood into place before turning to face Samara. "What is this, my boy? You've brought a mistress to Riverview?"

Samara's eyes widened. Should she be insulted? Before she could decide, however, a small giggle burst from her.

"You mischievous old dragon! Are you so ancient your memory has holes, or do you just like to cause trouble? This is Lady Samara Haughton, of course. Brentford's daughter. We are to help her find a husband," Easton said. "Lady Samara, this ill-mannered creature is my great-aunt Margaret Howard, Lady Morley."

Samara curtsied. "How do you do, Lady Morley?"

"Call me Aunt Madge, dear girl." Everything about Lady Morley was brown. She was a tiny sparrow of a woman, with a band of gray-streaked brown hair peeping from beneath the heart-shaped band of her French hood and tiny, pointed features. But her dark eyes were lively and her smile warm and friendly.

Cade took their arms in his and escorted the two women into the house. Betty scurried behind them.

"Thank you for coming, Aunt Madge. Apparently I am not considered a fit chaperone." His tone was teasing.

The older woman chirped a short, sharp laugh. "As if *you* could be trusted with the welfare of an unwed girl," she exclaimed. She waved her hand and turned to Samara. "I apologize, my dear, for asking if you were my nephew's mistress. I knew all along that you weren't. I've a rather wicked sense of humor, I'm afraid. You'll let me know if I offend you, won't you?"

"I like wicked," Samara said with a smile.

"Oh, then we shall get along famously! Cade, be a dear and get us some refreshments. I'm sure Lady Samara is exhausted from her travels."

"I am an earl now, madam," Cade countered. "You cannot order me about."

"Then tell Blackwell to get us some refreshments. With Jefferson at Easton Manor he is steward here now, is he not? Oh, I don't care who brings them. The day is hot, and I am parched. Lady Samara, have a seat." Aunt Madge sat on a bench strewn with plush embroidered cushions and gestured for Samara to do the same.

The fond grin on the earl's face, when Samara glanced at him, took her breath away. Fortunately he left the room before she forgot how to breathe altogether.

With luck, his effect on her would fade if they wed. If not, she would suffocate before she even got a chance to die in childbirth.

Aunt Madge's birdlike voice cut into her thoughts. "Tell me, child, how did you survive a trip across the countryside with only my scoundrel of a great-nephew for company? You appear unscathed, but then again, we just met."

"I have my maidservant—" Samara looked around, thinking Betty had followed her in, but she was not there. Perhaps she was taking Samara's things to her room. "—Betty for company. She saw that I behaved. Not," Samara asserted, horrified at what her words might have implied, "that I am incapable of behaving. In that way. It's just my first time away from home, and my father, I think, was afraid that I might bring shame upon him by acting oddly. But I didn't. At least, for the most part." She blushed, remembering her words about the innkeeper's daughter and the roughness of the branch in her hands as she swung it toward the earl's head.

"Always behaving oneself is not much fun," Aunt Madge remarked. A distinguished-looking man with silver hair that matched his livery appeared then with a carafe of wine, some goblets, and a tray of golden biscuits. The earl returned and seated himself on the bench across from them. He helped himself to a biscuit as the servant poured the wine. Aunt Madge took up her goblet and drank thirstily.

"Ahh." She beamed at the man. "Thank you, Blackwell."

"Yes, madam." He shuffled off.

"Aunt Madge, I instructed Blackwell to prepare the rooms next to yours for Lady Samara," Cade said.

"A wise decision." Aunt Madge glowered over her goblet. "She will be much safer with me."

Samara's cheeks blazed. She bit into a biscuit to distract herself from the memory of Cade at the lake.

"Safer, madam?" he asked. "Am I some shameless seducer of unwed girls, then?"

Samara inhaled a dry bite of biscuit and coughed.

Aunt Madge turned to her and pounded on her back in an attempt to dislodge the intruder.

Samara managed to swallow, and Aunt Madge handed over her wine. "Take a sip, darling. It seems Lady Samara already knows you well, nephew. My ears may not be as sharp as they once were, but I am quite sure I heard the lady laugh before she started to choke. What trouble can you have gotten into in that backwoods, tumbledown manor of yours? Again, it was wise of you to put her beside me. She is too lovely to be ruined by a rake like you."

"Lady Samara can hold her own, I assure you, Aunt Madge," Cade said, touching his cheek with a rueful smile.

"My hand or a large branch is all I need," Samara admitted once she could speak again.

"Oh, no," Cade said. "I see that if we are to live peacefully in the same household for the next few months, I must scour the surroundings for anything that can be turned into a weapon. And perhaps see to it that you are well stocked with drawing supplies so that your hands are otherwise occupied."

Samara deflated. Each time he mentioned her drawing it reminded her of how hard she would have to work to convince him of her suitability. And that she'd have to give up that which she loved the most to do so.

"What is this?" Aunt Madge asked, looking from her nephew to Samara.

"Another time, aunt," Cade replied. He stood, dusted his breeches free of crumbs, and drank the last bit of his wine before he put his goblet down. "I have to get to St. James's to attend the queen. Will you see Lady Samara settled?"

"Of course. Give Her Majesty my regards. That poor woman," she murmured. She turned to Samara. "Come, child. I'll show you to your rooms. Your maid should already be there unpacking your things."

Easton bent and kissed his aunt upon her wrinkled cheek. "I should be back by supper. If I'm not, eat without me." He nodded toward Samara. "Lady Samara."

Then he was gone, and Aunt Madge was halfway to the stairs. For such an elderly lady, she certainly was quick.

Aunt Madge led Samara through a series of rooms before she stopped in front of a heavy oak door.

"These are your rooms, my dear," she said. "Mine are just beyond if you need me. I know you must be tired, so I'll leave you to rest now. I'll tell Blackwell to have someone wake you before supper."

"Thank you, Lady—Aunt Madge," Samara said. The old woman patted her cheek and headed back in the direction from which they'd come. Samara opened the door.

The apartments were smaller than her rooms at home, but far more luxurious. The sitting room was spacious and comfortable, with walls covered in beautifully woven tapestries and lush Turkey carpets in vibrant shades of blue and green upon the tables. She would fawn over them later—there was far too much to take in to stop her explorations so soon.

The carved oak furniture was well-made and exquisite. Moving into the bedchamber, Samara gasped in pleasure as she took in the large, ornate four-poster bed in the center of the room. Gauzy ivory curtains fluttered around it like fairy wings, and a soft-looking cream velvet coverlet swathed the mattress. Deliciously plump down pillows were strewn carelessly about the head of the bed, contrasting with the rich red-brown wood of the carved headboard. A small, matching oak table rested beside it, and someone—most likely Betty—had placed Samara's wooden trunk by the window. It looked woefully plain and out of place in the lavish bedchamber, especially when compared to the larger chest at the foot of the bed. A beautiful dressing table, complete with a gilt-edged oval looking glass, sat on the opposite end of the chamber. She went to it, looked into the glass, and saw her face framed in gold and the reflection of the gorgeous room.

Once she won the earl, all of this beauty would be hers.

Chapter Ten

WHEN CADE RODE INTO THE COURTYARD AT ST. JAMES'S, THE sun was hovering just above the palace's red brick walls. Slender fingers of dusky pink, lavender, and gold reached for the stick-thin chimneys that jutted into the sky.

Cade paused a moment to gather his thoughts before he took Whitehawk to the stables, then hurried past the guards, through the arched entrance, and into the palace, anxious to catch an audience with the queen before she retired for the evening. She didn't know he was coming, but this was London: she certainly knew by now that he was here. She would be expecting him.

But what he had intended to be a quick, purposeful stride through the familiar maze of rooms was slowed by interruptions from people, both acquaintances and strangers, who had heard of the deaths of his father and brother and were eager to renew—or in some cases forge—a friendship. Cade was polite but noncommittal, graciously accepting condolences but not stopping for lengthy conversation. Still, by the time he reached the queen's Privy Chamber, nearly half an hour had passed.

She was just finishing her supper, and he was admitted to her presence by a secretary he did not recognize, a short man clad in dark velvet and wearing the chain of the royal secretary. Where was Sir John Bourne? The previous royal secretary had been a native of Worcestershire and a neighbor of sorts, though from a family much less important than Cade's own. *So much has changed.*

Once inside the Privy Chamber, he glanced around the room.

At least *some* faces were familiar. There was Jane Dormer by the fireplace, grown now and displaying the beauty at which she'd only hinted as a young girl. Her slender white fingers busily organized the queen's basket of colored thread. She offered him a small smile of recognition. The Countess of Lennox sat on a stool just a few feet from Jane, stabbing at her embroidery cloth with a savage-looking needle while shooting concerned glances at the queen.

Standing behind the queen's high-backed chair was Mistress Susan Clarinceaux—he remembered *her,* the greedy old crone, and clasped the beryl rosary beads, a gift for Her Majesty, tightly in his hand as if to protect them from her well-known acquisitiveness. She gave a barely perceptible dip of her head, as if she were unwilling to fully acknowledge him before learning if the queen still deemed him important.

Cade stifled a sigh. *Politics.*

There was little conversation among the few other ladies that bustled about the room, females he didn't recognize, but they noticed him: their shy smiles and the flushes that rose in their smooth cheeks gave them away. He grinned. Politics be damned; he was *happy* to be back! He'd escaped the papal prison. Easton could wait a bit. Cade, for the moment, was exactly where he belonged.

The queen dabbed at her thin lips with a white cloth and dipped her fingers into the bowl of water Mistress Clarinceaux held out to her. But when she finally struggled to her feet, with the help of the Countess of Lennox, his joy became horror and it took a great effort on Cade's part to conceal his shock at her appearance.

He remembered when the whispers had started in Rome, the ones that spoke of how Queen Mary of England again thought that she was finally to bear her Spanish husband a child. After the queen's first pregnancy had turned out to be a false one—to the delight of the parts of Europe that cringed at the thought of another Habsburg on the throne of England—news that she once again appeared to be with child, especially at her advanced age, was met mostly with scorn. How could such an old woman produce a living child, let alone a healthy one who would live to rule?

She couldn't. By the time he'd arrived in Paris, the entire court was laughing about the child that had been naught but another phantom, about the king who knew it and would not return to his wife's side.

But still her belly swelled—a horrific reminder of what might have been. She'd never been what one would call healthy. He knew that, of course. She'd suffered from headaches her entire life, and every time someone sneezed in her presence she was laid up for a week. But the difference between the queen he'd known three years ago and the old woman before him now was astonishing.

Her hair—once the lovely, shining red-gold of both of her parents—was a coarse gray band between the papery skin of her forehead and the edge of her pearled hood. Her blue eyes, in which she'd been nearly blind since childhood, were unfocused as they searched his face, and her skin, always more sallow than fair, bore deep creases that gave her the appearance of a woman with many more years than the forty-two she possessed.

What will happen to me, when she goes? The people I care about?

In 1547, Cade had been in London less than a year when he met Princess Mary, newly returned to the city following her father's death. She was not beautiful, but there was something about her, something serene and kind, which reminded him of his own mother. And the princess must have seen something in him—a wounded, virtually orphaned seventeen-year-old—for she took a great liking to Cade. After her brother Edward's accession, she returned to her principal residence of Beaulieu, bringing Cade with her to serve as secretary. And when news of her brother's failing health reached them, he accompanied her back to London, where Hayden joined their party and supported her claim to the throne over that of tragic little Jane Grey.

When Thomas Wyatt the Younger and his army stormed Southwark in the winter of 1554, Cade and Hayden waited with Mary's supporters on London Bridge. They helped beat the rebels back and eventually defeated them. Their loyalty did not go unnoticed. Mary knighted them both. She arranged for Hayden to wed Penelope Stockton, the only daughter of Sir Anthony Stockton, one of Mary's most steadfast supporters. Shortly after their wedding, in early 1555, Cade was sent to Rome with the English envoy. While Cade listened for the crown, then languished in the prison at Castel

Sant'Angelo, Hayden and his family lived happily—or so it seemed to Cade—in the country.

Of course, they knew that even God's anointed queen was not immortal. But Cade had given little thought to what might happen once she was gone. Without seeing her, it hadn't seemed real. But now...

Who will succeed her? If it is Elizabeth, will she even let me live?

"Lord Easton," the queen said in the deep voice that was always unexpected, no matter how many times he heard her speak—although weaker than he remembered. Cade dropped to one knee and clasped her proffered hand, pressing a kiss upon it.

"Your Majesty," he replied. "How many times I feared I would never again have the honor of being in your presence."

"You may rise," she replied, accepting the flattery, and he stood, forcing a smile to his face. "We are pleased to see you. We wanted to tell you personally how much we appreciate your service to the crown over the past few years."

Like being accused of aiding Morone in his heresy? Spending months in a prison cell with only spiders and rats for company? Ducking and weaving around the perimeter of France to avoid being captured by the French army, only to reach the coast and have to turn around and head to Paris to witness two children play-act at a wedding?

The bitterness of his thoughts surprised him. She was his queen, she favored him, and she'd trusted him with important matters of state. What was wrong with him? How ungrateful could he be?

If he was willing and able to think such things about the queen he loved, perhaps his father had been right about him. *Useless idiot. Worthless.*

"The honor of being trusted with such missions is one I'll never be able to repay," he said. There, that was better. And he even meant it, a bit. He held out his hand, the one that gripped the rosary beads. "Please accept a token of my appreciation and love, and my apology for going straight to Worcestershire upon my return instead of coming to pay my respects to Your Majesty."

The queen took the strand from him, held her hand close to her eyes, and rolled the beads between her fingertips. Mistress Clarinceaux, still standing by the queen's supper table, perked as she noticed the gift and craned her neck so that she could see it over the queen's hunched shoulder.

"How lovely," the queen said. "Such a wonderful blue color. What is the stone?"

"Beryl, Your Majesty, from a mine in one of the northernmost German states."

"Mistress Clarinceaux, these are beautiful beads, are they not?"

"Aye, they are, Your Majesty." The woman was almost salivating.

"Put them somewhere safe," the queen commanded, and handed over the beads. Mistress Clarinceaux took them and headed for a golden coffer on the mantle, but Cade kept his eye on her in case she decided that her pocket was a safer place for the treasure.

"So you are an earl now," the queen said.

"It would seem." He gave a little shrug.

"We were sorry to hear of the deaths of your father and brother."

He weighed possible responses. *I was not.* No, that wouldn't do. Despite the troubles she'd had with her own father and brother, family was family and she'd be appalled.

I was, too. No. She'd know he was lying. He'd confessed to her years ago why she'd found him when and how she had.

"It was God's will," he answered at last. She couldn't argue with that.

"It always is. His and no one else's." She passed a hand over her swollen belly. "Your cousin has already been to see us. He has faced tragedy as well in recent months."

"Aye, he has."

"At least he is lucky enough to have a child to comfort him." Something that looked like grief contorted her face, if only for a second.

This was getting uncomfortable.

"Yes," Cade said.

Half-blind, she squinted at him. "Hayden says you've brought a lady with you."

"I have," he said. "As a favor to her father. He wanted to send the girl to London to find a husband but could not come himself. He was of great help to me when my father died, and to repay him, I offered to escort her, as her trip coincided with my plan to return and pay my respects to Your Majesty. My aunt is acting as her chaperone."

"Hmm." She plucked at the lace circling her left wrist. "Who is her father?"

"The Earl of Brentford, Majesty."

"Brentford," the queen said thoughtfully. Her face lit at the memory. "Thomas Haughton?" Cade nodded, and the queen's mouth stretched into a ghost of a smile. "He wed with one of the Boleyn witch's maids. Anne Andrews, I believe. What is the girl's name?"

"He has three daughters, Your Majesty. Lady Samara is with me. She is seventeen. The others are Lady Katherine, who is fifteen, and Lady Cecily, who is twelve. It was Lady Cecily's birth that killed the countess."

"It so often does," the queen murmured. "What is she like?"

"She is artistic. Naïve, and a bit countrified," Cade said. "She is lovely. But I won't deny that she could use the polish only a stint at your elegant court can provide. She will need it if she's to make a proper match."

The queen looked hard at him, and an idea sprouted. What if the queen took Lady Samara on as a maid of honor or in another position that would keep the girl by Her Majesty's side? That way he would be relieved of his duty to her and could get on with his life—whatever his life might be now. He supposed he must return to Easton, to prepare it for winter.

And Her Majesty was a romantic. She enjoyed matchmaking. What greater honor for Lady Samara than to have her husband hand-picked by the queen herself?

But if the queen was dying, what would happen to Samara?

"Bring her to Mass tomorrow," she commanded. "Expect a page to summon you afterward. We should like to meet her."

"As you wish, Your Majesty."

"If we like her, we may find a use for her." The queen's eyes flickered over to Jane Dormer, still patiently unraveling thread. "Mistress Jane is to marry soon and leave us." The girl looked up from her thread and gave a shy smile, tainted with just a hint of ill-concealed sorrow. Surely she, too, saw the queen's time ebbing.

"My congratulations, Mistress Jane," Cade said. "Thank you, Your Majesty. I don't doubt Lady Samara would be thrilled to serve you in any capacity."

The queen extended her small hand to him. He kissed it again.

"Easton," she said before he could take his leave. "We may have further need of you. Do not leave the city without first asking our permission." She gestured to the Countess of Lennox, who returned to her side.

"Of course, Your Majesty. Goodnight." So Easton would have to wait. He backed from her presence. The last thing he saw was Lady Lennox helping the queen back to her chair, and the last thing he heard was a strangled cry of pain.

He was glad he'd escaped by the time reality slammed into him again.

The queen is dying.

She was dying, and her most likely successor was a co-conspirator in the rebellion that tried to bring her down. And she'd ordered him to stay in London. What could she need from him now?

Yet he knew that despite his new status and the fact that Easton needed him, he wouldn't, couldn't, refuse her.

Was it possible that only a few minutes before he'd thought of how glad he was to be back at court?

Now his future, cloaked in mist, yawned before him.

He took deep breaths to calm himself. She'd said nothing about sending him away again. And if, as it seemed, she had only months to live, he should be happy to spend them with her. He loved his queen.

Once he could breathe again, he took off in search of Hayden.

Cade found his cousin dicing with several courtiers, both male and female. Before he could make his way to Hayden a pretty little thing sidled up to him, wrapped her voluptuous self about his arm like a grass snake, and gazed into his face with melting brown eyes.

"Welcome back, my lord earl," she purred. Cade took in her round face and plump shoulders, the ash-blond hair that peeked from beneath her hood and her sweet, inviting smile. She looked familiar, and he ransacked his memory for her name. After a moment, her pink lips fell into a pout.

"Really, Cade, have you forgotten me? How is that possible, after the night we spent together at Whitehall? I know it's been a few years, but surely you *remember?*"

"Of course, I remember, Lady Beddington," he said as her name popped into his mind.

Beddington. How did I never realize the irony?

He gently detached her from his arm and headed toward Hayden, who crowed his joy at winning as he scooped coins into his pouch. Lady Beddington propped her hands on her hips and stared after Cade.

"We will play catch up later, my lord," she called provocatively.

He blew her an absent-minded kiss, reached Hayden, and fell into the chair beside him.

"You've seen the queen?" he said without preamble.

"I have." Hayden nodded as he shook the dice in his hand. He lowered his voice. "It won't be long, I think. False pregnancies aside, she's never recovered from the blow of losing Calais. And the king's been gone over a year. Everyone knows he's not coming back, but nobody will say it aloud."

Cade sighed and twisted the velvet cap in his hands, crushing all jauntiness from the feather that was pinned to it.

"It's a damned tragedy," he said. "She hasn't been the best queen England's ever seen, but her motivation is pure. And she's always been good to us."

"Word has it she's refusing to name Lady Elizabeth her successor," Hayden murmured.

Cade's eyes widened, and he dropped his voice to a whisper. "If not Elizabeth, then who?"

His cousin shrugged. "There's talk of Mary Stuart."

"Impossible." Cade shook his head. "Philip may not live here, but he's still England's king as well as Spain's. He would never allow a future queen of Scotland and France to take England as well. He would wed Elizabeth himself first."

Hayden shrugged again. "That's why I'm simply a courtier and not a politician. It's all far too complicated." He glanced around. "After it's over, I'm going home. There won't be a place for us here then."

"What will you do?" Cade imagined that Hayden's home, which had been part of Penelope's dowry, was nothing but a tinderbox of sad memories. How could he go back there?

"I suppose I should remarry. Molly should have a mother." Hayden cast the dice, but the toss was weak. They skittered mere inches across the table. The man across from them had to stretch to read the number.

"Don't rush it," Cade said. "You deserve to be happy, too." He stood. He ached to the marrow of his bones. "I'm going back to Riverview."

"I'm not far behind you." Hayden shook the dice again. "I'm losing too much coin."

"The queen wants me to bring Samara to the Mass tomorrow morning. Will you join us?"

Hayden laughed. "Would I miss her first foray into the court? Not a chance."

"I'll leave Blackwell with instructions to expect you tonight," Cade said. "Get home safely." He nodded to the other man, who was busy scooping his own winnings into his hands, and turned to leave.

Lady Beddington, across the room playing cards, caught his eye. In his shock he'd been rude to her and felt bad about it.

As if she'd heard his thoughts she looked up, met his gaze, and arched one eyebrow. Cade forced a grin and went to her.

"I do remember," he said when he reached her, and she got to her feet with a smile, her violet silk skirts making a tempting rustle as she did. "How could I forget? Whitehall, All Hallow's Eve, 1554. You wore a mask covered in diamonds, sapphires, and white plumes like angel's wings."

"Astounding," she purred as her lips curved into an inviting smile. "I must admit I have no recollection of your costume. I was far more concerned with what was under it."

Good Lord. He remembered her boldness now, too. It had been appealing to his twenty-four-year-old self. He wasn't sure if his current self liked it, though.

Oh, hell. She was beautiful. And married, so no harm would come of taking up with her again, would it? As long as they weren't caught.

"I am likely to be here until Christ's Mass," he told her as he touched a finger to her smooth cheek. "We will meet again. And soon."

"I look forward to it." Her cheeks stained pink, Lady Beddington took back her seat. Her card partner promptly started to whisper, and as Cade retreated, the tinkle of female laughter drifted from their small table.

He was probably mad for hinting at an assignation with all that was going on, but really, who would stop a man from trying to distract himself while his entire world rocked around him? If he was going to be forced by his queen to linger until she decided whether or not to use him, and while Brentford's daughter searched for some poor sap to be her husband, he could at least have fun while he was doing it. And if Lady Elizabeth became queen and reinstated her brother's laws and had him burned at the stake, at least he would have a good memory or two to which he could cling as he went up in flames.

❃

"It is the only solution, Robert," the Countess of Ashbury told her son. "I simply don't understand why you refuse to accept it."

Robert Hunter, Viscount Linton, looked from his mother to his father, the earl, who stood by the window and stared out at the river. Barges drifted lazily through the water, and Robert wondered if his father was thinking of his own flamboyantly decorated barge, which he had been forced to sell a few weeks ago to come up with the money he owed one of his many creditors.

"The queen has written that she will accept you at court, given the shame you feel over your father's treachery," his mother continued. By the window, his father shuddered.

"The only shame I feel," Robert said, "is that he did not try harder to rid England of papist evil! Even Princess Elizabeth is too ashamed of us to have anything to do with us, thanks to you!"

"That is enough," his father said, finally moving away from the window. "Would you rather I had tried harder and lost my head like Wyatt and Suffolk? Where would we be then?"

"Surely no worse off than we are now," Robert countered. "She fined you how many crowns for your part in the plot, my lord father? I don't know if I can count that high. That idol-worshipping bitch has taken everything from us! And now you put our future in *my* hands?"

"Robert!" his mother hissed. "While I am inclined to agree with you, you *will* watch your tongue. If your words fall on the wrong ears, we will all go up in flames. Or is that what you want?"

"Of course not." He rubbed his aching forehead. How many times had they had this conversation: Ten? Twenty? Ever since his mother got it into her head that he was their salvation, that the only way to ensure their survival was to send him to court to find a rich wife, she had spoken of little else. They had even taken to attending Mass, hoping that word of it would reach the queen and convince her of their repentance for Ashbury's part, albeit minor, in the dismal failure that was Wyatt's rebellion. It had been such a failure that Princess Elizabeth had written off the Ashbury family, who had risked so much for her. While Robert hoped it might be a show to keep her own skin safe while her sister was alive, there was no guarantee that they would regain her favor once she was queen.

If she is ever queen.

He had to go to court if he was to marry. His father was well known throughout the country for the role he'd tried to play in getting Mary off the throne. As matters stood, even those who shared Ashbury's views wouldn't marry their daughters into his family and soil their own names with his treachery. But if Robert went to court, it would show everyone that the queen had forgiven him, that Ashbury and his family were back in her good graces. He would become more appealing and would therefore have an easier time finding a girl to marry. Her dowry would fill Ashbury's coffers and keep them safe until the queen was dead and Princess Elizabeth took her rightful place on England's throne.

He knew all this. He was just having difficulty reconciling himself to the fact that he would have to serve the Spanish bitch in any capacity. It was hard enough to sit in Mass, surrounded by the riches that had managed to escape King Henry's greedy fingers when he sent his minions through the country to rip apart church lands.

Listening to the priest drone on in Latin while people knelt in their pews and prayed to statues. It was contemptible.

Robert tried one more approach, although he knew it was pointless. What his mother wanted almost always came to pass, whether he was a willing participant or not. Even if it meant possibly sending him to his death.

"What of my sisters, my lady mother? Surely they would welcome the chance to go to court. Comely as they are, they will have no trouble finding rich husbands."

His mother rolled her eyes. "Tell me you are not that stupid, Robin. Men, no matter how much gold they have, always want more. How do you propose we dower Isabel and Amy when we have *no gold ourselves*?"

She was right. And he hated the thought of his younger sisters wasting away in Ashbury Hall. They were beautiful, smart, sweet girls who deserved far better than their worthless father could provide.

He threw his hands in the air.

"As ever, I acquiesce to your wishes, my lady mother," he said with exaggerated formality. If anything, at least it would get him away from her and her constant scheming, away from his weak father and the belongings he had to sell off just to keep them in clothing that didn't make them look like the beggars they were.

"Good." His mother beamed. "The queen expects you tomorrow. We've rented this house through Candlemas. But I'm sure you'll find a bride before then."

Robert raised an eyebrow. "Through Candlemas? With what money?" And what if he'd said no? But of course, the idea of Robert refusing had never entered his mother's mind.

"Don't fret about that," she said, waving a beringed hand. She could have sold a few of her baubles, of course, but it was likely she'd just borrowed more money rather than part with her precious jewels. Or forced his father to sell something of his own. "It was necessary. And when you bring home a rich bride, it becomes moot. Just go to court, be the charming boy you've always been, and find a girl to sweep off her feet. Any one of them would be lucky to have you." She walked over to him and put her arms around him, apparently not noticing that he remained unyielding. She pressed a kiss to his cheek. Her lips were dry and cold.

"As long as you do *whatever* you must to win her," Lady Ashbury murmured.

Robert stepped from her embrace without returning it. Hurt flashed across his mother's face, but it lasted only a flicker of a second.

"What about you, my lord earl?" he asked his father. "What do you think of this scheme? Is it worth it to borrow more money we cannot repay if I'm not successful?"

"We just have to hope that you are," the earl said.

"I suppose we do." Robert shook his head. "I'll take my leave, then. I've much to do if I have to make an appearance at St. James's tomorrow."

He left the room without another word, which he supposed was very rude, but he couldn't bear another second in there with them. In his haste, however, he collided with his sister Amy, who was prone to listening outside closed doors.

Not that he could blame her. If he'd had the foresight to eavesdrop on his parents while they concocted this ridiculous scheme, he could have been far from London by the time his mother thought to mention it to him.

"Are you really going to court?" Amy asked, her eyes wide, not even bothering to pretend that she hadn't had her ear pressed against the door.

"It certainly looks like it."

"And the queen has promised to forgive us?"

Robert shrugged. "So they say."

"But why not just give our money back? Why do you have to go and serve her?"

"Because," he said, reaching out to ruffle her golden hair, "she hasn't *really* forgiven us. She only wants me there as a reminder of how *merciful* she can be."

Amy ducked out from under his hand.

"She is cruel and evil," she declared, with all the certainty of a thirteen-year-old. "I wish you did not have to go. I shall worry about you the whole time you're gone."

Robert smiled despite himself.

"I do this for you more than for our parents," he told her. "Don't you want to get married someday? Find a handsome prince to whisk you away so you can rule his castle?"

"I should rather die a spinster than have you whore yourself to Bloody Mary Tudor," Amy countered.

"Shh," Robert cautioned. "We do not know which of the walls have ears, little sister."

"She is right," Isabel said from behind him. "I do not trust the queen."

"Nor do I," Robert said, hardening his tone. "But we have no choice. Unless you want to work in a brothel on London Bridge or see me hawking salt cod from a market stall in Southwark, I will do this. If only so that we can escape the mistakes our parents insist on making."

Isabel's eyes, honey-colored like his and Amy's, filled with tears.

"Don't worry," he said. "I'll be fine. I know how to grovel. Besides, do you have so little faith in my ability to make a girl fall in love with me?"

His sisters giggled and the atmosphere lightened, if barely.

"I have heard the kitchen maids talking amongst themselves," Isabel said. "I don't doubt *that* ability at all, brother."

Laughing together—for what Robert hoped was not the last time—they left the hall.

Chapter Eleven

SAMARA SAT AT HER DRESSING TABLE AND TRIED NOT TO TAP HER slipper-shod foot with impatience as Betty labored behind her with a comb, muttering as she tried to coax Samara's hair into something resembling neat curls. A letter to Cecily—describing the journey, her arrival at Riverview, and her first impressions of the city—lay on her desk so the ink could dry while she was out. Samara was almost ready, gowned in silk the same shade as a pine tree in shadow, with ivory peeking between the split in her skirt, at the turned-back cuffs at her wrists, and lining the edges of her bodice. Her mother's necklace rested at her throat, and she had pinched her cheeks to give them some color. All that remained was her hair, and as usual it would not cooperate.

A soft knock sounded at the door.

"Yes?" Samara called.

The door opened just enough to admit a chambermaid.

"His lordship grows anxious, my lady," the girl said.

"I'm ready." She patted her head. "Betty, that's the best we can hope for. My hood will cover most of my hair anyway."

"I suppose you're right," Betty said. She fastened the pearl-trimmed hood to Samara's hair and straightened it. "There you are. Lovely."

Samara stood and took her cloak from Betty.

"The earl promises to have us back by nightfall." Samara followed the maid down to the great hall before Betty could say anything to make her more nervous than she already was.

The earl and Aunt Madge waited for her by the street-facing entrance, Aunt Madge seated on the cushioned bench of yesterday and Cade standing with his back to her, only his profile visible as he stared out the large glass window into the courtyard. Samara slowed her approach as she came upon them. She registered, just barely, that Aunt Madge wore a gown of deep wine-red, a color that helped alleviate some of her brownness. The earl, however…

God's teeth, he is beautiful.

His velvet doublet was the soft black of a cloudless night sky, and the dark hair visible beneath his velvet cap curled over the small silver ruff circling his neck. His legs were encased in black striped hose, which emphasized the strong muscles in his calf, and his sleeves were fashionably slashed to reveal a bit of silver fabric. The sun spilled in the window and cast him in shadow, making his square jaw look as if it had been hewn from stone.

Her gaze wandered over him, and for a moment her fingers itched for a pencil. She should capture him like this—quiet, lost in thought, without a shred of the arrogance that surfaced every now and then. *The way he was that night by the fire.*

The spell was broken by Aunt Madge getting to her feet and coming toward Samara with a smile.

"You look lovely, dear," she said. "That shade of green suits you."

The earl turned, and his gaze raked over her. Samara lifted her shoulders and fought the urge to touch her hood, straighten her skirt. She knew she looked beautiful. He couldn't deny it.

But he didn't offer any compliments on her appearance. He just nodded once.

"Wear your cloak," he said. "It's warm, and we'll be inside the coach, but I'm sure you saw how much dust a few horses can kick up. You'll want to protect your clothing."

"Thank you," she said, disappointed, and wrapped her cloak around her shoulders. Her fingers shook, and she struggled to fasten the gold frog at her throat. Why wouldn't it work? Had the seamstress sewn it on wrong? Then the earl was in front of her, his hands nudging hers away, and he secured her cloak with just the slightest brush of his roughened fingertips against her skin. She bit her lip as she felt her face grow warm.

"There," he said. "We must go."

She didn't want to go now. She wanted to lock herself in her room with the paper and pencils she'd sworn to forsake and draw her nerves away. But she had to break that habit. She *would* break that habit, so she held her ground as the earl helped his aunt to her feet. Besides, she must meet the queen. Her Majesty's approval would do wonders in terms of making Cade see her as marriageable.

The heels of her jeweled slippers made a delicious clacking sound against the polished stone floor, and the joy she took in that cheered her as they stepped into the warm September sunshine. Aunt Madge clung to Cade's arm as she teetered across the courtyard to the waiting coach. Cade made sure she was settled before he turned to Samara and offered her his hand. She accepted it, the roughness of his palm a thrilling contrast to the softness of hers, and he put his other hand lightly on the small of her back to guide her into the coach.

"Thank you," she said when she was safely inside—what was *wrong* with her; had she forgotten all the other words in her vocabulary?—and settled herself beside Aunt Madge on the deep blue velvet cushion.

"We're waiting for Sir Hayden," Cade told the driver. But before the words even left his mouth, Hayden was there, ambling across the courtyard.

"Good of you to join us," Cade said.

"I was counting my gold," Hayden replied. "I have considerably less than I did yesterday."

"That's what you get for dicing until the wee hours. To St. James's," the earl called to the driver.

The palace wasn't far from Riverview House, and for this Samara was glad, for the vile smell of the streets was something she didn't think she could take for long. She huddled beside Aunt Madge, who smiled and gave the floor a reassuring *thump* with her walking stick, and tried not to stare at the earl as he stared down at the clove-studded orange he rolled over and over in his hands.

He was so *handsome.* She wondered what Kat would do if she were there in the coach instead of Samara. Would she tell him the story of the time Samara had attempted to make laundry soap and had instead managed to dump the bucket of lye all over herself? Would she brag about her cherry preserves, which she considered the best in Worcestershire despite never having tasted any others? Or would she sit there and simper at him, fluttering her eyelashes and acting as if every word that fell from his mouth was a gem of uncontested beauty?

One thing was certain: she would say or do *something.* She would not sit there like a lump. But that was all Samara could do. She didn't want to speak—she might say something to remind him that she was odd. She couldn't move away from him; they were in a small vehicle. She could ask him about his relationship with the queen, since he obviously had one, but didn't know if he would consider that too personal.

You've seen each other almost naked. It doesn't get much more personal than that, you idiot.

She wondered what she had gotten herself into. If she couldn't speak to him, how would she make him want to marry her?

She felt so alone. No one understood her here. Not that they really did at home, either, but they mostly tolerated her and she knew what to expect from them. Samara sighed, tried to sink back in her seat but was stopped by her whale-boned bodice, and closed her eyes to force back the tears.

❋

Mass was tedious. It always was. The Chapel Royal was small, too, and aside from the interesting ceiling, not much to look at. That disappointed her. She had hoped the Chapel Royal would be far more elegant than the one in which she'd grown up attending Mass. That one was lovely, with its colorful stained glass windows and dark wood interior, but this was the queen's chapel! Should it not have been inlaid with gold, or pearl, or something more beautiful than plain old velvet?

But Samara's gloomy spirits were lifted as she furtively observed the courtiers in attendance. She had never seen anyone like them.

Most of the women wore gowns of rich, dark silks and other fine fabrics that dripped with lace. The men were dressed as elegantly as the Earl of Easton, in their striped hose and velvet doublets with the slashed sleeves and beautifully made slippers. Some of the men wore even more jewelry than the women. Was that normal? Her father never dressed so richly, and before coming to court, Samara and her sisters had not owned any really beautiful gowns. In fact, the pieces of her wardrobe Samara wore the most were the old dresses she'd inherited or the unadorned gowns she had designed and sewn to slip on and off over her head—life was ever so much easier when one didn't have to fuss with laces and tapes and hooks. But these people walked around so laden with gems and other fripperies she wondered how they were able to stand up straight. Did they do this *every day?*

She tried to keep herself from gaping.

It was only after the Mass was over that Samara realized that the earl hadn't pointed out the queen.

"Has the queen left already?" she asked him, and tried not to sound disappointed.

He shook his head.

"She wasn't there," he replied. Faint worry lines creased his forehead, but he smiled at her. "Should we take a stroll through the palace gardens?"

"I should like that." She glanced at his offered arm before shyly resting her hand in the crook of his elbow.

She more than liked it. The boring chapel and even the queen's absence from Mass were forgotten as Samara got her first view of the St. James's Palace garden. Despite the lateness in the year, the air was perfumed and the garden awash in such vivid color it was as if a rainbow had burst overhead. Sunny lady's bedstraw, white campion, and dusky purple bellflowers lined the path along which they walked. Further out, like a watercolor painting, were splotches of sky-blue, bright gold, pink, and midnight blue from the meadow cranesbill, rockrose, wild marjoram, and cornflower that grew there. Butterflies and small birds flitted and dipped like fairies from bloom to bloom. Gold and purple pansies lifted their cheerful faces to the sun, and for the second time that day Samara itched for her paper and pencils—no, not pencils. She wanted paint. It would be pointless to try and recreate this beauty in shades of black, white, and gray. It almost physically hurt to look at the scene and not be able to recreate it. But she couldn't tear her eyes away and got so lost in the view that she nearly tripped over the small boy that approached them.

"Lord Easton?" the boy asked a piping voice.

"Aye, lad, that's me," Cade replied.

"Her Majesty requests your presence and that of Lady Samara, my lord," he informed them.

Cade turned to Aunt Madge, who walked behind them with Hayden.

"Go on," she said, her hand waving like a bony white bird. "Hayden will guard my virtue."

"Indeed," Hayden agreed, tucking Aunt Madge's other hand into the crook of his velvet-clad elbow. "Come along. But you must behave. I have no desire to be challenged to a duel today." Their laughter echoed as they moved off.

The garden forgotten and her heart lodged in her throat, Samara trailed the earl and the page back into the palace and through a winding maze of rooms. She would have liked to stop and view the riches that passed through her peripheral vision in a blur of color, but the earl's stride was so long that she knew if she took even a moment to indulge her curiosity, she would lose him.

After walking a distance that *had* to be equal to the miles between London and the Malvern Hills, Samara found herself in the one place she had never expected to be, even in her wildest fantasies— the queen of England's Presence Chamber.

They were let into the massive room by a solemn little secretary, who departed immediately in a flurry of self-importance. The click of her shoes, so appealing in the Great Hall at Riverview House, echoed like cannon fire in the nearly empty chamber. Samara let her eyes graze walls draped with portraits and tapestries, the floor polished to such a shine she thought she might use it to fix her hair, the gilt-edged wainscoting, and came to rest upon a small woman sitting in a straight-backed throne draped in velvet and so large it seemed to have half-swallowed her.

Cade stopped and knelt before her. Samara realized at once that this tiny woman with the bulging belly was the queen and dropped into a deep curtsy, her silk skirts puddling on the floor.

"Rise, child." Samara had not expected the queen to have such a deep voice and was glad her head was bowed so Her Majesty wouldn't see her surprise. "Come closer. Let us look at you."

With Cade's help Samara rose from her curtsy. She glanced at him. He gave her an encouraging nod, and Samara stepped forward, aiming her gaze at the queen's purple-draped knees. *Her belly swells.* So she must be with child after all! It was extraordinary news. She'd known the rumors had been nothing but that—rumors! Her father would be pleased when she wrote him. She knew he worried about what would become of them if the queen's sister Lady Elizabeth took the throne. Now he would not have to worry. Her Majesty would birth a Catholic heir that would continue her work to turn England back to Rome.

She would not stare. She had no wish to make Her Majesty uncomfortable. But the queen extended a wrinkled hand and took Samara's chin between her cold fingers, turning it this way and that as if to ascertain which of her parents' parts made her up.

"Why, you look exactly like your mother," the queen said at last. "It's just like stepping into the past. You are lovely, my dear." She released Samara's chin, and Samara backed to her place at the earl's side.

"Thank you, Your Majesty," Samara murmured. *She would not stare.* But she was having such trouble keeping her eyes from the queen's belly! Even with Her Majesty in a seated position, it was swollen, misshapen, and looked far too much like Samara's mother's belly before she'd birthed Cecily and died. Perhaps the queen would die, too. She didn't look strong. Samara clenched her fists to keep from shuddering. Was there anything more dangerous than childbearing? Was it strange that the very thought terrified her?

If it could kill God's anointed queen, what was to stop it from killing her, unimportant as she was?

"What think you of our city, Lady Samara?" the queen asked.

Samara forced herself to abandon thoughts of her dim future and focused her attention on the watercolor garden that had enchanted her just moments before.

"I've yet to see much of it, Your Majesty. But the palace garden is wonderful!" *I am speaking to the queen of her garden. This must be a dream.* "I cannot get over all of the *colors*. And the river is so beautiful!"

"*Beautiful* is not a word often used to describe the Thames," the queen said with a smile.

"Lady Samara is an artist, Your Majesty," the earl interjected. Samara glanced at him again, hot shame making her skin prickle beneath the many layers of clothing she wore. Why would he say that? Samara wanted the queen to approve of her, not give her reason to deem Samara silly and unimportant. Surely a woman such as Her Majesty would not approve of a girl who spent her time drawing. "She sees beauty in everything."

"An artist, you say? How interesting." The queen's smile seemed genuine. But she'd said *interesting*. Not wonderful, or amazing. *Interesting* was just a way to say *stupid* without being rude.

"No longer," Samara said quickly. "My drawing was but a childish fancy, Your Majesty. It no longer appeals to me."

"Which is a shame," Easton said. "She's immensely talented."

"Thank you, my lord, but you exaggerate." Samara forced a laugh. "My drawings are amusing at best. And they matter little in the grand scheme of things, which is why I've given them up." Damn it. Her voice had trembled. She'd never be all right with the thought of giving up her drawing. If only Lord Easton would stop talking about it!

"So you've come to find a husband?" the queen asked.

"Yes, Your Majesty." Samara tried not to look at Lord Easton, standing so close she could smell the spicy clove of his pomander ball. "My father thinks I ought to have the chance to choose for myself."

Perhaps she should just stop talking altogether. She sounded like a child. God's teeth, she was better off when she could think of nothing to say!

"That's not surprising from a man such as he," the queen said. "He loved your mother very much. Anyone who saw them together knew it."

Of course, Samara knew her father had loved her mother. And she saw what that love had done to him. He was a shell of a man.

But she wouldn't say that to Her Majesty. It was well-known, even in Worcestershire, that the queen loved her Spanish husband, even if the rest of the country wished him back in Spain.

"We were saddened to hear of her death," the queen added.

"It was so long ago. I don't remember much about her," Samara admitted.

"I do." The queen face bore a hint of a gentle smile as she dropped her formality for a moment. "Come and visit with me again, and I will share with you every memory I have. She was a lovely woman, your mother. With many charming qualities."

"Was she?" She must have been, else her father would not have been so devastated at her death. But Samara had no solid memories, only snippets—a swish of brightly colored skirt as arms swooped down to save a toddler Samara from tumbling into the fireplace. The faint sound of laughter amid the fragrance of sunshine and roses. The echoing, drawn-out screams from behind a heavy door as she'd struggled to bring Cecily forth.

Samara shuddered. Maybe it was better that she couldn't remember.

"She was. I would like to tell you more about her, if you're willing." The queen's eyes were kind. "And if you'd like, we might soon have a spot for a new maid of honor."

A maid of honor?

Samara swallowed the shock that welled in her throat.

"I would like that, Your Majesty," she breathed. A maid of honor? This was certainly a dream! If the queen liked her enough to offer her the position, however noncommittally, didn't it speak well of her as someone worth marrying? Wasn't that why she'd given up her drawing?

She was thrilled that the earl was there to witness her triumph. Now he could not mock her, tease her, or deem her unworthy of being his wife. "I would like that very much."

"Good." The queen's hands drifted toward her swollen abdomen. "Run along now. You shouldn't be cooped up in here on such a beautiful day. Enjoy the gardens."

"Thank you, Your Majesty," the earl said. They bade the queen goodbye and the earl escorted Samara from the Presence Chamber.

"She liked you," he remarked as they navigated the palace, his stride so long Samara almost had to jog to keep up. "Do you realize how important that is? Once you have the queen's approval, finding a husband will be as easy as anything you've ever done."

Samara glanced at him. He stood straight and tall, his eyes on the path ahead of them. For a moment she wondered what would happen if she told him she'd already decided on a husband, and that she'd picked him.

"Slow down, please," she said instead. "If you get much farther ahead of me, I'll never find my way out. I will wander around until I starve to death, and a chambermaid will find my bones."

"My apologies." He didn't look at her, but he did slow his pace. A bit.

"Lord Easton?" she asked, once she was sure they were out of earshot. She had to ask. "I'm a bit confused."

"About?"

"Her Majesty's condition." He jerked to a standstill and turned to stare at her. "We all knew she was expecting a child, and that the child was due in March. And when we heard that she had not given birth but still appeared to be expecting, that it was not an heir she carried but a fatal illness, we chalked it up to malicious gossip from those who would wish her ill so that Lady Elizabeth could take the throne. But it is plain that she carries a child in her belly. What is going on? Why have we not received news of her pregnancy?"

The earl's face took on a sudden stillness. It horrified her. "It … it is a child, is it not?" It must be. If it was anything else, Her Majesty certainly would not be offering positions as maid of honor to young ladies newly come to London.

"Shh!" He glanced around, then grabbed her elbow and dragged her into a small alcove.

"What are you doing?" She tried to shake him off, but he was too close to her. Very close. She could feel his chest rising and falling with each breath he took.

"Teaching you a very important lesson," he replied in a harsh whisper. "No one speaks of the queen's health. To do so is dangerously close to treason, and becomes treason if you speak of

her death. Do you understand me?" His fingers dug into her elbow. The cold metal of the ring on his finger bruised her tender skin.

"Yes. Lord Easton, you are hurting me!" She tried to yank her arm from his grasp.

He stared at her for a second, as if she'd spoken a language he didn't understand, then glanced down at her elbow in his grasp. He flung it away.

"I'm sorry," he said. "I'm sorry. Are you all right?" He closed his eyes and gave a small shake of his head. "I don't usually ... I forgot myself. Forgot that you still have much to learn." He lifted his hand again, as if he were going to touch her, but let it drop.

"I'm all right." Samara rubbed at her elbow. Already the pain had receded, and from the look on the earl's face, he felt much worse than her arm did.

"I don't know if she's ill," he whispered. "But I think that it's possible. Probable, actually." He swallowed. "I don't think she will live much longer."

"Oh." His expression was so sad Samara felt tears well in her eyes. She had to stop herself from reaching up and touching his cheek. "You love her."

"Perhaps I shouldn't, considering, but I do. She was good to me at a time when I had no one else," he replied. Considering what? Her curiosity was piqued. He must have some interesting stories. "Besides Hayden." He shrugged and straightened. "It's in the past. She is human, not immortal, though she is a queen. Death comes for everyone, even for those of whom we cannot speak. Come along. We should be getting back to Aunt Madge."

Frustration swelled and overtook sympathy. Could he be more cryptic? Samara sighed. He was such a strange man. And people called *her* odd!

He was already twenty feet away when he must have realized she was still in the alcove. He stopped and turned around.

"Come," he demanded.

"I am." She hurried to follow.

One thing was certain. Once they were married, he was *not* going to talk to her the way her father talked to his hounds!

❀

"We may have further need of you. Do not leave the city without first asking our permission."

Cade felt like flinging his goblet through the window of his study, but he didn't. He was still trying to recover from his earlier mistake, when he had grabbed Samara's arm as he had seen his father do to his mother so many times. It was moments like that which reiterated that Cade was his father's son, even though the old man had always acted like Cade was a bastard foisted upon him. He would *not* give in to any more urges to physically express his frustration.

Even as his frustration mounted.

It seemed he'd escaped from one prison only to find himself shut up in another. He'd planned to stay in London for only a few days. A week at most. Long enough to pay his respects to the queen, see the girl settled with his aunt, and have some fun with Hayden—and perhaps with Lady Beddington—before returning to Easton and the people who relied on him to get them through the coming winter. His heart might belong to London, but his soul wouldn't allow him to set his duties aside while Samara tried to fool some poor, unsuspecting nobleman into believing that she would make him a decent wife. What a job *that* would be, he thought, with a snort of laughter. If she kept it up, she would be executed for treason first!

The thought sobered him. He also had no desire to linger until the queen died. He'd been through a similar experience once before and had no wish to do it again. Although the circumstances were different—he assumed he wouldn't be the one sitting by the queen's bedside and brushing her hair as she slipped into death—he was still about to lose someone dear to him.

Instead of hurling his wine goblet through the window, he drained it. He put it on his desk and slumped in his chair, rubbing circles against his temples with his thumbs. A pleasant haze stole over him, dulling his bitter thoughts. He poured another goblet-full and drained that too, then a third. He reached for the carafe again. He had trouble wrapping his fingers around it, for it seemed to be dodging his grasp, but eventually he got hold of it and tipped the dark red liquid into his cup.

"Hayden!" he bellowed when that goblet was empty. He was tired of drinking alone.

"What is it?" his cousin asked, appearing in the doorway.

With enormous effort, Cade pushed himself back from the desk. He grabbed the empty goblet and walked over to his cousin.

"Drink with me," he said, and held the cup out. It slipped from his fingers and hit the floor with a *thunk*. "Oh. Let me get you another."

Hayden chuckled. "How much wine have you had, Cade?"

"A lot," Cade responded. "Too much, probably. But you know how is. When bad things happen, drink wine! Ho, what are you doing?" Cade asked as his cousin's arm snaked under his arms and around his back.

"It's late," Hayden said. "I think it's time—" He grunted as he lurched out of the doorway. "—for you to find your bed."

"I can't," Cade said. He tried to lie down on Hayden's back. "Have to take Samara to meet the queen."

"You did that already. This morning." Hayden dragged him through the great hall.

"Oh." He *did* remember that, vaguely. "Where is she?"

"The queen?"

"Samara."

"Asleep, I would assume." Hayden withdrew his arm. "You're going to have to manage the stairs on your own, Cade. I'm not strong enough to drag you, and I have no wish to break my neck trying."

Cade looked up. The stairs were a spiral mountain, extending into the yawning dark of the second floor.

"I can do this," he muttered to himself. He heard a sound and looked over. Hayden was bent with laughter.

"Go on," he chuckled when he saw Cade looking at him. "I'm behind you. I'll catch you."

Cade braced himself on the wall and lifted his knee to his chest to take the first enormous step. Then he mounted the next. Hayden's presence was comforting behind him, and he went slowly and brought his knees high so he would be less apt to fall backward and crush his cousin beneath him.

For a mountain, he managed to climb it rather quickly and had his feet firmly planted on the ground in much less time than he would have thought.

"I did it!" he shouted.

"Quiet!" Hayden hissed. "You'll rouse the whole household, and I'm in no mood for Aunt Madge when she is suddenly awakened. Go to bed. I'll see you in the morning."

He turned to leave, but Cade grabbed him first and hugged him tightly.

"Thank you," he said. "You are my best friend."

Hayden patted him awkwardly on the back. "You're mine, too, Cade," he said. "Now get some sleep."

"Sleep. Yes." Hayden turned and descended the mountain.

Sleep sounded wonderful to Cade, but the floor of the chamber in which he found himself wobbled beneath his feet, and he was hesitant to walk the rest of the way to his rooms lest it open up and swallow him whole. A wooden chair beckoned from the corner. It was miles away. He'd never make it. Instead he stumbled the few steps to the safety of the wall and pressed his back against it.

"I'll just stay here until things are still again," he mumbled to himself. He slid into a sitting position and leaned his head back, which was how Samara found him the following morning.

Chapter Twelve

THE SUN WAS A SLIVER OF ROSE-GOLD ON THE THATCHED-ROOF-dotted horizon when Samara tiptoed from her bed to the casement window. Save for a few chambermaids and perhaps the cook, everyone seemed to be still abed. On bare feet Samara crossed the room to her wooden chest and withdrew one of the simple gowns she had made to wear outdoors. She knew such a dress was improper; Kat had chastised her more than once. She cared more about who saw her in it here than at home. But if everyone was still asleep, it wouldn't matter if she wore it simply to indulge herself in the beauty of the morning.

She stuck her head through the neck of the gown and tugged it down. It slipped over her chemise and fluttered to cover her to her feet. From another chest she took two ribbons—one she tied around her waist, to give the dress enough shape that anyone seeing her at a distance wouldn't think she was wearing only a shift. The other she used to tie her hair back after raking her fingers through it to remove any sleep tangles. She pulled on her old battered but comfortable leather boots and laced them up. Samara turned for the door, but before she could slip through it, something called her back.

Her paper and pencils, stashed in her small chest. They called to her as if they had voices of their own.

Yes, she'd told Lord Easton and Her Majesty that she'd given up her silly hobby. And yes, she was still aware that to find any husband, let alone the earl, she really would have to stop. But she missed it. Drawing was how she sorted through her feelings, and

God knew hers had been in a maelstrom since riding away from her father's courtyard. What if she drew less, and only in private? She could wean herself of the habit eventually. If the alternative meant repelling eligible suitors and being forced to marry Waltham, she thought she could live more comfortably without drawing than with that imbecile. It would just take time to learn to live without it. A little bit at a time.

She glanced toward the window. It was so early! Surely no one would catch her, not if she stole down to the river and concealed herself behind a tree. There were plenty in the spacious garden, fiery in their autumn splendor of crimson and gold, ochre and rust. The morning sky was so lovely, the ground draped in thin fog, and even though she didn't have the paints to portray the graceful arms of periwinkle and gray that stretched to hug the pale rising sun, she needed to be outside. She could capture the steely sheen of the river well enough, and the small boats she hoped would be out there even at this early hour.

Samara raced back to the chest, dug out her drawing materials, and again headed for the door.

She slowly, deliberately, lifted the latch. It swung open in silence and she slipped out, glad that she hadn't yet made a sound. But her attempts at caution nearly went for naught when she started through the sitting room for the stairs only to find the Earl of Easton, slumped on the floor and bathed in the small bit of milky sunlight that dripped from the tiny glass window above him. In yesterday's clothing. Motionless.

Is he dead?

But no. As she watched, his chest rose and fell in a steady rhythm. He was alive. Was he injured? She took a few steps closer and peered at him. There was no blood, no evidence of dagger wounds or anything suggesting he'd been struck. Besides, who would attack him and leave him for dead outside *her* door?

Samara inched even closer and sank to her knees beside him. His skin was pale against the inky black of his hair. His blue-veined eyelids twitched, and the normally tense set of his jaw was relaxed. He was beautiful in sleep; even more so than in waking. She supposed he did look rather ridiculous, curled up on the floor as if he slept atop the softest feather mattress, but that mattered little to her.

She should wake him. He couldn't be comfortable, and he would be sore enough when he did awaken and try to stand. But she couldn't yet. Want pulsed in her fingertips. She closed her eyes and prayed the temptation away. But God must have been sleeping as well. When she opened her eyes, the earl was still there, and so was the desire that raged in her blood.

She had to draw him.

If I manage to do it without being caught, I will never draw again.

Samara opened her case and flipped to the first clean sheet of paper. She hunted for the charcoal stick with the sharpest point. When she found it, she positioned it over the paper and studied the earl.

Best to start with his jaw. She did, drawing it as an almost perfect square, and from there her hand began to float over the paper. She sketched his ear and the black hair that tumbled over it, and his forehead—which, for once, was smooth and free of worry. She outlined his nose; it was strong and straight, without a hint of aquilinity. His mouth was relaxed, his lips neither full nor thin but gorgeously shaped. She drew his chin and shaded the tiny cleft in the center. He hadn't shaved in a few days. She smudged the charcoal around his jaw, his chin, and above his mouth to create a shadow of stubble.

Samara studied her work. It was good, but something wasn't quite right. She glanced at the earl again, and then back at her drawing. She bit her lip.

"Ahh," she said aloud as it struck her. His eyebrows. She'd drawn them too thin.

She bent over her paper and began to fill them out, scratching thin, tiny lines over the black curves she'd drawn above his closed eyes. She was so engrossed in her creation that when the earl pushed himself into a sitting position against the wall and groaned, she almost didn't notice.

"Samara?" he croaked. "What's going on?" His eyes were still closed, and his head lolled against the gilded wainscoting behind him.

Samara stifled a gasp and slammed her case shut, stuffing it under her arm as if she'd just been on her way out when she found him—which, essentially, was true. *Please don't let him have seen me drawing*, she prayed. *Please.*

"I should ask you the same thing," she answered, nerves making her sound more cross than she intended. "I found you here. Are you ill?"

"No." He struggled to push himself up from the floor with one hand but had no success. He drew his knees up to his chest and covered his face with his hands. "I mean, yes. God's teeth, yes."

Concerned now, her drawing forgotten, Samara crawled the few inches across the floor to him.

"What is it?" she asked. Now that he was awake, he looked awful. His face—at least the small bit that was visible beneath his hands—was blotchy even in the room's shadows. The hair on the side of his head that had been on the floor was matted to his skull. She reached her hand toward it, hoping with her whole soul that her fingers didn't come back stained with blood.

"Wine," he moaned.

She stopped mid-reach.

"You want some wine?"

"No." His fingers clutched at his hair; his palms pressed over his eyes. "No, no. That's what got me into this predicament in the first place."

"*Oh.*" Now she understood. "You got drunk!"

His hands fell to the floor and he winced. "Not so loud, please."

"I'm sorry." Now that she knew what was wrong with him, she wanted to laugh. "Can I help?"

"No, I'm fine. Thank you." The earl grimaced as he finally slid up the wall and into a standing position. He glanced down at himself, taking in his rumpled clothing, and chuckled.

"What were you doing on the floor outside *my* room?" Samara asked.

"If memory serves—and in these cases, it often doesn't— but if I remember correctly, Hayden helped me upstairs and then abandoned me. My guess would be that I didn't feel I could make it to my own rooms, or I may have thought this *was* my room, so I decided to fall asleep here." He shrugged. "Sorry if I startled you."

"It's all right." In fact, Samara was dismayed to realize that she was a little *disappointed*. What was wrong with her? Why would she think, even for a moment, that he'd fallen asleep *waiting* for her? Ridiculous. "You just worried me a bit. I thought someone had attacked you. It *was* quite a fright, actually."

"I'm sorry," he said again. "Really, I am." He laughed, and winced. He rubbed at his temples with his fingers. "We are very lucky that no one saw this. I can only imagine what they would have thought. Don't worry. You'll never find me near your rooms again."

His words shouldn't have ruffled her. She knew that. But her relief at finding him not only alive but uninjured turned their meaning upside-down. He would never again come near her rooms? Did he find her so undesirable, then?

"Good," she retorted, her injured pride overwhelming her reason. "I don't want you near them."

He dropped his hands and looked at her.

"Understandable," he said. "Servants gossip. When word got out that I spent my nights on the floor outside your bedchamber, you'd have a hell of a time finding yourself a suitable husband, and that's assuming the wrong person doesn't overhear you prattling on about things that could get you executed. Why don't we both act as if this never happened, just like we've been acting as if we'd never met before my father's funeral, and go on with our lives? The queen has ordered me to stay in London while she finds a use for me. And you're looking for a husband. The sooner both of those things are accomplished, the sooner we can move on and forget about how horribly we've disrupted each others' lives." His bloodshot eyes dared her to challenge him.

Samara already regretted her words but wouldn't give him the satisfaction of an apology. He'd dented her pride. It was somewhat comforting to know that she had the power to do the same to him.

"That sounds to me like a fine plan," she said instead.

"All right, then." He ran his fingers through his rumpled hair, and Samara cursed the hot tears that gathered behind her eyes.

"We will be supping at the palace tonight. There will be plenty of potential suitors about. Wear your best gown."

"I will."

"Until later, then," he said, and headed for the staircase. Was he so angry with her he would take the long way to his own rooms rather than cut through hers? Samara badly wanted to stick out her tongue at his retreating back, but she knew that with her luck, the chances of him turning around and catching her were too high. She satisfied herself by going back into her room and slamming the door as hard as she could. Only after the echo of the bang it made faded did Samara remember that it was barely dawn.

Her best gown, indeed. She knew exactly which one she would wear. And she knew how beautiful she looked in it. The Earl of Easton would be too full from eating his words to enjoy his royal supper, she vowed.

❀

Despite the fact that Robert towered over the queen by some eight inches, he was amazed—and infuriated—by how small she was able to make him feel.

After spending the better part of the day awaiting her pleasure in the room just beyond her Presence Chamber—which he suspected she had done on purpose, just to show him who held the authority and who did not—Robert had finally been allowed in to see her. He'd been escorted in by an odious little secretary so puffed up with his own importance he nearly floated through the door ahead of Robert. The man deflated a bit when the queen dismissed him with barely a wave of her hand, but Robert hardly noticed, as he'd dropped to his knee and pretended to be humbled at the so-called honor of being allowed into the royal presence.

"Rise," she ordered in a croak after he'd pressed his lips against her cold, veiny hand. He did so, trying not to let her see him cast his eyes around the chamber. Tapestries woven in rich colors and depicting bloody Bible scenes hung from the walls beside portraits of her ancestors. The floor was polished to a sparkling shine that would have put his mother's jewels to shame. The queen herself wore a lush but ugly gown of purple velvet and cloth of gold, with a gem-studded cross about her birdlike neck and a strand of rosary beads fashioned of pale blue gems in her gnarled hand.

Disgusting.

"You realize how fortunate you are that your queen is merciful, Lord Linton," she said. Her claw-like fingers, with their yellowed nails, worried the beads that snaked around them. "We could have left your father's head to rot on a pike on London Bridge with the other traitors."

Robert lowered his head. "Yes, Your Majesty."

Instead, you took every bit of gold he possessed. Gold you obviously did not need, if the treasures in this room are any indication.

"Be silent! You have not been given leave to speak." Her breath was hard and labored as it struggled from her lungs. "Let it be made clear. You are here because *we* wish it. Not because you deserve a place with your queen. However, because we are lenient, we are willing to give you a chance to atone for your father's sins. You must earn our confidence, and rest assured that there will never *not* be a time when our most trusted eyes are upon you. But we believe that a man can see the error of his ways, and are willing to give you the chance to prove your family's repentance."

Her patronizing words ignited a fury in Robert that he was hard-pressed to subdue. But subdue it he must, and did for the sake of his sisters. To hell with his parents. They had made their bed, and they could lie in it. But Isabel and Amy didn't deserve to suffer. He would do this for them—and only for them.

"Now," the queen continued. "You will be assisting the royal secretary, Master Boxall. He is responsible for the majority of our correspondence. You will be in close contact with him, and as such with important matters of state, so it is imperative that we are able to trust you. Do you foresee any problems with this, Lord Linton?"

She dared him. He knew that. The best possible place someone like himself could hope to be was a place where he would be privy to her most private information. And if any of it got out, she would immediately know that it was he who had leaked it and his sisters would be greeted by his decomposing head on a pike every time they looked out a window toward the river.

The queen was ill. There was no denying it. Her face was gaunt and drawn and her hands trembled on her swollen belly, which contained naught but another phantom child, as everyone knew. She was so old, it was laughable to think that she imagined herself capable of childbearing. But how long would it take her to die? Did he have it in him to serve her until it was time for Princess Elizabeth to take her rightful place on the throne?

"Do you foresee any problems, Lord Linton?" Her tone threatened.

"No, Your Majesty. Thank you." He trembled with anger and clenched his fists to keep it in check. It was amazing what simply being in this woman's presence could make him feel. He wasn't a violent person. He had never laid a hand on a woman in his life. But here, with his knee bumping the ground and an imperious old woman in front of him, he wanted nothing more than to put his hands around her neck and choke the idol-worshipping breath from what remained of her lungs.

"Good. You may rise," she said. As he did so, the queen turned to a woman he hadn't noticed until now, a young woman who sat quietly embroidering in a far corner of the room. "Mistress Jane, retrieve Master Boxall," Mary ordered.

The woman—no, a girl, younger than his twenty-four years—leapt from her stool to do the queen's bidding. But before she disappeared into the adjacent chamber, where the illustrious Master Boxall apparently was, he noted her prettiness—the copper sheen of the hair that peeked from beneath her hood, the pale skin that spoke of the fact that she was pampered, the richness of her clothing. A pretty girl whose family likely had money. But if she was in the queen's service, it meant that she too was Papist. Did he have it in him to convert a wife once he managed to find one? Or was her dowry more important?

He thought a curse at his father with all his might.

"Ah, Master Boxall," the queen cooed when Mistress Jane brought the man back into the Presence Chamber. "We hope we haven't taken you from anything important. This is Lord Linton, Robert Hunter. You mentioned a need for an assistant, did you not?"

"Indeed, Majesty," the man said. He eyed Robert. Robert stared back.

"Surely you've heard of his father, Lord Ashbury," the queen continued. Master Boxall must have known the name but, to his credit, didn't let on that he was aware of the negative connotations that name carried. "Fortunately, Lord Linton does not seem to share his father's views. We hope he will be of great help to you."

"Of course, of course," the royal secretary agreed. What else could he say to the queen? That he thought she was making a grave mistake, letting a traitor's son be privy to her correspondence? Robert almost laughed.

"Good. Take him away now, and we trust you to teach him what we expect." The queen turned her milky blue eyes on Robert. "Do not make us regret our good-heartedness."

"Thank you, Your Majesty," he said, keeping his voice low so she didn't hear the fury in it. Oh, this would be grand. If he could barely make it through one meeting with her, how on earth was he going to serve her in such a close capacity?

Master Boxall led him into the anteroom, where he kept a messy desk littered with papers and shelves of books. He pointed to a drawer.

"The quills are kept in that drawer," he said. "I'd like you to sharpen them."

With an obedience he didn't feel, Robert opened the drawer. It was stuffed to bursting with goose feathers, each tip duller than the next. There had to be at least a hundred quills in there!

Robert glanced at the mechanical clock on the desk. It was half-past nine in the morning. His stomach growled—he'd been too on edge to break his fast, and dinner was hours away yet. Would he even be allowed to eat if all the quills weren't perfectly sharpened by then?

With a sigh that he didn't bother to hide from the royal secretary, Robert picked up a quill and got to work. If anything, he could use it to stab himself to death if life became as intolerable as he was afraid it might.

❋

Cade's head still ached. Hell, so did just about every bone in his body; in his cups or not, what on earth had possessed him to sleep on the floor? But somehow he had managed to take his seat among the crowd of courtiers at St. James's Palace, most of whom were there for the rare glimpse of the queen they could expect during the meal. She sat at the high board, flanked by Mistress Jane Dormer on one side and the Countess of Lennox on the other, smiling between bites of roasted beef and sips of wine. Did anyone else notice that most of the food on her plate lay untouched? That her face was flushed, and probably not from the heat of the room or the wine in her goblet? That her hand gripped her belly more tightly than her other hand gripped her knife?

Cade glanced down at his own gilded plate. He himself had taken only a few bites of the dripping meat. The fine white bread was far more compatible with his stomach in the delicate state that organ was in, so he'd eaten several small loaves—without the mounds of butter to which he was accustomed. He couldn't touch his wine. He found himself longing for a mug of Worcestershire cider, with its clean, sweet apple taste to wash away the sourness in his gut.

Samara sat beside him, holding herself rigid as she lifted her goblet of wine to her lips. Her plate was clean, the beef's juices sopped up with bread. Cade swallowed hard to force back the bile that crept, burning, into his throat. If he hadn't felt so wretched, he would have appreciated the care she'd taken with her appearance tonight. Her mass of hair was caught back in the thin golden caul she'd worn at their first meal together, although the caul didn't look up to the task of containing her wild mass of curls. Her gown of rich tawny silk parted over an underskirt of gold and ivory brocade that twinkled like sunlight as she walked.

Twinkled like sunlight? Last night's wine still addles your brain, you blithering fool.

She'd obviously heeded his advice, though he felt bad about how he'd delivered it. He hadn't meant to snap at her. She was unfamiliar with the ways of the court. He shouldn't have expected her to know what she could and could not say.

And he couldn't help admitting that her disgust at finding him outside her bedchamber had wounded his pride.

She was so innocent. And damn it if he didn't find it appealing. Her world consisted of pretty dresses and fields of flowers, her paper and pencils and wishes and dreams. Had he ever been so naïve? He didn't think so. And he couldn't imagine it of anyone else he knew, not here at court. Those who peopled the court were exacting and capricious, manipulative and self-absorbed. He couldn't imagine any of them, save Hayden, doing something that didn't directly benefit them in one way or another.

To his right, Samara giggled with Aunt Madge.

Such a contrast from that morning, when her face had registered his hastily spoken words. *"You'll never find me near your rooms again."* It had tightened as if he'd slapped her. It almost seemed as if she'd taken his assurance as an insult. What was insulting about wanting to protect her? If he didn't, she'd be eaten alive. And he'd been in the wrong, not she. This time, at least. Thanks to Hayden. Why had his cousin taken him to the staircase that would require him to go through Samara's rooms to get to his own? Had he been so drunk his cousin hadn't thought himself able to drag Cade to the other stairs?

At least now the inappropriateness of their relationship was on a more even scale.

Anyway, he had done the right thing this morning, promising to stay as far away from her as possible. Her father had sent her to find a husband, hadn't he? Was she so naïve that she didn't realize what even a whisper of scandal could do to her chances of accomplishing that goal? Beauty would take her only so far. It would attract a man, but something would have to keep him there, and purity—and, all right, money—was held in highest regard.

Cade poked at the slice of beef with his dagger and grimaced as it slid around his plate. He swallowed hard and put the dagger down, patting his lips with the white cloth napkin that lay beside his plate. He couldn't wait to get back to Riverview, where his bed—a most comfortable structure, with a plump feather mattress and bed-hangings of such rich, thick velvet they could block out the entire world if he wanted—waited for him.

"Cade." Hayden's voice was urgent beside him. Cade turned his head painfully to the left and registered Hayden's wide eyes and the concerned set of his mouth. "I could be wrong, but I don't think I am. Look."

Hayden pointed discreetly with his own dagger—it dripped red with beef juices, and Cade was glad to avert his eyes—at a table across the hall from theirs, perpendicular, as theirs was, to the high board where the queen sat. He didn't recognize anyone at the table. They all appeared younger than he. Newcomers, most likely, arrived sometime within the last year.

"What?" Cade asked.

"Do you see him?"

"See who?" Cade squinted, which only made his head—and now his eyeballs—ache more fiercely. "I see a table of courtiers. None of whom I recognize."

"Are you sure you don't recognize any of them?"

"Hayden, I am in no mood. Please stop being vague. No, I don't recognize any of them." But wait; yes, he did. Or thought he did. A young man sat at the corner of the table, somewhat distanced from the rest. He didn't seem to be involved in their lively conversation either. He kept his head down, methodically cutting off pieces of meat and bringing them to his mouth. His clothing was well made but subdued and a little worn. He wore no jewelry. His wavy brown hair was cut short.

Cade's breath lodged in his throat.

"Viscount Linton. Ashbury's son," he stated.

Hayden's expression was grim. "That's what I thought."

"What is he doing here?" Cade demanded in a whisper. "They're a clan of heretics! The only reason Ashbury was spared is because of his distant cousinship with the chancellor. If Gardiner hadn't begged Her Majesty to spare Ashbury's pathetic life, she would have spilled his blood on Tower Hill like the rest of them."

"Guard your tongue," Hayden cautioned. "We don't know why he's here. I'm sure Her Majesty has a very good reason for allowing Viscount Linton into her court." He glanced around, but no one appeared to be listening. "At least, I hope she does."

"She must." Cade stared harder at the young man, so hard he was afraid Linton would feel his gaze and look up, but the other man kept his head bowed. "She has to."

Chapter Thirteen

"No, Betty. Not that dress." Samara restrained herself from pushing Betty away from the open armoire and digging out the gown herself. "The buttercup yellow silk. With the ivory brocade underskirt and sleeves."

"But, Lady Samara," Betty protested. "It's raining so hard you'll need Noah's own ark to get to the palace! You should wear something darker, to camouflage the water that will surely splash onto your skirt." Betty shook the sapphire-blue taffeta gown at her. Again.

It was a beautiful gown, of course, but better suited for evening than a midday appointment with Her Majesty. A shiver of excitement fluttered over Samara. She could still barely believe that she hadn't been dreaming when the messenger from St. James's arrived that morning, dripping rainwater and bearing a summons for Lady Samara Haughton to dance attendance upon Her Majesty that very afternoon.

The earl had glanced at it and smiled, a strange half-smile that could also have been a grimace, and congratulated her.

"So soon," he remarked. "You must have made a good impression on her, indeed."

"And why not?" Samara had asked, exhilaration coloring her words. "Perhaps I'm not the country bumpkin after all."

With that she'd fled to her room, knowing that it would now be only a matter of time before he begged her to marry him.

Now, nearly two hours later, Samara's stomach rumbled with hunger, but she wouldn't eat. Not if she wanted to be able to breathe once her stays were laced. In addition to the honor of attending the queen, this visit to the palace was Samara's first without Lord Easton by her side, and she needed to look her best if she wanted anyone to notice her. That was why her father had sent her here. She *would* return with the earl's betrothal ring on her finger. But he was different in London. He'd been so mean the previous morning and so surly at supper that she'd decided it wouldn't be such a bad thing for him to see her as sought-after. She hoped that without him dragging her around like a toddler in leading strings, someone might notice her and realize she was worth seeking.

"You're certain?" Betty asked, with a pointed look at the sapphire gown.

"I'm certain." Samara went to the bed, where Betty had laid a clean white chemise, and dropped her drying sheet. She pulled the chemise over her head and waited while Betty carried the sunny yellow gown to where she stood.

Twenty minutes later, Samara was dressed. Aunt Madge entered as Betty secured Samara's hood to her hair.

"You look like a daffodil," she said as she came toward Samara. "What a lovely gown. How are you traveling to the palace?"

"His lordship the earl has offered me use of his coach," Samara answered.

"Good. The roads will be muddy, but you'll have an easier time keeping clean than you would on the river. Still, be sure to wear your cloak. And mind your slippers."

Betty shot Samara a triumphant look, which Samara pretended not to see.

"You look beautiful," Aunt Madge said. "But something is missing. Ah, wait here. I'll be just a moment."

A moment to an elderly woman is so much longer than it is to me, Samara thought when Aunt Madge shuffled back into the room. In her hand she held a necklace. When she got closer, Samara saw that it was a large cross, several inches long, in silvery-black marcasite studded with topaz.

"It's beautiful!" Samara gasped, dropped it around her neck, and ran to the glass to admire herself. Even in the weak light that struggled to penetrate the window, it sparkled like sunshine.

Samara hugged the old woman. "Thank you, Aunt Madge."

Aunt Madge patted her back. "Of course, child. Now go on. It may be all right to keep a man waiting, but not the Queen of England."

As Samara descended the stairs to the hall, Betty in her wake, she allowed herself just a moment to think about how it would feel to keep the earl waiting for her.

✻

A smiling, pretty girl with red hair—coppery, not bronze like Samara's own—met Samara at the entrance to the queen's chambers and escorted her in. There seemed to be some sort of revelry going on. Two older women at a small table in the corner were playing a card game. The queen sat in a high-backed chair with a younger woman, lovely and sweet-faced with ash-blond hair, on a pillow at her feet, strumming a lute and singing. A few girls that seemed close to Samara's own age danced, their skirts swishing about their ankles, while the queen clapped.

"Lady Samara!" the queen exclaimed when she saw her. "Join us, won't you? Jane, find a pillow on which Lady Samara can sit. Do you play an instrument, my dear?"

"Only about as well as I sing," Samara confessed to a smattering of giggles. Her face flushed; she felt it. She hated to admit, in this room full of royalty and women who had been raised to serve royalty, that her father had been too concerned with his broken heart to see to it that she was properly educated for this world into which he'd thrust her. There wasn't much she could do that would impress anyone. Her dancing was passable, but when she tried to read aloud she sounded awful—she spoke too fast and her words tumbled into a mishmash of nonsense. She couldn't flirt. She could do nothing but draw, and that wouldn't get her anywhere. Already she could see how ill-suited she was for this life.

No wonder Lord Easton wanted to stay away from her! This was *his* world. She didn't belong.

But before she could feel too sorry for herself, the girl with whom she'd entered the room—Jane—took her elbow.

"You mentioned Lady Samara's love of art earlier, Your Majesty," she said. "May I show her the miniatures Mistress Teerlinc has done of us?"

"A wonderful idea, Jane." The queen's face was soft with affection.

Mistress Teerlinc? A woman painter? Employed by the queen?

Samara trailed Jane to the corner of the room, so astounded by the idea of a court-employed woman painter that she accidentally stepped on the deep blue skirt of the lute-playing lady at the queen's feet.

"Watch your step, you clumsy ox!" The woman hissed and yanked her skirt from beneath Samara's yellow silk slipper.

"Oh, I'm so sorry!" Samara's cheeks burned even hotter. How was that possible?

"It's nothing!" the lady replied, her tone changing from sibilant to merry as her voice went up in volume. "I should not have let my skirts fly about like a milkmaid in a hayloft. How uncouth. One would think I'd been raised in the country without any instruction on how to conduct myself in civil surroundings!" She smiled at Samara, but there was no kindness in it.

She is mocking me!

Samara opened her mouth to release the retort that sprang to her tongue. But before it could escape, Jane squeezed her elbow more tightly and pulled her along.

"Here they are," she said loudly. Then she dipped her head close to Samara's. "Pay no attention to Lady Beddington," she whispered. "She is not important. She is here only because her husband made it so. She married far above her station and since her wedding day has not let a soul forget it."

Samara cast a glance back at the lady. She was lovely, the epitome of beauty with her rounded figure and milk-pale skin, but there was a shadow of ugliness there. An ugliness even her fashionable prettiness and expensive clothing could not conceal.

"Thank you," Samara whispered back. "I'm not usually so ungraceful. It's my nerves. I fear I'm a bit out of my element." Even though she'd already realized she could invite more trouble by revealing weakness, she instinctively trusted Jane.

Let's hope I don't come to regret it.

"Here they are," Jane said. She opened a small wooden coffer and withdrew the miniatures, laying them carefully side by side on the shelf.

Samara had heard of the tiny paintings but had never seen one. They were smaller than she'd expected, fitting in the palm of her hand, dreamy watercolor on vellum framed with wood. Some of the frames were painted with gold and shimmered in the candlelight that illuminated the room. Samara reached out a fingertip. It was smooth beneath her touch, and she wondered what kind of painstaking time and attention went into creating something so beautiful.

Mistress Teerlinc, who, Jane informed Samara, had studied manuscript painting in her artist father's workshop in Flanders before marrying and coming to England, had painted all the ladies closest to the queen. Mistress Clarinceaux and the Countess of Lennox, the women engaged in cards in the opposite corner of the room, were represented. Lady Beddington, Samara noted with some satisfaction, was not.

Jane had one too.

"She's actually painted me twice," Jane confessed. "This is from the second sitting I did for her. The first was a gift for my betrothed."

"Your betrothed?" Samara, momentarily distracted from her fascination with the tiny paintings, glanced at her new friend.

"The Count of Feria." A blush stole over Jane's pale cheeks. "We met when King Philip came to marry Her Majesty. Our families disapprove, but Her Majesty has encouraged it, and so it will be. As soon as the king returns to England."

So Jane had chosen her own husband. With the queen's encouragement, no less! If she could do it, then surely Samara could. She began to feel better about her prospects of getting the earl to marry her. He didn't have to fall in love with her. She didn't *want* him to. But if they could like each other, and if the queen approved, then what could go wrong?

❀

After the coach had left for the palace, Samara safely ensconced inside, Cade retreated to his study to pore over his own message from the queen. He sat at his desk, eyed the wine carafe Blackwell had thoughtfully placed there, shuddered and pushed it away, and smoothed the crumpled note on the desk before him.

Easton, it read in the queen's scrawling hand. *At daybreak tomorrow Lord Feria will leave for Hatfield to visit with our sister, the Lady Elizabeth. It is our wish that you accompany him.*

Daybreak tomorrow.

He crumpled the note between his fingers.

"From the queen?" Hayden said from the doorway.

Cade tossed the note into the fireplace, as he thought she'd want him to do.

"I'm to take a trip to Hatfield with el Conde de Feria," he replied in exaggerated Spanish.

Hayden frowned. "For what reason?"

Cade gestured that Hayden should enter the room and close the door behind him. He trusted his staff, but there was no reason to ask for trouble.

"I assume it is to either confirm or contradict any report Feria might give her about the situation in Lady Elizabeth's household." He spoke in such a low voice that Hayden had to lean closer to hear him. "Feria is Philip's man. And everyone with eyes in his head realizes that barring accident or a sudden illness, Philip will outlive the queen. He'll not want Mary Stuart on the throne. He'll court Elizabeth as the next monarch. Quite possibly as his next wife, though I doubt he'll get a papal dispensation." Hayden chuckled. "And Feria will tell the queen whatever Philip wants her to believe about Elizabeth's suitability to get her to name Elizabeth her successor over the Scots queen."

"That sounds logical. Why did she choose you?"

Cade shrugged. "I suppose I must have proven myself capable of reporting the truth when in Rome," he said. It was the closest he'd come yet to telling Hayden what had happened to him.

And Hayden realized it. His eyebrows lifted.

"Reporting the truth?" he asked. "The word here was that you were just a secretary to one of the cardinals."

"I was," Cade said. "To Cardinal Morone. Pole's friend. I kept … records. Of events. And sent those records to the queen."

Hayden whistled through his teeth. "You're lucky the pope was too busy waging war with Spain to notice. Especially once Morone was imprisoned."

"That's true. He didn't notice." Cade watched his cousin, anticipating Hayden's reaction to what he would say next. "However, he *did* notice me trying to come up with a safe route through France which I could use to get home once my assignment was complete. He decided that I was attempting to construct a network of spies in France to report the doings of the French to King Philip. Ridiculous, of course, but I was imprisoned for a few months. I was only released once the commission found Morone innocent. Although he, poor man, stubbornly refuses to leave his jail cell until the pope admits he was wrong. I'll wager Morone dies there before *that* happens."

Hayden's eyes widened until Cade saw more white than blue.

"Cade!" he gasped. "You could have been executed!"

Cade's smile felt grim. "I know. But I was not. There was no proof to link me to any kind of spying. Certainly not the kind of which I was accused."

"When has a group of Inquisitors ever needed proof? God's teeth, Cade. Have you any idea how fortunate you are? I cannot believe she would ask you to do something else for her after you nearly lost your life in her service!"

"Why not? She is the queen." Cade shrugged.

That wasn't what bothered him, not really. What bothered him was his own reaction to her command. He'd had no problem putting his life on the line for her before, in the winter of 1554. He'd felt no qualms then. Even in Castel Sant'Angelo, he'd been frightened but not sorry.

Why now? Was it because he was an earl and no longer a throwaway younger son? Did he consider himself that much more important than before? Or was it because deep down he was afraid that if he brought himself to the attention of the Protestant woman who would likely be queen, she would remember him when she came to the throne and tried, as she undoubtedly would, to rid England of Catholicism once and for all?

"She is *my* queen," was all he said.

❋

The queen had dismissed all but Mistress Jane and Samara and the two older ladies that, Jane whispered, never left the queen's side. The room was quiet now, Lady Beddington having taken her lute with her. They sat in silence, Jane working on embroidery and Samara paging through a book called *The Christian Woman and Matrimony*. It was a dull book, insisting that a woman must acquiesce to her husband's every wish and talking of how her only business was childbearing, child rearing, soap- and candle making. Samara stifled a yawn as her eyes skimmed the words. At least the pictures in the book were pretty, colorful and serene. Each turn of a delicate page revealed a new image. She wondered who had done the illustrations, whether it had been a man or a woman.

"That book was a gift from your mother." The queen's voice, quiet yet deep, broke the stillness.

Samara looked up. Her Majesty had a gentle smile on her face.

"This book, Your Majesty?" she squeaked.

"That very book. She gave it to me at the New Year in 1540, when it appeared I might marry the Duke of Bavaria."

Samara closed the book and traced her fingers over its wooden cover. Her mother—her own mother, of whom Samara had almost no memory—had touched this very book. Had been close enough to a princess to gift it to her.

Astounding. She knew so little of her mother she hadn't even known of her relationship to the queen. Why had her father not told her?

"Were you close to her?" Samara asked.

"We did not know each other well, no. She spent most of her time with the court while I was—while my household was elsewhere. But on a few occasions, she accompanied my father's mistress to visit Hatfield. We met then. She was very kind at a time when few else were."

"I did not know her well either," Samara murmured.

"Yet you are like her."

Samara's head shot up and she stared at the queen—a gaffe that would mortify her later, when she relived this conversation. "I am?"

"You are an artist, are you not?" Samara wanted to deny it, but the queen's gentle face forbade her from doing so. "So was your mother. That book's interior illustrations were done by an artist in Belgium, but she painted the image on the cover."

Samara looked down at the book again. The cover portrayed a solemn-faced woman in an old-fashioned gable hood, clutching a cross and holding a Bible. But she hadn't really looked at it. Now she saw that the woman's face glowed as if illuminated by candlelight, while the fabric of her gown looked so rich Samara expected it to feel like velvet beneath her fingertips. The marriage ring on the woman's finger was a ruby so realistic it seemed to give off a soft red radiance.

"I never knew she painted," Samara breathed, so entranced she forgot she was speaking to the Queen of England. "My father never told me. He never talked about her at all." She bit her lip. "And he got angry when I asked."

She shouldn't have mentioned that last part. She might have been poorly educated in the ways of the courtly lady, but she knew her history. The queen knew all about angry fathers and dead mothers and Samara was ridiculously selfish to think Her Majesty might have any sympathy for *her*.

"They were deeply in love." The queen's cloudy eyes took on a faraway expression. "I imagine your father was devastated when she passed."

"He was."

"And you look much like her. She is in the tilt of your eyes, the shape of your face, and the beautiful color of your hair. I had red hair as a girl, but it wasn't half as lovely as yours."

Samara smiled as gratitude suffused her, warm and comforting. Why, she'd learned more about her mother from this stranger in five minutes than she'd learned from her own father in twelve years!

And she understood what the queen was trying to tell her. Her father *had* been crushed by the death of her mother. Samara had always known that. But while she'd always assumed that he was too lost in his grief to pay attention to his daughters, now she wondered if it wasn't more than that. If there wasn't something about them— about Samara herself—that made it too painful to give them that attention. It still suggested a weakness on his part. *But maybe he is not as selfish as I thought.*

"It is time for vespers, Your Majesty." Jane's soft voice rose from the other side of the queen's chair.

Samara and Jane trailed behind Mistress Clarinceaux and Lady Lennox as they hurried to the chapel. Samara, lost in thought, paid little attention to the service. She stumbled through the hymn, the psalms, and the Magnificat and hoped that the queen did not notice. She wasn't worried about God: surely He understood the reason for her distraction.

It had been only two days, but already she felt changed. As if there was more to life than sneaking out and drawing, letting herself live in a world of her own making. The real world was both bigger and much more interesting.

After vespers, the queen dismissed Samara.

"We will send for you again soon," she promised, patting Samara's cheek with her cold hand.

Betty emerged from an anteroom where she had spent the day gossiping with other ladies' maids. She was near to bursting with the information she'd gleaned from them.

"Betty, hush," Samara said. "I will never find our way out of here if I am distracted by your babbling." But she reached for her maid's hand and squeezed it to show that she wasn't angry.

She thought she had it. A doorway that looked familiar beckoned to her from the end of the empty chamber through which they walked. All she had to do was make a left, and she would reach the doors that opened into the courtyard.

"We're almost there." They reached the doorway, turned left, and—*whomp!*

Samara huffed as the breath was knocked out of her. Hands—large hands—gripped her waist and held her steady until her eyes regained focus. She was mortified.

"I'm so sorry," she exclaimed for the second time that day. What had Lady Beddington called her? A clumsy ox? Horrid the woman might be, but she must be right.

"*I'm* sorry," countered a rich, deep voice. "I should have been paying attention to where I was going. Are you hurt?"

Samara looked up into the face of the person with whom she'd collided. It certainly was a handsome face—oval, with smooth, lightly tanned skin that suggested he spent more time out of doors than locked behind them. She liked that. His hair, thick and wavy, was the rich brown of newly turned earth. His eyes, just a shade lighter than his hair, searched her face with concern.

She realized he'd asked her a question.

"No, I'm not hurt," she said. "Are you? I'm very sorry—I thought this was the way to the courtyard." She felt the heat in her cheeks. Of all the people that populated Mary Tudor's court, why did she have to collide with one of the handsomest men she'd ever seen?

"Hurt by such a delicate thing as you? Not at all." His lips curved to reveal straight, white teeth.

"Oh. Well, good." She was flustered, damn it. How did she keep finding herself in these situations? Why was it that the handsomer the man was, the more inappropriate their first meeting?

Then again, even plowing directly into a man's chest was more tolerable than having him catch her swimming in her undergarments.

"I know the way out," the handsome man said. "I'll escort you. Come with me." He led them in the opposite direction, matching his pace to that of Samara and Betty, who moved more slowly in their heavy skirts.

"I don't believe I've had the pleasure of learning your name," the man prompted as they walked.

"Lady Samara Haughton," she answered. "And you are?" Was that right? Should she have asked him, or let him offer it himself?

He paused before answering, then said, "Robert Hunter, Viscount Linton."

Samara smiled at him. "Pleased to make your acquaintance."

"The pleasure is mine." His gaze held hers. Time swelled and stopped.

Just in time, too. They'd reached the courtyard. Samara stood, uncertain of what to say or do.

"Lady Samara." Betty's voice, quiet but urgent, broke the spell. "It's nightfall, and you've not eaten a crumb all day. We'd best get back to Riverview House before supper is served."

The viscount's gaze flicked to Betty.

"Riverview?" he asked politely. "Is that where you live?"

"It's where we are staying while in town," Samara explained. "With the Earl of Easton. It is his house."

Lord Linton frowned. "The Earl of Easton is here? I was given to believe he was a bit of a recluse and hadn't been off his lands in years."

"That was the old earl," Samara said. "He passed in late spring, as did his heir. His younger son, Cade, has the title now. Do you know him?"

The viscount gave a start, as if someone had tied a string to his nose and yanked it.

"We are but casually acquainted, from years ago. Well. This is interesting, indeed." He smiled again at Samara. "And I assume you are Lord Easton's betrothed wife?"

"Oh, no," she said with a giggle. *A giggle? Who is this ninny that has invaded my body?* "He brought me here, but his aunt is my chaperone. The earl has little time for me. He is occupied with the queen's business."

Now, why had she said that? It wasn't true. They had been in London three days, and Lord Easton had yet to do anything other than greet the queen and take Samara to meet her.

This was exactly what she wanted. She couldn't ruin it with stories and exaggerations. The viscount was very handsome. He was here at court, so he must be in the queen's favor. She could get to know him, have a little flirtation, and let the earl see it. He would realize that at any moment she could slip away from him, and once he knew that, he would see how advantageous marriage to her would be. She would have her fun—innocently, of course—and still get what she wanted.

"I see," Lord Linton replied. He glanced at the little gold pocket watch in his hand. "I'm afraid I must run. The queen's secretary is waiting for me. I'm very pleased to have met you, Lady Samara. And I do hope we will, shall I say, run into each other again soon?" He cocked an eyebrow at her, and she laughed.

"Good evening to you, Lord Linton," she said. He executed a perfect courtly bow which sent a thrill up her spine, then reentered the palace, nodding at the guards who let him by.

Samara watched him go.

"He is very handsome," Betty noted as they approached the carriage that waited for them.

"He is," Samara agreed. "Not as handsome as the earl, though."

"But close." Betty waited as the groom helped Samara into the coach, then took his hand and heaved herself inside. "Do you still have your heart set on the earl?"

"Oh, I don't know." Samara pushed aside the curtain and watched the river pass them by as their carriage bumped along the street. "We've only been here for three days, Betty. My father gave me three months. Who is to say what could happen between now and Christ's Mass?"

Chapter Fourteen

WHEN SAMARA RETURNED TO RIVERVIEW HOUSE, ALL THOUGHTS of her day with the queen and Viscount Linton flew from her mind when she saw the earl drop an overstuffed saddlebag by the street entrance.

"Are you going somewhere?" she asked him.

"The queen's instructed me to accompany the Count of Feria to Hatfield. I leave tomorrow," he replied.

"Feria? Mistress Dormer's betrothed?"

The earl's forehead wrinkled. "How did you know that already?"

"I spent the afternoon with Jane. And the queen and a ghastly woman called Lady Beddington." A strangled sound came from the earl. Samara looked at him. "Are you all right? Oh, I am not supposed to say such things, am I?" Her heart fell. Of course not. A marchioness, no matter how rude, was Samara's better. Lady Beddington was even more noble than Cade.

"I'm fine." He coughed. "And as long as you're in here, and talking to me or to Aunt Madge, you may say whatever you like. Quietly. Just be sure it's nothing disparaging about Her Majesty." He glanced toward the dais, where a groom hovered with a loaf of bread and dish of butter. "Are you hungry? You're just in time for the evening meal."

"Ravenous," Samara admitted, relieved. The earl offered her his arm, which she took after only a moment's hesitation. It was warm and strong under her hand, the lawn of his sleeve soft on her fingertips.

"So you spent the afternoon at the palace? Did you enjoy yourself?" Cade asked once they were seated.

"Eventually, very much," she replied. Here was the Lord Easton she'd missed the last few days! "I don't think I made too big a fool of myself. Mistress Jane showed me some miniatures. Did you know that the queen employs a *female* painter?"

"Mistress Teerlinc," Cade said with a grin. "I haven't seen her in years. She is still around, is she?"

"So Jane says." Samara sipped her wine. "I should have liked to learn to paint. Back when I was still interested in art, that is." Her cheeks grew warm. She wondered if the earl had ever figured out what she had been doing, kneeling on the floor beside him the previous morning. "My father told me to be satisfied with charcoal."

"Mistress Teerlinc is a unique case," Cade agreed. "When she came here, King Henry's portrait painter had just died. He took her on to replace him. King Edward, then the queen, have kept her on. I imagine the next monarch, whoever it may be, will do the same." His eyes flitted around the room as he spoke, but they were very much alone.

"Where are Hayden and Aunt Madge?" Samara asked. Not that she very much minded their absence. It was the first time she'd been alone with the earl without any inappropriate circumstances causing awkwardness between them and without him wearing his courtier's mask.

"Right here," Hayden said, sliding onto the bench beside Cade. "Don't worry. I never miss a meal."

"Aunt Madge?" Cade asked.

"Taking supper in her room. Don't be concerned," Hayden replied. "She's not ill. Just tired. She's not used to so much excitement." He glanced up as the servant entered the room with a platter of food. "Finally!"

They began to eat then, and Samara sank into silence. She listened to their conversation. It meant little to her; she suspected they weren't speaking of anything of any importance, for her sake. She was disappointed but a little grateful. Her tongue was always miles ahead of her brain—why should they trust her with sensitive information?

She did have one question, though. And she waited until Hayden finished his story of a duchess who was cuckolding her husband right under his noble nose before she asked it.

"Cade?" she said. "What is in Hatfield?"

He swallowed his bread and took a gulp of wine before he answered.

"The queen's sister. Lady Elizabeth," he said.

She waited, but he didn't say anything more. After a while, she asked, "And why is the queen sending you to see her?"

Cade's voice, when he answered, was soft. "You remember what we talked about yesterday, in the palace?"

Samara nodded. "I do."

"Well, the queen has not yet decided who will succeed her. There are two main options—Lady Elizabeth and Mary Stuart, Queen of Scotland, who has just married the Dauphin of France." Cade took a drink from his goblet. "The Act of Succession makes Lady Elizabeth the natural choice, but perhaps not the right one. However, the current war aside, France is a natural enemy of Spain. As long as Philip is king, he will not allow England to ally with France, whether France is Catholic or not. So he will not want Mary Stuart on England's throne."

"I understand," Samara said. And to her surprise, she did. "But why is she sending *you?* Surely there are others who could go."

"Feria is a close associate of the king," Cade replied. "Since the king is not here, he sends Feria to visit Lady Elizabeth on occasion to gain some kind of understanding of her situation. But because the queen cannot trust that Feria is being completely honest with her, she has decided to send someone with him. Someone who has proven that he is loyal to her and no other, who will tell her the truth and not what the king wants her to hear." By the end of his answer his voice had dropped so low that Samara had to almost crawl across the high board to hear him. But she understood.

"Lady Elizabeth is a heretic, is she not?"

"It's not known for certain. She has had a Protestant education. But she also is said to attend Mass," Hayden offered. "She is certainly no zealot. Not publicly, anyway. But who knows what will happen if she becomes queen?"

Samara took a moment to digest the information, then a horrifying thought occurred to her.

"How long do you think it will be before we find out?" she whispered.

Cade shrugged. "There is no way to know. The queen has not admitted her illness, so no one really knows how sick she is. With luck, we will be able to stay as long as your father decreed and find you a husband before we have to leave. But if the unthinkable happens, and the queen names Elizabeth her successor and dies before we can do that, it will be best if we try to escape her notice and go home as soon as we can."

And I will have to marry Lord Waltham.

It was a selfish thought, certainly not the first one she should have had. But she couldn't help it. A monarch was a distant, untouchable figure. One was very much like another. Still, after spending the day with Queen Mary, Samara didn't want her to die. She was a kind woman, regal but real. She had only the best of intentions for the souls of her subjects. And to have a heretic queen replace her—well, it was unimaginable!

Samara was too young to remember well the turmoil of King Edward's reign, but she had vague memories of her father's fears for those who still followed the true faith. That king had died before any real changes could be implemented, save the Book of Common Prayer, but Elizabeth was young and said to be in good health. Even if Samara was forced to marry Waltham, would she live long after that? Or would Elizabeth hunt her down and burn her as Mary had burned the heretics?

"We've frightened her," Hayden murmured.

"It's a frightening situation," Cade replied. "But, Samara, I'm sorry if I've scared you. There's no need to worry just yet. I just think it's smart to be aware of the many different directions England could take in the near future. There are options. There are always options."

The servant brought out a plate of fruit and cheese then—sharp cheddar, one of Samara's favorites, and some crisp red apples— effectively ending the conversation. But Samara's appetite was gone. She nibbled on a slice of apple but swallowed none of it. She was beginning to wonder why she'd ever thought this might be easy. Though as a child she'd dreamed of going to court, she'd never thought it would happen. And when it had, she'd been blinded by fantasies of swooping in wearing jewels and beautiful gowns, making important friends and leaving with a handsome, sophisticated husband at her side.

She hadn't taken reality into account.

The death of the queen could have life-changing ramifications. And it imposed an even tighter time limit on her quest for a husband. What could she do? She still thought the Earl of Easton would be her best choice. Would she even have time to convince him of her worth? Or would she be whisked back home and wed to Waltham before she had any kind of a chance?

She couldn't lie to herself. She *was* frightened. But she could keep her fears quiet. She would have to if she was to achieve her goal. Cade wouldn't want to marry an idiot who ran shrieking from everything that scared her or didn't go her way. And if she didn't marry Cade, she would have to marry someone else. Someone who would take her far from her family and everything she'd ever known. Who wouldn't let her live her life as she wanted to but would keep her locked in the house where she would do nothing but make soap and preserves, perfumes and medicines. And babies.

Her time to win Easton was limited. And he would be gone tomorrow.

Hayden left them then, to write letters to his steward and daughter, though she was too young yet to read them. Samara considered escaping to the safety of her bedchamber but when Cade stayed seated at the high board nursing his mug of ale, she decided to stay too. She had to start making progress with him. Immediately.

"I want you to know that I understand why you were reluctant to tell me the circumstances of your trip," she said after giving him to speak first. "I have yet a limited understanding of this world. I agree that it's best for me and my untrained tongue to remain unaware of such delicate matters."

He gave her a small smile that made her chest feel as though a tiny bird fluttered inside.

"I did intend to keep it from you. But your inexperience with court life is only a small part of the reason why," he said.

Samara frowned. What other reason could there be?

"Do you think I'm too stupid to understand it, then?"

He sighed and looked to the ceiling.

"I doubt you'll find the words you seek written up there," Samara said. God, but he was infuriating. Maybe she should figure out how to deal with his quicksilver mood changes before she tried to make him want to marry her. She stood from the high board and smoothed her skirt. "Well, if you have no more to say, I'll leave."

He exhaled. "Wait a minute, firebrand. I do have more to say." He walked the few feet to where she waited, jaw clenched with frustration. When he stood so close, she was reminded of how tall he was; even though she was above average height for her sex, she still had to crane her neck to meet his eyes. "I wanted to keep the information from you because without it, you—you're *pure*. With no knowledge of how court life works, you can't help but be yourself. You have no idea how refreshing that is to someone as world-weary as I, even though we must watch you lest you get us all killed."

"World-weary?" she echoed. Why did his nearness make it so difficult to form a sentence? Parroting his words would have to do.

"So weary." He gave a soft laugh. "Until a few months ago, I thought this life was everything I wanted. After I was released from the cardinal's service, I set off for home counting the seconds until I would be back in London, ready and willing to do whatever the queen commanded. But now? I have responsibilities I never thought I'd have. Toward people who have no one else to look out for them, not just the queen. I hate it that those responsibilities have turned my life upside down, but not as much as I hate the fact that I've been forced to put them aside while I run around the country, doing everyone's bidding but that of the people I'm supposed to protect."

Like my father's? Does he really hate being here with me so much?

"But it's who you are," Samara protested. "Isn't it?"

"I used to think so." He shook his head. "I'm no longer sure."

He had stepped even closer to her as he spoke. Her back touched the cool stone wall.

"I've never said any of this aloud." He laughed again. "I've barely allowed myself the luxury of thinking it. Who are you that you make me throw everything I know to the wind? Are you some kind of witch?"

I, a witch? You are the one who seems possessed half the time.

She swallowed hard. "Not to my knowledge, my lord."

He lifted his hand, as if he meant to touch her face. Her eyelids fluttered closed, and she waited for the sensation of his fingers on her cheek. Rough, smooth, warm—how would it feel?

Instead, she sensed him moving away from her. When she opened her eyes again, the space between them was wide enough for an oak tree to grow there without either of them touching its trunk.

His face was closed off again.

"It's getting late," he said. "And I've much to do before I leave in the morning."

The lump in her throat made it hard to swallow. "Will I see you before you go?"

"It's unlikely. Feria wants to leave before daybreak." His eyes were bits of glass as he looked at her. "If you need anything while I'm gone, Hayden will be here. And Aunt Madge. I can't imagine I'll be gone longer than a few days, a week at most." He offered her a smile, but it was a poor, lopsided imitation of the soft laughter he had shared with her moments before. "I trust you to stay out of trouble until I get back."

Ordinarily such a statement would have raised her hackles, but she was too busy mourning the loss of him to respond cleverly.

"I'll try," she said.

He turned and was gone.

What just happened? Samara wondered, as her heartbeat picked up. Since she'd found him on the floor outside her rooms he'd been so careful about what he said and how he acted. But she imagined he'd just let more of himself be seen than he was used to. He had spoken to her as he would speak to a friend. And wasn't that what she wanted? A husband with whom she could be friends, without all-consuming love getting in the way and ruining everything?

Why did he pull away?

Usually Samara knew what she had done to make people angry with her. She was impulsive in her actions, but she always realized afterward when those actions were wrong. This time, however, she was at a loss.

Only later did she realize that, since meeting Cade in Riverview's Great Hall, she hadn't given a single thought to the handsome Viscount Linton.

❋

The morning air, crisp and bracing, hinted at autumn without surrendering to the passing of the seasons. Cade rode alongside Feria, a quiet man dressed in the height of velvety black Spanish fashion. On this, their third day as travel companions, Cade knew little more about the man than he had when they'd started out.

Cade suspected Feria knew why Mary had sent the two of them together. And if Feria resented his presence, well, so be it. It wasn't as though Cade could have refused.

"We should reach Hatfield in a few more hours," the count said, his English made melodic by his Spanish accent.

"Aye," Cade replied. Feria's coldness aside, he found himself strangely apprehensive about this little mission. He should have been grateful. He could find out what Lady Elizabeth was about and perhaps charm her a bit to win some time to figure out what he would do if she took the throne. And it wasn't as though he'd never seen Lady Elizabeth before. She'd been a prominent figure at Mary's coronation, and he had been one of the men on the banks of the Thames watching the night she was brought to the Tower to be imprisoned for her suspected hand in Wyatt's rebellion.

But had she seen him watching?

With every step Whitehawk took, Cade's enthusiasm for court life as a whole faded.

He didn't want this job. It didn't appeal to the man he was now—the man he'd realized he'd become only hours before.

He swallowed his sudden urge to burst into laughter. Who would have seen *that* coming?

Feria was right. The sun was almost directly overhead when Hatfield became visible to them. It was not an ostentatious palace—

more like an oversized house, built of mellowed red brick with several chimneys and casement windows. The knot gardens commanded more attention than the building itself. They traced a complicated design in the lawn, and the bloom of late-summer flowers offered an explosion of color.

Samara would love it.

Samara, who thought he was calling her stupid when he wanted to preserve her ingenuousness for as long as possible. Whom he'd come *that* close to kissing when the temptation of her innocence and the sight of her lashes fluttering angrily against her cheek became almost too much to resist.

And this time he would have had no excuse. He knew she was Brentford's daughter. He wasn't drunk.

He just wanted to. And Cade was used to taking what he wanted when it presented itself to him.

Sense had returned to him just in time. Not her. It would be a mistake. Brentford wanted her married; Cade would do what he could to make it happen, as quickly as possible, without a whisper of scandal touching her. Perhaps then he would even give some thought to getting married himself, if the queen didn't already have a wife in mind.

Thomas Parry greeted them in the courtyard, his cloak flapping in the breeze.

"The princess is just sitting down to dinner, and her afternoon is otherwise engaged," he told them. A frown creased his fleshy face. "She will meet with you on the morrow."

Feria bristled, but Cade bit back a rueful smile. Already Elizabeth would show who wielded the power here.

Parry shifted uncomfortably. He was reluctant to fawn over them.

"You can leave the horses here," he said after a short delay. "Someone will stable them. Have you eaten?"

"Not since daybreak," Cade replied.

"Come along, then," the man said. "If the cook has not yet cleaned up from his preparations of the princess's meal, I'll see if he can get some food for you." He turned and walked into the arched entrance, not waiting for them.

Feria looked at Cade and lifted a black eyebrow. Cade shrugged. Their presence here was unwanted, but what could they do? They were on the queen's business. Elizabeth was not queen. Yet.

They walked into the Great Hall, a vast room with an arched, timbered ceiling. Wrought-iron chandeliers dangled from the wooden beams and blue, red, and ivory tapestries covered the walls. Besides Feria and himself, there were no people, but long, narrow tables stretched from one side of the room to a high board at the other. Like an empty banquet hall. Lady Elizabeth held court but had no courtiers.

"What do you think are the chances we'll be given beds tonight rather than being housed in the stables?" Cade asked.

Feria grunted.

This trip will certainly be a pleasure.

❋

Three days after Robert met Lady Samara Haughton, the queen gave him a day off from his duties as Master Boxall's assistant. He went to the rented house on Fleet Street to sup with his family.

The meal was far more lavish than it should have been. Robert eyed the spread with annoyance. A roasted peacock adorned the battered wooden table, stuffed and reassembled with its glorious feathers draped over the plate like Joseph's multicolored coat. Carafes of sweet golden wine were passed around the table and drunk as if the supply was endless. After the meal, the cook sent out marzipan shaped and colored to resemble apples, pears, and quinces. A bountiful harvest indeed.

"Is it Christmas, then?" Robert drawled. "Last I heard, we couldn't pay a five-year-old hen to grace our table."

"Nonsense," his mother cried gaily. She stuffed a green marzipan pear into her mouth. "We are celebrating!"

"Celebrating what, pray?"

"Your success!" She washed the marzipan down with a swallow of wine.

"What success? That I have managed to keep the queen from executing me thus far? Because that's all I've succeeded in doing." He shot a glance across the table at his sisters. Isabel's eyes pleaded with him and he instantly felt sorry for mentioning execution. He knew that, despite his reassurances to them before he'd left, Isabel and Amy still feared for him.

"Don't be stubborn." His mother's scolding words were slurred. How much wine had she had? "Your success at finding the richest, most beautiful girl at the queen's court!" She raised her goblet in a toast.

"It hasn't happened yet, Dorothea," his father muttered into his own goblet.

Perhaps it has, though. The thought skipped merrily through his mind. Since meeting her, Lady Samara Haughton had developed a habit of intruding on Robert's thoughts. He would melt wax to seal Master Boxall's letters and the flame would remind him of her hair. He would catch a glimpse of some lady's bedstraw in the garden and think of the bright yellow gown she'd worn. When he unfolded and put on his doublet in the morning, he caught the faintest whiff of the perfume their collision had left on him—like violets, only somehow more exotic.

She was a source of much interest to the other men, too. By listening to them during the evening meal, he'd learned that she was raised in the country in Worcestershire, was the oldest of three daughters—no sons—and stood to inherit a third of her father's sizeable fortune. Unfortunately for him, she was also a Papist. But what else would he expect from a lady at a papist queen's court?

He wondered if she'd asked anyone about him after their meeting. She was brought here by the Earl of Easton—a man who certainly knew what he and his father had done. Had the earl told her? Was that why he hadn't seen her since the other night?

How stupid this whole plan was. No one would ever believe that Ashbury and his family were turncoats. Elizabeth wanted nothing to do with them; their name was still tarnished. And if Mary named the Scots chit her successor, there would be no hope at all.

"Send me to the Continent," he blurted out, dropping his dagger so that it landed with a clatter on the wooden trencher in front of him. "This is absurd. No one will ever believe we've changed sides. I will go to Sweden. I'll find a wife there and send for the rest of you once we're settled."

"Don't you understand?" his father bellowed, bringing his fist down on the table with such force his wife's goblet toppled over and both Robert's and Amy's trenchers clattered to the floor. "This is for England! Sweden adopted the pure word of God thirty years ago! It is *England* we must pry from the evil grip of idolatry!"

Robert took a deep breath and counted to five before he spoke—a tactic he'd developed in the years since realizing how idiotic his parents could be.

"I understand your fervor. Truly, I do," he finally said. "But, my lord father, I am *just one man*. And I am too busy trying to clean up your mess to take on England's mess as well."

"Stop, now," his mother said, the wine making her voice more petulant than soothing. "Come. We all want what is best for both the family and for the country. Don't we?"

The earl sawed with his dagger at the chunk of peacock carcass on his trencher.

"We do." Robert made a show of looking at the battered pocket watch he carried. "It's later than I thought. I must get back to the palace. Master Boxall has ordered me to report to him at sunrise tomorrow."

He escaped as quickly as he could, hugging his sisters and promising he would come back as soon as possible. Out in the street, he paused to take in a lungful of air. It stank, to be certain, but it was more breathable than the cold, angry air inside his parents' house.

A decision had to be made. His father's absurd dreams trapped him in England, serving a dying papist queen and having only papist maidens to choose as brides. He couldn't get to the Continent on his own, poor as he was. So his options were few. He would have to choose his wife from among the queen's ladies and hope he had it in him to show her the true path to God.

Lady Samara Haughton's perfect heart-shaped face flashed in his mind.

He'd heard that the queen had sent Easton to Hatfield with Feria to speak with Princess Elizabeth. No one had told him why; he was still the chief quill sharpener and not privy to any important information. But Easton's absence could benefit him in another way. If Lady Samara was out from under Easton's nose, she could be

Robert's for the taking. If he acted quickly. Hatfield was not far, and though Elizabeth would likely play with the men for a time, they wouldn't be gone long. He needed to formulate a plan, and quickly.

A grim smile on his face, Robert set off for St. James's.

Chapter Fifteen

LADY ELIZABETH TOOK HER TIME, AGREEING TO RECEIVE CADE and Feria shortly after noon on the day following their arrival. Thomas Parry led them through rooms bearing no decoration save carved wainscoting that must have dated from the building's inception in the late fifteenth century. They found her in the Great Hall, seated in an ornate chair not unlike a wooden throne, her simple gown of black velvet and pristine white damask highlighting the superior expression on her thin, pale—yet not unattractive—face.

"My lord of Feria," she said. "What a pleasure, and a surprise, to see you again." Feria dipped his head as Elizabeth's eyes, black as her mother's were said to have been, flicked to Cade. One side of her mouth curled into a hint of a smile.

"This is the Earl of Easton, my lady," Feria said in his softly accented English.

"I thought you looked familiar. We've seen each other before. You were no earl then, though, were you, my lord?" Elizabeth asked. Her gaze roamed over him. Cade thought this must be how a hen felt when it was being considered for a man's supper.

Her blatant appraisal caused a discomfort he tried to conceal. He'd heard she was a flirt. He should have been better prepared.

"At Her Majesty's coronation? No, my lady, I was not yet earl. Merely a second son." He tried his best rakish grin.

"How fortunes do change." Her fingers moved to her long white throat to touch a small gold cross that hung there. She kept her gaze on him.

"Indeed."

"But I've seen you on at least one other occasion, no? When my sister the queen had me confined to the Tower as her prisoner?" Well, that answered his question. At his reluctant nod Elizabeth's dulcet tone went sour. "Aye, I remember that as well. A whole crowd of you, standing on the bank of the Thames, watching them row me to Traitor's Gate like some commoner who couldn't pay her debt."

Beside him Feria shifted uncomfortably. Cade let the smile drop from his face.

So much for not putting himself in her sights.

"So tell me, gentlemen." Lady Elizabeth angled a pale golden eyebrow. "What have I done to warrant this visit? Of which plot have I been named mastermind this time?" Her tone turned playful as she leaned back in her chair, her black eyes sparkling. Only the slightly too-tight grip of her slim white hand on the chair's armrest revealed her tension.

Cade felt the need to shake his head to clear it. He risked a glance at Feria. Was she *always* like this? Alternating like quicksilver between venom and wit?

Feria's stiff posture gave no hint of a response.

"Your sister the queen sends her kindest regards," the count began.

"She does, does she? And how is she feeling? Word reached us that she was ill again." Lady Elizabeth's fingers tangled themselves in her cross's chain.

She had spies in the palace, Cade realized. Well, why not? Spies were commonplace among less contentious royal courts. Mary had banished her. If she was to be queen, she would have to be kept informed somehow.

"She is, indeed." Feria cleared his throat and crossed himself. "She wishes me to tell you that she intends to bequeath to you the royal crown, and all the dignity that comes with it."

Cade's heart thudded in shock. So Her Majesty would let her heretic sister take her crown? Had Philip talked her into it or was it a decision she'd reached on her own? Not that it was a completely unexpected decision. She had had few choices. But Mary Tudor must have seen the end coming if she was willing to make it official. He swallowed hard.

An expression Cade couldn't fathom flitted over Elizabeth's face. It was gone before he could even try to decipher it.

"I regret that the queen is ill," she said. "Truly, I do. But does she expect me to be grateful that she has finally deigned to officially name me her successor? She has no power either to bestow the crown upon me or to deny it. The Third Succession Act saw to that." The knuckles of the hand that gripped her chair drained even further of color.

"Of course, Lady Elizabeth." Cade could feel the fury rolling off Feria's black-clad figure. *Damn these pompous English,* Cade could almost hear him say. "In addition, Her Majesty wishes me to discuss the prospect of marriage with you."

"Marriage, you say?" Elizabeth demanded. She rose from her chair, and Cade and Feria backed away to allow her a path to the window. Her red-gold hair, which she wore loose and unadorned, tumbled in a mass of neat ringlets down her back. Her Majesty's hair had been almost the same shade once, he recalled. No longer, and it had never been so vibrant. Though even Elizabeth's hair paled in comparison to Samara's.

Elizabeth peered out at the flat gray sky before she whirled back to face them.

"Tell me, *comte,*" she said. Cade flinched at her use of the French term for Feria's title; undoubtedly she did it just to get under his skin. "Why now, when, except for a few earlier instances, my sister the queen has seen fit to allow me to retain my maiden state? Is it because she no longer sees me or an heir of my body as a threat?" Her black eyes bored into him. "Is it even the queen who wishes to discuss a marriage for me? Or is it your master the king?"

Cade took advantage of Feria's shocked silence to contemplate her questions. They were valid. As far as he knew, Mary had only pressed the suit of one candidate—the Duke of Savoy, King Philip's cousin. The reasons for this were quite simple. If Elizabeth had married and borne a son before Mary was able to, there would have been no end to the Protestant plots to overthrow Mary and install Elizabeth on the throne. Even if they married her to a loyal English

Catholic instead of a foreign prince, a child—especially a male child—could have destroyed any and all of the fragile progress Mary had made in stabilizing the country.

Philip, on the other hand, had to be aware—despite the fact that he hadn't seen his wife in over a year—that Mary's reign was almost at an end. Elizabeth alone on the throne would be more vulnerable to attack from other nations, particularly France. And he would want to keep England in the possession of his family, the Habsburgs, either by forcing Elizabeth to marry his cousin Savoy or by marrying her himself—assuming, of course, that the pope who hated him would grant him a dispensation to do so. Not likely.

So was Her Majesty suddenly interested in seeing Elizabeth wed only because there were no other viable options for the next monarch? Or did Philip want her wed so he could keep England for himself?

Cade was interested in Feria's answer.

"Of course, both monarchs wish to see you settled," Feria answered stiffly.

"With the Duke of Savoy, hmm?" Elizabeth laughed. "Will they never give up that ghost? My sister already once threatened to disinherit me and restore my illegitimacy if I did not accept Savoy's proposal. It did not sway me then. I imagine she is in no position now to insist on it."

She speaks treason! Cade dug his nails into his palm to keep from speaking. If he kept quiet, and Feria did not interrupt, they could give her enough rope to hang herself. And Cade would give her less to remember of him if she *did* become queen.

"With anyone with whom your ladyship would be happy, as long as he is suitable," Feria answered.

The tightening around Elizabeth's eyes as Feria called her "your ladyship" was barely perceptible, but didn't escape Cade's notice. Well, what did she expect? She was illegitimate, no matter what the Act of Succession said. She was fortunate to be part of the succession at all.

"Happy?" she echoed. Her eyes flashed. "I imagine my mother thought she would be happy married to my father. That is, before she knew he would cut off her head. And suitable?" She laughed. "A foreign prince of the blood, perhaps? Because my sister's marriage to Spain has worked out so well and has done wonders for England. Have you visited Calais of late, *comte?* I hear it is beautiful this time of year."

Cade could see that Feria's stoic demeanor was on the verge of shattering. Cade had to calm him before he ruined everything for them.

"Come, Feria," he interjected. "Surely you see Lady Elizabeth's point. She would see for herself the situation in which England finds itself, and only then will she know who will suit. There is nothing so wrong with someone wanting to choose whom he or she marries. Did Her Majesty the Queen not choose King Philip? And did you not choose Mistress Jane despite the misgivings of both your families?"

Feria glared at him.

"Neither Mistress Jane nor I have any claim to England's throne," he growled.

"True," Cade agreed. "But if you did, wouldn't you want to make sure you chose the best possible lady to rule beside you? The only way you could do that is if you were sure the situation was how it appeared, and not how people told you it was."

Elizabeth's laughter pealed through the wood-paneled walls as if someone had rung the dinner bell.

"Well, Feria," she exclaimed. "It appears my sister the queen has sent a diplomat with you. However will you survive not having the last word?"

Feria huffed.

"Lord Easton, I like you," Elizabeth declared. "God's toenail, whenever I hear that our dear *comte* is on his way to see me I almost die of boredom just imagining what it will be like while he's here. But you are a breath of fresh air. I would keep you if I could. Alas, I'm afraid you probably do my sister a greater service than you would me. At least while I am confined to Hatfield House."

"I consider it an honor to serve God's anointed queen in any capacity, my lady," he replied.

"I'm sure you do." Her eyes sparkled. "Join me for dinner, won't you, gentlemen? My cook has prepared some gorgeous perch caught just yesterday from the Lea. And later, we shall attend vespers."

Cade glanced at Feria, but the other man refused to look at him.

Well, he'd done the best he could. And while he was almost certain Her Majesty would approve of how he'd handled the situation, only God knew what would happen next.

"Thank you," he said, and offered Elizabeth his arm.

❀

This was court the way she'd always imagined it.

Samara had been right to save Betty's favored sapphire-blue gown for a special evening occasion. Cade had been gone for five days, and she hardly noticed his absence, she'd been so busy with the queen. She played cards with her, read to her, and helped Jane with the constant disarray that was Her Majesty's embroidery basket. These were things she would need to know, she supposed, if she took Jane's spot as a maid-of-honor. If it would even need to be filled. Her Majesty weakened visibly by the day.

But she wasn't always in charge of entertaining the queen. Sometimes the queen allowed Samara to entertain herself. That very day Samara had spent the hours before supper in Her Majesty's Privy Chamber, poring over the beautiful things that adorned the walls, surfaces, and even the floor. She touched a statue of the Virgin so lifelike she would have thought it a real person if it were not six inches tall and made of bronze. She stood in front of a tapestry depicting plump winged cherubs atop a cloud that floated in a flawless cerulean sky. She knelt before a low table draped in the luxurious softness of a Turkey carpet in vibrant shades of buttery yellow, brick red, ivory, and the fresh green of spring grass. Only afterward did she realize how foolish she must have looked and thanked God that no one, particularly that nasty cow Lady Beddington, had seen her on her knees on the floor like a common washerwoman. The queen, however, seemed inclined to indulge her, and for that Samara was grateful.

She had seen Lord Linton but once that day, as he walked past the open door of Master Boxall's office with a box in his hands. He did not seem to notice her.

The queen seemed to be in unusually good spirits, for she announced that after supper there would be dancing in the banqueting hall.

"Go back to Riverview House and nap," she instructed Samara. "We would like you see you enjoy yourself, not fall asleep during the pavane."

Samara did as she was told, and nightfall found her back at the palace, seated between Hayden and Aunt Madge at a long table while the most delicious food she'd ever tasted passed in front of her. She'd learned her lesson at her first palace supper, however, and took only small bites of everything that looked good to her, rather than a large helping of each. She wanted to dance, and if she was weighed down with food, she would make herself sick.

But the first dance was a galliard. It was the one at which she was worst. She decided to sit it out and participate in the next.

She watched instead, marveling over the intricate footwork and how no one seemed to trip over their own toes as she would have. Hayden danced hand-in-hand with one of the queen's maids— Samara, to her chagrin, had already forgotten the girl's name—and smiled down into her face as they circled the floor. Cecily would *not* have been happy. Samara would not mention it in her next missive to her youngest sister.

The galliard gave way to a pavane. It was not as exciting, but she did enjoy the better view she had of everyone's clothing. They were just as splendidly dressed as they had been at Mass. They wore velvets and silks, jewels and precious metals. The colors were not bright, but the fabrics so rich it didn't matter. She was entranced to the point where she didn't notice the man at her elbow until he spoke.

"Lady Samara," he said. "I had hoped to see you here tonight."

Samara looked up into the deep brown eyes of Lord Linton.

"Good evening, Lord Linton," she said as her heart skipped— just one beat. She allowed her lips to curve into a hint of a smile, as she'd seen other ladies do when talking to men. "How are you?"

"Very well, now." He didn't attempt to hide his own smile, and she was pierced by a sliver of doubt. Could he really be *that* happy to see her? He barely knew her. "Will you dance with me?"

"A volta!" the queen called from her spot at the high board, her deep voice carrying over the noisy chatter of her courtiers.

Her doubt fled. Of all the dances the dancing master had taught her, the volta was her favorite.

"I'd be happy to," she said, and this time she let a full smile bloom on her face.

"Aunt Madge, I—" Samara turned and was shocked to see a horrified expression on the older woman's face. "What is it?"

Aunt Madge shook her head, and her features settled themselves into a semblance of normalcy, although the set of her jaw was still tense. She gave Samara a small smile.

"It's nothing, darling. I thought I saw someone. I was wrong. Just my old woman's eyes playing tricks on me." She patted Samara's hand with her small, cold one. "Go and dance. Enjoy yourself."

Cade's aunt wasn't being completely honest with her. But now was neither the time nor the place to try and drag the truth out of her. Samara kissed Aunt Madge on her papery cheek before allowing Lord Linton to take her hand and lead her to the middle of the floor where the other courtiers had begun to assemble themselves.

She took her spot beside him, his hand warm on hers. He glanced down at her and grinned when, at the signal from the other dancers, they took the first sprightly steps. Samara's skirt fluttered around her ankles as she lifted one foot and then the other.

The viscount guided her around, and they danced back in the direction from which they'd come. Then he released her hand, put his other hand firmly on her waist, and she lifted her right hand to rest on the softness of his velvet-clad shoulder. He slipped the four fingers of his free hand beneath her busk—the warmth of them radiated through her clothing and her stomach tightened, almost involuntarily. Lord Linton lifted her high into the air, the breeze as she rose ruffling her curls. She gripped his shoulder for steadiness. She slid down again, and they took two more steps, then she was flying once more. On the next lift, he smiled up into her face. She couldn't help smiling back.

They twirled among the others, narrowly missing a collision at some points and laughing when they bumped into each other. She'd danced before, at home with her sisters and with the dancing master, but it hadn't been like this. Tendrils of hair come loose from her hood and stuck to the perspiration that beaded along the low neckline of her gown. His hands, when the steps required him to touch her, were warm and strong. This close to him she was able to see that his brown eyes were flecked with gold. Again she noted that his skin was lightly tanned—she liked that; he was not someone who sat on his behind and expected his servants to do all the work.

She was a strange mixture of disappointed and apprehensive when the dance ended. Disappointed for an obvious, though unexpected, reason—her hand felt bereft when he dropped it. Apprehensive because she wasn't sure where to go from here. Should they continue to dance if no one else approached her? If someone else *did* approach her, should she accept while Lord Linton stood in front of her? What was the proper etiquette? The dancing master had not taught her *this!*

She need not have worried, though, for before either of them could speak Hayden was upon them, a tall, gangly man at his side.

"Samara," he said, ignoring Lord Linton. "I want to introduce you to a friend of mine. This is John Blackner, Lord Parkhurst. Parkhurst, this is Lady Samara Haughton."

Lord Parkhurst grinned, revealing crooked yellow teeth full of the remnants of his meal.

Samara gasped. What, did he think he would be so hungry again later that he ought to smuggle extra food from the palace? In his *teeth?*

"Pleased to meet you," she managed to say. *Please, God, do not let him ask me to dance.*

Beside her, Lord Linton chuckled softly.

Hayden's eyes slid to the viscount as if he hadn't noticed him before.

"Lord Linton," he said, his voice as cool as Samara had ever heard it. "Quite a surprise to see you here."

"I imagine you're not the first to feel that way, Sir Hayden," Lord Linton replied, a sparkle of humor in his eyes.

"No, I don't think I am."

Samara's gaze shifted between Hayden and Linton. They knew each other? And why was Hayden being rude? She'd never seen him anything less than perfectly cordial.

"Things change," Lord Linton said with a pleasant smile on his handsome face.

"I know that all too well, Linton. Now, I hope you don't mind if I whisk the lady away. I've promised Parkhurst here a formal introduction." Hayden took up Samara's hand and for a moment Samara thought he meant to drag her by it.

"That's the price you pay when you've been monopolizing the attention of the most beautiful woman in the room." Linton shrugged and took up Samara's other hand, brushing his lips against the back of her knuckles. "Thank you for the dance, Lady Samara. I hope we'll get to do it again."

"So do I," Samara said, and found that she meant it.

"Goodbye," he said as Hayden pulled her away.

❋

Lady Elizabeth sent them on their way with no answer one way or the other about her marriage prospects, which Cade knew both Feria and the queen had to have expected. She knew she was about to inherit, that there were no other possible heirs. Her Majesty had no leverage. Elizabeth wouldn't be open to marriage negotiations now, and he'd tried telling Feria as much. But Feria was too much Philip's man. He would do what his master wanted, and nothing else.

Thankfully, the ride back to London from Hatfield took less than two days. He parted ways with Feria at the palace and rode Whitehawk the rest of the way to Riverview. He was tired. More than that, he was hungry. But most of all he was thinking of Samara and hoping she had managed to stay out of trouble during his absence.

The hall was empty when he entered. Sunset was visible through the tall, street-facing windows. It should have been close to suppertime, and indeed, the delicious scents that wafted from the kitchen made his mouth water. He figured he had time to wash before settling down to the meal. He started up the steps to his chambers and was greeted by Hayden, on his way down.

"Cade!" Hayden exclaimed. "You're back!"

"Aye. As I suspected, it was a wasted trip. Feria's instructions were to get Lady Elizabeth to agree to at least consider a few suitors. She refused, and quite smartly, I might add. Put Feria in his place. Come, I want to wash up before supper. Tell me what I've missed."

"We may have a problem, Cade," Hayden said. He followed Cade into his bedchamber and sat on a stool by the fireplace as Cade pushed up his sleeves and dipped his hands into the bowl of cold water on the table.

Cade groaned and splashed the water on his face. "What has she done?"

"I know you're joking, but I'm afraid she has done something." Hayden rubbed his forehead. "She's fallen in with Linton."

A chill rippled over Cade's skin. It might have been the water, but probably not.

"How?" he said.

"Honestly, I've no idea. I can only imagine she met him while she was at the palace. She never said a word about him to me, but last night we had supper at the palace and there was dancing afterward. I looked over at one point during the volta and he was lifting her into the air. It didn't look like she was struggling to get down."

Cade picked up the neatly folded drying cloth on the table beside the basin and rubbed his face with it.

"What did you do?" he finally asked.

"Parkhurst wanted to meet her, anyway. When the volta was over, I caught him and took him over to her. She seemed less than interested—I have to admit I don't blame her, the man carries more meat in his teeth than a dog at a bear-baiting—but the distraction worked. I got her away from Linton."

"Good." But Cade was only slightly relieved. He knew it wasn't over. Leave it to Samara to find the one man at Queen Mary's court from whom she should stay as far away as possible!

When she came down and saw him seated at the high board, Samara seemed as surprised as Hayden had been.

"I thought you would be a few days longer!" she exclaimed after they'd greeted each other, and he'd embraced Aunt Madge.

"As did I," Cade said. "But it wasn't difficult to get a feel for Lady Elizabeth. There's no doubt in her mind that she'll be queen. And she'll do it alone."

"Alone?" Samara asked. She settled herself at the high board. "How interesting. A queen has never ruled England without a king. Unless you consider Empress Matilda, but her claim was disputed.

Or Margaret of Anjou, but she was technically queen consort, though poor King Henry was unfit to rule by himself."

Her nonchalance was maddening. He had no interest in learning how well she had paid attention to her history lessons. He wanted to know what was going on with Ashbury's son.

"So, tell me. Did anything interesting happen while I was gone?" He used his thumb to spread butter on his bread, feigning ignorance. Sensing his aunt's gaze on him, he realized that she, too, had witnessed Samara's interaction with Linton and was concerned.

Samara considered. "Not especially. You were only gone six days. The queen was ill the day you left and did not want company." She brightened. "But I spent most of the day with her yesterday. She let me explore her Privy Chamber. Such riches she has there! Statues and tapestries, and Turkish carpets and jeweled boxes. I could have stayed a fortnight and not been satisfied."

Her face glowed as she spoke. Obviously she'd forgotten to keep up the pretense of not being interested in art anymore.

He allowed the beauty of her face, bathed in happiness, to distract him just for a moment.

"And last evening?" he asked. He took a swig of ale.

She was suddenly fidgety. "We had supper at the palace."

"Again? I'm happy to hear that the queen recovered from her illness of the other day. Was there dancing? I know there wasn't any the first night we ate at the palace, but the queen often likes to watch her courtiers dance after the evening meal."

"There was." Blood stained her cheeks, and her attention seemed irresistibly drawn to the capon wing on her plate.

"You're blushing, Lady Samara." He hoped he sounded teasing rather than nervous.

"Oh, I suppose Hayden has already told you, and that's why you're set on tormenting me. Yes, I met a man. Actually, I met him several nights ago. I know only his name, his title and that he is in service to the queen in some capacity, so don't ask me anything." She stabbed at her food with her dagger.

"I'm sorry," he said. "Hayden did tell me, and I suppose I was teasing. A bit. Do you like him?"

She shrugged and met his eyes, looking like a very young girl.

"I don't know." She bit her lip. "I barely know him. But he is likable."

"You met another man, too, Lady Samara," Hayden interjected.

She wrinkled her nose. "Lord Parkhurst? I'm sorry, Hayden, for I know he's a friend of yours, but no. He was nice enough, I suppose, but I think he was too concerned with snacking on the food that was left in his teeth to pay any mind to wooing me. The sucking sound he made was quite distracting. I'm afraid it deafened me to the point where I can't tell you anything he said."

Thoughts of Linton fled as Cade burst out laughing. Even without a pencil in her hand, Samara could draw quite a picture.

Hayden laughed too. "You're right, and I'm sorry, Samara," he said. "I don't know what I was thinking, bringing him over to you."

"What about Lord Rennington?" Aunt Madge piped up. "You danced once with him."

Samara shook her head. "He lives in Northumberland. I don't want to be that far from my family. And I can barely understand him when he speaks."

"Lord Grimsby? He is from Warwickshire."

"His clothes never match. I saw him yesterday in a blue doublet and black hose with yellow stripes. He looked like a bumblebee that forgot to light the candles before he got dressed."

Cade had to fight to control his amusement. He swallowed his laughter, for if she thought he agreed with her, she would never choose a husband—an outcome more important than ever now that Linton had set his traitorous eyes on her. Brentford would see him hung if he allowed the viscount anywhere near her.

But he wouldn't do anything yet. If her reaction was to be believed, it wasn't as if she was enamored of Linton. They'd only met a few days ago. As the queen's health deteriorated she would not ask Samara to attend her, so Samara would not see him. Cade would keep an eye on the situation and nudge her in another direction. But he hadn't spent the last few years in the company of as many different women as he wanted without picking up one important tidbit about them.

If you told a female directly what you wanted her to do, chances were good that she would do the exact opposite.

But could he risk encouraging the match? It might be the one time his theory failed.

He wouldn't let Samara know who Robert Hunter really was, or had been. He was willing to give the younger man the benefit of the doubt until he had reason to believe otherwise. In the meantime, he would try to find a few decent men who might be interested in her. Whether or not she would be interested in them was another story. She had to find someone, though. What would they tell her father if she didn't?

But if Linton tried something with Samara—anything—he would pay.

Chapter Sixteen

THE NEXT MORNING, CADE MET FERIA IN THE CORRIDOR OUT-side the queen's Privy Chamber.

"Good morrow to you, Feria," Cade said when he arrived and found the dour, black-clothed man on his way out.

Feria grunted at him.

Still annoyed at me for appearing to take Lady Elizabeth's side, are you? Cade wanted to ask. But he bit his tongue. Aggravating the man was hardly in his best interest. Instead he tossed his clove-studded orange pomander in his hands until the Countess of Lennox, with an apologetic smile, opened the door to the chamber and waved Cade in.

The queen was worse, he saw. Her skin was more jaundiced than sallow; even the whites of her eyes were yellowed, like old paper. Her hand trembled as she held it out to him. Cade kissed the quaking knuckles and waited for her to speak.

"Lord Feria says that our sister is as obdurate as ever," the queen began.

"He does not lie," Cade confirmed. "She seems to have little interest in marrying. She insists that as Your Majesty has not taken serious issue with her maiden status thus far, she does not understand why the issue is now of such importance."

The queen gritted her teeth.

"Feria said as much. The wench is as pig-headed as her whorish mother," she declared. "Of course, we did not take issue until now: any marriage she made could have garnered support and an attempt might have been made to usurp our throne!"

So he'd been correct. And hearing Her Majesty speak of her impending demise jarred him.

"She promises to consider any potential suitors Your Majesty might suggest. But no more than that," Cade said. "I'm sorry I don't have better news."

The queen closed her eyes. A thin coating of perspiration gave a sheen to her forehead in the brightly lit chamber.

"We did not expect a miracle," she muttered. "Still, that she would continue to put her own desires above that which is best for England! It is a tragedy. After all we have done to restore the true faith, to save the eternal souls of our subjects, that she would so casually…"

The queen trailed off. Her twisted fingers plucked at her misshapen stomacher.

"Feria also mentioned that the lady implied that we might not be in a position to insist." Her Majesty lifted her chin. "Did you witness this?"

"I cannot be certain that her meaning was that clear," Cade said carefully. He would not lie to his queen. But though his first impression had been that Elizabeth spoke of Her Majesty's impending death, after thinking about it, he'd decided that her words could have other implications as well. Wasn't that what Elizabeth was known for? Cloaking her true meaning in words that could be taken several different ways?

"We would know exactly what she said."

Cade took a deep breath.

"Her words were much as Feria reported them, Your Majesty," he began. "That Your Majesty is not in a position to insist on her marriage. I can see how those words might be taken. However, before I continue, I would plead that Your Majesty give me leave to speak bluntly."

God's foot, he hoped he wasn't making a mistake.

"You have it," the queen answered. He heard her curiosity.

"I cannot in good conscience insist that she spoke treason. She could have meant several things," he answered. "For example, that there is no one else better suited to inherit the throne. She *is* part of the Act of Succession. Of those with any claim to the throne still remaining in England, they have no following. And Mary Stuart might be Catholic, but to unite England with France and Scotland would spell disaster, as Your Majesty well knows. As it is, Lady Elizabeth loves her country. I don't doubt she'll marry the man she feels will do the best job as her consort."

He held his breath as he waited for the queen's response. For all he knew, he could have just signed his own death warrant.

"I see," she said. "Lord Easton, were you anyone else we should not have liked to hear what you just said. But you have proven yourself time and again." He let his breath out. "We will think on it, and you will answer one more question for us."

"Of course, Your Majesty."

"We want to know about her faith."

He took a moment before answering her. Again, he wasn't certain. Her manner of dress suggested that she subscribed to the reformed faith, but had they not attended vespers? And it wasn't as if he'd found a Book of Common Prayer on his bedside table.

"I cannot say for certain," he said. "She attended Mass, as Lord Feria will confirm. I saw a few things that hinted at her possible subscription to the reformed faith, but nothing that would confirm her allegiance one way or the other. If I may speculate, it would seem that perhaps she hopes to court both those of the true faith and Reformers. But again, Your Majesty, that is nothing but my own conjecture. I honestly do not know her intentions."

His heart raced. He knew he hadn't told Her Majesty what she wanted to hear. He also knew that he had probably opened Lady Elizabeth to even more scrutiny. They both had reason to be angry with him. But he would not lie. Surely his queen had her own spies at Hatfield. She would know he had been honest, and she could not fault him for that.

He was so weary of this. He'd lost his diplomatic touch. He no longer wanted anything to do with the court.

You're useless, his father sneered from inside his head.

The queen dismissed him, and Cade backed from her presence, struggling to keep himself from running once he was free—it wouldn't do if someone came upon him fleeing like the headsman's ax was behind him. Those in a hurry usually looked guilty. He was guilty of nothing but speaking the truth to his queen, but he couldn't trust anyone to believe that, so he slowed his pace.

From the unseen chamber ahead of him, he heard women's voices.

"...don't know who she thinks she is," one of the women said in a lofty tone. "Why, even Her Majesty falls all over her as if she is the Blessed Virgin herself."

The other woman giggled.

They emerged as he neared. One he did not know. The other was Bess, Lady Beddington.

Her eyes lit at the sight of him, and she stopped in her tracks, her flattering burgundy skirts fluttering around her ankles.

"Cade!" she exclaimed, blood staining her cheeks. But she caught her composure quickly and allowed a cool smile to bloom on her face. "Now, where exactly have you been? You arrived nearly two weeks ago, and I've yet to have the pleasure of even a moment with you."

The other woman, the one Cade didn't know, giggled behind long, white fingers.

He gave only a moment's thought to the situation that presented itself before making his decision.

"I'm here now," he said, injecting just the right amount of teasing into his tone. *This* was easy. No woman would ever dare call him useless.

"So you are," she purred. She shot a glance at the other woman, who, to her credit, seemed to grasp the message behind it right away. The woman mumbled an excuse and swept away, leaving Cade and Bess alone.

"The marquess has been summoned back to Beddington to solve the mystery of an illness that has been taking the lives of our breeding horses," she murmured, fingering the jeweled cross around her neck and keeping it from disappearing into her plump white bosom. "It's been rather ... lonely without him here."

Cade laughed. "Lonely?" he asked sardonically. "Bess, there's no need to pretend with me. You've made your feelings about the poor marquess known on several occasions."

She laughed too. "It's been so long, I'd forgotten."

"And yet you accused me of having a poor memory," he taunted. "What is it you want, Bess? There is no need to be obscure with me. Whatever you want, chances are I'm more than willing and able to provide it."

He grinned as blood rushed to her cheeks again, staining them a faint pink under the white makeup she wore.

"Well," she said. "The queen has been kind enough to give me the evening off from her services. I have a houseful of servants, to be sure, but no one with whom I can … converse."

He nodded solemnly. "I'm quite good at conversing."

She sighed. "I remember."

"If you are so starved for good conversation, though," he asked, "why wait for this evening?"

With that, she gasped as he gripped her by the waist and hurried her backward to the nearest alcove.

❋

He couldn't do it.

Not that he was physically incapable—no, that part of him functioned just perfectly, a fact to which the stubborn ache in his groin attested. No, it was something else.

It had to be his mood. He hadn't felt himself since his return the evening before. The longer than necessary trip to Hatfield and the hours spent engaged in a war of wits with a stubborn Lady Elizabeth had taken their toll. The news that Samara could allow herself to be wooed by a possible former traitor who might be spying for Elizabeth did not help.

And he worried about the future. Queen Mary would not last much longer, and Elizabeth had confused him. Was she or was she not a heretic? If she was, it could spell doom for him and those for whom he cared. Especially since she'd been reminded of his existence. She would know him solely as a messenger of her Protestant-burning sister. Would it make a difference to tell her that Cade did not share his queen's fervor? For he did not. He was of the opinion that a heretic was still a human being. He didn't share Her Majesty's conviction that all who wandered from the path of the true faith were permanently lost and deserved to die for it.

But as time had shown, those who followed the reformed faith did not take kindly to attempts to lead them back. Irritating Elizabeth could prove fatal for anyone who still followed the true faith—including himself, Hayden and his family, and Samara and hers.

Which brought him to his heart.

He couldn't stand the thought of Samara living a life of fear, waiting for Elizabeth's wrath to come down on her head. Would she even realize danger threatened? Or would she continue to live in the innocence of her fantasy world, blissfully unaware until the moment the flames began to lick at her feet?

Lady Beddington stood in the alcove with him, her back pressed against the wall, her gray-blue eyes narrowed. Whether it was in anger or concern for him, he didn't know, and found he didn't much care.

"It's the red-headed chit, isn't it," she said—her first words since it became apparent that Cade wasn't going to provide her with what she wanted, after all.

Cade rubbed his forehead. "What do you mean?"

"The girl. The one you've *escorted* here to find a husband." She sneered the words. "I'm not blind, Cade. She's beautiful. Childish and green, to be sure, but lovely." The venom in her voice made him realize that Samara was the topic of the snippet of conversation he'd heard before coming across Bess and her friend, and that Bess was the one speaking. She laughed. "Well, I never thought I'd see the day."

"What day?" he demanded. She was beginning to get on his nerves.

"The day Cade Badgley had his heart stolen out of his chest so completely he couldn't even be counted on for a meaningless tryst."

He gaped at her. "Have you taken leave of your senses?"

"No, but I think you have," she shot back. "Then again, from what I've heard, love will do that."

"Don't be ridiculous. I do not love her. I'm protective of her, certainly. Her father made me swear I would be, and his help was valuable to me so it was an easy oath to take. But believe me, I cannot get her married off quickly enough. She is keeping me from more important duties. For Christ's sake, I'm an earl who was barely able to stay on my land long enough to see my father buried. She has turned my life upside-down and caused nothing but one inconvenience after another."

"Cade." Lady Beddington's voice was a low warning. "Are you trying to convince me? Or yourself?"

His hand itched to slap her, and it frightened him that that instinct was his first. But he managed to tuck it away quite nicely.

Instead, he kissed her.

Her lips were hard and unyielding at first, then softened under his assault. Her arms, which she'd had clenched to her sides, lifted and entwined themselves around his neck. She pressed herself against him and, despite the layers of clothing that separated their bodies, he waited for the return of the heat that would prove to both of them that he was not, in any way, in love with Brentford's daughter.

It never came.

The realization hit him almost immediately, but he continued to press kisses against her lips in hopes that something, anything, would happen. It didn't. He could have been kissing a tree trunk for all the reaction she coaxed from him.

Disgusted, he reached up and disentangled her arms from his neck. Gripping them softly but with determination, he pushed her back, making sure to be gentle. It wasn't her fault, after all.

Well, in a way it was. If she hadn't brought up Samara, he would not have felt like he had something to prove. He could have explained that his audience with the queen had left much on his mind and he was far too distracted to do anything but return to Riverview and ponder this recent turn of events. But no, she'd had to goad him. All his life, whether it was his father, his brother, or even the pope, there was only one way he responded to that. *Prove them wrong.*

And this time, like so many others, he had failed to do so.

Lady Beddington eyed him and he stared back, trying to find whatever it was about this woman that had attracted him in the first place. At a glance, she was the epitome of fashionable beauty. Her hair was smooth and thick, its ash-blond color the envy of women who were forced to use dyes to even approximate it. Her eyes were wide, giving her a deceptively innocent appearance. But her skin was slathered in white makeup which, while fashionable, effectively wiped any trace of life from it. Her clothing was ostentatious—the gown she wore was covered in beads and embroidery to the point where Cade imagined it must have taken a team of seamstresses six months to create it and a dozen of them to lift it. And she was so tainted by life at court that he could never be sure when it was truth spilling from her heart-shaped lips and when it was not.

He wanted nothing to do with her.

"I'm sorry, Lady Beddington," he said, hoping that she would infer his meaning when he used her title and not her Christian name. "Whatever it is you want from me, I'm afraid I can't give it."

"Can't? Or won't?"

"Both." He had nothing to lose by being honest.

She nodded, twisting the cross around her neck in her fingers.

"Well, if that's how you feel." She shrugged.

Cade breathed a sigh of relief.

Then she flew at him, her plump fists pummeling his chest.

※

Samara hurried through the palace, disappointment dogging her steps. The queen had not summoned her that day—word had it that she was ill—but she'd woken that morning to a message from Jane Dormer, inviting Samara to accompany her on some errands. As Samara had seen very little of the city in the short weeks since her arrival, she'd jumped at the chance, dressing in a peacock blue suit and having Betty painstakingly fix each of her curls so that they were perfect.

But when she'd reached Jane's apartments, the other girl's maid told her apologetically that Jane was ill too, and while it was nothing more dangerous than a migraine, her mistress was in no condition to go traipsing through the London streets.

Samara agreed, of course, and asked the woman to pass along her wish that Jane feel better soon. When the door closed on her, however, she realized that she now had the entire day free and had no idea what to do with herself. Betty went to arrange for a coach, since the one in which they'd come was surely halfway back to

Riverview. Once she'd left, with instructions for Samara to meet her in the courtyard, Samara thought she might take the opportunity to seek out Lord Linton.

She hadn't seen him since they'd danced, though she'd harbored a small hope that he might try to call on her. Even though her goal was still to show Cade that other men found her desirable, she had to admit that Lord Linton fascinated her a bit. He was the first—handsome—man to pay attention to her of his own volition without the influence of wine or mistaken identity.

But she couldn't find him, and at last she realized—feeling quite stupid about it—that he was probably with Master Boxall, the Royal Secretary. Glum now, for the day yawned in front of her, she set off for the courtyard in the hopes that a coach might be waiting for her.

She turned. Out of the corner of her eye she saw a flash of burgundy skirt and heard gasps, grunts, and heavy breathing that caused the blood to rush to her cheeks. She lowered her eyes and hurried past to avoid the scene that was surely taking place. It amazed her how often these nobles dallied with each other in almost plain sight, though she'd never come across them in the daytime before. Had her father been aware of the type of place to which he would send her? Surely that wasn't the *polish* he'd hoped she would get.

As she approached the alcove, a woman stumbled out, a man clutching her tight to his velvet-clad chest. Samara stopped in her tracks as her heart plummeted to rest in her heeled silver shoes.

Cade and Lady Beddington.

"Samara," he gasped, and released his hold on the other woman.

Lady Beddington eyed Samara with an expression that made her look like a cat that had swallowed a particularly tasty canary. Her lips curved into a smile, though as her gaze swept Samara in the conciliatory way she had, the smile turned to a sneer.

Samara, however, graced the woman with only a glance before deeming her unimportant—right now, anyway. She was more distressed to find that Cade had been the one in there with her. She'd thought he was better than that.

Was he really, though? She knew little about him. And much of her past experience with him suggested that no, he really wasn't better than that. He'd attempted to seduce her when he'd thought she was just a peasant, hadn't he?

Her heart thumped angrily. She stared at him, hoping he could see the disappointment in her eyes.

His face flushed.

"Believe me, Samara, this is not what it looks like," he said, gesturing to Lady Beddington.

Samara forced herself to shrug. "Of what import is it to me? You are a grown man. She, a grown woman. A married woman, but grown nevertheless." She was proud of herself. Her voice didn't tremble even a little bit as she spoke. But hot tears stung her eyes and she blinked, refusing to give either of them the satisfaction of knowing how deeply affected she was by what she'd witnessed. Her breath came in short bursts.

"I promise you—" Cade began, but she held up her hand to stop him.

"Cade, please." She forced herself to smile. "You don't owe me anything. You are not my husband or my betrothed. We are barely even friends. You are only here with me because my father asked it of you. Do you think I don't know that? If not for me, and the inconvenience with which I've saddled you, you could be living your own life. And so you should. Please don't let me or my presence here keep you from doing what you would if I had stayed in Worcestershire and you'd come here alone."

Each heavy thud of her heart seemed to force the tears closer to the surface of her eyes, but she managed to keep them at bay. Her words were solemn and sure.

Lady Beddington's round blue eyes flitted between Cade and Samara, and her expression shifted into something sour. Cade's gaze was intent, his jaw set, his forehead creased into the tense lines with which Samara had grown so familiar.

She had to get away from here. From him, from his whore … from everything.

"Please, forgive me for interrupting," she said. This time her voice quavered—only slightly, but it was there. "Betty is waiting for me in the courtyard—with some kind of transportation, I hope. I'll see you at Riverview. Or perhaps not."

With that, she hurried away, not waiting for a response.

Betty waited, grumbling, with a hired coach. When she saw Samara's expression, she stopped muttering and came toward her, concern on her kind face. But Samara shook off the embrace her maid offered. She was a child no longer and had to learn to deal with disappointment on her own. The carriage ride back to Riverview was silent, though Samara could feel Betty's worried gaze on her.

Only when she was safely ensconced in her bedchamber did Samara allow her tears to flood her eyes. They streamed down her cheeks, scalding her already hot skin.

Her first impression had been correct. He was a pig! He cared nothing for her; all his kindnesses—keeping her secrets, supporting her drawing, bringing her to the queen, trusting her with delicate political information—had been lies. She couldn't for the life of her understand why he'd acted as her friend. Obviously he saw her as nothing more than a nuisance! If he was so quick to run away to Hatfield when the opportunity presented itself, she couldn't mean anything more to him.

"Ugh!" Samara yanked one of the beautiful silver slippers from her feet. She hurled it at the oak door.

Kat could have him! They deserved each other!

The shoe hit the door with a thud and dropped to the floor. She reached down, removed the other slipper, and launched it at its mate. As it sailed toward the door, to Samara's horror, the door swung open.

Cade leapt aside and the slipper narrowly missed him, gliding past his forehead and into the chamber beyond, landing inches from where she'd found him sleeping that morning that already felt like a lifetime ago. She'd knelt beside him that day and committed him to paper, so beautiful was he in sleep. She'd been so stupid!

"You dropped your shoe," he remarked, turning his head to stare at it.

"I didn't drop it. I threw it," she retorted. "What do you want?"

"A chance to apologize. You denied me back there."

"I told you, Lord Easton. You don't owe me any apology."

He flinched at her use of his formal title rather than his Christian name, which she had only recently begun to use. "But you were upset. You *are* upset. Obviously something affected you. It had to be what you saw."

"Do not flatter yourself," she flung back at him. "I am upset because I had plans to go shopping with Jane Dormer today, and she developed a migraine, so those plans were thwarted."

He stepped into the room tentatively. When she didn't attack, he seemed relieved.

"So you are crying because you could not go shopping?" he asked gently.

She scrubbed at her face with her fist. "I am not crying."

"Well, it's not raining. Something's got your face all wet."

She glared at him, her heart rate picking up speed again as her anger welled.

"Samara, what you saw—it was not what you think it was. Lady Beddington wanted it to be, but I did not. What you witnessed was me fending off her blows. She came at me when I turned her down."

Samara rolled her eyes. "Your arrogance is unbelievable. She *attacked* you because you rejected her advances?"

"It's the truth. Would you like to see? I would have to remove most of my clothing, but I can show you the bruises that are almost certainly blooming there." He lifted his hands, moving as if to take off his jerkin.

"That's not necessary," Samara said stiffly. She'd already seen what was under his jerkin, anyway. And she wanted no part of something so many other women had seen.

He dropped his hands and took another step toward her. His expression was wary, as if he expected her to throw something else at him. But she didn't. Instead, she folded her arms over her chest and stared at him.

"What?" he asked.

"You wanted to apologize. I'm allowing you."

"Oh." He took a deep breath. "I'm sorry."

She waited, but he said nothing else.

"That's it?" she asked. "Do you even know what you're apologizing for? Because I do not."

"I'm sorry that you came across Lady Beddington and me. I swear to you that it wasn't as it appeared. We did have a sort of relationship a few years ago. But it's over now. I told her that, and she didn't react well to the information."

"Why?" Samara asked.

The earl looked confused. "Why didn't she react well? I don't know."

"No. Why is it over?"

Cade shrugged. "A few reasons. It's going nowhere. She's not particularly nice. She's already married and has several children. I, on the other hand, need to start looking for a wife if I'm to make Easton successful again."

Despite it all she couldn't help a tiny thrill of hope. Tiny, yes, and tainted with disgust at the idea of Cade having any kind of relationship with a woman of such dubious morality, but it was hope. He was admittedly in the market for a wife. But how could she make him *see*? She was not like Lady Beddington. She had none of the marchioness's bovine charm, her experience, her polish. But she had *something* to offer, didn't she?

Before she could come up with an example, however, a soft knock sounded at the chamber door. She looked up to see Blackwell with a note in his hand.

"Excuse me, Lady Samara. This was just brought for you."

An apology note from Jane, probably. Samara took the note from the steward and smiled at him.

"Thank you, Blackwell," she said, and opened the small folded square of parchment as the steward ducked from sight.

Dear Lady Samara, it read. *I hope this note finds you well. I realize that this may be a bit unorthodox, but as our chances of meeting each other at the palace are not high, I thought I would write and invite you to a late-morning picnic on the bank of the Thames tomorrow. The queen has been kind enough to give me the day off from my duties to her, and as the weather is supposed to be unusually fine for late October, I jumped at the chance to see you outside of the palace. I would enjoy that more than you could possibly know, and hope you will consider taking me up on my offer. Please send your reply to the palace. Your faithful servant, Robert, Viscount Linton.*

Samara suddenly felt as if one person had her left arm and one had her right, and she was being pulled by them in opposite directions.

Cade stood silently a few feet from her, gloriously handsome. He was hot and cold by turns and she could never be sure how he felt about her, but perhaps his kindnesses hadn't been lies after all, and he did care a little bit.

Lord Linton, on the other hand, was also handsome. He didn't take her breath away like Cade did, but surely it was better if he didn't—she would be better able to keep from falling in love with him. He was charming, going out of his way to spend time with her and get to know her. More than Cade had done. In fact, Cade had promised to go out of his way to leave her alone. If he thought there was any value in her at all, he would not have done that.

Cade stood, politely patient, undoubtedly waiting for her to either accept or reject his apology. But she'd already pushed it to the back of her mind.

She was confused. She'd thought Cade would be the perfect husband—her social equal, her father's neighbor, a man with whom she could get on well enough to have a comfortable, if not passionate, marriage. But he'd never once said or done anything to make her think he felt the same. Then there was Lord Linton, who wrote her notes, invited her to picnics, danced with her, and despite his distance let her know she was in his thoughts. On paper he was just as good a prospect as Cade—possibly even better. She wasn't sure she would always love the way he seemed to let her dwell in his mind, but right now, it was flattering. Perhaps she could learn to live with it.

That settled it. She would accept Lord Linton's invitation, and not only so that Cade would see her as the object of another man's interest. She would do it because the viscount himself was a viable candidate and deserved a chance.

"There was one more thing I wanted to apologize for," Cade said, his voice causing her thoughts to scatter once more.

She folded her hand around the note.

"Yes?" she asked.

"You told Bess—Lady Beddington—that we were barely even friends. Is that what you believe? Because I thought we had at least progressed to friendship. We've turned each other's lives upside-down, certainly, but I had assumed that we were making the best of what we've been given." He gave a sad little smile. "I know I swore to stay away from you. But that was for your own protection, so that your reputation did not suffer. I'm sorry if I've given you the impression that I did not consider you a friend. I do."

And just like that, her hardened heart melted.

"No, I didn't realize you felt that way," she said. "I thought I was just a chore to you, something you had to do to repay my father. I assumed you wouldn't be here if not for me."

"Well, I wouldn't," he said with a little laugh. "I'd be on my lands trying to figure out how to do the damn job. But I don't consider you a chore, either. You deserve a good husband. And I'm going to do my best to help you find one."

It just won't be me. He didn't say the words aloud, but he didn't have to. She heard them.

She forced herself to smile and hoped it didn't look as confused and hopeless as it felt.

"Thank you," she said. "Now, if you'll excuse me. I have a letter to write."

"Of course," he replied. "Will I see you at supper?"

"Of course," she echoed.

He left then, and she went into the bedchamber to dig out her writing materials. She sat down at the desk, spread out a sheet of vellum, dipped her quill in ink and began to write.

Dear Lord Linton, she began.

I would be happy to accept your invitation.

Chapter Seventeen

ROBERT LAY ON THE SMALL, HARD MATTRESS IN THE TINY BED-
chamber he'd been given to use while serving the queen. The note in
his hand was crumpled from repeated reading, the loopy, feminine
handwriting already faded and illegible in spots. But he would save
it, for it was his first tangible proof that he was on his way to achiev-
ing his goal. He'd managed to interest Lady Samara Haughton to
the point where she was willing to accept a rather intimate invitation
from him.

That had been a risk, suggesting a picnic. He didn't know how
strictly she'd been raised and if she would demur at the idea of being
alone with him so soon after meeting him—except for her woman,
of course. But luck was on his side. She *had* agreed.

With the small amount of coin he'd won during a lucky game of
Primero the previous evening, he went down to the cook shop and
purchased a roasted chicken, a loaf of white bread, some cheddar
cheese, and a cask of spiced wine. He couldn't let her know how
poor he was—not until they were married and her dowry became his
fortune. She clearly didn't know, and he wondered, not for the first
time, why Easton—or Sir Hayden, or anyone else—hadn't told her
anything about him. It wasn't hard to imagine that if she'd known
his family history she'd have wanted nothing to do with him. The
fact that she was willing to spend time with him could mean one of
only two things. If she *was* aware of his situation, she didn't care,
and he knew from experience how unlikely that was. If, however, she
wasn't, it either meant she hadn't spent enough time at court to hear

the gossip he knew ran rampant—which was entirely possible—or Easton had decided to keep it from her.

That possibility in itself was puzzling, and more than a little intriguing. Was Easton so anxious to be rid of her? Or was he just willing to give Robert the benefit of the doubt?

Robert laughed. If *that* was the case, then the man truly was a fool.

Not that he'd been anything but a perfect assistant to Master Boxall. He wasn't involved with the actual reading and writing of correspondence, but he had taken advantage of rare private moments to scan several of the queen's letters, hoping to find some tidbit he could send to the princess to show his loyalty and perhaps earn back her favor. Only later, when he had found none, did he realize it was probably a good thing: if Princess Elizabeth made it known that she was privy to information the queen had sent to someone else, he would be the first person accused. That wouldn't help his family at all.

At any rate, it seemed Boxall was already in regular communication with William Cecil, at Hatfield with Princess Elizabeth. That boded well for the future. It looked like the queen had finally realized there was no one else to succeed her, unless she wanted her legacy to be an England ruled by Spain, or by Scotland and France. He chuckled to himself. God Himself obviously knew in which direction the wind blew. The rest of the world would find out soon enough.

He rolled off the small cot and went to the battered wooden chest that took up most of the south corner of the room. In it he kept his clothing, the small amount he had. He would have to choose wisely. In the candlelit chambers and halls of St. James's Palace, the shabbiness of his clothing was easier to mask. Faded velvet, loose seams, and stains would be much more obvious in daylight.

He dug until he found what he was looking for—a velvet doublet of dark gold with minimal signs of wear. If he combined it with a green and gold embroidered jerkin, green trunk hose, and gold-striped nether hose, he would cut a dashing figure. Dashing enough for a lady who was undoubtedly the most beautiful at court. He hadn't been exaggerating when he'd said that.

He even had a thick gold chain to put around his neck. He'd stolen it a year ago from the neck of a nobleman who slept off his drunkenness beside the Cheshire Cheese. He had thought to sell it, but something had told him he might need it one day. Now he was glad he'd listened to his instinct. The chain was simple but elegant, bearing but a plain ruby medallion and, as far as Robert could see, nothing indicating it had belonged to someone in particular. At any rate, he would wait until he was well out of sight of the palace before putting it on. No need to invite trouble.

Through the small, dirty window by his bed, he saw that the palace lawns teemed with people enjoying the last bit of fair weather they were likely to see that year. He contemplated his basin of three-day-old water and wished for a real bath. He sighed. Only a few more months, if that. He could do this for Amy and Isabel. Once they were safe and settled, this wouldn't feel as if it was all for naught.

❁

In his bedchamber, Cade paced. He hadn't slept well and a dull yet persistent ache thumped in his temples. The pain was frustrating. He hadn't even had anything to drink. If his head was going to throb, he should have at least gotten some fun out of it first.

He couldn't get Samara out of his mind.

Not the usual random images he had of her when he let his mind wander too far—his first glimpse of her in the lake, for instance. The way she'd sprawled carelessly in the grass the day he'd left her father's house, or how her eyes lit up when he'd given back her lost drawing materials. Or the way he'd caught her kneeling over him when he woke from his drunken slumber, her hair mussed from sleep and her body clad in that ridiculous blue gown that hung off her shoulders in a way no proper lady would allow but which was, nonetheless, enticing. No, he wasn't having *those* kinds of thoughts.

It was the look on her face when she'd discovered him and Bess in the alcove. Wounded, as though he'd slapped her. Her hands clenched into small white fists at her sides, her eyes swimming with tears she hadn't let herself shed. With emotions she hadn't allowed herself to express.

She cared about him.

Perhaps that realization, and the force with which it had struck him, was responsible for the ache in his head.

He didn't know what to do with the insight. He cared about her, too. But like that? No, he didn't think so. She was beautiful; naturally he reacted to that. Any man with blood in his veins would. But she was more trouble than she was worth. He couldn't trust her to tell the difference between harmless gossip and that which should remain a secret one guarded with one's life. She was lost in her own world, a place where the way the light fell onto a bowl of strawberries took precedence over seeing that her people would be properly fed and clothed. And her instincts were questionable at best. Why was *Linton* the only man with whom she didn't seem to have a problem?

He hadn't managed to shake his bad feeling about Linton's presence at court. He hadn't heard anything. Nothing more than the usual whispers, finding their way to Cade's ears as he moved through the palace and failing to convince him either way that Linton's purpose there was innocent or nefarious.

Yet his doubts remained. Whatever the queen thought, Linton's goals could not be as benign as she assumed they were. Mary was an intelligent woman, but she was also soft-hearted. She probably thought she was doing a good thing by giving Linton, and by association Ashbury, a chance to purge their souls of the sin they'd committed against her when they'd decided to support Wyatt. But Cade, who had seen firsthand the blood lust in the eyes of the men who *hadn't* abandoned Wyatt, thought differently. Men who were willing to kill for their cause were not often in the habit of giving up that cause simply because they didn't get their way in the end. Linton was up to something—he had to be—and Cade wondered if and how Samara fit into those plans.

He had told Hayden he would keep an eye on the situation as it developed. But now that he'd hurt Samara, however inadvertently, she was more apt to respond to Linton's advances. He had no idea what to do, short of marrying her himself, and he didn't think anyone would end up happy in that situation. She might think she cared about him, but she didn't know him. All she saw was his handsome face and the exciting life she thought he led. She was bound to be disappointed if she married him thinking he would continue that life when all he wanted to do was return to Easton, if only to purge it of bad memories. He was stuck with it for life—he should at least try to make something good out of it.

Besides, Samara hadn't known his father. Not the way he had. He wondered how much of the old man had been passed to *him*—at least some, as was evidenced every time his temper rose and he had to beat down the urge to put his hands on someone or through something. He'd been successful so far. Grabbing Samara's elbow had been more of an anxious gesture than an angry one. But yesterday, with Bess? He'd wanted to draw his dagger as if she was a man who'd impugned his mother's honor. That scared him. He would hate himself if he ever hurt Samara.

He *wouldn't* let himself become the old man. Even if it meant dying without issue. Maybe Easton, despite the bad spirits that haunted its halls, would be cleansed by reverting to the Crown and eventually given to some other family.

He shook off his melancholy. He had nothing of importance on his agenda today, and thought he should take the time to send a message to Jefferson at Easton and update him on the situation. And he would make a list—a list of eligible men suitable to become Samara's husband. She would choose one of them, and everyone's life could go on.

❋

The day had dawned bright and sunny, but as the morning went on, clouds rolled in. As the sky grew darker, so did Samara's mood. She had been looking forward to spending some time out of doors—a rare experience since her arrival in the city. And she'd looked forward to doing it with Lord Linton, to having the chance to test her feelings for him.

But now it looked as if it wouldn't happen. Samara peered through the glass window at the sky over the river. It was even darker now than it had been a few minutes ago. So much for fine weather! And she'd worn a new dress, too—a bright grass-green satin over her ivory and gold-embroidered underskirt. What a waste. She should take it off, and save it for the next important event that came up.

She could spend her afternoon writing letters. She hadn't written Cecily in days, and her sister's natal day approached.

She turned to head up the stairs to her rooms, but as she put her foot on the step, Blackwell entered the hall.

"Viscount Linton to see you, Lady Samara," the steward said.

Her heart gave an excited little thump.

"Thank you, Blackwell," she said, trying to keep her surprise out of her voice. "Show him in."

Blackwell nodded, and before Samara could blink, Lord Linton was there, a large woven basket in his hand.

"Lord Linton!" she exclaimed. "I didn't expect to see you!"

He grinned, revealing a small shadowed dimple in his left cheek.

"We planned on a picnic, did we not?" he asked, jiggling the basket in his hand.

"Yes, but when I saw the sky—it looks ominous—I thought a picnic would be out of the question."

"I do not recall Parliament passing a law stating all picnics must be held outdoors." He took his other hand from behind his back and showed her a blanket.

Samara laughed. "Indeed, I don't think they have. Blackwell, have someone bring some more wood for the fire, please? With the sun gone, the room grows chill." She stepped aside as Lord Linton set the basket down and spread the blanket over the smooth flagstones. He seated her as a groom entered with an armful of chopped wood and dumped it into the hearth before departing. Then Lord Linton seated himself, reaching into the basket and drawing out his bounty.

He set out a cold roasted chicken, a lovely loaf of fine white bread, hard cheddar—her favorite—and some wine. He filled a goblet and handed it to her. She sniffed it, and the bouquet of spices that assailed her nose was pleasant.

"It smells delicious," she said. "I don't believe I've ever tasted this kind of wine."

"It's from Spain," Lord Linton answered. "Made from grapes grown exclusively in that region. They are called *lairén*." His tongue rolled over the word.

"Oh." How sophisticated he was! She put the goblet to her lips and sipped. Hmm. It was rather watery, and the spices were a bit overwhelming. But perhaps she was just used to her father's country wines. Her palate was unrefined, after all. If this was what courtiers drank, she would train herself to like it.

She took another sip.

"Very good," she lied, and smiled at him.

He looked pleased.

"Are you hungry?" he asked.

She was ravenous, in fact, but was it ladylike to tell him that? She'd observed ladies eating only a few times since arriving in London. They took small bites and seldom cleared their plates. So she suspected no, she shouldn't let him know how hungry she'd gotten while waiting for the picnic.

But he'd purchased so much food! Surely he didn't mean to eat almost all of it himself. She warred with herself while her belly rumbled.

"A bit," she answered when she thought she could delay no longer. Her stomach growled a loud contradiction.

A gentleman, Lord Linton did not acknowledge the crude sound even as she flushed and struggled to conceal it. Instead he removed a pewter plate from the basket and laid several thin slices of chicken on it. He tore a chunk from the loaf of bread and set it on the plate, then used his dagger to slice off a portion of the cheese. He handed the plate to her before filling his own.

"A toast before we eat?" he suggested. He poured a bit more wine into her cup and gave it to her. Then he lifted his own goblet.

"To new friends," he said. "And perhaps someday, if the lady will be so kind as to give me a chance to court her, something more." He tapped his goblet against hers as her brain struggled to absorb his words.

Court her? He wanted to court her? But how could he have decided that already? They had met twice—danced once. What could he know of her except that she was beautiful, which she was not ashamed to admit, and able to dance without falling over her own feet?

Misgiving bloomed. And what of herself? Was this what she wanted? Was *he* what she wanted?

Then again, if he was in the market for a wife, he had to make his move before Queen Mary died. He might not keep his place at court if—when—Her Majesty passed. He couldn't afford to waste time, any more than Samara could.

She looked into his eyes, which crinkled at the corners as his expression tensed in anticipation of her answer. He truly was adorable. And kind, and romantic. And he liked her! Why on earth did she hesitate?

"I should like that," she said in a voice so shy she was surprised to hear it come from her own mouth.

His expression melted into a smile. He took her goblet from her hand and put it down, along with his, on the floor next to their blanket. Then he inched closer to her, until his face was so close she could feel his soft breath on her cheek.

"May I kiss you, then?" he asked.

She nodded, afraid to speak. Her eyes fluttered shut.

His forehead bumped hers once, gently, before his lips touched hers. They were warm and soft but somehow not what she had expected. She didn't know *what* she had expected. A shower of sparks, perhaps? A complete melting of her bones? She had never been kissed before but had witnessed others doing it. It seemed a pleasurable experience. What Robert was doing was very nice, but she didn't feel as if melting was in her immediate future.

He lifted his hand and cupped the back of her neck, drawing her closer. He pressed his lips against her more insistently, and she realized he expected some kind of response—not that she sit there like a statue. She imitated what he did. But when he nudged her lips apart and brushed his tongue against her bottom teeth, she jerked away, knocking her wine goblet over in the process.

"Oh!" she gasped, embarrassed, but at least she'd distracted him from her reaction. She hoped. What a child she still was!

"It's fine," Lord Linton said with a smile, removing a cloth napkin from the basket and sopping up the wine that puddled between the stones.

"I'm rather glad my kiss got you so flustered," he added in a teasing tone.

Samara smiled and clenched her hands in her lap to try and stop their trembling. So that was a kiss! Not the earth-shattering experience for which her girlish fantasies had prepared her, but altogether nice. And next time she would be better prepared for what it entailed. She'd had no idea that *tongues* were involved!

"Shall we eat?" the viscount suggested, and she nodded.

Her mouth felt different as she went through the familiar motions of putting food between her lips, chewing, and swallowing. She wondered if she looked different too.

"Tell me about yourself," Lord Linton suggested. "I should like to know more about the lady who has captured my heart."

Pretty words—even prettier when directed at her. She couldn't help the hot blush that crept into her cheeks.

"There is not much to tell," she hedged. "I am seventeen and the oldest of my father's three daughters."

"There are three of you?" Lord Linton asked. When Samara nodded, he chuckled. "Lord help your father if your sisters are as beautiful as you are."

"My sisters are very beautiful," she assured him. "We are all different. Katherine is fifteen, and she has my father's coloring— golden brown hair and light blue eyes." She would not mention Kat's temperament. "Cecily is twelve, and she is blonde with dark blue eyes. We do not know from where she gets her coloring. My father has said that an elf left her at our door."

She probably shouldn't have said that. It was true that her father had made that jest a few times over the years, but it suggested that perhaps Cecily's father was a stranger—an untruth that redounded to neither her father's credit nor her mother's. She hurried on before Linton could pay too much attention to her words.

"And I have been told that I am the very portrait of my mother," she said.

Lord Linton smiled. "Then your mother must be one of the most beautiful women alive." He continued before she could tell him her mother was dead. "But I want to learn more about *you*, Lady Samara. I've no desire to court your sisters or your mother. Only you. Tell me what you consider most important about yourself."

Most important? About herself? Samara frowned. She knew what *she* thought was most important but wondered if he would feel the same. Still—there was always the existence of Mistress Teerlinc on which she could fall back. Surely if the queen supported a woman painter, Samara's love of art wouldn't be the mortifying thing she'd been led to believe. And it would set her apart from all the other nondescript, virginal girls prowling for a husband.

"I'm an artist," she confessed.

Lord Linton raised an eyebrow.

"An artist?" he asked.

She nodded. "Like Mistress Teerlinc," she boasted. "Well, not exactly like her, for I don't know how to paint. My father would not allow me the materials. But I draw." She wondered if he would ask to see her work. She didn't know how she would respond. Her drawing was immensely personal. But if she was to marry him, shouldn't he be privy to her innermost thoughts?

The notion chafed.

"How charming." Lord Linton smiled and laid a slice of cheese on his bread. "Of course, you know that once you're married, it's unlikely your husband, whoever he might be, will allow you to continue with your art. There is too much that goes into running a household to waste time on childish fancies."

Samara's spine stiffened. How dare he call her art a childish fancy? She might have told Her Majesty the same thing, but to have someone else, a virtual stranger, say it, was something else entirely.

"The queen employs a woman painter," she pointed out.

"She does," the viscount agreed. "But Levina Teerlinc is not nobility. She is a Flemish immigrant. Her income and that of her husband depend on the commissions she earns by painting miniatures for Her Majesty. A noblewoman has no time to squander on such activities."

He was wrong, and she knew it. Just because she would not earn a living from her drawing did not make it a *childish fancy*.

"But—" she began to argue, before he silenced her by placing a finger against her lips.

She fought the urge to slap his hand away, and won. Fine. She would let him think for now that he could have any say over what she did when she was married—to him or any other man. *The queen employed a woman painter.* That was all the information she needed to know that her art was not a childish fancy but something to be proud of. Cade realized it. Why didn't Lord Linton?

"Tell me something of yourself," she suggested when he removed his finger, before he could further insult her. With luck, he wouldn't say anything else that would sour her on him.

"There's not much to tell," he echoed with a chuckle, and she laughed, relieved. At least he had a sense of humor.

"I've two younger sisters as well," he told her. "Amy and Isabel. Isabel is nineteen, Amy fourteen. They're not married yet. But my parents are working to secure matches for them. They are good girls and mean the world to me."

"I'd like to meet them," Samara said.

"Perhaps you will," the viscount said with another smile. But his expression lasted only a few seconds before it faltered.

"There is something else I should share with you," he said. He took the wine goblet from her hand and put it down, along with his, before covering her hand with his. "I hate to bring this up so soon, but I'd not have our relationship start without total honesty between us. I don't want you to feel taken unaware should someone with a less than noble cause take it upon himself to inform you."

She felt cold. *What could it be? Did madness run in his family? Witchcraft? Murder?*

She scanned the room for a defensive weapon, should she need it. The fireplace poker was too far away, but the wine bottle was close. The fingers of her free hand inched toward it.

"What is it?" she asked hesitantly.

He sighed. "Having an earl for a father as I do, I'm sure you know how difficult it is to defy him once he gets a certain idea in his head."

Samara did. She wouldn't even be here if she'd been able to convince her father what a terrible wife she'd make. She might have started to warm up to the idea, but still...

Linton went on. "My father, several years ago, decided that the tenets of the new faith appealed to him more than that of the true one." She gasped, and he searched her face with his gaze. "You've heard of Wyatt's rebellion?"

A lump of dread that had formed in her throat prevented her from speaking. She nodded.

Lord Linton sighed again. His grip on her hand tightened. "He was misguided, and deluded. I participated only to stay close to my father and make sure he was kept safe. It was a stupid idea in retrospect. The rebellion failed—no surprise there. And when it was over, no one cared why I'd joined, only that I had." He smiled a little. "Her Majesty was generous in sparing our lives. Many others lost theirs. But ever since, despite returning to the one true faith, we've been stained by our association with Wyatt and his cohorts. That's why I wanted to tell you before anyone else did. I wanted you to hear the truth of the matter and not someone else's idea of the truth, lest it poison you against me."

"But why would anyone lie? You're a member of the court now. Surely Her Majesty would not have given you a position if there was any way you were still associated with—them," Samara managed.

Robert smiled. "Your innocence is one of the most charming qualities you have," he informed her, lifting his hand from hers to stroke her cheek with the backs of his knuckles. "But the royal court can be a cesspit of intrigue. I'm glad you haven't been tainted by it." He wrapped a curl around his finger and lifted it to his lips. "We're just like any other family, trying to make our way in the world. Our title is fairly new, only a few generations old, and my father didn't help matters any by taking up with Wyatt and Suffolk and their ilk. But I will change that. When I am earl, the Ashbury title will come to mean something."

"I'm sure it will." Samara smiled. And perhaps she would be the countess helping Robert achieve his goal.

"You really hadn't heard any gossip about me?" Linton asked. He dropped the lock of hair and moved to refill their goblets.

"Not a word," she admitted. "I haven't spent much time in the palace, you see. The queen has been so ill she's stopped sending for anyone outside her innermost circle, as I'm sure you know. Jane Dormer has become a friend of sorts, but she is very close to the queen and has been spending most of her time with Her Majesty."

"What about Easton?" But before Samara could respond, heavy footsteps pounded on the stairs. Samara glanced up from Lord Linton's intense gaze to see Cade come to a skittering stop in front of them.

Samara blinked, unsure if she should introduce the men to each other or if they were capable of doing it themselves.

"Linton," Cade said in a strange tone. It didn't sound like a greeting.

The viscount scrambled to his feet, brushing his padded hose free of crumbs.

"Lord Easton," he replied. "It's long since we met."

"Indeed." Cade's gaze flickered to Samara as she struggled to rise from the floor in her heavy skirts.

He extended a hand to her, but Lord Linton stepped in front of him. He gripped Samara's hand and pulled her to her feet.

"I didn't realize you were acquainted," she said as she straightened her skirt.

"The courtiers' circle is small," Cade said.

"It certainly is!" The carefree warmth in Lord Linton's tone contrasted sharply with the ice in Cade's. "Congratulations on your accession, Easton."

Cade nodded his acknowledgment. "And congratulations are in order for you too, it would seem."

"For what?"

"Your *reacceptance.*" He smiled, but in a way that didn't reach his eyes. Samara had never seen him smile in such a way before, and she shivered.

The skin around Lord Linton's eyes tightened. But his laughter was natural.

"Aye, I am lucky," he agreed. "Evidently not bound to repeat the mistakes of my father. We should all be as fortunate as I."

Cade's hands, hanging by his sides, clenched into fists for just a moment before relaxing. She thought she saw him shudder and take a deep breath.

"I hope your luck holds." Cade's eyes went to Samara again. His gaze swooped appreciatively over her dress, or so she thought.

Well, she hadn't worn it for him! And it wasn't as if she could fill it out the way Lady Beddington filled out *her* gowns.

"What's the occasion?" he asked.

"A picnic," she told him with a smile she hoped was dazzling. "We'd planned to hold it on the bank of the river, but the weather did not cooperate. So Lord Linton brought the picnic indoors."

"How ingenious," Cade said dryly.

First Hayden, now Cade. Why were they so rude to Lord Linton? Was Cade jealous?

No. Not possible.

Though she couldn't deny the tiny thrill that rippled over her at the idea that he might be.

"I refused to be denied another chance to see Lady Samara," Lord Linton said. "With the queen's illness, the lady hasn't been at the palace, and I found that I'd grown more accustomed than I thought to the happiness a mere glimpse of her face brings me."

Well! His kiss had not made her melt, but his words certainly had potential.

"I see." Aside from a quick twitch of his jaw, Cade's face was stony.

"Although I must say, the happiness I feel at seeing her is nothing compared to the joy I experienced when she agreed to allow me to court her." A grin slid over Lord Linton's face. Samara's heart gave a thump in her chest.

Cade looked at Samara. "Is this true?"

"It is," she said, feeling as if her arms were being pulled in opposite directions again.

"Isn't that wonderful?" Lord Linton drawled.

Cade glanced at the doorway. Samara followed his gaze and stopped at the sight of Hayden, who had entered the hall with alarm on his face.

"Hayden, you remember Lord Linton, I'm sure?" Cade said.

Hayden came into the room. "I do," he answered. His normally open blue eyes were shuttered. "Welcome to Riverview, Linton."

"It's good to see you again, Sir Hayden." The viscount's tone was jovial, as if he knew the punch line to some colossal jest. But judging from the strained expressions on Cade's and Hayden's faces, Lord Linton was the only one privy to the joke. "A shame we couldn't all spend time reminiscing, but I have to be on my way. For those who serve the queen, their time is never their own. As you know."

"I will walk you out," Samara offered, desperate to escape the waves of tension that swirled around the hall. And, she had to admit, for a few more minutes alone with Lord Linton. She bent and gathered the blanket, goblets, and remnants of their meal, tucking it into the basket and handing it to him.

"Thank you for such a wonderful day," she told him shyly when they reached the street entrance.

"The first of many, I hope." He smiled. "I shan't stop thinking of you all evening. Will you think of me, even for just a moment?"

"I promise," she told him. It was likely she would spend more than a moment on him.

He kissed her again, lightly this time, with no pressure or invading tongues. She still didn't melt but thought that kissing Lord Linton was infinitely better than kissing Lord Waltham would be. Yes, if Lord Linton turned out to be the one she married, she would not repine.

God's teeth. Am I in love with him?

When she returned to the hall on slightly trembling legs, Cade and Hayden stood in front of the hearth, so close their shoulders touched. They stared, stone-like, as she made her entrance.

They couldn't be more of the same mind if they shared a head. For such handsome men, they had no difficulty assuming annoying facial expressions.

"Well, out with it," she told them. "You obviously have something you want to tell me. You'll not get anywhere standing there staring at me like a pair of gargoyles."

Hayden snorted. Cade silenced him with a glance.

"There's something you ought to know about Viscount Linton, Samara," Cade said.

"We only want what's best for you," Hayden added.

It had to be the story of his father, and his attempt to overthrow Her Majesty. They thought she wouldn't have heard. *Well, you hadn't, before today.*

Samara crossed her arms over the bright green bodice of her gown. "If it is the tale of the Earl of Ashbury's involvement in Wyatt's rebellion, then I am already aware of it," she said.

The men exchanged glances.

"And you still agreed to let him court you? Samara, the man is a heretic!" Hayden exclaimed.

"He is *not*," she countered. "He told me the whole story. His father made a foolish decision to follow the Protestant faith and join with Wyatt. Robert went with his father to protect him. Robert knows his effort was in vain, and his father has seen the error of his ways."

"Are you certain?" Cade asked. His tone was maddeningly calm. "Did he tell you why, or how, he got a position at court so close to Her Majesty?"

He hadn't, she realized. But what did it matter? He had returned to Catholicism. The queen would not have given him such a position if she didn't trust him.

"He did not," she replied. "But he *did* inform me that there are certain factions that would see him discredited for their own gain." He hadn't said that exactly, but wasn't that what he'd meant?

The men glanced at each other, and Samara's annoyance, bubbling beneath the surface until then, boiled over.

"Stop trying to turn me against him!" she exclaimed. "He is the only man who's shown an interest in me that I can picture myself marrying. Would that there were suitable candidates knocking down the door, but there are not. And I like him!"

"We only want to keep you from harm," Hayden said.

"I'm not in any danger," she insisted. Hot tears of frustration stung her eyes. "Only of ending up wife to a man my father chose in the event I'm unsuccessful here. I'm nearly a woman grown. I'm not stupid. Go back to your cards, your wine, and your whores. I don't need your help."

Chapter Eighteen

"I NEED INFORMATION," CADE SAID.

The short, plump tavern wench giggled. "It'll cost you, m'lord."

"I came prepared," he said with a grin, and dangled a pouch in front of her so she could hear the jingle of the coin inside.

A suggestive smile bloomed on her rosy-cheeked face. She bent, resting her dimpled elbows on the table and letting him have a view of the treasures that threatened to spill from the ruffled neckline of her chemise.

"What can I do for you?"

On the other side of the table, Hayden rolled his eyes.

Cade swallowed his laughter. The girl overplayed her part, it was true, but he did need information, and it was important.

"I need to know if you've heard anything about the Earl of Ashbury staying in town."

She pursed her pink lips and gave the question thought.

"I believe I have," she said. "Haven't seen 'im though. Me mum sells meat from a stall in Southwark. She sold a peacock to his lady countess a week or two back."

"Excellent." Cade handed her the pouch of coins. "Do you happen to know where they're staying?"

"I might, but the information'll cost extra," she said.

"But I just gave you all the money I brought with me."

"Did I say it would cost gold?" She laughed.

"I see," Cade replied. Hayden snorted into his mug. "Tell you what. You share what you know of Ashbury's whereabouts, and I'll come back when you're done working tonight. We'll talk payment then."

"Fair enough," she said as her cheeks pinkened in the dark of the tavern. "I've 'eard they're rentin' a house on Fleet Street. Not far from Temple Bar."

Cade met Hayden's eyes. "That shouldn't be hard to find."

"Not at all," his cousin agreed.

"Thanks, sweetheart," Cade said. He swallowed the remainder of the ale in his mug and stood as Hayden did the same. "Would you look at that? I do have an extra coin on me." He dropped the half-sovereign down the girl's bodice, and she squealed as cold metal touched her bare skin.

Cade blew her a kiss as he and Hayden left the inn.

"Well played," Hayden laughed. "Although I don't think you'd regret it if you did pay her back the other way."

"I don't know," Cade mused. "It was just for fun. But lately I've been wondering if I'm still that man. I don't think it's worth a dose of the clap to find out."

Fleet Street. All this time Ashbury and his family had been mere yards from him and he hadn't known. The mystery could have been solved the day after he'd been alerted to Linton's presence in court, but he'd solve it now.

If he could figure out a way to get the information necessary. The wench back at the tavern surely wouldn't have that kind of knowledge. And the family had done a superb job of keeping itself out of sight.

"Hayden," he said as they meandered down Drury Lane toward Aldwych. "Have you any opposition to a flirtation with one of Linton's sisters? He has two, if memory serves."

"A flirtation?"

"An entirely harmless one," Cade assured his cousin.

"Not really, no." Hayden laughed. "What, pray, do you think that will accomplish?"

"I'm not sure yet," Cade said. "I am weighing my options. Trying to figure out exactly what Linton is up to."

"What if he's not up to anything?" Hayden asked. "The queen gave him a position as assistant to her secretary of state. That, to me, says that she trusts him. You're saying he's convinced her of his repentance, but not you?"

"That's exactly what I'm saying." Cade lowered his voice. "The queen, the few times I've seen her, has seemed lucid enough. But she's ill. What if she's lost her ability to tell when she's being lied to? Why wait until now to infiltrate her inner circle, when it is obvious she won't be with us much longer?"

"I don't know," Hayden answered. "Maybe that's the way it worked out. Remember she thought she was with child. Perhaps she thought that by surrounding herself with those who had wandered from the path of the truth only to return, she would show the prince or princess that anyone can be saved from damnation."

"Doubtful. She knew she was *not* with child by the time she brought him on."

"Well, then, perhaps Ashbury has been appealing to her for years, and she refused to respond until a few weeks ago. For whatever reason. Ashbury only kept his head because of his distant relation to the Lord Chancellor—and he's been dead nigh on three years. Perhaps Ashbury waited until Gardiner's death to avoid dragging him in farther, and it has taken until now for Her Majesty to become convinced that he truly regrets his part in the rebellion. However much of a failure it was."

"Maybe," Cade replied, but he wasn't convinced of that either. "But why send Linton? Why not vie for an appointment for himself?"

"Her Majesty's terms, perhaps?" Hayden suggested as he sidestepped a beggar slumped against the wall. "Since Linton himself was not a direct participant, as he was quick to tell Samara, maybe she thinks his repentance is more likely than that of his father's."

"Hmm." It was entirely possible, but Cade still didn't believe it. Nothing about Linton's performance yesterday in front of Samara suggested repentance of any kind. He'd seemed more smug than anything else. Though Cade had decided there was no way Linton was there on Elizabeth's behalf. It would be far too obvious.

Then it hit him.

"Samara," he exclaimed.

"What about her?"

"He's courting her. What if she marries him?"

Hayden shrugged. "I have to admit I don't think he knows what he's getting himself into, but what of it? If they've really converted to the true faith, having their oldest son marry a Catholic girl like Samara can only help them convince people that they're sincere."

"There is that," Cade said, feeling frantic now. "But think back. Ashbury kept his head because of his relationship to Gardiner. But Her Majesty still punished him. Do you remember how?"

"She fined him," Hayden said slowly.

"She confiscated nearly all of his property. I'm sure he's managed to stay afloat these past three years thanks to whatever meager income his remaining land generates, but Hayden, that won't last forever. And they have two daughters to dower. How can they do that if they're destitute?"

"With Samara's dowry," Hayden finished.

"Exactly."

"What can we do?"

Cade felt frustration begin to bubble in his veins. "Not much until we have solid proof. Acting against Linton with nothing to back up our suspicion will likely do nothing but anger the queen, who would not want to be told that she had given a coveted position to a lying, traitorous fortune-hunter. My first inclination is to get Samara out of the city and safely home to Brentford, but again, without proof, Brentford will not be happy that I've thwarted his plans."

"Nor will his daughter," Hayden added with a chuckle.

Cade allowed himself a brief smile, imagining Samara's reaction when he told her he was taking her home two months before the limit her father had imposed on her, and while the queen still drew breath.

Then his smile faded. If she'd agreed to let Linton court her, then it probably meant she had some kind of feelings for him. Which could be good—if it meant any feelings she might have had for *him* were fleeting, the result of girlish fancy and nothing more. He wasn't good for her. He knew that. But if his suspicions were correct, then Linton was even worse for her. How could he make her see?

"I suppose we can only wait for Linton to hang himself with his own rope," Cade said. "And if possible, keep Samara away from him without her noticing."

❀

The next few weeks drifted by in a haze. Samara wasn't able to see Lord Linton as often as she would have liked, and she found herself missing him. Which was strange. The queen kept him busy with duties at the palace, and those duties increased as her illness progressed. And as the queen grew sicker, her invitations to Samara to attend her, always sporadic, stopped altogether. She wouldn't become a maid of honor after all, it seemed.

Moreover, Cade decided that there were many things in the city he thought she should see. He took her to shops that sold beautiful fabrics, rare books, and jewelry, and she was able to purchase a small silver ring for Cecily's natal day. He discovered a group of strolling actors and recruited them to perform a play in Riverview's hall, which was delightful. He took her to a bear-baiting, which she found so horrifying she refused to speak to him for nearly a week, until he confessed that he hated them too but had not wanted to deprive her of everything London could offer. He was amusing to be with, and sweet to do so much for her, but if he didn't want her, he was eating up valuable time. Christmastide grew closer every day, and the queen's health worsened. Samara's options dwindled by the hour.

October melted into November, and the queen no longer left her bed. Word had it that she, at long last, had recognized that she was not likely to recover from whatever illness she suffered and bear an heir to the throne. However, she still refused to choose—publicly, anyway—from the list of possible heirs at her disposal. Cade and Hayden, their faces taut with worry, dropped names and reasons why the queen would not choose from among them. The Countess of Lennox and Mary Stuart, the queen's cousins, were the only reliably Catholic possibilities. But the countess had no following in England, neither was featured in the Act of Succession, and Philip would never agree to Mary Stuart with her connections to France. That left Catherine Grey, sister of the ill-fated Nine Days' Queen Jane, whose cousin King Edward had included her in the Act of Succession but who had nothing else going for her. It was becoming common knowledge that the only real possibility was Lady Elizabeth, who was said to be busy assembling her own government even as the queen lingered among the living.

Samara wondered how they were able to keep it all straight—the names, the relations, the history. It made her head whirl.

News fluttered through the city streets like pigeons. Jane Dormer, unable and unwilling to leave the queen's side, sent Samara missives in which she described the daily happenings in the palace.

My lord Feria has been to see our dear queen today, she wrote. *Her Majesty recognizes him but is unable to read the letters he brings from the king.*

Her Majesty apologized to me today for making me wait to marry my lord. She regrets that we have wasted this time, but I have convinced her that even marriage would not take me from her side.

And then—

Her Majesty has decided to send me to Hatfield to appeal to Lady Elizabeth personally. If she is to be queen, all Her Majesty asks is that Lady Elizabeth pays Her Majesty's debts and works to maintain all of the progress she has made in reinstating the true faith.

That news set Cade to pacing the floor of his study. But it was the last Samara heard from Jane.

The seventeenth of November dawned gray and chill. The winding Thames was flat and dull, like the sky above it. The house was silent and still when Samara woke and dressed in one of her simple gowns, combed her hair, and slipped down the stairs to take in the clean, cold morning air.

There was a stone bench in the garden that faced the river and Samara perched herself on it, contemplating the drawing materials in her hand. Should she? There was something beautiful about the starkness of naked branches against the flat sky, the gray-white fog that leached the color from just about everything in sight. That would be easy enough to replicate with her paper and charcoal. Besides, if she had more drawings—good drawings—to show Lord Linton, perhaps he would no longer think of her art as a childish fancy.

She opened her case and slid from the bench into the morning grass, damp with dew, unheeding of her skirt. The dress was old. She lifted her pencil and eyed the bare, bony limbs of the oak tree that rose in front of her. She lifted the pencil and let it hover just a hair's breadth above the paper as she considered the best angle from which to begin.

A weak but pitiful shriek interrupted her.

Samara's concentration shattered at the sound, and she dropped her pencil. It left a harsh black gash on the clean paper.

"God's toenail!" she cursed. Paper was not easy to come by! She would wring the neck of whatever creature had caused her to destroy a perfectly good sheet. But the shriek sounded again, more pitiful than before, and the sound pierced her heart. Samara dropped her things and got to her feet. It was clearly not human, but whatever it was, it needed help.

She started across the manicured lawn toward the river, in the direction of the sound. She dodged tiny clusters of sleeping flowers and wound her way around the small but well-kept knot garden. From where did the sound come? The wind off the river, damp and biting, picked up the tiny shriek and threw it in another direction.

I'll never find it, she thought. But then she saw it on the edge of the riverbank. She went down on her knees and crawled, afraid that the closer she got to the water, the muddier the ground would become. But she inched on.

There, at the base of a tree and huddled in a sad pale-orange ball, its fur damp and matted, was the tiniest kitten Samara had ever seen.

It saw her and opened its mouth, revealing small, needle-sharp teeth. But it must have shrieked itself hoarse, for no sound came out.

"Oh, you poor darling!" Samara exclaimed. She reached out and scooped up the kitten. It trembled—either with cold or fear. Samara would do her best to ease both. Leaving her materials in the grass where she'd tossed them, she fled up the lawn and into the house, the tiny animal cupped safely in her hands.

"Betty!" she cried, bursting into her bedchamber. "Where are you?"

"I'm here, Lady Samara," Betty said, emerging from her small room attached to Samara's chamber. "What is it?"

Samara held out her hands. The kitten, seeing Betty, mewed pathetically.

"Oh!" Betty gasped. "Where did you find the wee thing?"

"About to drown in the Thames," she said. "The poor dear needs a bath and a big bowl of milk. Will you help me?"

"Of course!"

Together they submerged the creature in a basin of warm water, gently washing bits of mud, dead leaves, and grass from its fur. When the kitten was clean, Samara rubbed it dry with a linen cloth until its fur was dry and fluffy. She checked for any signs of injury and was grateful when she found none. The poor thing seemed healthy enough, despite its adventure.

Betty brought a bowl of milk and a dish of chicken that had been cut into tiny pieces so the kitten's small throat could swallow it without danger of choking. The animal ate its fill, swallowing every last morsel of chicken and almost emptying the bowl of milk, and then scaled the coverlet of Samara's bed with its needle-sharp claws. It daintily stepped into her lap, turned a few circles, and curled into a ball. Within moments, the kitten's large blue eyes were closed and its purr resonated through Samara's skirt clear to her leg.

"What will you name it?" Betty asked.

"I don't know," Samara mused. She stroked the soft fur between the kitten's ears. "I haven't checked its sex yet." She lifted the kitten, and it mewed a sleepy protest. "A female," Samara declared before setting the animal back in her lap, where it promptly returned to sleep.

"I had a cat named Daisy as a child," Betty offered.

"Daisy." Samara tasted the word and looked at the kitten. She shook her head. "It's a lovely name, but it's not this cat's name." The sleeping kitten emitted a delicate snore, and Samara giggled.

"Where do you think she came from?"

"I imagine," Samara said before pausing, reluctant to acknowledge that anyone could be so cruel, though she was aware that such a thing happened with regularity. "I imagine the intent was to drown her, probably with her siblings. She is strong to have made it to a safe place where I was able to find her." Inspiration struck. "I shall call her Danaë."

Betty looked askance at her. "Dan-ay-ee?" she asked, dragging out the pronunciation.

"Yes." Samara scratched the kitten under her tiny chin. "In Greek mythology, Danaë was the mother of Perseus. Her father placed them in a box and sent them down river in hopes that they would drown, but they were rescued. This kitten is no Perseus. Thus, Danaë."

"If you say so." Betty shook her head. "Seems a mouthful for such a tiny thing."

"Still, it's her name." Samara looked down at the sleeping creature in her lap, and her heart swelled with love. She'd never had a pet to call her own before. She shared Lady with her sisters, but the dog's heart and soul belonged to Cecily. They kept cats in the barn, but they were independent creatures, darting away at the slightest hint that someone might come to force a hug on them. But this kitten—Danaë—would belong to Samara and Samara only.

As if in agreement, the kitten stretched and snuggled down.

❋

Outside, the chime of the church bells cut through the damp gray day, announcing the arrival of the noon hour and calling the London populace to pause and recite the Lord's Prayer.

Inside, Riverview's inhabitants were too stunned to even recall the words of the familiar prayer.

The queen was dead.

The messenger from St. James's stood silent in the doorway of Riverview's study. Hayden sat at Cade's desk, his face in his hands, while Cade stood and stared out the window at the winding gray snake of the Thames. The November morning was dull, and a cloak of solemnity hung over the city. Mary had not been popular, but London did not rejoice in her death. Or perhaps it was too soon for a celebration to have been arranged.

"What now?" Cade asked, turning from the window.

"Pembroke and Arundel have been dispatched to Hatfield to inform Lady Elizabeth of her sister's death, my lord. Sir Nicholas Throckmorton is but an hour behind them and carries the necessary proof. She will be brought back to the city. Planning for the coronation has already begun."

Even before the funeral. If this is the kind of sister she is, what can we expect of her as queen?

Cade signaled a servant passing by the door to the study.

"My lord?" the servant asked.

"This man comes from the palace. Take him to the kitchens and see that he is fed before he departs."

"Yes, my lord." The servant bowed and took the messenger away.

Hayden stood. His eyes were red, but dry.

"I should write my father of the news," he said.

Cade waved toward his desk. "Go ahead," he told his cousin. "Everything you need should be there. I'll be back." He left Hayden in the study and headed for the staircase. He wanted to tell Samara before she heard it from someone else. She hadn't had the time to grow sufficiently close to Her Majesty, but she'd been fond of her, and he knew the news would sadden her.

Not as much as it worried him, however.

He'd been unsuccessful in figuring out Linton's true aspirations. Time and circumstances had not been on his side. But he *had* succeeded in keeping Samara as far from the viscount as possible. The queen's illness helped. She wanted no one around her for the final weeks of her life save important members of her government and the women who had been with her for years. So Samara had not been invited to court, and Linton had been busy there, working with Master Boxall to communicate with William Cecil and ensure a smooth transition of power.

They would have to stay in London long enough to attend the queen's funeral, but Cade hoped to be on the road back home to Worcestershire as soon as he swallowed his last bite of food from the banquet that would surely follow. If Samara hadn't found a husband by then, she would return to her father's home a single woman. Let Brentford decide who she would marry; he was her father, and that was his duty. Cade wasn't going to endanger his life and the lives of those he cared about simply because Brentford had been too blinded by grief to do his duty by his daughters.

He approached Samara's chambers. The door to the main chamber hung open, and Samara was on her knees on the floor, wearing that old blue dress she'd had on that day by the lake. The image of her in a drenched chemise flickered into his mind, and he shook his head to be rid of it. Now was not the time. What was she doing on her knees? She dangled a string in the air, and as he watched, a tiny ball of fur leapt into the air and batted at the string with a clumsy paw. It missed and fell to the floor before rolling over on its back. Samara crowed with laughter and bounced the string in front of the animal, which continued to try and catch it.

He felt one corner of his mouth quirk into a smile as he watched her. He hadn't known she liked animals. In fact, he still had much to learn about her, despite sharing his house with her for almost two months. She liked to draw, but she couldn't be too attached to the activity, since she'd seemed more than willing to give it up in exchange for a husband. She had two sisters, but she seldom spoke of them. Aside from the rivalry he'd seen between Samara and Katherine, he had yet to get a real sense of her relationship with them. And she liked to do things that her father would lock her up for doing if he heard about them. Although she hadn't done anything like that here. In fact, except for her association with Linton, she had made few demands on him as host. Could she have matured that quickly?

Inexplicably, the thought made him sad.

He shook it off and rapped his knuckles against the open door, alerting her to his presence. She dropped the string, and the orange kitten pounced on it. Samara's hair was a mess, curls sticking out in every possible direction from the ribbon that struggled to contain them, and the hem of her blue skirt was muddy.

Her face flushed when she saw him and her hands went to her hair, her fingers trying in vain to press down the curls.

She was adorable.

He hated having to break sad news to her.

"Good morning," she said awkwardly, getting off her knees. "Or, rather, afternoon—I heard the noon call to prayer, didn't I?"

"You did," he said. He gestured to the kitten. "And who is this?"

She reached down and scooped up the kitten, cuddling it in the crook of her arm.

"Danaë," she said proudly. "I found her this morning by the riverbank. Half-drowned, the poor little thing."

The kitten struggled to scale her shoulder. She allowed it, and it climbed up to perch by her neck, poking its nose into her ear. She giggled.

He was unable to keep from smiling. But the smile fell from his face as he remembered why he'd come up to see her.

"I'm sorry to interrupt you," he said. Her giggles faded too when she saw his solemn expression. She plucked the kitten from her shoulder and set it on the floor, where it immediately pounced on her booted toe.

"What is it?" Her green eyes were dark with curiosity.

He gestured to the chairs and table set by the fireplace, indicating that she should sit. She looked frightened now but did as he suggested. He took the seat opposite her and leaned forward, resting his elbows on his knees and taking her small hands in his. She glanced down at her fingers resting on his palms, and her eyes flew back up to meet his.

"Cade, what is it?" she asked again.

He swallowed hard. He'd known this was coming, of course, but the words were harder to say than he'd thought they would be.

"The queen died this morning, Samara. I'm so sorry."

Her expression was blank for a moment before tears bubbled to her eyes. She blinked furiously—trying to fight them, he guessed. Heat stung Cade's own eyes.

"I see," she said. She straightened and, removing her hands from his, swiped her eyes with the back of her hand. "What does this mean?"

He was surprised. He hadn't expected her to dissolve into tears—she hadn't spent enough time with Her Majesty for her to have such a reaction—but he also hadn't expected a rational question from her so soon. It was something a seasoned courtier might have asked, not a naïve girl.

"I don't know for sure," he replied. "Her funeral. We must stay for that. But once it's over? Well, I would suggest we leave London as soon as possible."

She nodded, and he could see more questions in her eyes, but she didn't ask any. He was glad. He had no desire to field questions about her marriage prospects or lack thereof now that her time was up. He didn't know if she realized the extent of his involvement in keeping her away from Linton and was not prepared to address that topic either. She had not, however, expressed interest in any other man while she'd been in the city. And aside from the smattering of available Catholic men in London at the moment, no others had approached her. Was the writing on the wall so clear? With a Protestant all but sitting on the throne, were they afraid to take a Catholic girl to wife?

Maybe he'd been wrong to concentrate on keeping her from Linton. Should he instead have distracted her with other possible suitors, had he been able to find any?

What would her father do if she went home without a betrothal ring on her finger, and it was all Cade's fault?

Chapter Nineteen

ROBERT WANTED TO DANCE.

He couldn't while he lodged in the palace and posed as a repentant heretic. Celebrating the queen's death inches from her lifeless body would not endear him to anyone who happened to see him, which in such a crowd someone inevitably would. So he bit his lip, clenched his hands, and lowered his eyes, hoping that those who saw him would think he was too full of grief to make eye contact rather than striving to conceal the pure, unadulterated joy that had been flowing through him since ten o'clock that morning.

The papist bitch was dead!

Long live Elizabeth!

Would it be possible to leave the palace? The rented house on Fleet Street was the only place where he could safely express his glee.

The sobbing women who streamed from the queen's rooms took no notice of him as he slipped past them. Robert emerged into the courtyard and tugged his shabby cloak around him to keep out the biting wind. He glanced around for a coach he might hire to take him the nearly two miles to the house near Temple Bar, but there were none to be found, so he pulled the hood of his cloak over his head and around his face and set off on foot.

The streets were eerie in their silence. Surely by now the news had started to trickle through the city by way of market stalls, churches, and taverns. Was everyone mourning? Or were they busy planning their celebrations? As he considered this question, movement caught his attention from the corner of his eye. He glanced toward the west, where in the distance on top of a hill a bonfire's flames danced. A smile stretched over his face.

His steps slowed as he walked down the Strand. Palace after opulent palace blurred until he could only focus on one street-facing façade—Riverview House. Samara was inside. Did she know yet of the queen's death? If she did, was she sad?

Easton mourned, lapdog of the queen that he'd been. Hayden too. That went without saying. But Samara had arrived six weeks ago, and for most of that time the queen had been ill. There hadn't been time to forge much of a bond.

Nor had she had time to forge a bond with *him*. The queen's business had kept him busy these last few weeks, and he couldn't be sure, but it felt like Samara had been avoiding him. But why would she do that after agreeing to let him court her? Theirs hadn't been much of a courtship due to circumstances, but they had time. The queen would lie in state for several weeks yet. Without her to keep him busy, he could spend the time wooing Samara away from Easton and start laying the groundwork for her conversion to the new—and real—faith.

And for the conversion of her dowry to my coffers.

He stopped in front of Riverview. The townhouse was beautiful but nowhere near as ostentatious as the palaces that lined the fashionable street. He felt a begrudging respect for Easton for that. He hovered before the gate house. Should he pay Samara a visit? It would do her good to think he cared about how she coped in the wake of the news.

"Ho!" called a voice as he dithered. Robert glanced up. A face peered at him from one of the turrets atop the gate house. "Who goes there?"

It seemed the decision was made.

"Viscount Linton, to see Lady Samara Haughton," he replied.

The head disappeared. A moment later the portcullis creaked as it was lifted. Robert strode beneath it and through the modest courtyard to Riverview's main entrance. The door in front of him opened as if by magic, and a man Robert guessed was Riverview's steward looked at him with one feathery gray eyebrow raised in expectation.

"I wish to see Lady Samara," Robert repeated.

The man stepped aside and extended his arm, waving Robert into the Great Hall.

"Welcome to Riverview House, my lord," he said. "Make yourself comfortable, and I'll tell Lady Samara that you're here. May I take your cloak?"

Fully conscious of the shabbiness of his old cloak, Robert shook his head.

"No, thank you," he said. "I don't intend to stay. I wanted to make sure Lady Samara was doing all right in wake of the news."

The steward dipped his head. "It's a tragedy for all of England."

Another Papist. Well, he wouldn't be for long. Robert forced a tight smile and a nod.

He waited in the Great Hall, taking a moment to go over to the hearth, where a fire blazed merrily, and warm the November chill from his hands.

Only a moment passed before he heard the distinct sound of footsteps behind him. Lord, but she was heavy-footed. Beautiful, yes, but she had none of the grace a lady should possess.

No matter. He wanted her gold, and he would have it with or without a graceful wife. Manners could always be taught afterward.

He plastered a sad smile to his face and turned to face Easton himself, his expression enough to chill any warmth that had seeped into Robert's bones.

He pretended not to care.

"Easton," he said, inclining his head.

"Linton." The earl, alas, made no gesture of respect, faked or otherwise. "What can I do for you?"

"I'm waiting for Lady Samara," Robert replied.

"She's indisposed at the moment. May I give her a message for you? Or simply tell her you stopped by?"

What Robert wouldn't give for the opportunity to punch the self-righteousness off Easton's face. Who did he think he was, anyway? Simply because he had been in the queen's pocket since before her accession, he thought he was something special. Well, the world would see how special he was once Elizabeth took her place on the throne and went to work finally eradicating idolatry from

English soil. How smug would he be when the flames started to lick up his legs, consuming those rich silver-striped hose of his?

"Robert?" A female voice drifted up from behind Easton, whose jaw tightened before he turned.

"Samara," he said. "Are you feeling better?"

"Yes, thank you." She walked around Easton and came to stand in front of him, her back to him. The ghost of a smile haunted her heart-shaped face. "Robert, what are you doing here?"

"I came to see how you are. I assume you've heard the news?"

"I have." She folded her hands demurely at her waist. "It's very sad, but I'm all right. It's sweet of you to come, though. Especially when I know you must be devastated yourself."

"Why wouldn't I be?" He lowered his voice, mainly to annoy Easton. "I've missed you these last weeks. The queen's final duties kept me far too busy for my taste."

She stiffened. *Damn! You shouldn't have said that. Especially not with Easton hovering like an overprotective father.*

"Because they kept me from you," he added. Her shoulders relaxed again, and her cheeks pinkened.

"I do regret we haven't been able to spend as much time together as I would have liked," she said. Behind her, the motion of Easton's right hand as it clenched into a fist caught Robert's attention and he had to swallow his amusement. Was his ire really due to Robert's presence? Or was he jealous? Did he have feelings for the girl?

Now he wished with even greater fervor that he'd been able to see her more, if only to assess the competition. She didn't *seem* interested in Easton, but who knew what went on behind Riverview's closed doors? It *was* a strange situation. Easton was a skirt-chaser—always had been. He could have seduced her. Did Robert want to take the time to win her over if she was damaged goods?

Idiot. It's not her virginity that's the prize here.

"Well, we will have plenty of time over the next few weeks," he said. "With Her Majesty's unfortunate death I've been released from my duties, and there will be no social gatherings at the palace until Queen Elizabeth's coronation. What do you say to another picnic? Or perhaps a masque? My family has rented a grand house on Fleet Street, and my mother leaps at any opportunity for a party."

Now, why had he said *that?* His family could barely afford to feed itself, let alone an entire house full of party guests.

"I don't know." Samara sounded doubtful. "Isn't it in rather poor taste to have a party when we are in mourning for Her Majesty?"

"A subdued affair," he assured her. Now that he'd mentioned it, he would have to follow through, damn it. "A celebration in honor of her life, and all of the good she was able to do because of it." God's teeth, what nonsense spilled from his lips! "We will wear only black aside from our masks. And you will meet my sisters. You will love them. And they will adore you, as I do."

Saved, he thought as he watched her blush deepen and steal over her lightly freckled cheeks. He wondered why she did not cover them up with artifice, as a fashionable woman would do. But again, he decided not to waste time on such things now. There would be plenty of time for such teachings once she was his wife.

"I think I should like that," she said. "I've never been to a masque."

Easton remained silent, but his hard eyes were on Robert's face. They made him uncomfortable, but Robert would not give the earl the satisfaction of letting him know that.

"Good," he said with a genuine smile. He liked the idea of having her in his house. He would propose marriage to her then. He could come up with a backup plan to force her hand in the event she turned him down, though he didn't believe for a moment she would.

"I am glad you're not despairing," he said, stepping forward, close enough take up her hand and press it to his heart. "I hate the thought of you being sad. I'll do what I can to see that you are not." He brushed his lips against her knuckles. "I must go. My family is expecting me."

"Thank you for coming, Robert," she said.

He tipped his velvet cap to her, quickly so she didn't see how ragged it was.

"Expect an invitation to the masque within the next few days," he promised. "For all of you." Easton would never let her go without him. "I look forward to celebrating Her Majesty's life with those who loved her best." He started for the doorway. To his annoyance, he had to squeeze past Easton. "Good day to you, Easton."

"And to you, Linton." He felt Easton's eyes on his back even after he shut the heavy door and found himself back on the street.

A masque. He shook his head. Well, it must be done now. They would come up with the money somehow—didn't they always?

❀

"A party!" his mother exclaimed, clapping her ringed hands. "What a brilliant idea, Robin."

"Oh, very," he said dryly. "Quite possibly the most brilliant idea I've ever had." But her enthusiasm was catching. He might actually succeed. Lady Samara already liked him, he knew that. If he could get her to meet Amy and Isabel, she would adore them. They were wonderful girls; one couldn't help loving them.

"Stop that," she scolded. "We will borrow the money. Now that you've found the perfect marriage candidate, money is not an issue. You have done very well, my darling. I only lament that the girl is a Papist—well, there isn't much we can do about that. A Catholic queen would surround herself with Catholic girls. A woman should do as her husband says, anyway, and I know you will do your duty by her and get her to see the error of her ways."

"That is if she agrees to marry me," he reminded her. "I haven't asked her yet, and even if I had the time, I cannot write her father and ask his approval. He'll not know of my so-called *conversion*. This will be no conventional betrothal, my lady mother. As you said in the beginning, I must do whatever I can to win her. If relying on her naïveté doesn't work, drastic measures may have to be taken."

To his chagrin, the wheels in his head already turned, formulating ideas that would help him get Lady Samara to marry him. None were pleasant, but all had potential.

"I trust you," his mother said for the first time he could remember.

❀

"Remind me why this is not ill-advised?" Cade asked his cousin as he passed a filled goblet of wine across the desk. But his words were careless. Of course, this was ill advised. The only reason he was allowing Samara to go was so that she could see with her own two eyes that Linton did not need or want *her*—just her dowry.

"Because she'll go regardless," Hayden said. "Short of locking her in her apartments, which might result in the house burning down, she'll find a way to get to the party if she really wants to go. And I think she does. She likes him. But if we go *with* her, we can stay near her at all times and, with any luck, discourage Linton from making advances." He sipped his wine.

Cade sighed. "I know you're right. She's the most headstrong girl I've ever met, though being here has seemed to mature her a bit." He swirled the wine in his goblet before taking a long drink. "But I still think we should tell her our suspicions. Linton has been nothing but circumspect in his dealings with her, but we don't know how desperate he is. She's such an innocent. It would be cruel to send her in there with less than complete information."

"I agree," Hayden said. "And maybe this time she'll believe us."

"Perhaps." Cade chuckled. "Or perhaps she'll send us off to our wine and whores again and ignore every word we say."

Then he sobered. "I feel bad, Hayden. She hasn't liked any of the other men who've approached her, and I can't say I blame her. She's too special to be wasted on a man like Parkhurst or Grimsby. But no others have come near her. Do you know why that is? Is it because they all knew Elizabeth would succeed Mary, despite Her Majesty's hesitancy, and they didn't want to tie themselves to a Catholic?"

"Probably." Hayden brushed his fingers up and down the silver stem of his goblet. "Most people are in it only for themselves, and to hell with everyone else."

"I wish Brentford had never gotten it into his fool head to send her here."

"Don't speak too hastily, Cade." Hayden grinned. "If he hadn't, you might never have fallen in love with her."

❈

Samara's mind whirled as she dressed for the masque—or attempted to, for Danaë made it a point to attack the hem of Samara's hastily sewn black satin gown as if it were lined with field mice. In the end,

Samara plucked the kitten from the floor and placed her in a tall basket. It would not hold her, for with her sharp baby claws she could climb anything in a matter of seconds, but perhaps it would delay her long enough that Samara could get downstairs and into the hall where Cade waited, for he would not let her go without him.

"But I won't be alone," she'd protested. Not that she didn't want him there—in fact, she was strangely exhilarated at the prospect of walking into a party with Cade, even if the party was at the home of the man who'd been courting her (did that make her fickle? She hoped not)—but because he and Lord Linton so obviously disliked each other. She wished Cade would open his eyes and realize that Robert was not a danger, not a person of whom to be wary. He was a good man. He'd risked death to protect his father! "Aunt Madge will be with me."

"Nonetheless, I am going," Cade said, and would tolerate no argument. "Hayden too."

She'd sighed but was strangely grateful for it. Maybe a few hours in the company of both Cade and Robert would sort out the feelings she had for the two of them. She was torn. She hoped that seeing Cade on Robert's territory for once, instead of the other way around, would give her new insight. If the evening went well, perhaps she could enter into a marriage with Robert without wondering what might have been if she'd managed to win Cade.

The scrabbling of claws told her that Danaë struggled to scale the side of the basket. The kitten's head peeped over the side, and she meowed.

"All right, you little monster. I'm leaving. Have your fun, but don't torture Betty." She blew a kiss to the kitten and swept from the room, closing the door. The last thing she saw was Danaë tumbling over the side of the basket to the floor.

How many times had she descended a flight of stairs to find Cade anticipating her arrival? Several, at this point. But every time she did, she found it necessary to pause for a moment to look at him, in awe of the fact that such a glorious-looking man was waiting for *her*. Never mind that he had no interest in her and no idea how much sense a marriage between them made; if he had, he would have proposed already. Well, she wouldn't waste time being disappointed about that. Perhaps he and Kat would suit each other better. Anyway, she had Robert. She would be very happy with him.

She hoped.

As for Cade, may Kat be worthy of him.

She descended the rest of the stairs. Blackwell greeted her and offered up her black velvet cloak.

"Thank you, Blackwell," she said. She pulled the cloak over her shoulders and fastened the gold frog at her throat. For a moment the gesture swept her into the memory of Cade performing that service for her just before her first trip to the palace.

Then he was beside her. "You look beautiful," he said, his voice a low caress that turned her bones to water. "Well! Is everyone ready?"

"Yes," Hayden drawled from his spot in front of the fireplace. He did not look excited.

"Yes!" Aunt Madge echoed from beside him. She looked less of a sparrow and more of a blackbird in her ebony silk gown. She carried a feathered black and smoke-gray mask in her bony hand.

"Yes," Samara whispered at last. *This is it.* Her last chance to make her choice.

When she returned to Riverview House this evening, it could be as a woman betrothed to marry.

"Let's go, then. Samara, don't forget your mask." Cade took it—a delightful confection of black lace, paste jewels that looked like diamonds, and black satin ribbons—and handed it to her. Then he ushered them out of the house and to the courtyard, where the coach waited.

When they were settled inside, the horses had not even begun to move when Cade cleared his throat.

"This won't be a long ride, so what I have to say, I will say now. Samara, Hayden and I will do our best to flank you at all times. But if Linton manages to get you alone and broaches the subject of marriage with you, you will turn him down." Cade's jaw was set, his lips thin with tension.

"Oh, not this again!" Samara cried. Why would he try to ruin her evening before it had even started?

"Listen to him, Samara." Aunt Madge's voice drifted up from the corner of the coach. Samara glanced at her in surprise. Aunt

Madge had been reticent on the subject of Lord Linton. Why would she speak up now? "I know you like him, dear girl. And by all appearances he's the perfect husband for you. But please, heed those of us who were here for the rebellion and its aftermath. Those men and women died for their beliefs."

"Robert and his father didn't," she pointed out.

"Because they were cousins of the Lord Chancellor. He pled with Her Majesty for leniency for them, and she granted it," Hayden said. He bounced his pomander ball in his hand.

"But why would she grant it if they weren't sincere?" They were wrong. They had to be!

"To show her detractors that she could be merciful," Cade replied. "She fined them, though. Took nearly everything they had, and rightly so. The family is in debt up to its ears. At this point it must be desperate for money." He paused. "For your dowry."

His words hung in the air. No. It couldn't be. Her Majesty was not stupid. She wouldn't put a heretic into her service! And Samara was not so naïve that she would fall for a fortune-hunter.

They were wrong.

But something inside her, a nearly imperceptible sensation in her belly, whispered to her. Lord Linton had come on strong. She wasn't familiar with courtship rituals, but he had barely taken the time to make her acquaintance before he was asking if he could court her. How had he known she would suit him? Hadn't she felt just the tiniest doubt almost from the beginning?

No. It was nerves. *They are wrong. He cares for me, as I care for him.* She felt their eyes on her. She kept hers fixed straight ahead.

As Cade had promised, it was not a long ride. Mere minutes had passed by the time the carriage slowed to a stop in front of a rather nondescript house.

"Are you sure Lord Linton lives here?" she asked, confused. Riverview was not a palace by any stretch of the imagination, but it was far grander than this. Robert lived *here?*

"Positive," Cade said. He glanced quickly at Hayden, and she knew he thought she'd missed it.

Samara's hands, inside her soft scented kid gloves, began to tremble.

Inside, once they'd been welcomed in by a servant in gaudy red and gold livery, was only slightly better. The visible bits of wood floor showed signs of wear, and the wainscoting on the walls appeared to have been painted to cover up the same. Samara could see where the shining gold paint dipped into scratches and gouges. The wall above the wainscoting, instead of being draped with beautiful, colorful tapestries, was stark off-white plaster. She gave a delicate sniff. At least the rushes on the floor were fresh.

No statues, no artwork, no pretty coffers like the ones the queen, and even her father, had strewn about their rooms. No personality.

Nothing to reflect their riches. Unless she'd misunderstood, the wealthy *always* displayed their riches.

Were they telling me the truth after all? Does Robert only want my dowry?

Her pulse hummed; her limbs weakened. She felt hot and slightly faint.

"Coming?" Cade asked.

Should she dig in her heels, request that he take her back to Riverview? No. She wasn't quite ready to admit defeat. Perhaps Robert's family didn't want their goods damaged or stolen by their guests. That would explain the lack of treasures on display, wouldn't it?

Besides, Robert had been kind to her. She owed him at least a little of her loyalty. When she saw him, she would demand he tell her the truth himself.

They drifted into the Great Hall, which teemed with people. A small gallery filled with tattered musicians played joyful music. The guests wore masks—Samara slipped hers over her eyes, as did Cade; his was solid black with no adornments—but the colors did not suggest mourning. A woman in a dazzling mask like a Mary's Gold blossom flitted by on the arm of a man in a feathered mask of crimson and sapphire. Another woman, her mask dripping in feathers dyed the exact shade of a robin's egg, danced with a man in grass green and bronze. Colors swirled about them. Samara would have been enchanted, had she not been so dumbfounded.

"What is this?" Samara breathed.

"A party," Hayden answered from behind her, his tone grim.

Beside her, Cade shook his head.

"They couldn't keep up the pretense long enough to achieve their goal," he muttered.

Samara's stomach ached.

"You were right," she whispered. "He's not in mourning at all. None of them are." Hayden put a comforting hand on her shoulder.

"Stay with us," Cade murmured. "Don't let us lose sight of you."

She was growing more frightened with every word he said.

"What do you think will happen if I do?" she asked.

"You won't. I'll find him first." Cade's expression implored her to cooperate, and though fury and humiliation had her blood racing and her heart pounding, she felt compelled to help him in any way she could. She realized now what he'd been doing the last few weeks with all the activities he wanted her to experience. He'd been suspicious of Robert, for whatever reason, from the moment she'd mentioned his name. He'd wanted to keep her safe. Why had he even allowed her to attend the party?

Because he knew you wanted to go, and trying to stop you would be pointless.

How did he know her so well?

Though they were already forced by the crowd of party goers to stand huddled together, she inched closer to him. His tall sturdiness was comforting.

But given the opportunity, she *would* confront Robert herself. She deserved to hear the truth from his lips, hear him say that he cared nothing for her, only for the dowry her father had set aside for her.

Hopelessness washed over her. She would have to marry Waltham after all.

❊

Cade left the women with Hayden, trusting his cousin to keep them safe without attracting suspicion. He circled the room, disgusted at how many faces he knew. Not that he'd expected honesty from Linton for a moment, but this obviously was *not* a celebration of Her Majesty's life. However, he was surprised that Linton hadn't tried harder to keep up the appearance just a bit longer. Long enough to ensnare Samara, which was almost certainly his plan.

So be it. If Linton wanted a fight, he would get one.

"Excuse me," he said, as his distracted musings caused him to collide with a woman in a crimson gown. "I didn't see you."

"It's all right," she said. She lifted her eyes and smiled at him. She was young—Samara's age or a year older—and very pretty. But he was far too absorbed by the situation to find her any temptation. He nodded and started to walk away.

"I seem to have spilled my wine, though," she continued. She frowned as she looked at the floor, where a pewter wine goblet rolled between people's feet.

"I'm sorry," she said. She lifted her eyes to him once again. "But my stays are laced so tightly that I'm afraid if I bend to retrieve it, I'll never get back up. Do you mind?"

That earned the young woman a glare, though perhaps it was undeserved. Still, he did *not* have time for this. He had to find Linton, confront him—beat a confession out of the wretch if it came to that, which he fervently hoped it didn't—and get Samara safely out of there.

"Please," she pleaded, rather prettily.

Chivalry and general human kindness won out. He could spare a second to bend, pick up the goblet, and hand it back to the girl. It wasn't as if Linton would leave the premises. And Samara was safe with Hayden.

"At your service." He sighed and reached for the goblet, but someone's dancing foot kicked it from his grasp. He chased after it and watched as it rolled under a table whose cloth reached the ground. Cade scrambled after it, reached beneath the long table skirt, and felt his fingers wrap around the stem of the goblet. Triumphantly he pulled it out of its hiding spot and stood, brushing dust from his knees. He turned to hand the goblet to the girl, but she had vanished.

He rotated in place to see if the girl had stepped aside to talk to someone, but it was as though she had evaporated. Cade's annoyance grew. He threw the goblet to the floor and strode off, finishing his surveillance of the room as he moved. Linton was nowhere to be found. The fact relieved him somewhat. Samara was safe from him for now.

He made his way through the crowd, gently using his elbows to maneuver himself to the spot where he'd left his cousin with the women. But wait—they'd moved too. Again he turned in a circle, his eyes sweeping the room. He searched for Hayden's blond head, Aunt Madge's hood, Samara's vibrant curls. Nothing.

The three of them had disappeared.

Chapter Twenty

THE AIR IN THE GALLERY HAD A CHILL THAT CUT RIGHT TO SA-
mara's bones. She shivered and rubbed her hands up and down her
arms, wishing she hadn't given her cloak to that groom.

"Are you cold?" Lord Linton asked solicitously.

"No, I'm fine," she lied. She heard the strange note in her own
voice and flinched. She forced herself to appear natural, besotted
even, and turned toward him.

He chuckled and reached out, wrapping his arm around her
shoulder and pulling her close. She fit nicely in the space between
his body and his arm. It was just too bad that the feel of him against
her made her even colder. And a little nauseated.

She shouldn't have come up here. Cade would have her head
if he knew where she was. But she wanted to be the one to make
Robert tell the truth. If he had lied to her, made her nearly fall for him
through meaningless pretty words and deceit, she would at least have
the satisfaction of a confession even if she had to marry Waltham
and move to Yorkshire, never seeing her family again while she bore
that disgusting man's children. Perhaps she *would* die in childbirth. It
might not be something to fear under those circumstances.

"This is my great-great-grandfather, the first Earl of Ashbury,"
Robert said, pointing to a dour-looking man with chin-length brown
hair and a pointed nose. "He was granted the earldom by King
Edward of York after fighting alongside him at the Battle of Barnet."

"How fascinating!" Portrait galleries were still a rather new
phenomenon, and under ordinary circumstances she would have

loved a lengthy tour of Robert's. He knew that, of course. Certainly he must have thought it would be the perfect way to get her alone. He planned to propose, she knew it. She waited for it. She was anxious to see the look on his face when he realized she was aware of his treachery.

"His wife, Lady Joan," Lord Linton said, drawing her along to the next painting. Samara hoped the sound of her heels clicking against the floor drowned out the steady thump of her heart.

He took her along the long, narrow gallery, naming faces as he did so. She retained none of the information. What was he waiting for? A herald to announce his intentions by bleating a horn?

"You shall meet him," Robert promised. Meet whom? She had no idea. She hadn't been listening. Samara forced herself to nod and smile.

"Are you interested in seeing more?" he asked when they reached a doorway at the end of the gallery. "My parents keep most of their paintings in this room. There are many. Scenery, still life…" His voice trailed off. "I had hoped you would want to see them, given your love for art."

A love you would squelch if I were so stupid as to become your wife. Samara wished he would just ask her and get it over with. She longed to return downstairs—no, to Riverview, where she was safe. At Riverview she could pretend she still had all the time in the world, and Lord Waltham was still a faraway threat that she could elude by picking out her own husband.

"I don't understand," she said instead. "If you have so many paintings, why not hang them on the bare walls downstairs? Those walls could use some decoration."

He paused before chuckling once more. "One of my father's small quirks," he explained. "They are so valuable, he is afraid to expose them to sunlight and dust."

He reached out and pushed open the door. The room beyond them was dim but not entirely devoid of light. There was enough to see that the small chamber contained no paintings—just a battered wooden chair in the middle of the floor.

Before Samara could comprehend the situation, she felt Robert's hand, firm on her back, shoving her into the room. She stumbled forward, only narrowly saving herself before she fell to her knees. He came in behind her and shut the door. Barred it shut.

Samara righted herself as her heart raced. What was he doing? Oh, she'd been so stupid coming up here with him! She took a deep breath, gathering strength in her throat to let out the blood-curdling scream she knew she was capable of.

He was on her in an instant, one arm around her waist, his other hand clapped against her mouth.

"Don't scream," he begged. "Please. No one would hear you anyway, what with the celebration going on downstairs." He sighed. "I was hoping it wouldn't come to this, but you've left me no choice. You and your *protector.*" He spat the word. "If Easton had just let it go, and been himself—the same carefree skirt-chaser I've always known him to be—this would have been so much easier. You would have been free to fall in love with me, and I would have convinced you to marry me in secret as so many others have done, and there would be nothing anyone could do about it."

The pressure of his hand on her mouth loosened as he spoke. She opened her lips and clamped her teeth down on the fleshy part of his palm. He yelped and jerked his hand away, leaping away from her.

"And have my dowry, too?" she snarled at him. She stared at his hand. Damn! She hadn't broken the flesh.

He smiled, and the wistfulness made her want to simultaneously claw his eyes out and burst into tears. How dare he try to soften her? Would his treachery never end?

"So you've figured me out, have you?" he said. "Either you're smarter than I thought, or Easton gave me up. Don't cry," he said as her traitorous eyes allowed themselves to fill with scorching tears. "I do like you, Samara. You're a bit childish, but that can be charming under the right circumstances. No, I don't wish to harm you. Please believe that."

"Then let me go." She was relieved that her voice didn't tremble.

His gaze was soft with regret. "I can't do that," he told her. "I need you. That papist bitch took every piece of gold my family had. We have nothing. Nothing! Not even a dowry for Amy and Isabel. We need money. And you, Samara, have it. You're innocent enough that I could have convinced you to consent to a clandestine marriage.

And you were alone in not knowing what my family did to incur the queen's wrath. That made you my only option. No other girl in this town—in this country!—would dare be seen in public greeting me, let alone give me the opportunity to court her."

He stopped rubbing his injured hand and took a few steps closer. Instinctively she backed away, only to stumble into the chair. She tried to read his intentions on his face.

Is he going to rape me? Oh, God. Oh no.

"Please," she whispered.

"Sit in the chair," he ordered.

Perhaps if she cooperated, he would consider setting her free. She sat in the chair. It creaked as it accepted her weight.

"You don't have to do this," she told him. "My father will pay any ransom you desire."

Robert's eyes were sympathetic. Damn him.

"I'm sorry, but it's not a measly ransom I want from him," he said. "It's his daughter to wife and her dowry. You see, my family and I put our lives on the line when we agreed to aid Wyatt with his ill-fated rebellion. A Catholic queen on the throne would have destroyed all of the progress made since King Henry broke from Rome. The papist way is done. There is no place for idol worship and superstition in England anymore."

"But it is the true faith," Samara argued. She felt sick with the knowledge that he'd lied to her.

"It is not!" he shouted. Blood stained the skin of his neck and crept toward his jaw and cheeks. "You mean to tell me you honestly believe that a piece of *bread* becomes the flesh of Christ? That souls linger in Purgatory when there is no mention of such a place in the Bible? That only a priest can tell you what the Bible says? It is not so. You have been fooled. The Church is corrupt. We have a duty to clean it up and to call no man our Father on earth."

He was mad. A Protestant zealot. Terror lodged like rocks in her lungs, making it difficult to breathe.

"Please don't be afraid," he pleaded. "Once you have been made to see that you have been worshipping false idols all your life, you will understand. And even be happy. With me. I promise you that."

He stalked toward her.

❀

"Where is she?"

"Cade, I don't know. I'm sorry!" Hayden's eyes were wild with panic and regret. "She was there one moment. Aunt Madge and I bent to help a girl who had been knocked to the ground, and when we stood up, Samara was gone."

Cade put his hand on the hilt of his dagger, but a warning glance from Aunt Madge, seated on a bench against the wall, made him stop short of withdrawing it from its sheath.

"We were distracted on purpose," he said grimly. "Linton has included his sisters in whatever nefarious plot he's cooked up. Well, he can't have taken her far. We will find her."

He wished he believed his own words.

The number of people in the Great Hall seemed to have multiplied since they'd realized Samara was gone. Cade scanned the crowd, looking for anyone he might recognize—Lord or Lady Ashbury, one of their so-called helpless daughters, or Linton himself. He saw none of them.

He uttered a loud curse. A gray-haired woman in a blue and gold gown turned to glare at him.

"Cade." Hayden put a comforting hand on his arm. "We'll find her."

Where to start? Cade glanced toward the entrance. The crush of people that blocked it would have made it difficult for Linton to whisk Samara into the street, but not impossible. They would start there.

"Lord Linton," he demanded of the servant guarding the entrance. "Have you seen him?"

The servant shook his head. "No, my lord."

Cade appraised the young man, wondering if he was lying. If he was in on it. Then he shook his head. They did not have time to waste interrogating a mere groom.

"Back inside," he said to Hayden, and they went in, battering their way through the crowd.

"I've never been inside one of these houses," Cade said. "I'm not familiar with the layout. I don't know where to start."

"The stairs," Hayden suggested. "Perhaps he's got her in one of the chambers up there."

A knot formed in Cade's gut as the possibilities of what Linton could be doing to Samara in one of those rooms occurred to him. He felt his fingers clench involuntarily into a fist. When he found that criminal, whether he'd laid a hand on Samara or not, Cade would see to it that Viscount Linton's handsome face would not be handsome for a long, long time.

"Aunt Madge," Cade said. "Will you be all right? The coach is just outside should you need to get away."

"I'll be fine," she assured him. "Don't waste a moment worrying about me. Find that precious girl before that devil does something he'll regret."

With a curt nod, Cade gestured to Hayden and they raced up the nearest staircase to the first floor. They found several rooms with their heavy oak doors barred shut. They pounded on each door in turn. Nothing. Not even a whimper to suggest that Samara might be inside.

Cade's panic grew.

"Second floor," Hayden said.

Up they went.

❀

It had all been so easy it would have been funny if he hadn't been so desperate. He'd been watching for their arrival from the minstrels' gallery. Waiting. That Hayden and Easton had figured him out and informed Samara of their suspicions was obvious the moment their small group entered the hall. It angered him. He'd been so close!

The pastor he'd recruited had been willing to conduct a secret marriage ceremony. Samara was so naïve she wouldn't have realized it was illegal until it was too late. But with Easton and Hayden stuck to her side like burrs Robert knew he'd never get her away long enough to do it. Luckily he'd had the foresight to come up with a last-minute contingency plan. He'd dreaded having to use it. His sisters, too, hated the idea of tricking Samara, but they realized there was no other option, not if they wanted a future, and had played their quickly assigned parts well. He'd had to assure them he wouldn't hurt

Samara to convince them to participate, but it wasn't a hard promise to make. He didn't want to hurt her. He had no plans to lay a hand on her, except to do what was necessary. No, it would be enough when the people his sisters planned to bring to the portrait gallery saw him in the tower room with her. Only one conclusion could be drawn then, and like it or not, she would be forced to marry him, because no other man would have her once word got out. As it inevitably would.

His captive sat as if tied to a stake in the old chair he'd dragged up from the cellars. Neither he nor she had spoken for a few moments, but her eyes followed him as he paced back and forth, listening for sounds of movement in the gallery. He glanced at his battered pocket-watch. Only a few more minutes. It had been easier than he'd thought to get her to come with him.

Why did she come, if she knew of my intentions?

Was she so guileless she thought she could confront him herself? He almost laughed out loud. Well, it had worked in his favor, hadn't it? She was here. Easton and his cousin were not. She was his.

His hand throbbed. He glanced at it. The marks her teeth had left were fading, but he would have a few small bruises. He acknowledged her spirit with grudging admiration.

Her chest heaved above the neckline of her gown, the ivory skin rising and falling with each shallow breath she took. She was terrified. He regretted that. That was why he stayed closer to the door than to her; he didn't want his nearness to frighten her further. He was rather surprised she hadn't screamed, but maybe she believed him when he told her how futile it would be to scream from a tower room on the third floor when the only people in the house were several stories below her, dancing to the minstrels' merry music.

"I won't be a bad husband to you," he offered. "Things have worked out quite well, in fact. With the dowry you'll bring me, even after my sisters are married, we'll be able to live quite comfortably. Ashbury Hall is grand, and it's in a beautiful part of Devonshire. And with Elizabeth taking her rightful place on the throne, I am guaranteed a place at her court." Although that wasn't necessarily true, was it? His father's missives to Elizabeth had gone unanswered. It seemed she had written them off. But he found it difficult to believe that she'd done so for any reason other than to distance herself from the families involved in the rebellion. Surely once she was safely ensconced on the throne she would welcome them to her court.

"As my wife, you'll be welcome too. Perhaps Elizabeth will even make you a lady-in-waiting. Wouldn't you like that?"

She didn't speak. She just continued to stare, her green eyes following his every step as he paced a pattern in the floor.

Robert glanced at the small gold watch again. Then he moved closer to the door, straining to hear. Footsteps and voices. Faint—they were probably at the other end of the hall. He gave a small smile. It pleased him to know that he had the support of his sisters, that they were willing to help him with the scheme he'd hoped he wouldn't have to devise. Everything he did, he did for them.

The footsteps grew closer. Robert turned from the door to face the terrified girl in the chair.

"Stand up," he commanded. "It's time."

❀

"Time for what?" Samara demanded. Instead of standing, she wrapped her legs around the chair, hooking her ankles so that even if he tried to drag her into a standing position, the chair would follow.

"I don't want to hurt you," he said again, staring pointedly at her ankles. "But if you don't cooperate, I may not have a choice."

She took a deep breath. She didn't want to be hurt. But she didn't want to give in, either.

She'd never been in a situation like this. Wasn't it better to be brave, even if it meant a few bruises?

She let the breath out. She stayed where she was, lifting her chin and glaring at him.

He sighed.

"If that's how you want it, then." He strode the short distance to the chair. He grabbed the back of it, hooked his foot under one of the legs and flipped it.

Samara—and the chair—went tumbling to the hard floor. Her elbow cracked against the wood when she landed, and she yelped. Pain radiated from shoulder to wrist.

"I'm sorry, but you should have done what I said." Robert tore the chair away. Samara scrambled to her hands and knees and tried to crawl away from him. Her skirts did not make it easy. Her elbow throbbed. Robert reached down with both hands and tugged her over onto her back.

She gasped as bare skin touched cold floor. Her skirts bunched around her knees, exposing the pretty silk stockings she'd put on for the first time tonight. Lord Linton loomed over her, a strangely regretful expression on his face—how could she have ever found him handsome?—and he climbed over her, sitting down with a knee on each side of her hips, pinning her firmly in place.

She wanted to scream. She *had* to. But fear sucked the moisture from her throat, rendering her voice useless.

"I'm not going to hurt you," he said yet again. He'd said it so many times now it sounded as though he wanted to convince himself more than he wanted to convince her.

He reached out and unlaced her stomacher.

"What are you doing?" she cried in a dry rasp, the best her throat could produce. He *was* going to rape her! She pummeled at him with her fists. He brushed off her blows as if they were flies.

"What needs to be done," he said. Her stomacher detached, he moved on to the tiny hooks that kept her stays fastened. Her breath was coming shallower now and she couldn't quite get enough air into her lungs. The room's bare walls spun around her.

Cold air burrowed beneath the fabric of her exposed chemise, causing gooseflesh to rise. Or was it fear? Linton glanced at the door. The expression on his face was expectant. Then he stood, grabbed her hands, and yanked her to her feet. Samara pulled her arms up to cover herself, but he tugged them down and wrapped both arms around her waist. She responded by beating at him again. But he pushed her toward the door—no, toward the wall next to the door—and, using his body, pinned her against it. He leaned over and lifted the bar.

She saw the fierce determination in his eyes, and she drew in a breath, intending to at least try to scream. But before she could he stopped her by kissing her, closing her lips off with his.

The door beside them swung open.

❀

They'd found her.

Cade had expected the door to be barred shut, but instead of using his shoulder to plow through it as he'd initially planned when he'd heard the murmur of voices behind it, something told him to push it first. He was surprised when it swung open.

The first thing he saw when he rushed into the room was Linton pressing Samara against the wall, kissing her. Or something. Her gown hung loose, her chemise dropped so that one ivory shoulder was revealed.

The second thing he saw was red.

He flew at the viscount, yanking him away from Samara and hurling his fist into Linton's face, where it connected with a satisfying crunch. Linton fell away, blood spurting from between the fingers that covered his nose.

Cade went for him again. He grabbed Linton's wrist, which was slick with blood, and pulled it away from his face. He hit him a second time, catching him square in the mouth. Linton fell to his knees, swayed, and toppled face-first to the floor. Cade gave him a swift kick in the ribs, eliciting a groan from the fallen man. Then another.

The red haze swirled in front of his eyes. *You're useless.* He kicked him again. *Damned accident.* Cade dropped to his knees and began to throw his fists at whatever he could find.

It should have been you.

He didn't know how long he pummeled the man on the floor. It could have been a few seconds, or it could have been hours. Every frustration he'd ever felt emerged with each swing of his fists, each wound he inflicted. But at last the haze lifted. As it did, Cade became aware of his surroundings again. It wasn't his father on the floor.

He heard a voice.

"Cade. Cade!" It was Hayden. Samara was screaming.

It was the sound of her screams that had caused the haze to dissipate. He looked at the viscount, who was curled into a moaning ball on the floor. It took a moment to realize what he was looking at.

When he realized what he'd done, he scrambled backward on his knees, staring at the gory mess he'd made of Robert Hunter. He raised his hands and gazed at them in horror. His knuckles were mangled, a torn mass of flesh and blood. It was like looking at another man's hands. He didn't even feel pain.

"Cade." Hayden was beside him, his hand outstretched. "Come. He won't be getting up anytime soon, and Samara needs our help."

Wordlessly Cade accepted his cousin's hand and allowed Hayden to pull him to his feet. Samara had stopped screaming but stood with her back against the wall, her arms folded over her chest, her hands balled into fists and pressed to her mouth. Her eyes were wide, her face pale. For a second the scenery around him changed, and he was again on the grassy bank of the lake that straddled the line between Easton and Brentford lands, watching a strange and intriguing chit of a girl trying to cover herself so that he couldn't see beneath her wet chemise.

Nothing had changed. Everything had changed.

She trembled as he approached her, and he cursed himself for losing control. She didn't need to see that—to see what he really was beneath the carefully constructed veneer of the courtier and diplomat. He'd tried hard to keep that from her. But tonight he'd effectively shattered any illusion she might have had about him. Reality had come crashing down on her twice tonight.

Had he not been such a coward, he might have tried to fall on his own sword.

Slowly he reached out a hand, his eyes asking her permission. She gave a barely perceptible nod and let her arms drop to her sides. Cade took the neckline of her chemise between his thumb and forefinger, careful not to poison her with his touch, and pulled it back up to cover her shoulder. But before he could decide what to do about her unlaced stays, she collapsed against him, burying her face in his chest, shaking and sobbing into his velvet doublet.

He met Hayden's gaze over his head. His cousin's eyes were troubled. Cade had never felt so lost, so helpless in his life. Not when his father died. Not even when his mother died. Samara trembled against him, her sobs coming in tiny gulping hiccups, and he couldn't help himself. He lifted his arms, wrapping them around her and letting her cry out her fear.

"Her cloak," Hayden mouthed, and disappeared when Cade nodded. By the time he returned, Samara's sobs had dwindled to sniffles and Linton was trying to push himself up from the floor. Hayden tossed Samara's long black velvet cloak to Cade.

"Here," he said softly, releasing her from his hold and draping her cloak over her shoulders. She gave him a grateful little smile, though it was pathetic with her swollen eyes and tear-stained cheeks, and pulled it tight, holding it closed at her throat.

"Stay back," he told her, and she nodded. He turned his attention to Linton, who had managed to struggle to his feet, and withdrew his dagger.

Linton spat a bloody tooth on the floor. It would be a long time before another unsuspecting girl was conned by the viscount's handsome smile.

"Game's over, Linton," Hayden drawled.

"I could kill you right now and toss your mangled corpse into the Thames, and nobody would ever question it," Cade announced. "Give me one reason why I shouldn't do just that."

Despite his blackened jaw and bloody mouth, Linton somehow managed to arrange his destroyed face into an expression resembling scorn.

"Because your bitch queen isn't here to protect you anymore," he replied before spitting more blood onto the floor. "What do you think all those people are downstairs celebrating? Don't pretend you haven't heard how happy the people are that we finally have a Protestant queen. Elizabeth would love to make an example of you. What's one Catholic convicted of murder and beheaded? Nobody would fault her. In fact, they would praise her."

He might be right. But Cade would be damned before he gave him the satisfaction of knowing it.

"Personally, I don't think she'd care," Cade answered. "She hasn't done much to help you, has she, even though your family lost its fortune and prestige trying to support her? No, I don't believe she cares at all. The only reason I'll let you stumble out of here is because it will amuse me to watch her dangle you like a pike on a fisherman's hook. You'll learn soon enough that a queen's favor is only worth as much as she wants it to be." He was satisfied to see uncertainty pass over Linton's face. "I'm taking Samara home now. And if I ever get wind of you sniffing around her again, I will kill you. Do not for a second think that I won't."

He touched Samara's elbow. "Come. We're getting you out of here."

"Just a moment, please," she whispered. Clutching her cloak, she stepped around Cade and went to Linton. He stared at her from eyes that were beginning to blacken around the sockets. She gazed back for a few seconds.

Then she lifted her knee and jammed it between his legs with such force Cade flinched as if he'd felt the blow himself. Linton dropped to his knees before toppling.

"That's all." She drew a deep shuddering breath and turned her back on Linton, curled in a ball and whimpering. "I'm ready to leave."

Cade and Hayden flanked her as they escorted her back into the gallery, where a crowd of party guests—headed by the girls Cade now realized were Linton's sisters—gaped at them. Samara didn't seem to notice their attention, or that of the guests who still danced in the Great Hall. They collected Aunt Madge and went out to the street, where their carriage waited, the horses' breath puffing white in the cold night air.

"Come," Cade said, so exhausted he felt he could curl up in the street and fall asleep. Samara clung to him. "Let's go home."

Chapter Twenty-One

December 1558

IT HAD BEEN A DRY AUTUMN, A SURPRISE AFTER SEVERAL WET ones, and for that Thomas, Earl of Brentford, was grateful as he, his men at arms, and the coach carrying his two younger daughters rumbled down the road toward the London city wall.

"Dickon," Thomas called. The man-at-arms at the front of the party wheeled around and rode to meet him, the horse beneath him surprisingly comfortable supporting Dickon's considerable weight.

"Yes, milord?"

"I want you to ride ahead and let the Marquess of Wexley know we should reach him several hours past nightfall." Thomas scanned the skyline in front of him, made jagged by the houses. God's teeth, how many people called the city home nowadays? They were miles from the wall, yet Thomas could hear the stubborn lowing of cows dragged to market, the squawk of chickens dodging squeaking cart wheels, the cries of children and those hawking their wares. London was the same; it had just spread like a stain.

He didn't want to be here. He had grown too accustomed to the quiet comforts of home to be happy among the filthy sprawl of the capital. He should be sitting before the fire drinking cider pressed from the last apples of the season, preparing for Christ's Mass and, perhaps, Samara's wedding.

But as Earl of Brentford it was his duty to attend Her Majesty's funeral, and he couldn't deny to himself that he was anxious to see how Samara fared. He'd heard little from her in the three months since she'd left his house and couldn't decide if that was a good thing or a bad thing. Either she was distracted by the many eligible candidates for her hand and found little time to write, or she had nothing to report.

He supposed if Easton had come to his senses, Thomas would have had a message from him, at least. But he'd had nothing, save a reply to his own letter, in which Easton regretfully informed him that Riverview House did not have room to host Thomas, his daughters, and the myriad others who had accompanied them to London, and that Thomas would have to take Hal up on his offer to let them stay at Wexley House.

Their party rolled down Aldersgate Street, toward Cheapside and eventually Fenchurch Street, where Wexley kept his London townhouse. Thomas wished he could hear Katherine and Cecily's reactions to the sights—the spire of St. Paul's Cathedral, the bustling Cheapside markets, street-facing facades of close-knit buildings unlike any they'd ever seen. If only he could have brought them into a happier situation! With the city in mourning for Her Majesty, and wary of the new queen who even now was said to be settling herself into Whitehall with her own government, there would be little amusement for his daughters.

Sundown was but a distant memory by the time they drove through the opened gate into the vast courtyard of Wexley House. Thomas had been here several times before, but in his long-gone youth, and he marveled at the opulence of the house. Hal, for all his bluster, had an eye for beauty and had designed his townhouse to reflect it.

It was the only thing that caused Thomas to regret that a match would not be made with Waltham: Samara would have adored the house.

He dismounted and handed the reins to a hovering groom in crimson and gold livery, then turned to see his daughters being helped out of their coach by identically clad male servants. Cecily gazed at her surroundings, her mouth agape in wonder, but Katherine was more circumspect. A slight widening of her eyes was the only thing that gave away her awe.

"Welcome to Wexley House, my lord. My ladies," said the steward when they entered the hall. "His lordship the marquess will be in to greet—"

"Tom!" came a bellow from one of the cavernous archways that led, if Thomas remembered correctly, toward the Great Chamber.

"—you in a moment," the steward finished.

"Glad you made it, Tom. Hello, Lady Katherine. Lady Cecily." They curtsied prettily. "If only it wasn't under such circumstances!"

"What is the situation?" Thomas asked, keeping his voice low so not to scare his daughters.

Hal swiped at his mouth, where a rather large crumb of bread stuck in his mustache. It dropped to the floor. "There isn't much of a situation, Tom. Save gossip and speculation, city's been quiet as a church mouse since Her Majesty's passing." They crossed themselves. "The lady—I mean, Queen Elizabeth—has been at Whitehall for days. She hears Mass daily. She has promised to undo none of Her Majesty's work in reinstating the true faith. But her government is already hard at work. Doing what, nobody knows. Yet. She has issued a summons to members of Parliament to convene in January. I suppose we'll find out then."

"I suppose we will." Thomas glanced at his daughters, standing off to the side, their eyes lowered, waiting patiently to be shown to their rooms. What would become of them? Could he get them safely married and living somewhere else in the event the new queen decided that England's Catholics must burn?

"It will work out," Hal said with certainty. "It must. God's teeth, Tom, she's giving the late queen a Catholic burial in accordance to her wishes! She wouldn't do that if she had plans to kill us all."

Hal's voice rose with his excitement. Thomas had to change the subject.

"So where's young Waltham, eh?" he asked.

"He went to a party or a masque of some sort," Hal replied. "He got in shortly after the clock struck midnight. The boy's not really one for merrymaking. I think he's already sleeping it off. Speaking of sleeping, Tom, you look like you haven't in weeks. I'm a beast for keeping you up, and your pretty little daughters, too. I'll call servants to show you to your rooms."

Thomas smiled in gratitude, and before he knew it he was in a lavish bedchamber with his body servant and a groom Hal's steward had sent to help Thomas unpack and prepare for bed. The Wexley servant set up a screen in the adjacent chamber, and Thomas stepped behind it to change from his dusty traveling clothes into a nightshirt.

From the bedchamber, the idle chatter of two chambermaids reached his ears.

"And when the door opened there she was, her gown torn so she was bared to the waist!" one of them exclaimed in a whisper.

"No! An earl's daughter would never let herself be found like that," the other one cried aloud. "He must have exaggerated."

Thomas chuckled. Servants thrived on gossip, be they city folk or country. He pitied the earl whose daughter was the subject of the tale, exaggerated though it probably was.

"Aye, it's the truth. Benjamin told me." The first maid sounded certain that this Benjamin was a paragon of honesty. More likely he had told her the story to win a few minutes under her skirt.

"And with Viscount Linton? The Earl of Ashbury's son?" the other maid asked.

"Aye. The party was at his house. His family has rented one on Fleet Street, Benjamin said." A pause. "The best part, though, is that the Earl of Easton found her. And it wouldn't surprise me if she's been dallying with him too. She's been staying at his house while searching for a husband, you see."

Thomas stopped with his gown half over his head. His breath stuck in his throat.

Samara? Were they talking about Samara?

"She'll never find one now," the second maid said, and they both giggled.

The swish of skirts told him when he'd been left alone.

The blood rushed to his head, roared in his ears and blurred his sight.

His Samara? The subject of cruel and salacious gossip? It couldn't be true—his daughter had far too much pride to allow anyone to take liberties, let alone a traitor! Ashbury's son? What in God's name was Samara doing at *his* house? Where the hell was Easton to have allowed it?

It couldn't be true. Not his daughter.

But he knew how the world worked. True or not, she was probably ruined.

No, no probably about it. Word of the incident, whatever had happened, was out.

She *was* ruined. And her sisters too.

How could I have raised a daughter so prone to carelessness? And why didn't Easton stop her?

He hadn't felt such fury since the midwife told him Anne wouldn't survive Cecily's birth.

He called for his body servant in a voice he barely recognized as his own. Told the man to help him dress again; he had to go out. Avoided the servant's knowing glance—he knew too? already?—and stepped into the simplest clothes he could find. He wouldn't be long. He was going to Riverview to fetch his daughter from the home of the man he'd trusted to protect her.

❋

Samara couldn't stop shaking.

At first, she had felt only fear. Would she ever forget her shock as Robert shoved her into that room? The hopelessness that flooded her when she realized what he intended? She doubted it. Her perceptions of the world had been effectively shattered the moment she found out his true intentions toward her.

But when Cade and Hayden burst in to rescue her, the terror that gripped her gave way to relief, and she'd trembled against Cade's warmth. His arms around her assured her that even though she would never again look at life in the same way, she was safe. She'd be all right. When they'd led her away from the knowing eyes of the party guests and into the street, she was just aware enough to shiver at the cold judgment in their stares. And when she'd gotten home and into the warm, comforting bath a tearful Betty had prepared after hearing of her ordeal, she shuddered with the agony of knowing she'd failed. She'd been made a fool. She'd always *been* a fool.

Now she shook with fury.

She'd dismissed Betty and begged Aunt Madge to seek her bed. Samara was in no mood for company, or any bit of weak comfort they might try to offer. She wanted to scream. Hit something. Break something.

Cry.

How could she have been so *stupid*? Why hadn't she listened to Cade when he'd tried to warn her? She'd been awful to him, and Hayden too. Why, she'd actually told them to go back to their *whores* and leave her alone!

What kind of person *was* she? No wonder Cade didn't want her!

Which was the worst part of all, now that she realized she loved him.

She'd never loved Robert. Not even close. She hadn't had time. He had been but a passing infatuation—a result of the thrill of having such a handsome and, by all appearances, important man pay attention to her. But although she was furious to find out he'd lied to her, she was not furious in the way she would have been if it had been Cade. That would have hurt. There was no hurt from Robert's betrayal. She just felt so *stupid.*

And to have Cade know of her stupidity—that didn't bear thinking of.

She'd never been so happy to see someone as she had been to see him when he burst into the room where Robert had her. And not just because she knew he was there to rescue her, but because he was there at all. She felt safe in his presence. Protected. Cared for, even when he had never said anything to make her believe he did care. She'd come to the stunning realization that as long as Cade was there, no harm could come to her. And she would never allow harm to come to him.

And when he'd led her away from the shocked and judging eyes of the party goers, she hadn't wanted to let him go. He'd allowed her to cling to him the entire walk to the courtyard, the ride home, into Riverview and up the stairs to her rooms. He'd only disengaged her once Betty was there to take over, and she'd immediately missed him, as though he'd taken a piece of her with him. Is that what love felt like? No wonder her father had wandered for so many years, bereft, when he'd lost it.

She groaned and flung her arms across the table set by the hearth, sweeping a few pewter plates, a goblet, and her scent bottle to the floor with a satisfying series of crashes. But the clatter of metal hitting stone had barely faded before she regretted the action. They weren't her plates to dent. And it was late. No doubt Betty, or some other servant, outraged at being woken, would soon come running into the room to see what had happened.

As if in response to her thought, someone tapped on her closed chamber door.

"I'm sorry," Samara called. "I don't need any help. I'm fine. I apologize for the noise."

"Samara?"

The voice on the other side of the door was not that of a servant, or even Aunt Madge.

It was Cade.

Her heart leapt into her throat.

She wasn't anywhere near ready to face him yet. But her soul screamed out for him.

"Really, Cade, I'm fine," she said. She cursed the tremble in her voice that revealed her lie.

"I'd like to talk to you."

She cast an agonized glance at the mess on the floor and for at least the third time that night blinked away tears. She couldn't push him away. He'd risked so much for her, and it could be one of the last moments she got to spend with him. Surely once he was certain that she was all right, he would abandon her. Not that she'd blame him. Why would he tarnish his own name by associating with her?

"A moment," she said, and dug a robe from her chest to cover her sheer chemise.

She went to the door and lifted the latch to reveal him. And though her heart filled at the sight of him, she couldn't meet his probing gaze, instead fixing her eyes on the decorative sconce on the wall behind him. She focused on the dancing flame and the slight, sweet fragrance of beeswax.

"May I come in?" he pressed gently.

Samara folded her trembling arms over herself, then almost laughed at the ridiculousness of the action. Why was she trying to hide? At this point, the only person who'd seen more of her body was Betty, who'd changed her nappies.

"Of course. This is your house," she said, and retreated. She knelt on the floor and began to pick up her mess.

She stopped when she felt his hand on her shoulder. The warmth seeped through the thin lawn of her robe and chemise.

"Leave it," he said. "I'll send someone to see to it. We need to talk about what happened tonight."

"What is there to say?" She got to her feet, grudgingly accepting the hand he offered. His knuckles were bandaged. She hoped they didn't hurt. "I'm a fool. You warned me, and I paid you no heed. In fact, I was downright insulting. Do you remember the things I said to you, Cade?"

"I remember," he assured her. The prickles of guilt reminded her she wasn't worthy of him. "But Samara, there are so many things I could have done to keep this from happening but didn't. I should have written your father from the start. He knows what Ashbury did. I could have tried harder to find out what Linton was after once he set his sights on you."

"You were busy doing the queen's work," she argued. "It's not as if you could deny her to cater to me. Besides, my father asked you to accompany me. Not hover like an overprotective nursemaid."

"My protection, I believe, was part of the deal," Cade replied. "Your father didn't ask for it, but I don't think he'd have wanted me to bring you here if he didn't expect me to provide it when I could."

"It doesn't matter." Those stubborn tears were back, swelling behind her eyes. She looked away from him and hoped he didn't notice the violent trembling of her bottom lip. "I'm ruined. People saw me, and they will tell others, and no one will want to marry me because of the reputation this incident will bring me. Even the horrible Lord Waltham won't want me now, though in that case this whole thing might be seen as a blessing. Anyway, *it doesn't matter.* I'm done."

"That's not necessarily true." His voice was soft.

There was something in his voice, something that distracted her from the anguish inside her that strained to be freed. She swung her gaze back to meet his.

"What do you mean?"

"You don't—you're not ruined." He swallowed hard—she watched the muscles in his throat tense and relax with the action. "I will marry you."

She stood stock-still, her breath caught in her throat. Hours seemed to pass as her pulse hummed and she couldn't, not for the life of her, put together a coherent string of words in response.

He would marry her? After everything she'd done, everything she'd put him through?

There was no one else quite like him, she was certain. Her blood sang in her veins.

But—

"Why?" she asked, when she'd meant to say *yes*.

He looked taken aback.

"Because it makes sense," he answered, his eyes clouded with his confusion. "I'm an earl who needs a wife. I can't imagine the new queen having any use for me, so I'll be going back to Easton. And you need a husband more than ever. Who better than myself? We're friends. You won't even have to leave your family, really. It's the most convenient solution." He chuckled, softly and a little sheepishly.

Convenient. Not a word about affection. Could he not even pretend?

"You don't want to marry me," she said.

His jaw twitched. "I wouldn't have offered if I didn't."

"No, maybe not," she replied slowly. *What are you doing?* her inner voice shrieked. *This is what you've wanted! Say yes!*

"I realize it's not the epic, sweeping romance you hoped for," he said. "But I thought it might be mutually agreeable."

Mutually agreeable. As if she were a business deal he was trying to make.

Her heart, already bruised, began to crack. He could not, under any circumstances, find out how she felt. Even if she could convince him, and she was entirely sure she couldn't. Only a week ago she'd thought herself if not in love, then close to being in love with Robert Hunter. Why would he trust her if she now said she loved him? Could she even trust herself?

"Oh, Cade," she said. "It's so kind of you to want to help me. Really," she said. Her voice, in her sorrow, shook. "You've done nothing *but* try to help me from the very first day. But are you sure this is what you want? Do you honestly think you can live with me?"

Can I live without him, *now that I know?*

"What are you afraid of, Samara?" he asked gently. "What happened with Linton will not happen again. Especially not if you're married. But if you refuse to face what happened tonight, it will eat you alive. What then?"

And if she didn't marry him, who knew what would happen to Katherine, and especially Cecily? They needed her to do this.

"I am terrified," she whispered. "Of it all. Of being an adult, responsible for not only myself but for other people. Of being a wife. I know nothing of being a wife, you know. And children? Nothing scares me so much as bearing children. Women die, Cade. In childbirth. Sometimes before, sometimes after." He opened his mouth to speak but she continued before he could. "I am not prepared to die. I enjoy life far too much to give it up so soon."

The sympathy in his eyes was almost more than she could bear.

"What happened to you tonight was terrible, and I will always blame myself for not stopping it when I had the chance," he said. "But Samara, you cannot always expect someone to come to your rescue." He passed a hand over his forehead, and when he dropped it back down to his side, he looked exhausted. "Yes, adults die. Every day. There is always the chance when we wake up in the morning that it could be the last morning we see. I could leave this room, fall down the stairs, and break my neck. You could go outside to draw, step too close to the river, and drown. Hayden could catch a chill. One of your sisters, the sweat. The new queen could burn us all for our faith. Death comes for everyone! Failing to accept that will not keep you a child forever. It will simply render you unable to deal with the reality of life."

She listened to his monologue with the dawning realization that he was absolutely right. This entire time, since she first set foot in the city, she had been play-acting at being an adult without assuming any of the responsibility. She was lucky that Linton was the only bad thing that had happened to her and that Cade, who she now knew she loved with her entire heart and soul, was offering her marriage.

"Cade," she began, but faltered when a knock sounded on the door.

He ignored it. "Yes, Samara?"

"I—" The knock came again. Smothering a curse, Cade flung it open to reveal Blackwell.

"I apologize for the late hour, my lord. My lady," he said with a nod in Samara's direction. "But the Earl of Brentford is here."

✳

It took a moment for Blackwell's words to register.

"Brentford? Here? At this hour?" He was exhausted. He was confused. He could not deal with Brentford right now.

"He's heard."

The horrified whisper came from behind him, where just moments ago Samara had stood confessing her deepest fears to him, the faded remnants of her sunny freckles the only color on her pale, tear-stained face.

"Don't be ridiculous." Cade heard the frustration in his own voice and winced. She'd had a horrible night, and he knew he'd shocked her by proposing. Hell, he'd shocked himself. He certainly hadn't known he'd been thinking it until the words fell from his mouth. Her refusal to answer, however, had him just a little piqued. "How could he have heard? We were not even made aware of his presence in the city, so he can't have been here long enough to hear anything. We've been home no more than two hours."

"He knows."

Cade bit back his sigh. Stubborn, always stubborn.

"Stay here," he ordered her. "I'll tell your father you're asleep. He can't see you like this. He will ask questions."

"All right."

Her immediate agreement was a surprise, but one he welcomed. Without a backward glance he left the room, pulling the heavy door shut behind him.

Blackwell must have sensed the tension but kept politely silent as he accompanied Cade to the Great Hall. Sure enough, Brentford waited bent by the hearth, his gloves tucked under the arm of his cloak as he waved his bare hands before the fire.

"Brentford!" Cade said, forcing as much pleasantry as he could muster into his voice. "We'd no idea you were in town already. Welcome to Riverview."

Samara's father straightened and jerked his head toward Cade. The blazing fury in the man's gray eyes sent Cade a step backward. He tossed his gloves to the floor and stalked toward him.

Whatever this late-night visit meant, it couldn't be good.

"What have you done?" Brentford asked.

"What have *I* done?" Who did the man think he was? "I've no idea what you mean, Brentford."

"I've spent the last nine days traveling with my daughters to a city I can no longer stand to attend the funeral of a queen who might be the only reason we spent the last few years practicing the true faith without fear for our lives. I finally arrive, hours past sundown, hungry and exhausted, to hear that Samara was just tonight discovered alone in a room, half-undressed, with the son of a known traitor. I demand to know, Easton, *how this happened!*"

He roared the last sentence and Cade took another step backward. Damn it to hell, Brentford *did* know! How was it possible?

"How did you—"

"Find out? Easily. I had barely dismounted my horse before the Marquess of Wexley's servants started whispering about it. They made an attempt to appear discreet, of course, but you know servants. Gossip's worth more to them than the shillings they receive on quarter days. How *they* heard so quickly is an entirely different question, but they did, and I can only assume others have as well." The man's face was crimson verging on purple. Cade wished desperately for some wine.

"I can't imagine how word traveled *that* quickly. It happened less than two hours ago." Brentford's mouth opened, undoubtedly to spew forth more ill-directed rage. Cade stopped him by raising his hands. "What you've said, however, is true. Robert Hunter, Viscount Linton, has been courting Lady Samara for the last few months. This evening, at a party held at his house, he was able to compromise her—"

Cade paused as Brentford twitched like he wanted to shove Cade but changed his mind. A wise decision. Cade had more than a head's worth of height on the man and the benefit of youth.

"Knave," he growled instead. "I sent Samara with you because I thought you would keep her safe. After all I've done to help you, *this* is how you repay me? By allowing a traitor and a heretic to have his way with my daughter?"

"Allow me to finish," Cade interrupted. His blasted head ached. He wished Riverview empty so he could get a moment of peace. "He didn't lay a hand on her. Not in the way you think. She remains— untouched." Heat flooded his face. He'd never spoken about a woman in such a way. Especially not with her father. "It was a ruse. His sisters were in on it. They distracted Lady Morley, Hayden, and me, and as they did so Linton tricked Samara into thinking he would show her some portraits. When she went with him, he dragged her into an empty room and tried to assault her. Hayden and I discovered them before any physical damage was done. But she was seen by party guests in a state of disarray. There's only one conclusion they would have drawn. We got her out of there and brought her directly back to Riverview. She's asleep now, but she has not left her rooms since we returned."

"She went with him *willingly?*" It was a valid question—Cade himself wondered why she had gone with Linton when she was aware of his true intentions, and after he had told her to stay clear of him—but did Brentford have to be so loud? Cade was surprised that the sheer volume of Brentford's voice didn't rattle the precious glass in the windows. Soon the entire household would be gathered in the hall to see what was going on. "He was courting her? How was he able to get near her? What is wrong with you that you would allow such a thing?"

"It was not for lack of trying," Cade shot back, although his time, he knew he deserved Brentford's wrath. He should have tried harder. Locked her in her rooms. Offered for her earlier. "I warned her several times about his reputation. But the man was able to convince Her Majesty of his repentance. He was assisting Master Boxall, after all. If he could convince a queen, why not a naïve young girl dazzled by her first romantic experience?"

Brentford's face, so hard it appeared hewn from granite, crumbled.

"My poor Samara," he moaned. "She is ruined. No one will have her now. Not even Waltham."

"It's not necessarily true that no one will have her," Cade said. He wondered how Brentford would react to *this*. "Just moments ago, *I* offered her marriage."

The other man's visage brightened ever so slightly.

"You did?" he asked. The change in his toned was marked. "That was good of you, Easton. And I won't lie. It's what I wanted from the beginning. I'm too much a sentimental fool. I thought she'd enjoy the experience of court and the idea of choosing for herself. I always hoped she'd choose you."

So Cade had gone from knave to savior. He would have laughed if this entire night didn't have him so damned bewildered.

"She has not answered me." He gave a little laugh. "In fact, I think she might refuse."

The smile froze on Brentford's face. "I'm sorry?"

"She has not given me an answer." Cade shrugged. "She is scared to death of adulthood. I don't know what happened to her as she was growing up to make it so, but she seems to want nothing more than to take care of you in your dotage and die a maid in your house."

"She…" A strange look crossed Brentford's face. "The entire city of London thinks her ruined, yet the most suitable candidate for her husband has offered for her anyway and she *will not answer?*" Brentford's face again took on a tinge reminiscent of the skin of the damson plums Cade's mother used to make into preserves. "That idiot girl. What am I to do with her? She is sleeping, you say?"

"No, my lord father."

Brentford's gaze lit on something behind Cade and over his shoulder. Cade heard Samara's light footsteps on the smooth stone floor as she entered the hall and came to stand behind him.

He turned to look at her. Her face was scrubbed clean of tears, and her hair was as neat as it could be, but her eyes were still red-rimmed, and she had obviously dressed in a hurry. She wore one of the old-fashioned gowns he'd seen her in a few times.

"Samara." Brentford narrowed his eyes. "Explain to me what happened tonight."

"Cade told the truth," she said. "Lord Linton and his family have no money. Her Majesty fined them heavily for their roles in the rebellion. She took their property. They have almost nothing. Lord Linton learned of me and my dowry and lied, telling me that his family had reverted to the true faith. As Cade said, he managed to convince Her Majesty. Why wouldn't I believe him?" Her voice trembled ever so faintly. "A countrified bumpkin such as I would believe anything a man told her so long as he worded it prettily enough."

Cade felt a pang in his chest.

Brentford closed his eyes, obviously collecting his wits.

"Fetch your cloak, and Betty. I am taking you back to Wexley House with me."

"But, my lord father—"

"*Now.*" Brentford's tone left no room for argument.

She stood there. For a moment Cade wondered if she would defy him, and what her father's reaction would be if she did. He hadn't seen such a range of emotion from the other earl in the entire time he'd known him and found it impossible to guess. But without a word Samara whirled and fled back up the stairs.

Brentford rubbed his hand across his forehead. When he took it away, he looked so tired Cade wondered if he shouldn't offer the man a bed for the night. He didn't really want to send Samara away with him either. Brentford was angry. What would he do to her in his fury? Hadn't she been through enough for one night?

"I don't blame you entirely for this, Easton," Brentford said. "Surely there must have been something you could have done to keep her from falling prey to Linton, but my daughter has always been headstrong. She would have found a way to be with him if it was what she wanted."

"Those were my thoughts exactly." A vision of her fashioning a rope from her gowns and dropping catlike into the garden forced the hint of a smile to his face. "I thought if I couldn't stop her, it would be enough to stay near her. But Linton was a step ahead of me, always."

"I just don't know what I'll do with her now." Brentford shook his head. "Even if Waltham will still have her, I don't wish it. She's too good for a fool like him. But I have nothing else with which to threaten her. Perhaps I'll try talking her into accepting your proposal.

I had sincerely hoped the two of you would come to some kind of an agreement without the hindrance of my meddling. I was certain she had some kind of affinity for you, even before I sent her off."

"Oh?" But before he could ask why Brentford thought that might be, or tell him that he wanted Samara to *want* to marry him, not be talked into it, Samara returned with her cloak, a bleary-eyed Betty with a small trunk, and a meowing basket.

"What is that?" Brentford asked.

"My kitten. Danaë."

"No. There's no way to take it with us. I was in such a hurry to get here and find out if what Wexley's servants said was true that I brought only Dickon, and we rode horseback. The animal stays here. I'll have Wexley send someone for it and the rest of your things tomorrow."

"As you wish, my lord father. Betty, put the basket down." Her eyes sparkled in the dim light of the hall. Was she about to cry again? "Help me put on my cloak."

Cade turned from the sight of Betty helping Samara into the long, marten-lined cloak he'd thrown over her earlier to cover her state of disarray. God, had that really been just a few hours ago? This was turning into the longest night of his life. Even those nights spent in the dark of Castel Sant'Angelo with only rats and fleas for company hadn't taken nearly as long to turn to sunrise.

"Thank you for everything, Easton. I'm sorry to have brought so much trouble upon you. Samara will stay with me at Wexley House from now on. We've much to discuss." Brentford grasped Samara by her upper arm. "Come. I've no wish to cause an uproar in Wexley's house by strolling in just before dawn." With her arm in his hand, he began to walk toward the courtyard entrance.

Samara turned one last time to look at him, and he was floored by the hopelessness in her eyes. Her spirit was battered and bruised, but he hoped it was yet unbroken. That she should look that way seemed a crime to him. She had made one mistake! A major one, to be sure, but certainly the rest of her life shouldn't hinge on one error. There had to be another solution.

There is, and you offered it to her, a voice in his head reminded him. *She did not respond. Her situation is entirely her fault.*

Maybe. Maybe not.

Samara's lips parted as if she would say something. But her father dragged her from sight, and Cade soon heard Brentford shouting to his companion to take Betty up. Moments later the clopping of horses' hooves started and faded as they rode away, out of the courtyard and to the street.

She was gone.

Cade wished for a bed to materialize right behind him so he could drop onto it. Exhaustion threatened to overwhelm him. This horrible night had finally ended. He should march right up the stairs to his rooms, fling himself into his bed, and not get out until the queen's funeral.

Or he could have a few goblets of wine to try and forget, even for a few hours, about all that had happened. Samara's face. Her tears. Brentford's fury.

As he started for his study where he kept a jug of wine for such occasions, he laughed at the idea of even pretending there was a choice.

Chapter Twenty-Two

SAMARA PRESSED HER CHEEK AGAINST THE SOFTNESS OF HER FA-
ther's cloak, allowing the wool to absorb the tears that had been
scalding her cheeks since they'd cleared the gate at Riverview. They
galloped fast and hard through the streets, quiet now at this late hour,
and Samara realized her father must have been in a hurry to get her to
Wexley House, for he hadn't even attempted to make her ride pillion.
Whether his speed was out of concern for her safety on the London
streets or eagerness to get her to a place where he could beat her for
her idiocy, she didn't know but suspected she would soon find out.

Nothing was going the way it should. She should have shrieked
her acceptance of Cade's proposal the minute the words left his
mouth. Instead she'd wavered, allowing her fear to override the tiny
bit of good sense she possessed. So what if he didn't love her? That
could come later. If she'd said yes, they both would have what they
needed. He would have gained a wife to run his household, if she
could learn quickly enough, and bear his children so long as one of
their births didn't kill her—both things she had never before wanted
any part of but would gladly do for him. She, on the other hand,
would have not only a husband but one she loved.

Now, instead of celebrating a betrothal she had made her goal
months ago, she was bound for the Marquess of Wexley's home where
she would, presumably, spend the remainder of her time in London. It
was the worst possible thing that could happen. Away from her, Cade
would have ample opportunity to rethink his proposal and would no
doubt come to the conclusion that he'd spoken in haste. He'd realize

what a mistake he'd made and count himself fortunate that he'd found an escape. And Samara would either be married off to Waltham—assuming he'd still have her—or to someone else, and who knew what would happen to Katherine and Cecily? Her stupidity could have cost them their futures. For that, she would never forgive herself.

The cold November wind bit at her wet cheeks.

The trip seemed to last both seconds and hours. Eventually her father and Dickon directed their horses into a courtyard dimly lit by the silvery full moon overhead. Instinct nagged her to look at the walls around her, and for a moment she allowed herself to marvel at the strange architecture that echoed some of the illustrations she'd seen in one of her father's books on ancient Greece and Rome. Had there ever existed a more beautiful structure? She never would have suspected the boorish Marquess of Wexley would have such exquisite taste in buildings.

Then again, one should not judge a person based on casual acquaintance. A lesson she'd certainly learned that night.

"Come," her father commanded, and strode toward the entry.

She didn't follow at once, instead pausing to reflect on her options. She couldn't go back to Riverview: she had no idea where she was in relation to it, and it wouldn't do to get lost. Anyway, Cade wouldn't want to see her again tonight. Perhaps ever. She *really* didn't want to go inside and face a household that already seemed to know everything that had happened to her at Robert's party. Had her sisters heard? How could she face them, knowing that her idiocy could have ruined their lives?

She could hide. Stake out a spot in the stables until daybreak, when she would make a run for it. She could disguise herself, find work as a lady's maid. She was a lady herself, she knew what the job entailed.

"Samara!"

Her father's roar from the entrance to Wexley House brought her crashing back down to reality. A lady's maid? What was she thinking? She could barely take care of herself, let alone someone else.

Whatever happened, she must deal with the situation. No matter the consequences. *She was an adult.* She could do that much.

Samara squared her shoulders and started toward her fate.

❀

At least she could be grateful that the household was silent, its residents apparently gone to bed. She was already mortified. She would never be able to live with the idea of the entire Wexley family and its staff being privy to the admonition she was about to receive.

They were alone in what Samara guessed was the marquess's Great Chamber. Two lit candles illuminated the room, leaving her even more embarrassed that someone had anticipated her father bringing her in here. Betty was gone. Samara hoped she was off somewhere seeing a room prepared, because once this traumatic night was over, she wanted to burrow down in bed and never come out again.

"I want to know everything that happened between you and Viscount Linton." Her father's voice was dangerously low, a tone she'd never heard him use before but which instinct told her did not bode well.

Samara swallowed hard.

"Everything?" she asked, her voice little more than a birdlike squeak.

"Everything."

Where to begin? With their first meeting at St. James's Palace, when he'd helped her find her way out? It had seemed an innocent enough event at the time, but had she known just how things would end, she would have decided to wander lost rather than let him help. Oh, but she was disgusted with herself. Robert had met all the criteria she'd established for her future husband. Handsome, of course, but also kind—or so he'd seemed—and a member of the court. Who would have seen him for what he really was?

Cade did.

Maybe it was a good thing she was ruined. She would never again be able to trust her judgment in such a situation. Not that she would want to be in such a situation again, now that she'd fallen in love with Cade. And even if she hadn't, it wasn't as if her father would be eager to again leave the choice up to her. No, despite her father's assurances that he believed her intelligent enough to choose wisely, she had proven herself incapable of *that*. How disappointed he must be.

Haltingly, Samara told her father of the entire courtship, such as it was. She told him of their first meeting. She talked about dancing with the viscount on the last night the queen had felt well enough to stay up, and the picnic he'd brought to Riverview on that rainy October day. She told him of how Robert stopped to see her after word of Her Majesty's death got out and how he'd invited her to a party in celebration of the queen's life. Even now her face burned with shame. She marveled that she could be so stupid. A party, when they were in mourning? How had she not seen through him?

Her father listened calmly, only the occasional twitch of his cheek or clenching of fists revealing his feelings about what she said. When she had finished her story, ending with Cade and Hayden bursting into the empty room but leaving out the part about Cade beating the viscount to a bloody pulp, her father closed his eyes for a count of ten before he opened them again. Samara's heart thudded painfully against her ribs at least fifty times before he spoke.

"It's partly my fault," he surprised her by saying. "I should have prepared you better. Dance lessons and a new wardrobe were necessary, but I should have also warned you not to lose your head to the first man to show you attention. I know you're intelligent for a woman, but you are yet a woman. You need more guidance than I provided. I had hoped Easton would take up the reins once you were here. I did not expect him to abandon you to your own devices."

But he didn't! The queen had him doing things for her. And he did try to help me, though I didn't know it at the time. Even I know that if he'd come right out and forbade me from seeing Robert, I would have defied him.

Her father sighed and rubbed his forehead, where the hair that fell over was now more gray than brown. When had that happened?

"Perhaps if your mother had been here to teach you," he said. "But there is no point to wondering about that."

He fell silent again, and the pause lasted so long Samara thought he'd forgotten she was there.

"My lord father?" she asked. "If I might say something?"

He lifted an eyebrow and nodded.

"Lord Easton did not abandon me. Her Majesty had him doing certain jobs for her, and he was not always able to be near me. And he did try, several times, to warn me about Lord Linton. I did not want to believe him. Please don't blame this on him. It is entirely my fault." She lowered her eyes.

"You are both somewhat to blame. It doesn't matter. What's done is done." He sighed again. "It's late. Both of us need sleep. Perhaps tomorrow we'll know better how to handle the situation."

By tomorrow, Cade will have forgotten about me, Samara thought as she entered the candlelit chamber that had been prepared for her. Her body throbbed with exhaustion as she removed the old blue gown and untied the ribbon in her hair. She glanced at the bed, which was large and inviting, but knew there was no way her mind was quiet enough for sleep. And she couldn't draw, either, for she'd left her case in Danaë's basket, hadn't she?

Frustrated tears filled her eyes and spilled over cheeks already stiff from earlier bouts of crying. But no sooner had they started than she realized what she *could* do. There was no way she would sleep tonight, which meant she would be up with the sun. If she could find a way to sneak out of Wexley House first thing in the morning, she could get to Cade before he had time to change his mind about his proposal. She could tell him how right he'd been about her and that he was correct, a marriage between them made perfect sense, and the only reason she'd hesitated was because fear had clouded her judgment. If his offer still stood, she would be proud to be his wife.

Samara took her blue gown from where she'd thrown it on the floor and draped it over a chair. Beside it, on the floor, she set her soft, worn leather boots. The ribbon that had earlier tied her hair back from her face went into the pile, as did her cloak and a pair of gloves. She would need to bribe a groom to accompany her, for she had at least learned enough not to roam the city unaccompanied, so she dug a pouch of coin from the trunk and hoped it would be enough to buy not only an escort but his silence.

She surveyed the items and hoped she wasn't forgetting anything. She couldn't afford to have to turn back. She needed to be out at first light if she was to avoid detection and get back before anyone noticed her absence.

Samara splashed her face with water, hoping to erase traces of tears and minimize any swelling around her eyes. She had to at least try to look decent. She ran a comb through her hair. She dug her scent bottle out of the trunk and put it on the table next to her ribbon. Then, unable to think of anything else to help pass the few hours until sunrise, she sat on the bed to wait.

And she waited.

In just a few short hours, she would know her future.

❀

Halfway to the library, Cade turned back.

The cat.

The basket in which Betty had carried the creature from Samara's rooms still sat on the floor by the staircase. What was he supposed to do with it? He couldn't leave it there. He might be an idiot, but he wasn't cruel.

But did he want a cat running around Riverview? It wasn't as if there was any point to letting it out to catch mice. How many could it catch in the few hours before someone came to pick it up, as Brentford said they would? And though Riverview was a fraction of the size of some of the other homes along the Strand, it was still large. A cat that small could get so lost it might never be found.

If he lost Danaë, Samara would never forgive him.

Assuming he ever saw her again.

Cursing, he grabbed the basket and carried it to the library. It wouldn't kill him to watch it for the night.

Cade shut the heavy door behind him and set the basket down on the desk before he lifted the cloth that covered it. The kitten lay on another folded length of cloth, curled into a tiny ball of orange fur, whiskers trembling, its forlorn blue eyes staring at Cade with what he would have sworn was accusation, if such a thing was possible from a cat.

"I'm sorry," he said to the animal. "Her father made her leave you. It wasn't my choice. I don't even like cats."

The kitten got to its feet and stretched daintily. It yawned, revealing tiny, needle-like teeth. Then it crouched and wiggled before it leapt to a precarious perch on the edge of the woven basket.

"Look at you," Cade murmured, charmed despite himself. "What magic do cats have that allows them to perform such feats, hmm?"

As if in response, the creature opened its mouth and squeaked.

Cade chuckled. He hadn't lied to the little beast. He didn't like cats. Never had. They were self-involved and self-sufficient, never thinking they needed a thing from anyone and too good to accept it when it was offered. Dogs, loyal and patient, were much more to his taste.

But this cat had personality. Maybe it was its youth. He stretched out a bruised and aching finger to scratch it under the chin. No, not it. She. Danaë was the mother of Perseus, right? The classical reference surprised him. Another insight into Samara's mind.

Before he could make contact, Danaë jumped from the basket's rim to the surface of the desk and butted her small head into his palm. Again and again she nudged him, pausing only to rub her face against his hand. He swept his thumb over the soft fur between her ears and a contented purr rumbled from her throat. She stepped with her two front paws onto his wrist, her sharp claws digging through his linen shirt into his flesh, and scaled his arm before settling on his shoulder like the tamed parrots he'd seen in Rome and France. She gave his cheek a quick bump before settling herself. His shoulder was broad enough that she seemed able to do so quite comfortably.

Her purr sent a soothing vibration through him, which settled in his heart. With that, she had him under her spell.

Cade moved carefully, not wishing to dislodge the small beast that had made her bed in the crook between his neck and his shoulder, and went to the shelf behind his desk where he kept a decanter of wine and a goblet for moments such as this. His battered knuckles screamed as he removed the items, setting them down on the desk beside the basket. Then something inside the basket caught his eye. Something Danaë's body had hidden, something the size and shape of a book but thin. And familiar.

Samara's drawings.

She'd left them here.

Did she know?

He'd had a feeling her insistence that she'd given up drawing had been an act. She was a terrible liar. She loved it too much. That was clear in every line and shadow; he'd seen it the very first time he'd looked at her work. It was her lifeblood, the thing that gave her purpose. She might say what she would; she might even have honestly tried. But there was no way he would believe that she'd given it up entirely.

And he couldn't shake the foggy bit of memory he had, of her leaning over him as he slept off his drunkenness on the floor outside her bedchamber. He'd barely been able to get his eyes open, and when he had, his head throbbed as if someone had removed the top of his skull and speared his brain with a dagger. Had she really been checking him for injuries? He'd probably never know.

He glanced at the door and back at the case. Would he?

"I'll feel guilty later," he promised Danaë as he lifted the cover. She snored delicately in response.

The top drawing was a sketch of the river as seen from the lawns, barges and cargo boats drawn so realistically he could almost hear the splash of water against their hulls. A swan, its regal white neck extended, soared in the sky. He shook his head. Her talent was immense. No matter what her father told her, what kind of man would seek to stifle it in favor of fruit preserves and properly darned stockings?

He moved to the next drawing. This one gave him pause. It was a hand. A man's hand, obviously, the strong fingers wrapped around the stem of a goblet. On the middle finger of the hand was a ring—a solid band studded with bits of onyx. Cade glanced at his own hand, at the ring on his middle finger. At the goblet perched on the table beside him. Next to a decanter of wine.

Shame flooded him, hot and nauseating. So that was how she saw him—as a man who always had a cup of some kind of spirit in his hand. And she was right, damn it. He didn't remember consciously making the decision to numb himself with wine and brandy, but if she thought he did, then he did. He had met a few artists in his travels. They saw things normal people did not.

Cade set the drawings down, uncorked the wine bottle, and went to the window, where he poured the dark red liquid into the hedges and threw the empty bottle out onto the lawn. He'd kick it into the river tomorrow.

Satisfaction was a far more comfortable emotion than shame. He returned to his desk.

The next sketch was Danaë in mid-leap, straining for a ribbon that dangled just out of her reach. He smiled. The kitten's fur was so detailed and lifelike he could have sworn the paper would feel soft if he touched it. Instead he lifted his hand and stroked the subject of the drawing, still nestled against his neck.

He glanced out the window. The sky was beginning to lighten to the same flat grayish-purple as the river at dusk. The household would stir soon; chambermaids would light fires and the cook would start making the day's bread. Life would go on for him, but what would become of Samara?

Don't worry about her. You offered her a way out. She did not take it. She's her father's problem now.

His heart heavy, he turned to the next drawing in the case, the last one, and his breath caught in his throat.

That's me.

To see his own face reflected on a sheet of opaque vellum was jarring, to say the least. How had she done it? She had captured the exact shape of his jaw, the curl of his hair, the line of his nose and— he had to laugh—the thickness of his eyebrows. As he'd never seen himself in sleep before, he couldn't be sure that his mouth really looked that relaxed or his expression that calm, but as everything else was eerily accurate, he had to assume it was a perfect rendition. So she *had* been drawing him when she pretended only to worry that he was sick or injured. He hadn't been dreaming.

"You might never have fallen in love with her."

Words from Hayden that had seemed strange at the time, and that Cade hadn't had a moment to think on all evening. But he had a moment now. *Had* he fallen in love with her?

It was ridiculous. He'd never thought himself capable of loving someone. Making love, yes. But the kind of love where the heart was involved? No. He was too much like his father in that way. He barely had enough heart for himself, let alone to share with someone else.

But then why had he proposed to her? God knew it hadn't crossed his mind before tonight. He'd gone in just to see if she was all right. But one glimpse of her tear-stained face, the sorrow in her voice as she spoke of her ruined life, the thought of her growing old alone in her father's house—or worse, the thought of her being foisted onto someone who would not care about her—had propelled him into action. The words fell from his mouth before the idea even had time to settle in his head.

And she'd rejected him.

Well, not outright. But she'd asked him why. What did it matter? It was a perfect situation. That she didn't see it that way meant only that she didn't see *him* that way. Maybe he'd been wrong about her reaction when she'd caught him with Bess in the alcove. Maybe she was honestly in love with Linton. He glanced down at his bandaged knuckles. Maybe she hated him for the violent drunkard he was. His gut twisted.

Perhaps it was better this way. What kind of husband would he be? Certainly not the kind she deserved. The only example he really had to look to was his father. And though there had been plenty of times when Cade had thought he couldn't possibly be related to the old bastard, there had been several times when he heard or saw himself saying or doing something right out of the old man's playbook. His injured hands would attest to that. Samara didn't deserve the life his mother and Stephen's mother had lived. Maybe she had known exactly what she was doing when she'd said *why* instead of *yes*.

But she didn't say no.

She should have. He was a hypocrite. All those things he'd said to her tonight, about being afraid to grow up, applied to him too, didn't they? He was no paragon of maturity. He might have headed to Easton as soon as he found out he would inherit, but hadn't he come running back to the city at the first opportunity, leaving the souls who depended on him bereft, yet again, of their lord? He had complained mightily of Brentford's demands but had never once offered an alternate solution. And he'd mourned for his old life, a life he hadn't even really stopped living, as he would have mourned the death of a living, breathing person. Certainly harder than he'd mourned his own father.

He was a fraud. No wonder Samara wanted nothing to do with him.

He touched a trembling finger to the vellum and traced where her hand had fondly recreated the curve of his chin and even the dark stubble that shadowed it after a few days without shaving.

The kitten mewed in his ear.

"I know," he said, scratching the scruff of Danaë's neck. "I already miss her, too."

Chapter Twenty-Three

CADE EYED THE MUG OF ALE, LOAF OF BREAD, AND HUNK OF yellow cheese a servant had left on the table in the room attached to his bedchamber. His stomach turned. He had no appetite. By his estimation it was still far too early to be awake after the night he'd had, but the servants from Wexley House would arrive at any moment to pick up Samara's belongings, and knowing that every trace of her was about to be removed from his house made it difficult to return to sleep.

He could have joined Hayden while his cousin broke *his* fast, but he had no desire—at least not yet—to let Hayden know he'd been right. That Cade had fallen for her. He was still having trouble acknowledging it himself. Aunt Madge's company, too, was out of the question. She was much too perceptive and would have asked questions, questions he wasn't ready and frankly had no idea how to answer.

So instead he paced, animal-like, within the confines of his bedchamber, glad that Samara's rooms were not near enough to his that he would be able to hear the sounds of the servants erasing her presence from Riverview.

"My lord?" Blackwell's voice accompanied a knock at the door. "You have a visitor."

A visitor? Who the hell would be calling at this hour of the morning? "Who is it, Blackwell?"

Silence but for some muffled words. Then—

"Lady Samara, my lord earl."

Cade dug his fingers into his hair, pressed his palms against his temples, and squeezed his eyes shut, trying unsuccessfully to ignore the tiny thrill that went through him at the sound of her name. What was she doing here so early? Why was she here? Did her father know where she was? No, of course he didn't. She wouldn't be here if he had any clue. She'd sneaked out, then. What was *wrong* with the girl? Had she learned nothing?

"Cade?" Her voice, soft but persuasive, floated through the closed door. "I don't have much time, but I must speak with you."

Why? He wanted to ask. *So you can reject my proposal in person?* His bitterness surprised even him. Would he be in a better mood if he'd slept?

Well, best to get it over with.

"Come in," he said, his voice dry.

The door slid open, and Samara slipped inside. His gaze scanned her for marks, any evidence that her father had beaten her, and was relieved to find none. Still, she was a mess. Her hair was tied back but still managed to be wind-tangled, her skin pale but for purple shadows framing red-rimmed eyes. She wore the same dress she'd left in the night before, and it needed brushing. She was the most beautiful thing he'd ever seen.

She smiled at him hesitantly. Although he was still hurt at her failure to jump at his offer and not keen on the idea of her knowing what he felt for her, the upward turn of his lips was almost involuntary. She saw it and brightened, which sent a tremor of misguided hope running through him. Was it possible she *wasn't* here to reject him?

Was she stupid enough to have decided he would make her a good husband?

"Does your father know you're here?" he said by way of greeting.

"No," she replied, "which is why I haven't much time. I need to get back to Wexley House before anyone notices I'm gone."

"Well, say what you must," he said. He shifted his weight, held his breath. Waited.

She closed her eyes for a long moment, drawing a deep breath that lifted and dropped her slender shoulders before she opened her eyes again and looked at him.

"Last night you told me things I've long needed to hear," she said. "And you were right. I've been far too desperate to remain a child. My drawing *is* a silly fancy. I never was able to give it up, for all my blathering that I would. And I made no serious effort to find a husband; I merely latched onto the first kind and handsome man to pay me any attention. If I'd given a moment's thought to what my instincts, and you, were telling me for weeks, you never would have found me in that room with Linton last night. I might have ended up wed to Waltham, but at least my reputation would be safe and my sisters would have prospects for marriage." She drew a deep breath. "I spent most of the last few hours at Wexley House realizing that I've been helping no one, least of all myself, by pretending to be an adult while longing to remain a child."

Well, it wasn't an answer to his proposal, but it surprised him nonetheless. He wondered what it had taken for her to come to such a conclusion, for her to feel she needed to vocalize it. To him. She'd grown up in the hours since he'd seen her last. He was proud of her.

"You are not the only one," he admitted. He wouldn't let her take all the blame. "I too spent the hours after you left last night ruminating over my own pathetic position. I was so desperate to escape my father even after his death that I slipped right back into the life I used to lead with barely a thought to the people who now depend on me. Is that something an adult would do? I think not."

She favored him with another little smile. "Then it would seem we are well matched."

His heart gave a short thump. "Are we?"

She nodded. "I hope you still think so," she said. "Cade, I cannot imagine what it took for you to offer me marriage. After all the mistakes I've made, after everything I put you through. You were right. I hesitated only out of fear. But I've vanquished that fear, or, at least, I will make a valiant effort to do so. If…" She trailed off.

He waited, watched as she bit her lip.

"If?" he finally prompted. *She is going to say yes.*

She took another deep breath. "If your offer stands, I accept."

"My offer?" Yes, he would torture her a bit, just to give her a taste of what the last hours had been like for him. Just a taste was all that was possible. It wasn't as if she returned his ardor.

"Yes. Your proposal." Her unwavering gaze met his. "I would be honored to be your wife. If you will have me."

Of course, he would have her. His heart aside, his terror at the thought of being like his father notwithstanding, it *did* remain the most practical solution.

But he had to know.

"Did your father convince you to accept?" he asked.

He almost buckled under the relief that swept through him at the shake of her head.

"No," she said. "We did not speak of your proposal last night. This decision is entirely my own." She lifted her chin just a bit. "An adult decision."

"Yes, it is," he agreed. He couldn't help his grin. "A solid first step."

"I thought so too." She plucked at one of her sleeves. "So, you are still willing? To have me as your wife?"

They would regret this. He felt it in the very marrow of his bones. But the sight of her in front of him—messy hair, shabby gown, flushed cheeks, hopeful eyes—took any common sense he'd once thought he had, turned it upside down, and dumped it on its head.

"I am, yes," he said. "My offer stands. I will marry you."

"Oh." Her breath escaped her in a *whoosh*. "Thank you. I was so afraid you had decided it was a mistake, and that you could do much better for yourself than me. I still think you could. You—you are so much more than I deserve." She blurted out her last words, as if she hadn't really meant to say them, and they puzzled him. But before he could ask her for clarification, she was speaking again.

"I must go. I cannot afford to have my father find me missing." She turned to leave, but at his laughter, whirled back to face him. "What?"

"How exactly do you plan to inform your father of our betrothal?" he asked, still grinning. "Unless you *do* intend to confess your early-morning escapades?"

"Oh, no," she breathed, her hand going to her heart. "I hadn't thought that far ahead." Blood stained her cheeks, and she cast him an apologetic glance. "I'm afraid I'm not off to a good start."

He chuckled again. Laughter? Where was the grim, dejected man who'd woken in his bed that morning? Gone with the morning fog, apparently. Was it because his future was taking shape at last?

Or was it because of her?

"Don't worry," he said. "Just get home as quickly and as safely as you can. I'll write him a message begging him to ask you to consider my offer. When he comes to ask you, tell him you've decided to accept. He'll be so thrilled he won't even think to question your answer. Not that he would, for it wasn't as if you rejected me the first time."

"That's true. I didn't," she said.

"Right. So hurry back to Wexley House. I'll send my message with the servants who are here even now retrieving your things. Just try to avoid being seen by them."

She smiled, and with that his misgivings melted away. They would return, he felt certain, but for now he was willing to bask in happiness.

When was the last time he'd been able to do that? Had he ever?

"Wait," he said to her retreating back. Her hand already on the door, she turned to face him again. He went to the table in front of the fireplace and retrieved her drawings. "You don't have to give them up. I don't want you to. Here."

She accepted the small portfolio with trembling fingers. Her eyes lifted to meet his, and they were filled with such joy his heart gave another thump.

Dear God, do not let me do anything to make her look any other way than how she looks right now.

"Thank you," she breathed. "Really, Cade. Thank you. For everything."

And then she was gone.

❋

Samara slipped back into her rooms at Wexley House undetected, adding to the joy inside her, which already threatened to overflow.

He didn't change his mind. He still wants me for his wife.

He might not love her, might have offered her marriage only out of pity—points on which she would *not* dwell—but that would change in time.

She hoped.

Washed, combed, and dressed in a simple but blessedly clean gown, Samara forced herself to stay inside her rooms to wait for her father to appear with Cade's request. She drew a bit, sketching from dim memory the dreamland that was Wexley House's fantastic courtyard. When she realized she could not concentrate on that she practiced acting surprised, as she would have to when her father told her the contents of the message Cade would send. Hours, or what seemed like hours, passed before a patter of footsteps approached her door and slowed to a stop.

A soft knock sounded. Softer than her father's would have been, especially if he was still angry with her.

"Samara?" called a voice.

Not her father. Cecily.

Which was almost as good.

"Come in!" she called, and the door slid open, revealing a tall, slender girl Samara mightn't have recognized if not for the unique color of her hair and eyes.

Cecily's face lit with joy, and she hurled herself across the room and into Samara's arms.

"I missed you!" she cried.

"I missed you too, Ceci," Samara said, tightening her hold on her sister's shoulders before releasing them. "Step back. Let me look at you." Her younger sister complied, and Samara took in the lithe, curving figure, the nearly hip-length hair, the high cheekbones that had been obscured by childish roundness just three months before. Samara shook her head. "You are a stranger! Where did my little sister go?"

Cecily giggled, a babyish sound that reassured Samara that the young girl she loved still lived inside the almost-woman's body.

"I am still here, I promise," she said. "Although it's little comfort to poor Millie, who spends most of her days taking down the hems of my skirts."

"I can imagine. Millie always hated sewing. Oh, I'm so glad to see you. What think you of London?"

"I haven't seen much of it. But it is noisy! And the smell—what *is* it?"

Samara laughed. "It is noisy. And the smell, I am told, is because housewives empty their families' chamber pots into the streets each morning."

Cecily lifted a hand to her mouth. "Into the *street?*" she breathed.

"So I've heard it said. You get used to it, though."

Her sister shook her head with vehemence. "I would not."

Samara smiled fondly. "You would be surprised at what becomes commonplace when you live in the city." Dearest Cecily, with her charming naïveté. Samara hoped she would never lose it, but of course, she would. As had Samara herself. At least she could hope that Cecily didn't lose her innocence in the same way. Samara would kill anyone who tried.

"I have so many things to ask you!" Cecily exclaimed. "I know from your letters that you met the queen, God rest her soul. But I got the sense that you were holding back when you spoke of her."

"I was," Samara admitted. "It is treason to speak of the queen's death, even when she is obviously dying, so I didn't mention it. At any rate, I met her on only a few occasions before she became too ill to send for me. But she was kind. She made me feel welcome. And she knew our mother."

"She did?" And with those words the cloak of impending womanhood slipped away, and Cecily was a little girl again—a little girl who lived with the knowledge that she had been given life in exchange for that of the woman who had birthed her, a knowledge that, though she never spoke of it, had haunted poor Cecily since she was old enough to understand what it meant.

"She did. She even had a book with a cover painted by our lady mother. A beautiful painting. She was a talented artist."

"Like you."

Samara thought of Cade, his words as he handed back her drawings, and warmth stole over her. "Better."

Cecily fell silent, her face thoughtful. Her fingers worried the ivory fabric at her turned-back sleeves.

"I always wondered—" she began, but was interrupted by the creak of the door as it swung open again.

Samara's heart leapt. This was it. She would have liked to talk with Cecily more, but that could wait. They had plenty of time.

"Hello, Samara."

Her heart sank as quickly as it had risen. Not her father. Katherine.

She forced a smile to her face as her other sister entered, looking woefully provincial in a plain, dark green wool gown, her hair loose and unadorned down her back. That was fine if she was to stay inside Wexley House, but if she had any plans to go outside, even into the courtyard, something would have to be done.

But then she chided herself for her mean thoughts. She hadn't seen Kat in months, and maybe she had changed. There had been little evidence of that in the few stilted letters her sister had sent, but it was possible. Besides, Samara had won, hadn't she? She would have Cade. She could afford to be magnanimous.

"Kat," Samara said warmly, embracing her sister. After a moment's hesitation, Katherine hugged her back. "It is so good to see you."

"And you," Kat replied, but her chilly tone immediately set Samara on edge. She disengaged her arms, stepped back, and took in Kat's face, which, unlike Cecily's, looked exactly the same—right down to the angrily narrowed eyes.

"It's funny," Katherine said after a moment of awkward silence. "I've never seen a fallen woman before. I thought you might look different, but you don't."

Cecily gasped. Samara's blood hummed in her ears before rising to a roar. Her face burned, her fists clenched the fabric of her skirt.

She took a deep breath. Counted to ten. Opened her mouth.

"Perhaps it is because I'm not really a fallen woman, as you so cleverly put it, Kat," she said.

"That's not what every servant in Wexley House is saying!" Katherine snapped. "Samara, what on *earth* were you thinking? Did you think at all, or just about yourself, as you usually do? Did you think of poor Lord Easton, how you must have embarrassed him by carrying on in such a way under his very nose?" Poor Lord Easton, indeed! Did *Kat* think of anyone else? "Did you give a moment's thought to the welfare of Cecily and myself? Your actions reflect on us too, and you have quite possibly ruined our chances at any kind of a future. I hope he was worth it."

Months ago—no, just a few weeks ago—Samara would have resorted to her own sharp retorts, or perhaps sent Katherine sprawling to the ground again. But those were childish actions, and she was a child no longer. Katherine didn't know what had really happened. Of course, she would believe what the servants, and others, were saying.

Still, it stung that Kat was not willing to give Samara the benefit of the doubt. To hear *her* side of things before drawing conclusions.

"Kat," Cecily said. "Can this not wait? Can you not be happy to see our sister?"

"Happy?" Katherine spat. "Cecily, darling, do you not see? She has ruined not only herself but us! Who will marry us, with a sister who thinks nothing of stealing off to dark rooms with *traitors!* God's teeth, Samara, could you not even find a Catholic man with whom to dally?"

The red haze that only Kat was able to make her see hovered on the edges of her vision, threatening to take it over. But again they were interrupted by a knock on the door, and this time Samara knew it could be no one else but her father. Her anger subsided, knowing that in mere moments Katherine would have to eat her words with the same vigor she had when presented with custard tarts.

"Come in," she called.

Her father the earl entered, a mewling basket in his hand. He set it down when Samara cried out in joy. She rushed to it, lifted the lid, and scooped out her kitten, touching the little pink nose with her own before setting Danaë on the floor.

"Oh!" Cecily cried, immediately enchanted. She dropped to the floor, heedless of her skirts, and the two began to play.

"Good morning, daughters," her father said. "Samara, I must speak with you."

Kat glowered. Samara pretended not to see.

"Yes, my lord father," she said, lowering her eyes demurely.

"The Earl of Easton sent a message with the servants who retrieved your things," he began. "He is a good man, Samara. Better than any of us knew."

"*I* knew, my lord father." Katherine's voice fairly dripped with honey.

"I am talking to your sister," their father said. "Perhaps I should be speaking with Samara in private."

"No, my lord father," Samara said. "My actions affect all of us, as Kat has so succinctly pointed out. She may stay."

Her father eyed her, as if he knew what she was up to. She saw him wondering. Had the royal court taught her the art of subtle verbal warfare? Or had she possessed the knowledge before she left, and he hadn't noticed?

She smiled at him innocently. He gave a tiny shake of his head.

"His offer stands, and he wishes you to think on it," he said.

"His offer?" Kat squeaked.

"Lord Easton asked me to marry him," Samara murmured. "Last night, after the incident at the party."

Silence. Samara glanced at Katherine. She looked as if a mouse had crawled into her mouth.

"You know I'm loath to force you to wed against your will," her father said. "But Samara, I'm of the belief that this is the best possible thing for you. I want you to think long and hard on this."

"There is no need, my lord father," Samara said. "I thought of nothing else as I tried to fall asleep last night. You are right. Lord Easton is right. A marriage between us is the best option for everyone. I accept his offer, and I'm very fortunate that he is so kind and generous. You may write and tell him so."

Beside her Kat hissed, a sound their father either did not hear or purposely ignored.

"It is settled, then," he said. "I'll write the earl and inform him of your decision. After the funeral, when things have calmed down, we will work out the details." Relief was plain on his face. One daughter spoken for; two remained.

"Thank you, my lord father," Samara said. She watched his retreating back, waiting until the door closed behind it before turning to Katherine. "So you see. Not so fallen after all."

"You bitch," Katherine whispered. Her eyes glittered with tears.

Had the situation been different, Samara would have hated hurting her sister. But she felt certain that Kat saw Cade as a means to an end—not unlike the way in which Samara had first viewed him. If Katherine had loved him, Samara would have stepped back. But Kat didn't. And she knew nothing about what had really happened.

"Cecily, may I have a few moments alone with Katherine?" she asked. "You may take the kitten with you. Her name is Danaë." Samara smiled at her sister, wanting to ease the discomfort evident on Cecily's face. "We'll talk more later."

"All right." Cecily picked up the wriggling cat and left the room, shutting the door softly behind her.

"Whatever story you're about to make up, Samara, I have no interest in hearing," Katherine said. "I know you want Cecily to believe you are a true and virtuous woman, but even she is not so naïve that she will ignore the gossip about you. Sending her out of the room will not protect her."

Samara stared at her sister, anguish welling up inside her. Katherine had always been prickly and a bit sour, but when had she become so poisonous? What had Samara done to make Kat hate her so much?

Was there even a point in trying to explain the horror she had experienced last night?

It didn't matter. She had to make the effort.

"Oh, she will find out the truth one day," Samara vowed. "Just not today. I sent her from the room because she is too young to hear what I have to tell you." She folded her hands. "And whether you want to hear it or not, you will listen."

Chapter Twenty-Four

KATHERINE'S EXPRESSION WAS SHUTTERED, THE TEARS GONE from her stony blue eyes.

"I've no interest in listening to your lies," she said.

"I have no intention of lying," Samara said. "Don't worry. My tale will give you plenty of opportunity for gloating. It does not paint me in a flattering light."

Katherine crossed her arms over her chest. "Yet you still managed to wrangle a marriage proposal out of poor, unsuspecting Lord Easton. What did you do, arrange to be found in a compromising position so he, honorable man that he is, had no choice but to offer for you?" She sniffed. "What a good man he is, that out of pity he is willing to saddle himself to you forever."

That stung. It was too close to the truth. Samara knew that pity was the only reason Cade had offered for her. But she would not allow Kat to think it too.

"He does not pity me," she flung back. "We became friends. We care about each other, in our own ways. He offered for me because he didn't want to see me suffer the results of my own stupidity." Which was the same as pity, wasn't it? Damn it. "But believe it or not, Kat, you have it almost correct," Samara said. "Except for the part about me arranging it. I had no plans to end up in the situation in which I was found. Only my foolishness allowed it."

A flicker of interest crossed Katherine's face. "Go on."

Kat *would* be interested in a story that painted Samara as a fool. She hoped she would not regret this.

"I met a man," she began. "A very handsome viscount, Robert Hunter, Lord Linton. He is the only son of the Earl of Ashbury."

She continued the story, telling Katherine the exact tale she'd told her father the night before, and watched Kat's face change as she talked. It went from passively interested to disgusted, amused to horrified, before settling on what appeared to be dumbfounded.

"And there you see," Samara finished. "I was not so stupid that I thought I could dally with a man and have no one find out. I was stupid because I thought I could get him to confess his treachery, not realizing how desperate he was." Her voice quivered. Telling the story again had brought it all back. Only the knowledge of its outcome—betrothal to Cade—made it bearable.

"Oh, Samara," Katherine breathed.

"And perhaps this isn't the time, but while I'm making confessions, I should say that I'm sorry you hate me," Samara added. "I don't pretend to know why. We were good friends as children, and for the life of me I cannot remember anything I could have done to make you despise me as you do. But if you feel you must, then do so. Just please hate me for something I've actually done. It would be much easier to endure that way."

"I don't hate you," Katherine shocked her by saying. "I never have, and I do miss our girlhood friendship. But we are not little girls anymore, Samara." The muscles in her throat tensed as Kat swallowed hard. "Truth be told, I envy you more than anything."

Samara was so surprised that the brush of Danaë against her ankle could have knocked her over. "Envy *me?* Why?"

"Because of who you are!" Katherine burst out. "You are not afraid to do whatever you like, and our lord father permits it. You can spend your days sketching by the lake or playing with your roses, while I oversee the household, and our father never says a word."

"But I thought you enjoyed household duties!"

"I do. And it is good that I know how, so I can make someone a good wife someday. But there are times I do not want to make soap or perfume or medicine. Sometimes I too would like to sit in the knot garden for hours and stare at the sky without a care, as you do. And our lord father allows it! Do you know why, Samara?"

"Because I have no talent for housewifery, would confuse the milk with lye, and end up poisoning us all?"

"No." Katherine shook her head, her eyes again glittering with tears. "Because you remind him of our lady mother."

"I do not."

"You do." Katherine swiped at her eyes. "How could you not? You look almost exactly like her. I heard you tell Cecily that she was an artist. You are a dreamer, as she was. All the things that made our father love her, you are. And he has made no attempt to hide the fact that you are his favorite daughter."

"His favorite daughter!" Samara exclaimed. "Kat, that is not true. Why, after our mother died and before he got it into his head to send me here, he never expressed one whit of care for me."

"Perhaps you didn't see it," Katherine replied. "But Cecily and I watched him refuse to scold you for disappearing for hours on end, grant you drawing supplies whenever you asked, and send you to London to choose your own husband. Why else would he allow you those things, if you were not his favorite?"

Guilt was a feeling with which Samara had never been comfortable. It crept over her now, hot and prickly, as she looked at her sister in a way she never had before.

"God's nightshirt, Kat, if I were you, I would have hated me too," she said.

"I don't hate you," Kat repeated. "Envy, yes. And I resented you. But hate? No. You are my sister. I could not hate you if I tried. And believe me, I did try." She smiled a little. "I am sorry for making your life so miserable. And for the horrible things I said to you today. I was just so angry at the idea that your tendency to do as you wish had affected Cecily and me. Deep down I knew there had to be another explanation. You are no idiot."

Samara smiled. "Well, thank you, though I think I am. And for my part, I'm sorry too. I should have been a better sister. If it is any consolation, I am so ill-prepared for marriage I don't doubt Cade will regret making his offer before the wedding celebrations are over."

"We shall see." Kat favored her with a little smile. "I don't know, though. I have a feeling that Lord Easton knew exactly what he was getting into when he proposed. Before that, even. I saw the way he looked at you when he stayed at our home last spring."

They might have come to an understanding and even started toward healing their sisterly bond, but Samara still would not tell Kat about her first meeting with Cade, which was the only reason why he had looked at her at all.

"He probably just wondered why I acted so strangely compared to the women he knows," she replied. "I may not be anything like you or any proper noble girl, but I am no courtier either. I don't fit in anywhere, I'm afraid."

"You fit with him," Kat told her. "I saw it then. Perhaps that's why I decided I wanted him for myself. To prove that there was something I was more worthy of, something I could have that you couldn't. Even though I suspected even then that you would win him."

A memory assailed Samara then, of her sister whispering into Cade's ear and the eruption of jealousy she felt when she saw it.

"Kat?" she said. "Do you recall what you told Lord Easton the day I left for London? I was standing by the coach, and I saw you whisper something into his ear. Do you remember what it was?"

Katherine gave her another little smile. "I told him to take good care of you."

❋

The group inside the queen's Privy Chamber was smaller than Cade had expected. It was a depressing place, to be sure; walled off by thick black hangings that blocked out any weak afternoon sunlight that had managed to pass through the windows, it echoed with the weeping of those who were truly sorry Her Majesty was gone and those who merely wished to put on a show. But it was still the room where the body of the first Tudor queen regnant lay in state. There should have been more than the dozen or so mourners who surrounded the display of her royal body. Had so many of the court hangers-on already switched allegiance?

Though it *had* been several weeks. In just a few days he would have to return to accompany the coffin to the Chapel Royal, the first step in its progress to Westminster Abbey for burial. Perhaps these particular mourners were second- or third-time visitors instead of stragglers like himself.

Beside him Hayden absently rolled his pomander ball in his hands, sending a welcome whiff of warm, spicy nutmeg to Cade's nostrils. Though his decision to wait had been based on both a selfish desire to avoid crowds and gossip about the party at Linton's and reluctance to admit that his much-loved monarch was gone, he shouldn't have taken so long to come and pay his respects. Although it was winter, with the mourning draperies preventing any fresh air from entering and the lingering scent of the many human bodies that had passed through the room, not to mention the three-week-old corpse they'd all come to see—preservative herbs and spices could do only so much—the level of odor in the chamber approached unbearable.

Cade lifted his own pomander to his face and gratefully breathed in the sharp scent of fresh lavender. With it came a thought of Samara. Faint and fleeting, but it was there.

My betrothed wife.

He'd heard little from her in the week since they'd reached their agreement—just a message from Brentford telling him that she'd decided to accept his proposal, and a quick note from the lady herself informing him that she was well and grateful for his kindness.

His kindness? Is that all she thought it was? Although he had to admit, it was better that way. The less attached she was, the better off she would be.

"Cade." Hayden nudged him with an elbow, and Cade realized that space had opened up in front of the trestles on which Her Majesty's coffin rested. They could approach.

All the cloth-of-gold and beeswax candles in the world couldn't mask the sight before them. Cade had seen dead bodies before. Hell, it hadn't even been a full half-year since he'd buried his own father, and that in summer and without the benefit of court physicians and their concoctions to preserve the body as long as possible. A corpse was never pretty. But the corpse of a woman who had been dead for weeks, whose countenance when alive had been considered pleasant at best, and who had spent the last few months wasting from illness … well, it wasn't something he wanted to see again anytime soon.

Beside him he heard Hayden gulp.

"Just close your eyes," Cade murmured to his cousin as they took their place on their knees beside the coffin.

Cade followed his own advice, closing his eyes and crossing himself before turning his thoughts to the queen he'd loved. It wasn't difficult to switch his focus to pleasant memories. Despite his ordeal in Rome he'd been lucky to have her. If not for her, who knew what would have happened to him once he'd arrived in the city? The money from Glenwood wouldn't have kept him afloat, not if he wanted to maintain a lifestyle at court. He would have had to return to Easton, tail tucked between his legs like a kicked dog, while he figured out another way to get out from beneath his father's thumb. Either that or hire himself out as a cut-throat, which at times seemed the better option. He'd been so fortunate to meet the queen, to gain her support, respect, and approval. Without Mary Tudor, his life might have ended before it ever began.

More people entered the chamber. Cade opened his eyes, saw them fidgeting uncomfortably, those who were lucky enough to have their own pomanders pressing them to their noses.

"Let's go," Hayden murmured. "We can pay our respects just as well in our own home."

"Agreed," Cade said, and they got to their feet. With a final glance at the coffin and the body of the queen who'd given purpose to the last decade of their lives, they left the Privy Chamber.

"How soon after the funeral do you think we should leave?" Hayden asked once they had escaped into a relatively clear corridor.

"I had planned on immediately," Cade replied.

"You're certain it will be that dangerous for us?"

"I'm certain of nothing. I merely wish to secure our safety." He thought back on his brief meeting with Elizabeth. She had not worn her faith as a badge on her sleeve, had played at conforming to her sister's laws, but he had little reason to believe she would continue Mary's work of reestablishing Catholicism as the national faith. And the death of Cardinal Pole, on the very same day as the queen, seemed to put the proverbial final nail in the coffin of England's subscription to the true faith. "I don't think it's a chance we should take. We were vocal in our support of Her Majesty five years ago. Elizabeth has not forgotten that. Besides, we both have responsibilities. You to your child, and I to my people. According to Jefferson, Easton has been doing unexpectedly well, but running back to the city the first chance I got can't have given those who live there a favorable impression of me. They need to know I care more than my father did. And that I will try not to get executed."

"And you'll take a wife." Hayden's words were accompanied by a good-natured jab to Cade's ribs with his elbow. "She ought to keep you busy for a few years."

"Cade."

His heart stopped, then lurched back into uneven rhythm. The object of his cousin's jest stood before him on the arm of her father, perhaps more resplendent than she should have been in mahogany and cream.

"Good day, Lord Brentford. Lady Samara," he said. She smiled at him, a tremulous and uncertain upturn of her lips. Christ's bones. She was having second thoughts.

"Hello, Easton," the other earl said. "Good to see you. And you, Sir Hayden."

"Lord Brentford," Hayden said easily. Thank God for him and his unflappable nature. Cade felt like a green lad partaking in his first love affair. "How d'you do, Lady Samara? Riverview House has been far too quiet without you."

"I am well, Hayden, thank you." Cade sneaked a glance at her. Her cheeks were pink, but she held her head proudly. Her eyes flicked to him, and she held his gaze for a moment before lowering hers to the presumably safe region of his knees. "How is Aunt Madge? I've missed her."

"And she you. I'm sorry we haven't been able to see much of each other. Cade and I will be walking in the funeral procession in a few days, and we've been busy helping to make arrangements."

"There are always arrangements to be made," Brentford said. "Today 'tis a funeral, tomorrow a wedding. Someday soon, with God's blessing, a birth."

Cade angled another glance at Samara. Her shuttered expression and stiff posture gave no hint to her thoughts. When had she learned to do that? What had happened to the girl who'd slapped him on the shore of the lake just seven months before, who'd once thrown her shoe as if she hoped it would knock off his head?

What had the royal court—and Robert Hunter—done to her?

"Still, it's a pity we haven't been able to enjoy each other's company," Cade offered. Though he could certainly think of better ways to spend an evening than across the high board from a fiancée who could not bring herself to make eye contact with him and a father-in-law who seemed not to know his own mind from day to day. But they *would* be family. She would be his wife. He would make them happy if it killed him.

God's blood, but he'd thought his eagerness to please would have died with his father. Instead it would be the death of him.

"We'll be family soon, Easton," Brentford said, echoing Cade's thoughts. "There will be plenty of time to enjoy each other's company then." He lifted his hand, lowered his voice. "We must go in. I've witnessed my share of royal deaths, and this is always the part I dread the most. Come along, Samara. We must pay our respects."

Cade wanted to stop her long enough to warn her of what she would find inside the Privy Chamber. Surely a girl who had been so sheltered would be taken by surprise at the sight of the corpse on its bier. He even reached out to put a hand on her sleeve, to stop her and give her some encouraging words, but though she turned another sorry attempt at a smile on him, her father whisked her away and she was gone, only the faint scent of lavender lingering on the air reassuring him that she'd ever been there.

❁

The thirteenth of December dawned chill and gray, the sky heavy with the threat of snow. Early in the morning Queen Mary's funeral cortege gathered in the courtyard of St. James's Palace to prepare for the procession to Westminster, just a mile away, where she would be buried in the Lady Chapel of her grandfather, King Henry VII.

Samara, among the ladies who contributed to the company of lesser mourners, scanned the large group of gentlemen mourners for Cade. She wished to see him, to see how he fared. She had been so wrapped up in her own sorrow—and fear, she had to admit; she had not seen many dead in her short life and certainly not a dead monarch—at the palace the other day that she had barely been able to manage a smile for him. Selfish of her. It should have occurred to her that this would be much harder for him, like losing his mother again. She gazed hungrily for a glimpse, but the crowd must have swallowed him, for by the time the procession began she hadn't seen so much as a flash of black curl, pale cheek, or angled jaw. She faced forward, taking her place in the mass of bodies, and waited for her cue to move.

It was all very formal, very rigid and grand. The queen's household officers, clad in black and carrying banners of the royal arms, led the procession, paired and marching according to rank order. This first part of the procession was long, for a monarch needed many souls about her to help carry out the business of the realm, and Samara was relieved when it ended—until she noted Lord Linton, his face painted in mottled bruises of purple and yellow, one of his lovely brown eyes nearly concealed by swelling even now, more than a week after the incident. She shivered, almost able to feel his strong hands on her again. Covering her mouth, unlacing her stays. By now the story was probably out. Only Cade's chivalry kept the mockery away.

Next came five heralds carrying another banner of the royal arms. Standards bearing images of the dragon, the greyhound, and the lion fluttered like the wings of brightly colored birds. Mourners clad in black drove their horses forward with purpose. The sweet, solemn voices of the gentlemen of the queen's chapel rose over the din of the crowds that lined the street, over the biting November wind. Under other circumstances, it might have been beautiful.

A chariot carried the coffin and an effigy sculpted to look like the queen—although the artist had failed miserably, in Samara's opinion; she could probably have done a better job herself if she knew anything about sculpting. It showed Her Majesty dressed in velvet of her favorite color, crimson. A crown topped the painted head, and white plaster fingers, decorated with rings, gripped a scepter. One glance was all Samara needed. It was almost worse than the sight of the poor queen's body.

Behind the chariot came Lady Lennox, the queen's cousin and chief mourner, her elderly face streaked with evidence of her sorrow. She was accompanied by Her Majesty's ladies-in-waiting. The Marchioness of Beddington's face was lovely and serene, a direct contrast to poor Mistress Jane Dormer's pale, tear-stained cheeks and red-rimmed eyes. Presumably the presence of Jane's betrothed, the Count of Feria, in the honored position nearest the coffin was the only thing keeping her from tumbling from her horse in her grief. Samara's heart clenched. She hoped Jane and her count would be able to marry before Elizabeth got it into her head to stop them.

The group of gentleman mourners brought up the end of the procession. Samara knew this, though she couldn't see them from her position, toward the middle. Still, she drew strength knowing that Cade was back there.

The procession slowed as it approached the ornate northern entrance of Westminster Abbey. As the chariot drew near, four bishops in pointed miters and an abbot came out through the great arched door to greet it. They carried golden censers in their hands from which the sickly-sweet fragrance of incense emerged. They swung the censers over the coffin as Samara watched in wonder. She had never seen anything like this before. How different were the funerals of a royal and her subjects!

The bishops and the abbot, old men who visibly strained beneath the weight of the royal coffin, turned with it and went back through the door of the abbey. It closed behind them. From what she had heard, a hundred poor men would stand guard over the coffin overnight until the mourners returned in the morning for the funeral Mass.

Samara's part was over, and no matter how small, she was honored to have performed it.

❋

"This is a day of sorrow," the Marquess of Wexley boomed that evening, over the dessert course of gingered bread and fresh cream. "But just because we are mourning the loss of our good queen does not mean we cannot feel joy over other things."

Samara forced her gaze from the designs the dancing candlelight painted on the lovely gilded wall. The marquess grinned, and crumbs dropped from his bristly mustache. What was he talking about? She looked to her father, who wore a pinched smile.

The marchioness's smile was weak. No clues there; her expressions were always feeble. Lord Waltham, however, his orange hair fashioned in a style reminiscent of a milk thistle, sprawled in his chair, an indolent grin on his blotchy face.

She shuddered. Even if Cade never looked at her as anything other than a friend, Samara would forever be grateful to him for rescuing her from the clutches of Lord Waltham.

"First Lady Samara managed to snag the Earl of Easton for her husband," the marquess said crudely. Samara cringed. Heat suffused her face, her cheeks, and even her scalp. *Snag? Can he be a bigger boor?* "And now, another happy occasion. Lord Brentford and I came to an agreement just yesterday." He raised his goblet. "My son, Viscount Waltham, will marry Lady Katherine."

Samara's breath caught in her throat and she shot a glance at her sister, who sat as straight and stately as one of the old oaks in their father's park, her rosy complexion drained of color and frozen in shock. How cruel of their father to tell her this way! Kat was not Samara. He had no cause to worry that she would make a scene upon hearing the news. He could have done her the courtesy of giving her time to digest such a horror before making the announcement. But to Kat's credit she didn't flinch, nor vomit as Samara thought she would have in the same position. She instead dropped her eyes respectfully to the table, but not before Samara saw the telltale glitter of tears.

"I see," she said, and her voice was so soft Samara had to strain to hear her. "Well, I thank you, my lord father. In this, as in all matters, I acquiesce to your wishes."

Samara met Cecily's eyes across the high board. There would be plenty of sisterly chatter tonight, of that Samara had not a doubt.

Chapter Twenty-Five

THE MOOD IN THE ABBEY WAS SOMBER, THE AIR HEAVY. NORmally Samara would have been enthralled by the old king's Lady Chapel—the spiny Gothic-style exterior, the splendid fan vault ceiling with pendants dangling like jewels strung on spiderwebs, the rainbows painted on the floor by the pale December sun spilling through the stained glass—all right, perhaps she was just a tiny bit enthralled. It spoke well of her, didn't it, that she was able to find beauty even in the midst of sorrow? But the drone of the Bishop of Winchester's voice soon dragged her attention from the splendor around her and reminded her why she was there.

The bishop, in his heartfelt eulogy, had nothing but good things to say about the queen who had been not only his monarch but his friend. He praised her devotion to God and her people, her love of children and her desire to protect the souls of her subjects, her many virtues and all the altruistic deeds she had performed in her lifetime. Samara fought back a surprising surge of tears. She had seen evidence of that altruism herself, had she not? She had been invited into Her Majesty's most intimate chambers. Allowed to admire priceless treasures and the queen's personal effects. Complimented on her art and encouraged to pursue it. Why else would the Queen of England do these things for a perfect stranger, if not because she was kind?

"I verily believe," said the bishop, a tremor in his deep voice, "the poorest creature in all this city feared not God more than she did."

A tear rolled warm and silent over her cheek. Others in the chapel were affected too, a fact to which the muffled sniffles and sobs around her attested.

She hiccupped. Cade, a comforting presence to the right of her in the pew, shifted as he placed his hand over hers and squeezed gently. Unable to help herself, she squeezed back. She was glad he was there. He had to be mourning even more deeply than she—he, who had had a personal relationship with Her Majesty, the depth of which Samara would probably never grasp. He was sweet to comfort *her* when he must be hurting so much more.

"I praise the dead which are already dead more than the living, which are yet alive," the bishop continued. "The dead deserve more praise, for they have chosen the better part. Yet our beloved queen has left a sister, also a lady of great worth, whom we all must obey, for *melior est canis vivus leone mortuo.*" Beside her Cade sucked in a sharp breath. When Samara glanced at him in question—her grasp of Latin had ever been tenuous—he leaned in to her.

"The Bishop of Winchester has just said that a dead Mary is better than a living Elizabeth and likened Elizabeth to a dog," he murmured. "I fear he will pay for that." Indeed, those in the pew around her looked uncomfortable. Her father's eyes were closed. Beside him, Aunt Madge's lips moved in what Samara assumed was prayer.

"What do you think she will do?" Samara whispered back.

"I do not know. But I imagine we'll soon have an idea of what Elizabeth intends to do about her Catholic subjects."

"She is royal like Mary and holds the realm by the like title and right," the bishop went on. "I wish her a prosperous reign in peace and tranquillity, if it be God's will."

Cade, and Hayden on his right, sighed. Samara's father gave a minute shake of his head.

The eulogy concluded, and the offertory Mass followed. The mourners in the chapel watched as Her Majesty's coat of armor, sword, shield, and banner of arms were given back to God. The effigy, scepter, rings, and other royal tokens were taken from the coffin for safekeeping, and the coffin itself was lowered into the vault that had been opened in the north aisle of the chapel. The symbolic earth was cast upon it; the officers of Mary's household broke their staffs of office and tossed them into the grave.

"The queen is dead, long live the queen!" cried the heralds. At their words a great mass of people rose and tore at the banners and cloth hangings, dismantling them with swiftness and, to Samara, complete and utter disrespect for Her Majesty.

"It's what normally happens," Hayden said to her. "It was the same at the funeral of old King Henry and Edward the boy king. They want souvenirs."

"It's awful," Cecily declared. Hayden grinned at her.

The trumpets blasted, signaling the beginning of the funeral banquet, which would take place at the lodging of the Abbot of Westminster. Elizabeth had been very generous with the royal coffers—what was left in them, after years of war with France—and the amount of food available to the mourners and guests was amazing. But aside from the marquess, of course, Samara and her party merely picked at the food.

Their group departed the banquet as soon as was possible without looking as though they disrespected the late queen. Night had fallen, and the cold air bit through even Samara's heavy mourning robe. They moved as a group, silent and careful, to the several coaches that waited for them. Waltham had attached himself to Kat's side like a boil, and Kat looked none too happy. Cecily trailed after Hayden like a duckling behind its mother, her eyes full of an adoration that Hayden seemed not to notice. The marquess strode half a dozen paces ahead of his wife while Samara's father allowed Aunt Madge to support herself on his arm. Samara herself clung to Cade's elbow, her fingers digging into the soft velvet of his doublet.

"Are you all right?" he murmured in her ear.

The warmth of his breath as it danced through the curls that had sprung loose from her hood sent a shiver racing down her back. Probably not a proper reaction to have on a day of mourning, but one she couldn't help.

She swallowed hard. "I'm fine," she said. "It was a sad day, but I hadn't expected otherwise. And you?" Her fingers, seemingly of their own volition, pressed into his strong forearm in what she hoped he would take as a comforting gesture.

He smiled. "Fine," he said. Then he lowered his voice. "It speaks well of the new queen that she would allow such a grand funeral. I hope it bodes well for our future as followers of the true faith."

That hope was dashed rather quickly the next day, when word came that the new queen had, for the offenses committed in his sermon, confined the Bishop of Winchester to his house at Her Majesty's pleasure.

❀

Samara glanced at the woven basket at her feet. Danaë's pitiful meows could be heard even from beneath the length of linen Samara had draped over the basket to keep her safely inside.

"Shh," Samara whispered, bending down to put her face close to the basket. "Not much longer. Once we're in the coach, you can come out."

The kitten shrieked again at the sound of Samara's voice. Samara longed to peel back the linen cloth and let the creature out, but she knew she might never catch her again before they had to leave. Danaë was curious by nature, even more so than a cat usually was, and if she got it into her tiny orange head to explore, it was nearly impossible to keep her contained.

"Just a few more minutes," she begged. Danaë made a pathetic squeak. Samara couldn't help it. She lifted the cloth, and the kitten's small face immediately peeked over the edge of the basket. Seeing Samara, she deftly climbed out and scaled Samara's arm, perching herself on her shoulder and pushing her nose against Samara's cheek.

"You spoil her." Cade's amused drawl came from the stairs as he descended. He leaned against the doorway. "Something tells me that creature will have more authority over my home than I will."

"You would want to be spoiled too if someone had dropped you into the Thames to die," Samara retorted. She tried to pluck the kitten from her shoulder, but Danaë dug her tiny claws through her dress and into her skin. "Damn."

"Don't think it hasn't almost happened." He came toward her. "One doesn't spend as much of his life in this city, among the court, as I have without coming close to losing it a few times."

"Duels over a lady, I assume?" She tried to make her voice sound nonchalant, but even she could hear the note of jealousy it held. She hoped he missed it.

"More often than not," he agreed. "And when I was in Rome, the pope accused me of spying. Locked me up in the papal prison where I was refused even a glimpse of sunlight for several months."

She stared at him, wondering if she should take him seriously or not. She decided he couldn't possibly be telling the truth. He was a good Catholic. Popes didn't imprison their own. "You are impossible," she said, shaking her head with a laugh.

"You'll soon find out just how impossible," he promised. He gave her a crooked grin.

She flushed and distracted herself by trying to peel Danaë from beneath her hair, where the kitten had made herself comfortable.

"Do you need help?" he asked. "That creature certainly has an affinity for that particular spot. I think she must be part parrot." Without waiting for an answer, he went to her and pushed her hair aside. His fingers brushed against the soft skin at the juncture of her neck and shoulder. She jerked away, sure that if he noticed the gooseflesh that sprang up at his touch, he would realize her true feelings and she would be at a permanent disadvantage. That couldn't happen—not if they were both to be happy.

He glanced at her, curiosity in his eyes, but detached the kitten without ripping skin or silk and handed Danaë to her.

"Thank you," Samara managed when the kitten was safely returned to her basket, howling her protests as fiercely as her tiny throat allowed. Samara was so distracted that she couldn't even form the words to ask him what a parrot was.

"My pleasure." He looked as though he wanted to say more but before he could, Katherine and Cecily entered the hall.

"This is a beautiful house, Lord Easton," Katherine said.

"Thank you, Lady Katherine," he replied. "It's been in my family for generations. And now that you will be family, you may stay here when you visit the city, if you're so inclined."

"Thank you," Kat said primly. "But Lord Waltham has his own family residence." Her cheeks paled a bit as she spoke his name. The reality of her betrothal to him still hadn't sunk in, she'd admitted to

Samara, but every now and then she saw a glimpse of her future as his wife. Those glimpses were like tiny waking nightmares.

The clatter of wheels over the stone courtyard interrupted their conversation. Cade glanced toward the street entrance. "The coaches are here," he said. "Are you ready to go?"

The marquess and his family planned to accompany Cade, Samara, and her relatives north. It would be easier, her father explained, to travel together rather than separately. It eliminated the risk of their belongings becoming separated and stranding someone without certain articles of clothing or other necessities, and with such a large party, bandits would be less inclined to attack them. The ascension of a new monarch brought upheaval to her subjects even under the smoothest of transitions. This time, when fear of new religious policies and no indication of what they might entail had an entire country on tenterhooks, more people might fall prey to desperation about their situation. That could lead to more danger on the roads. Three families traveling together would be too much for anyone hoping to rob them and get away alive.

Samara barely listened to his explanations. She was just glad to have one last glimpse of Riverview—the place where everything had changed, where her new life had begun. She had spent her brief visit circling her room, knowing she'd never look at it the same way again. She would be a married woman the next time she was here, if they were ever able to return to London.

She'd trailed her fingers along the lovely wainscoting, touched the softness of the bed hangings and the smooth oak of the carved furniture she'd loved at first sight. It was partly hers now. She still found it hard to believe. Even though, as a woman, she had no real claim to the Badgley property, these things, this house, the furniture in it, the man who owned it all were part of her now. Part of her family. Of her future.

"Samara?" Katherine prompted, shattering the reverie. "Are you ready to go?"

She stood, taking one final look around the hall. She hoped to see it again, but it might not happen. Still, as long as she was with Cade, she would be safe.

"Yes, I'm ready."

Katherine and Cecily went ahead of them. Cade picked up Danaë's basket and reached for Samara's hand with his other hand. She hesitated a moment before letting him take it. The way her fingers intertwined themselves with his felt so natural she had to remind herself that it hadn't always been that way. That it wasn't really meant to be that way, and that she should count her blessings that things had worked out as they had.

The smile on Betty's face was embarrassingly wide when they emerged behind Samara's sisters and she saw their joined hands. If Samara was happy about the way things had turned out for her, Betty was over the moon.

"Not to take anything away from your own dear mother, my lady, but you are like a daughter to me. I want nothing more than your happiness. And you will find it with him. You care for him."

Samara smiled ruefully. "Have I been that transparent?"

"Not to him," Betty replied with a laugh. "But to me, yes."

"The real test was Kat's reaction when she found out," Samara said. "I am fortunate that she was so willing to step aside. She had set her heart on the earl almost right away."

"Well, it seems to me that he would rather have *your* heart," Betty said.

"It's not a love match, Betty," Samara said quickly. "It's convenient, and we've become friends, but that's all. I have no illusions about Lord Easton, and I don't believe he has any about me."

Betty's reply had been a smile.

"I'll take that," the maid said as Cade and Samara reached the coach. "Your sisters are in your father's coach." She took the basket from Samara's hand and put it inside. Aunt Madge, already inside the coach, poked her head out.

"Please tell me that the little beast will spend the majority of the trip inside her basket," she said. "I'm wearing my good marten-lined cloak and have no desire to see it covered in cat fur."

As if she'd understood, the linen cloth covering the basket slid aside, and Danaë's large blue eyes peered over the rim. She leapt agilely from her woven prison and scrambled onto Aunt Madge's lap, where she turned a few times and settled into a small, purring orange ball.

"That answers that, Aunt Madge," Cade said, laughing.

Aunt Madge, whose bark was far worse than her bite regarding the kitten, shook her head and scratched Danaë between her ears.

"Up you go, Betty." Cade offered the maid his hand and helped her into the coach. Then he turned to Samara.

"Your turn." He gripped her fingers in one strong hand, and the other snaked around her waist to hold her steady as she stepped into the coach. He released her so she could settle herself. "Are you comfortable?"

"Fine," she assured him, though she wished she was in the coach with Katherine and Cecily. They still had much to discuss, stories to share. But her father had thought it might be a good idea if she started to distance herself, since she and Katherine would soon be married and gone from each other. So Samara would see her sisters only when they stopped to rest.

Betty tucked a heavy blanket over their laps to keep them warm until they reached their first destination, an inn along the road in Middlesex.

"Good," Cade said. "We'll stop around midday to rest the horses and take care of certain necessities. We should reach the inn by nightfall. Alert the driver if anyone needs to stop for any other reason."

The similarity of his words to those he'd used when they'd first left for London was striking compared to how their situations had changed. Samara smiled to herself as Cade shut the door to the coach and folded her arms over her chest to keep the irrational happiness from spilling out.

❀

By the sixth night of their journey all were exhausted—Cade and Hayden, Wexley and Waltham, Brentford, the horses, and even the women, though they'd spent the trip cloistered in the dubious comfort of their coaches. Samara's eyes, when she alit each night, had begun to look somewhat wild, and he could only imagine how she must be going mad cooped up in there for hours on end with only two old women and a rambunctious kitten for company. He knew she was sad to be spending the journey away from her sisters—they would so soon be permanently separated; he thought that it would do them good to spend this time together. But Brentford had spoken, and though Samara was Cade's betrothed she was still the other earl's daughter, and his wishes were more important.

He had a surprise for her, though, and hoped she would like it.

They had taken a small detour. Instead of rolling up to an inn, the coaches, led by Cade and Hayden on their horses, drove into a small courtyard.

"I miss my daughter," Hayden had said on the third day of their journey. "I'm beginning to feel that it was a mistake to desert her so soon after Penelope died. She's probably already forgotten her mother, and now she won't remember me."

"Then we'll stop at your house," Cade said. "It's not too far out of the way. A few miles, that's all. And I'm sure the women would love a chance to sleep in a proper bed for a night."

The grin that creased Hayden's face let Cade know what a good idea he thought it was.

"Where are we?" Samara asked once her feet were on solid ground. She cast her gaze to the familiar outline of the Malvern Hills in the distance.

"Hill House," Cade replied.

"*My* house," Hayden added. He tossed the reins to a groom that had materialized beside him, bounded across the courtyard and disappeared through the entrance.

"Welcome, I suppose," Cade said.

Their party crossed the courtyard and entered Hill House, a building in which Cade had only spent a minimal amount of time. It was on the small side, with a hall about one-third the size of Easton's that boasted a beautifully carved screen depicting men and women dressed in the flowing garb and laurel head wreaths of the ancient Greeks. He watched Samara's jaw drop open as she took in the sight. Her reaction was exactly as he'd expected.

"Magnificent, isn't it?" he asked.

She turned to him, her eyes wide with wonder. "I've never seen anything like it," she breathed.

The archway under the screen led to the private parlor, and it was there they found Hayden, a small, golden-haired girl in his arms.

She had flung her arms around his neck, and his face was buried in her hair as he hugged her.

Cade's heart contracted. He wondered if, once he was a father, he would feel the kind of love for his child that Hayden had for Molly. Or would he be like his own father, treating the child as the worst thing that could have happened to him?

Perhaps he would simply be indifferent. That might be best for everyone involved.

Hayden took note of them and set the girl down on the smooth marble floor.

"Molly, here are some friends and relatives you haven't met before," he said. "The Marquess of Wexley and his wife, the marchioness. Their son, Viscount Waltham. The Earl of Brentford and his daughters—Lady Samara, Lady Katherine, and Lady Cecily. Our cousin the Earl of Easton and Aunt Madge, Lady Morley. Make your curtsey to them, please."

The tiny girl spread her dark blue skirts and performed a perfect curtsey.

"How d'you do," she lisped.

Hayden grinned at the child, pride on his face.

"It's a pleasure to meet you, Mistress Molly," Cade said. "With your father's permission, I think you should call me Uncle."

Hayden turned his smile on Cade. Cade shrugged and grinned back. He hoped his cousin knew what he implied—that Hayden had been more a brother to him than Stephen had ever been.

"And—Aunt?" Cade turned to Samara, who stood nervously beside him, her eyes on Molly. "Since you're to be my wife. What do you think?"

"I like it," Samara said softly. "I've never been an aunt."

"I like your hair," Molly said to Samara. "It looks like fire. May I touch it?"

"Margaret!" Hayden said, aghast, against a background of soft laughter. "It's very rude to mention another person's physical appearance."

"Well, she's right," Cade pointed out.

Samara smiled. "There's no denying that it is red," she agreed. "And I like that she compared it to fire. Perhaps there's a bit of the artist in you, Mistress Molly." She knelt and beckoned the child closer. "Of course, you can touch it."

Molly approached, and when she reached Samara she extended a chubby, dimpled hand. She took a gleaming curl between thumb and forefinger.

"It's not hot," she said, sounding surprised. Another smattering of laughter ensued.

"No, it's not," Samara replied. "And do you know something? Your hair looks like sunshine. It's lovely."

The little girl smiled.

"Say thank you, Molly," Hayden prompted.

"Thank you," Molly said.

Samara grinned and stood, patting the top of her head.

"Thank *you*," she replied.

"What a little darling," Samara said once Molly had been taken away to bed and they were sitting down for a meal.

"She remembered me," Hayden said, and his face glowed with happiness. "I was terrified that she would not. But she knew me immediately."

"Children are much smarter than many people give them credit for," Wexley remarked.

Cade glanced at the marquess's son, attached to poor Katherine's side like a boil that would not burst. Surely the young man had a redeeming quality—he must. Whatever it was, though, was buried deep beneath the odious surface.

"To be sure," Cade said. Beside him, Samara emitted a dainty cough.

A servant appeared at his elbow. "Wine, my lord?"

Cade glanced at his betrothed. She didn't appear to have noticed, her quicksilver focus having been drawn again to the screen. What else was he to drink? Water might kill him. Ale, if drunk in large enough quantities, had the same effect as wine.

"Have you any cider?" he asked. "Apple or pear, it makes no difference."

"Of course, my lord." The servant moved on to Aunt Madge, filling her goblet with deep red liquid, then retreated to the pantry. He returned with a mug emitting the sweet-tart scent of apples and spice.

"Very good," Cade said. He took a long drink. Hell, it tasted so much better than wine! Why didn't everyone drink this?

They lingered at the table long after their places had been cleared, talking of everything but the subject that was at the forefront of everyone's mind—the new queen's religious policies. They would find out soon enough what she had in mind for them as followers of the true faith. All those rumors of her being a reformer had to come from somewhere, did they not? Surely the Bishop of Winchester, still confined to his house, would agree. And she had to know that there were still those, Cade included, who considered her a bastard, the product of a union illegal in the eyes of God and country. No pope, or Catholic nation, would recognize her as a legitimate queen. What would happen? A coup? An assassination? A civil war?

He looked once more at Samara, whose dreamy eyes flitted around the room as she took in the tapestries, the ornate oak paneling, the patterns made by the unusual black and white marble floor. She was so innocent despite the last few months. He wondered what it was like to live in her world, a world where everything was beautiful, where evil intentions failed to exist. Even her experience with Linton had frightened her but not scarred her. She seemed able to escape the darkness by turning to her art, whereas he was only able to escape by tumbling headfirst into his cups.

The next morning they rose early. Though they were close, it would be another ten hours or so before they reached Brentford Hall. Hayden would not come with them, instead making the journey out in time for the wedding.

"We have only just been reunited," he said as they stood in the courtyard, his hand possessively on his small daughter's head. "I'm not anxious to leave her again so soon. But write me when your plans are settled, and I will be there."

In just a few short hours little Mistress Molly had made a friend of Danaë and was distressed to part with her. Tears rolled down her rounded cheeks as Samara picked up the cat's basket and prepared to take it home.

"Margaret," Hayden said. "There are plenty of kittens in the barn for you to play with. Danaë belongs to your Aunt Samara. Stop your tears."

The little girl nodded desolately and sniffled.

"Yes, my lord father," she said.

Samara knelt before Molly and placed the basket on the floor.

"You and Danaë have become fond of each other, have you not?" she asked gently.

Molly nodded. "Yes, Auntie."

"Well, here is my dilemma. I am going to my father's house now but will soon move to another home. I'm afraid that moving so much might confuse the poor thing." Cade watched, unable to help smiling. "I think Danaë might be better off with just one home. Do you mind if I leave her here? She will be happier to stay in one place, and I know you will take very good care of her."

Molly's eyes widened, and she looked to her father. Hayden nodded his approval.

"Yes, Danaë may stay here," he said. "But she will be *your* responsibility, Margaret. I do not want to hear of Joan being saddled with the care of her."

"Yes, my lord father!" the little girl exclaimed. "Thank you, Aunt!" She hugged Samara briefly before pouncing on the basket, tearing the linen covering aside and scooping Danaë into her arms.

"That was kind of you," Cade said to his betrothed.

"I'll miss her," Samara admitted. "But I have an entire new life ahead of me. She deserves to be with someone who can pay attention to her. Molly will."

Hayden, Molly, and Danaë stood together in the courtyard while the remainder of their party rolled under the portcullises and across the drawbridge, then headed back out to the main road that would take them to Brentford Hall.

Chapter Twenty-Six

THAT NIGHT THEY GATHERED AROUND BRENTFORD'S HIGH board for yet another meal—one during which Cade could finally relax, as his journey was almost over.

He thought back to the first time he had sat there. Glancing around the long table, it looked as if nothing had changed—but in reality, everything had. Where before Samara had been engrossed by the vivid red of early strawberries, she now watched Lady Katherine carefully as the younger woman, who seemed a bit happier since her husband and future in-laws had decided they were too exhausted from traveling to eat with the family, directed the servants. Where Brentford had then been too busy questioning him about Glenwood to pay attention to his daughters, now he beamed at Samara, obviously happy with her choice, however forced it might have been. And where he had been at a loss, trying to insert himself into his new position as the penniless and ignorant Earl of Easton, he now felt more comfortable in his skin and, more important, as part of a family.

"So, Easton," Brentford said cheerfully as a groom brought out the sweet—a delicious-looking quince custard tart. "When would you like to marry my daughter?"

"I hadn't thought that far ahead, to be honest," he confessed. "I was mostly concerned with getting her home safely and out of the sight of Elizabeth."

"Foresight for which I'll be eternally grateful," Brentford said, "no matter which way the winds blow in the near future."

"I assume we'll know sooner rather than later," Cade said grimly. "Although, who knows? She has seen both sides of the fight. She is an intelligent woman. She might surprise us all."

"Be that as it may, I'm still grateful for your concern about my daughter's safety." Brentford used his dagger to saw off a chunk of the tart. "London has ever been a pit of vipers. And it doesn't seem to be getting any better."

Then why did you send your daughter there? Cade wanted to ask. *Knowing how innocent, how naïve, how unsuited she is for life as anything other than a gypsy?*

But even as he thought the questions, he knew the answer. Brentford had admitted to having Cade in mind for Samara since the very first day. He might have wanted to give Samara the chance to choose her own husband, but Brentford had wanted her to choose *him.* And he'd thought the best way to do that was to push them together and send them somewhere where Samara might get the polish she hadn't succeeded in learning at home, and where Cade might feel inclined to be protective of her.

"You do realize, Brentford, how incredibly fortunate we all are that things worked out the way they did?" Cade asked.

"Of course." Brentford chuckled. "I did not say my reasons for sending my daughter there were good ones."

"Just so we understand each other." Cade raised his cider-filled goblet to the older man.

"*What* are you talking about?" Samara demanded. Her expression, and that of her sisters, was mystified.

"Politics," Cade said smoothly, and Samara rolled her eyes.

"But we should get down to the business of your marriage," Brentford interjected. "Easton, you know I've no sons. I've also no remaining male relatives. Samara stands to inherit a third of my estate. In addition to that, she also brings with her a generous dowry. We'll discuss that later. However, I think you'll be happy to know that as part of Samara's dowry, I shall be returning Glenwood to you. It still thrives, but I've found that raising sheep is not to my liking, nor do I have a talent for it. So Glenwood is yours again."

The bite of tart Cade had taken stuck in his throat. He dislodged it with a hearty gulp of cider and swallowed before trying to speak.

"You are returning Glenwood?" he asked, his voice thick with disbelief.

"I am." Brentford nodded.

Cade wondered if it wouldn't be a little strange for him to throw himself at Brentford and hug him. The older man would probably think so. Instead, Cade nodded. He couldn't trust himself to form the words that would convey to Brentford how happy the news made him.

"Thank you," was the best he could manage.

Brentford acknowledged the gratitude with a nod.

"So what do you say to a wedding the Sunday before Candlemas?" he asked. "That leaves enough time to call the banns, and Samara's natal day is the first of February, so it can be a double celebration." Brentford beamed at his daughter.

"I don't see why not," Cade agreed. He looked at Samara. "I just realized I did not know when your natal day was."

"Now you do," she replied. "And as our wedding anniversary will be so close to it, you'll never forget it."

"It will be highly unlikely," he agreed. They exchanged a smile.

❀

Christmastide at Brentford Hall had never been a rowdy affair; there was no Lord of Misrule as other great households had, although Samara's father did invite the villagers in for wassailing. Samara and her sisters, Katherine desperate to escape the greedy paws of her betrothed husband, spent one particularly brisk morning hunting through the woods for pine boughs, holly branches, and sprigs of rosemary with which to decorate the hearth in the great hall. Cecily discovered a box of bayberry candles and set about distributing them throughout the house. Cade, who had returned to Easton to prepare for Samara's arrival, came back to celebrate with them and stayed for a week after.

"I feel so terrible for Kat," Samara confessed to Cade as they sat together in her private chamber on New Year's Day, a game of chess between them but abandoned to conversation. "She is miserable about having to marry Waltham. I was so happy to escape him that

I didn't give a moment's thought to the idea that my father might arrange for one of my sisters to marry him."

"He is a lout," Cade agreed. "But unfortunately Katherine is not the first to be given to a man who disgusts her, and she won't be the last. I wouldn't worry about her, though. She is of strong stuff. I don't doubt that he will be cowering under her thumb within a month of their wedding." He smiled at her. "It would be almost easier, wouldn't it, if she had never explained herself to you and she was still the nasty little sister she was before?"

"Almost," Samara said. "Though I am glad to have her, and Cecily. I'd be lonely without them."

As soon as the words left her mouth she felt awful. Cade's brother had died! A shadow passed over his face so quickly she wasn't even sure she'd actually seen it. But when he spoke, his voice was steady.

"My own brother and I were not friends," he said. "He could say and do some very cruel things. But I don't know if he did those things because he meant them, or because he saw my father doing them. Stephen was a little soft in the head, and very much my father's pet. My father liked to make that known. He had little time for me and even less love. Stephen, for the most part, followed his example. I like to think that my brother and I could have had a very different relationship if my father had been a different man."

"How horrible!" Samara exclaimed. "My father has not been as attentive as he might have been. But even though at times I was convinced he did not care about me, some part of me must have always known that he did, for he was never cruel. I cannot imagine how it must feel to know for certain that your parent doesn't love you." She ached for him. Would it be improper to hug him? It would only be for comfort, after all. Mostly. And Betty was in the next room.

He smiled a little. "I've gotten over it, I think," he replied. "And for nearly every bad memory I have of my father and brother, I have a beautiful one of my mother. And you have helped, too."

"I have?" What on earth did he mean?

"You have." He nodded. "Before your father gave me the responsibility of you, I was very much a lost soul. I did things for the Crown, but it was because I had nothing tying me down. I had fleeting affairs with unavailable women simply because they were unavailable and could not make me settle down with them. I've never been so terrified of anything as I was when I found out I was to inherit Easton. And even though I made my best effort to fix things, I didn't argue when your father asked me to take you to London. I could have. I would have had a good reason for saying no. Your father had already purchased Glenwood, so I had the gold I needed. I suppose I felt I still owed him something, but in reality, I guess I was looking for an excuse to flee to London, where I was comfortable. And then, there was you." He laughed. "Since my mother's death I haven't felt that protective of anyone. But when I saw how overwhelmed you were by the court, and when Linton made his move ... I couldn't help it. My whole reason for being was to keep harm from befalling you. I almost failed." He looked pleased. "But in the end I didn't."

"No, you didn't," she whispered. Her blood sang in her veins. He did care about her. He might not love her, but he cared. That was enough. For now. "Thank you."

He shrugged. "To be honest, I'm glad I discovered that I have that in me. Too often I see shades of my father and..." He trailed off. "Well, I can work on it. I have been. But that's enough of this. I'm growing maudlin. It's New Year's Day, and I haven't given you your gift."

She was horrified. "Oh, no! I have nothing for you!"

He laughed. "Please don't worry. It's nothing extravagant. I didn't even spend any money on it. Although," he said hurriedly, evidently afraid she was one of those women who expected a man to empty his coffers for her, "had I had the time, I certainly would have."

He rummaged in the leather bag he'd dropped by the chair in which he sat, triumphantly withdrawing a long, narrow, fabric-covered box.

"Stand up and turn around," he commanded.

She held her breath as she obeyed, and he came to stand behind her. He draped it—*a necklace!*—over her collarbone and fastened it, gently reaching beneath her hair. Then he took her by the shoulders and turned her around.

"Perfect," he said, sounding pleased. "I thought it would be, but couldn't be sure until I saw it on you. Go to the glass and tell me what you think."

Betty knelt on the floor in Samara's bedchamber, organizing garments for her trousseau. She looked up as Samara flew through the open door that separated her bedchamber from the sitting room. She shook her head.

"It's beautiful!" Samara gasped. "Oh, Betty, look!"

"Then you like it?" came Cade's voice.

"I love it!" This time she threw restraint to the wind as she ran back and flung her arms around him. She felt him laugh as he returned her embrace, hugging her tightly.

He had never kissed her. It would be so easy to do from this position. All she had to do was pull back an inch or so, turn her head slightly...

Betty, from the bedchamber, cleared her throat.

Chagrined, Samara stepped out of the warm circle of Cade's arms. She touched the cool metal around her throat and went back to the glass. It was gorgeous—oval emerald cabochons set in diamond-shaped gold filigrees.

"Where did you get it, if you didn't purchase it?" she asked. "If you don't mind me asking. Never mind. That was horribly rude." She turned in the mirror, allowing the weak winter sunlight that streamed in through the window to bounce off one of the stones.

"It belonged to my mother," he answered. "But don't worry, it wasn't a gift from my father. Even if he *had* given her anything over the course of their marriage, I wouldn't give it to you. It was a gift from her father."

"I love it," she said again. "Thank you."

Leaning in the open doorway, his eyes on her, he smiled.

❋

Once Twelfth Night had passed, the days began to fly. For three successive Sundays the banns were called and, as expected, no one presented any reason why Lady Samara Haughton should not wed with the Earl of Easton. Her trousseau was finished, the marriage contracts signed, and before she knew it, Samara woke one day in late January to bright, cold sunlight pouring through her bedroom window and puddling on the stone floor.

It was her wedding day.

She shot out of bed as the sound of servants in the sitting room floated through her closed door. She padded over on bare feet and opened the door to see Betty directing them to fill the heavy oak tub that she'd dragged to a spot by the blazing fireplace.

"Good morning," Betty said merrily when she saw Samara standing there. "Did you sleep well?"

"Well enough," Samara said. "I had no nightmares, anyway." She watched the servants trail out of the room, the last one shutting the door behind him.

"I should hope not!" Betty exclaimed. "Not after all you've been through with the earl. You know him. There's no reason to be afraid of marrying him." She waved Samara into the room and helped her disrobe. "Get into the tub now, before the water cools. You don't want to catch a chill on your wedding day."

Samara obeyed and climbed into the hip-high tub. The hot, scented water felt wonderful on her chilled skin. She sat as long as she could before Betty scolded her to stop dallying and get out of the tub so she could dress.

She had only managed to slip into a new, clean chemise before the door opened and Cecily flew in, followed by Katherine, who moved at a much more reluctant pace.

"It is your wedding day!" Cecily exclaimed. "Are you excited? How do you feel?"

Samara considered before answering.

"Numb," she said at last. "I have yet to allow myself to think about it." Cecily's shoulders slumped—surely she'd been expecting a more ecstatic response.

"But I am happy," Samara added. She smiled. "Very, very happy."

"That's enough chatter," Betty said. "Let's get you dressed. Come along!" she called to Cecily and Katherine as she hustled Samara back into her bedchamber, where the gown she had chosen to wear lay flat on the bed.

"You look so beautiful," Cecily breathed when Samara was laced, tied, and ribboned. "That color is perfect for you."

Katherine, who had been silent all morning, nodded her agreement.

"May I see, Betty? Please?" Samara begged.

"Not yet. Lady Cecily, get the hairpins, please. That's a good girl." Betty stood in front of Samara and placed something on her head. She took the pins from Cecily and secured it to Samara's unbound hair. "There. Now you're perfect. Now you may look."

Careful not to muss her gown, Samara tiptoed to the glass. The vision that greeted her almost took her breath away. Cecily was right—the ivory gown with the forest green and gold underskirt really was perfect. It brought out a golden undertone in her skin, made her eyes more vivid, her hair brighter. Her long, flowing curls were topped with a delicate wreath of woven rosemary sprigs and snowdrops, picked yesterday morning and kept cold so they would stay fresh.

There was just one thing missing.

"Betty? Get my necklace, please. The one that was a gift from the earl."

Betty brought the gold and emerald choker to her and helped her put it on.

Now she was perfect.

"I have never wanted to draw myself before," Samara confessed. "Now I find myself wanting to take a few minutes just to capture the details of my dress."

"Well, there's no time for that," Betty told her. "You're to be married. The procession is waiting."

Samara's heart leapt into her throat. Her breath got stuck behind it and for a moment she couldn't breathe. She cast a wild glance back at her bed. She'd never sleep in it again. Tonight, the bed in the master chamber.

After that, Cade's.

❋

The January morning was crisp, cold, and fair. A fine dusting of snow glazed the low-hanging branches of the juniper tree in the churchyard. At the church door, with only Hayden for company, Cade waited for his bride.

At times he felt like he had floated out of his own body and was watching rather than participating in the event. When he was *in* his body, the thudding of his heart, the racing of his blood through his veins and the slight tremble in his limbs reminded him that he wasn't ready for this—he had only just learned he was earl; he needed more time!

Brentford's village church was not unlike Easton's, with its soft red brick walls papered with climbing green ivy. Stained glass windows caught the milky sunlight and threw it back to the ground, where it littered the frost-covered grass with a mosaic of colors. The sight was beautiful. Samara would love it.

Samara.

He heard the musicians before he saw anything. A merry clatter of horns and strings crested the hill upon which Brentford's church squatted. After a few moments the coach followed, slowed to a stop, and she emerged, wrapped in a rich fur-lined cloak and flanked by two small girls in crimson robes with white snowdrops in their hair and clusters of gilded rosemary, tied with silver ribbons, in their kid-gloved hands.

Her sisters, in matching jewel-toned gowns—Lady Katherine in ruby and Lady Cecily in sapphire—were behind her, lifting the hem of her gown so it didn't drag in the snow.

She grew closer, and he saw that her lips were compressed, her knuckles white around the bouquet of fragrant rosemary and holly she held. Was she scared? Having second thoughts? Not that it mattered, the contracts had been signed and the betrothal ceremony held, but still … he didn't want her to do anything she didn't want to do. His knees felt as if they were filled with quince preserves rather than bone. He fought the urge to reach out and grab Hayden for support.

Then her eyes caught his, her face lit up with her smile, and the world stopped spinning. His limbs stilled, his heart returned to its normal rhythm, his blood slowed, and everything was right. She was his, and he loved her.

He loved her.

Then she was beside him, sweeping with her procession into the church to meet the priest where he waited at the altar. Hayden flashed Cade a grin before entering the church himself and joining everyone else—Samara's father and sisters, who carried the cloak she'd divested, Aunt Madge, villagers who had come to witness the event—in their pews. Cade sucked in a deep breath before he went in to join his bride.

She stood to his left—as she should, since Eve had been created from one of the ribs on Adam's left side—and the priest recited the words that would bind them. Cade repeated his part of the script as if by rote but stopped to listen when Samara said her lines. Her voice carried and flowed over the heads of those who had congregated to witness the winter's biggest social event.

He had no memory of placing his mother's ring—gold, set with tiny, smoky gray faceted stones—on the Bible, but there was the priest sprinkling it with holy water and instructing Cade to slide it onto her finger. He did so, holding her hand lightly in his, placing it first on her forefinger, then her middle, then her fourth finger.

He had been to weddings before. Hell, he'd been there when the queen wed King Philip! Why could he not remember what came next?

Oh. The kiss.

He looked at her, trying to gauge what she was feeling. Reluctant? Nervous? As bone-chillingly, stomach-churningly terrified as he was? She gave him a little smile and he relaxed. She wanted to be here. And he wanted to kiss her. Perhaps not with an audience, but he would take what he could get. They were in church, after all.

He took her face in his hands and brushed her lips lightly with his own. He felt her eyelashes flutter against his cheek. He held back—after all, the purpose was to seal the union between them, not to get an early start on the consummation aspect of the whole thing. She smiled against his lips, coaxing a smile from him, and it was over. They were married.

Now they just had to get through the Mass.

It wasn't easy, kneeling there with her under the linen draped over their heads to keep out evil. It was too much like being alone with her. If not for the priest's droning Latin, he might have forgotten they were in church. Samara, for her part, kept silent. He was desperate to know what she was thinking. He wondered if she was able to sense the difference in him. Surely realizing the depth of his feelings had changed him outwardly as well as inwardly. Could she tell?

They took communion. His mouth was so dry the bread stuck, and he had to take more wine than was necessary to dislodge it. A few more moments of incoherent droning from Brentford's priest, and Mass was over. The wedding was over. He was a married man.

They emerged from the church to a smattering of cheers from the villagers gathered around the porch. Cade would have thought it too cold for a large gathering, but apparently many of the locals wanted to see Brentford's daughter marry the elusive and much-gossiped-about Earl of Easton. He hoped they were satisfied, and that they knew he would treat her like she was precious to him. After all, she *was*.

Back at Brentford Hall, a grand wedding feast had been laid out while the ceremony and Mass were taking place. Long tables and benches that had not been there before now crowded the floor of the Great Hall, leaving only enough space for the wedding guests to dance after they had gorged themselves on Brentford's bounty. The musicians that had taken part in the bridal procession arranged themselves in the minstrels' gallery that extended over the hall and struck up a lively tune. The high board looked near collapse beneath the feast that had been arranged there—dozens of roe deer, suckling pigs, salmon and shrimp, whole roasted chickens, and flaky meat pasties. Vegetables were scarce, this being a wedding feast for the nobility, but bowls of shiny red apples, golden quinces, and green pears provided a colorful contrast to all the meat dishes.

Cade and Samara were seated in the lord's and lady's chairs, where they were able to look down upon their guests. After a moment of watching those in attendance, Cade leaned over to whisper to her.

"Do you know all these people?" he asked.

She nodded. "Most of them, yes. Families from the village who have known me since I was born. And some of the local gentry. There is Sir William Southbridge and his wife, and his daughter Agnes."

Agnes. Now why did that sound familiar? Cade squinted at the girl to whom Samara had discreetly gestured.

"He is having trouble marrying her off," Samara murmured. "They have no money, and poor Agnes is hardly likely to get by on her looks or charm. She is a sweet girl, but Sir William has yet to find a man who cares only about that."

Ahh, yes. Now he remembered. The mousy Mistress Agnes from his father's funeral.

"Let the bride and groom begin the dancing!" Brentford called over the din of the crowded hall. "A galliard, I think." He clapped his hands twice, and the musicians shifted to another lively melody.

"Shall we?" Cade held his hand out to his bride. His heart gave an erratic little thump when she accepted it. He wasn't nervous about the dancing; of the many things he'd picked up as a courtier, dancing had come most easily. Thumping just seemed to be what his heart did when she was near.

He led her from the high board to the floor, released her hand and bowed as she curtsied. In response to the notes drifting down from the gallery, they joined hands again and began the galliard.

She laughed as they whirled around, her rosemary-and-snowdrop wreath sliding dangerously to one side of her head. Others soon joined them. From the corner of his eye he noticed Cecily grab Hayden's hand and drag him into the activity. Hayden loathed dancing, said a man was not supposed to prance about like a damned leprechaun. Cade caught his eye, and Hayden shrugged good-naturedly before taking the girl's hand and joining the growing group of wedding guests that hopped and twirled across the floor.

The festivities lasted late into the night, and Brentford must have noticed how his guests were drooping with fatigue—or vomiting from excess of wine—for he called for the musicians to stop.

"This part of the celebration is over," he announced. "I believe it's time for the bride and groom to retire for the evening."

His words ignited another round of whooping. Cade glanced at Samara and saw that her face was scarlet. A wave of pity washed over him. He had participated in the bedding ceremony several times, but he had never considered what it was like to be the one being bedded. And it had to be far worse for her. He, at least, knew what was coming, whereas she had to deal not only with the embarrassment

SOME RISE BY SIN

of being publicly put to bed but the fear of the unknown she, a virgin, surely had.

The crowd rushed them up the stairs to the master bedchamber, which Brentford had kindly given them for the evening. Cade gripped Samara's hand, trying to comfort her as well as keep her from tripping on the steps, for the people around them were serious in their intent. The crowd of wedding guests swelled around them, pushing them up and over the final step and into the attached sitting room. Someone lifted the bedchamber's latch. The door swung open, and Cade and Samara were shoved inside.

"Stop!" Brentford shouted. "Unless you want to witness the consummation with your own eyes?"

Samara's eyes widened. Cade squeezed her hand comfortingly.

"I didn't think so," his father-in-law chuckled when the group settled down. "On account of my daughter and her new husband I thank you all for being here to celebrate with us. Of course, the marriage is not legally binding until it's been consummated. Easton, what are you waiting for? Take your wife to bed! The rest of us will continue the celebration. Back to the hall, all of you!"

Cade caught several ribald jokes over the laughing and cheering that accompanied the guests back down the stairs. Katherine and Cecily were two of the last to turn. Katherine's eyes raked over them with a certain resignation, while Cecily's were bright with curiosity.

"Goodnight!" she said merrily.

"Cecily!" Katherine hissed. She rolled her eyes. "Come."

They disappeared down the candlelit stairwell. Cade lingered by the open door. If there was any moment in his life he hadn't imagined ever happening, it was this one.

"Finally," he couldn't help saying.

Chapter Twenty-Seven

CADE FIRMLY SHUT THE DOOR TO THE BEDCHAMBER AFTER Katherine and Cecily disappeared. Samara stood by the bed, as motionless as a corpse, and waited for him to turn around. When he did, she found herself unable to speak. She could only look at him.

Dear God, that was mortifying! Her face burned.

"Are you all right?" he asked softly, coming toward her.

She gulped. "Yes."

"Of all the ridiculous traditions, that has to be one of the worst." He came to stand near her—not so near that she could touch him but not so far that he felt distant. "Do you want me to call Betty to help you undress?"

"I—no," she said. Her voice had dropped to a whisper.

You ninny! You are not the first to go untouched to the marriage bed. And you certainly won't be the last. Besides, look at him. Are you honestly going to act like you don't want him to touch you?

He tilted his head. "Do you want me to do it?"

Did he even have to ask? She nodded.

"I'm certain you know how," she added in an attempt to show him she wasn't scared.

He laughed, a low chuckle, as he came to stand behind her.

"I do," he agreed as he unlaced her bodice. "Although never under these circumstances."

"I should hope not!" Her fingers trembled as she attempted to help him unhook her heavy skirt from her loosened bodice. He placed his hand over hers to still her fingers and proceeded to undo all the hooks himself. When he was finished, her skirt puddled with a swish at her feet.

He moved on to her sleeves, untying each of the ivory silk bows that bound the sleeves to her bodice. He drew each from her arm and laid it over the carved oak chair. He removed her bodice and placed it with her sleeves, then unlaced her brocade kirtle.

A fire blazed in the fireplace, but with each layer of clothing that disappeared, gooseflesh rippled over her skin.

She wasn't cold, though. It was because of him.

After a while, he took away her petticoat and put it with the other pieces of her gown. She stood shivering in her chemise and black silk slippers.

"Are you cold?" he asked, concern softening his voice.

She shook her head. "No."

He smiled a little. "Sit on the bed."

Trembling, she obeyed.

He knelt on the floor and drew her slippers off.

"You make an excellent lady's maid," she told him. God's toenail! Was that throaty voice hers?

He laughed again.

"I'm glad to hear that," he said, standing, "because for the next few hours I don't want to share you with anyone, including Betty." He drew off his own clothing—first his black velvet, gold-trimmed robe, then his matching doublet. He kicked off his black leather shoes and drew off his hose, leaving him standing in nothing but a thigh-length, ruffle-collared linen shirt.

Her eyes drank him in as he undressed, not caring for the moment if it was improper. She wanted to *see* him. His legs were muscular, not too thick or too thin, and covered in a mat of fine black hair. Very nice indeed. Her gaze drifted upward to the hem of his shirt, but the blood rushed to her cheeks and she skipped up to his face. She didn't know why she was feeling so uncertain. She'd nearly seen him naked before, in the lake. If she had allowed herself to look, little of this would be a surprise to her now. Damn the gentle upbringing that had made her shield her eyes!

Still clad in his shirt, he turned to her.

"Why don't you get under the coverlet?" he suggested.

"But I'm not cold." She realized what he was getting at and stopped arguing. "Oh. Yes. I will."

He went to the small table by the fireplace. "Wine?"

God, yes. Anything to calm the churning in her stomach.

"Please," she said. She arranged herself beneath the velvet coverlet.

He filled two goblets—one with wine from the carafe, and one with liquid from a separate pitcher—and brought the goblets to the bed. He handed her the one with the wine and tapped the rim of his goblet against hers.

"A toast to our marriage," he said. "May we never find reason to murder each other in our sleep."

She giggled and drank deeply from her cup, the wine sinking into her belly and warming her blood. Cade drank too, then took both goblets and set them on the table beside the bed.

"I don't want to frighten you," he began. "You are aware that it will hurt the first time?"

She swallowed hard and nodded. "Yes. Betty told me."

"Only the first time, though. And I'll do whatever I can to keep from hurting you any more than necessary," he promised.

She stared into his face. His light blue eyes were full of concern, and his brow, as usual, was furrowed. She reached up with one hand and laid it against his clenched jaw.

"I trust you," she said.

The worry melted from his face. He smiled.

"I'm glad," he said, and kissed her.

It wasn't at all like their first kiss, that day in church. Had it only been a few hours? His mouth tasted of cider, not wine, and that surprised her. She felt herself going languid as his lips brushed over her cheek, her jaw, her throat. She lay back against the pillows without really thinking about what she was doing. He followed her down, stretching his legs so they lay against hers, one hand warm on her cheek, the other gently twisting one of her long curls in his fingers.

Samara lifted her arms and wrapped them around him, entwining her fingers in the soft, slightly too-long hair at the nape of his neck. She hugged him close, and his hand abandoned her hair, instead moving downward just to sweep back up along her side, catching the hem of her chemise and drawing it up to lie at her hip.

She trembled, but only partly with fear. She released her hold on him and allowed him to pull the chemise over her head and toss it to the floor. The linen bedclothes were soft against her skin. Her breath came and went in short bursts.

"You, next," she managed to say, and helped him sit up so that he could remove his own shirt.

Gently, with one hand, he pushed her back down to the pillows. His long body covered hers. She ran her fingers over his bare shoulders and down his muscled arms, up his back and down the smooth skin along his sides. How many times had she refused to allow herself to imagine touching him like this? Now she could. He shivered, the muscles tensing beneath his skin, and she dropped her hands.

"I'm sorry," she whispered.

"No," he ground out. "You have nothing to be sorry about." He kissed her again, and she marveled at the way her lips already seemed to know what to do in return. They continued like that, his hands brushing over, or lingering on, spots on her body she never even looked at, let alone touched, until an aching fire that erupted in her belly threatened to consume her.

"Cade," she gasped, frightened.

He shifted so he could look at her. She knew she must look frantic, but she had no idea what was happening to her.

"Shh. It's all right," he comforted her. He brushed a curl, matted to her skin by the sheen of sweat that had formed, from her shoulder, then kissed where it had been. He shifted himself so that he hovered over her, his elbows propping him up. "Remember," he told her. "There will be pain, but it only lasts a moment, and I'll try to make it as easy as possible."

She nodded, closed her eyes. He didn't seem afraid—this must be what was supposed to happen. It was all right.

His kiss absorbed most of her gasp, but it was more a gasp of surprise than pain. That receded quickly, as he'd promised. In fact, it felt rather nice, once she grew accustomed to the bizarre situation in which she found herself. She almost wanted to laugh, but some deep-rooted instinct told her that might not be a good idea. At any rate the urge to laugh receded almost as quickly as the pain of her lost virginity. It was replaced by the urge to maybe move with him, help him along, instead of letting him do all the work. But she had no idea what to do. So instead she raised her legs a little, pressing her knees against his hips and wrapping her arms around his shoulders, and held him while she closed her eyes and let herself float away.

It didn't seem to last for very long, although she had nothing with which to compare it. She was strangely disappointed when he rolled off her, wrapped her in arms that were damp with perspiration, and pulled her close to him.

Well, *that* part was nice. She snuggled into the circle his arms made around her and closed her eyes.

"Are you all right?" he asked again, his voice soft.

Somehow she sensed he would be disappointed to know that the longing he'd caused had merely eased rather than gone away entirely. But she wasn't lying when she whispered, "I'm wonderful" in response to his question.

"Tired?" he asked, stroking her hair.

She hadn't thought about it until then, but yes, she was exhausted. What a day it had been! And she hadn't slept well the night before. She'd had no nightmares, as she'd told Betty, but sleep had been hard to find and harder to keep. Even as she thought about it, she stifled a yawn and her eyelids fluttered shut.

"Very," she murmured.

"Go to sleep, then, *wife*," he whispered. He kissed her on her temple, and she felt him shift his body. Her eyelids flew open again.

"You're not leaving?" she asked.

"No," he promised. "Just pulling the coverlet back up."

"Oh," she said. He brought the blanket up and over them, tucking it against her shoulder as he settled himself. One of his arms lay beneath her and the other circled around her front, cradling her against his chest. The soft sound of his rhythmic breathing lulled her.

Very nice indeed.

Within moments, she slept.

❀

The pale, weak sun was high in the gray-white winter sky when the baggage cart and the small coach carrying Aunt Madge and Betty rumbled out of the courtyard on their way to Easton Manor. Samara, flanked by Cade and Hayden and seated atop her favorite horse—which her father had allowed her to take to her new home as a wedding gift—watched them go. As they disappeared among the trees, she felt the remnants of her old life go with them.

"Take care of my daughter, Easton," Samara's father said.

"I will cherish her," Cade vowed, and Samara's cheeks burned. She sneaked a glance at Katherine, who stood in the courtyard with them, but her sister didn't look resentful. In fact, her eyes were red-rimmed, a clear indication that she'd been crying. Or was trying very hard not to.

Cecily had been less inclined to hide her emotions.

"You just came back," she'd sobbed that morning as she helped Samara pack the bag she would carry on her horse. "And now you're leaving again."

"I'm not going nearly as far this time, Cecily," Samara soothed her. "I'm only a half-day's ride away. We shall see each other so much you'll get sick of me and wish I'd married someone on the Continent."

Cecily sniffled in response.

Samara had glanced toward the bed, which was stripped bare. The bloody sheet waved proudly in the January wind and alerted everyone that she was legally married to the Earl of Easton. She was a countess! *A countess who has no idea how to be one.*

She'd sighed. Cade was going to regret his moment of chivalry once he saw what kind of woman he'd taken to wife.

Now she bid goodbye to her family even as the wind emerged from the brown, bare gardens, carrying with it the scent of snow.

"I hate to rush this, but I'm afraid it will storm," Cade said, his tone full of regret. "We should be on our way before it hits."

"Of course," Brentford agreed. He backed away from Samara's horse and stood between his unmarried daughters. "Have a safe trip, and we shall see you for Katherine's wedding in the summer."

"I hope before then." Samara exchanged a meaningful look with Katherine, who smiled in return.

"Ready?" Cade asked, and Samara took a deep breath and nodded. She could do this. She wasn't unintelligent. She could learn. After all, Cade had never expected to be the earl. They would learn together.

"Goodbye!" they called as they set off down the oak-lined drive. Her family's chorus of goodbyes echoed after her, until they were too far away to hear them anymore.

The cold air cleared both her lungs and her head as they rode together. It had been far too long since she'd been atop a horse—her trips to and from London, not to mention the few excursions she'd made through the city, had happened while she'd been stuffed inside a coach or a barge. There was something to be said for fresh, clean air and beautiful scenery. London had been wonderful in its way, but Samara realized she belonged here in the country, not catering to the whims of people who wouldn't know a juniper tree if one sprouted in the middle of their hall.

Their horses cantered into the village of Easton at sunset as fat white flakes of snow drifted from the sky. They wouldn't stick—they rarely did—but they were beautiful nonetheless as they fluttered toward the ground. At least Samara assumed they were; she saw nothing except the faces of people lined up along the village road, staring at her as she made her entrance as the new Countess of Easton.

Her heart thudded against her rib cage as she met the stares of the people. *Her* people. She wondered if she met their expectations, or if they saw through her. Certainly she was beautiful, but did that mean anything? Could they tell simply by looking at her that they terrified her?

As if in answer to her fears, they threw flowers at her as her small party made its way through the village. Snowdrops and crocus, the only blooms one could find at this time of year, but also sprigs of fresh rosemary and even dried rose petals. That touched her. She smiled and waved, and her small gestures were met with cheers. Parents lifted children onto their shoulders so they might see her better, and the children left on their feet scrambled toward her horse and reached out with tiny hands. She made it a point to graze as many of those hands as she could with her own, and by the time they reached the white-haired woman, emotion filled her throat to the point of pain.

The woman, however, almost stopped her in her tracks. Dressed entirely in black with a shock of white hair providing the only contrast aside from her sallow, wrinkled skin, the woman let her milky eyes follow Cade and Samara as they cantered along the road. She stood with a small group Samara assumed was her family—a stodgy female who appeared to be in her mid- to late thirties, a man who looked similar in age to the stodgy woman, and two boys who seemed to be teetering between childhood and adulthood, perhaps close to Cecily's age. The four younger people wore tentative smiles, but the old woman's face was etched in a scowl so deep Samara feared it might be permanent.

Samara glanced at Cade, wanting to see his reaction, but he simply inclined his head toward the woman and her family. The crone gave no signal that she'd seen it. She just stared, her gaze trailing them as they moved past. Even once they had their backs to her, Samara felt as though she could feel the woman's gaze boring into her.

Moments later they rode into Easton's courtyard, and thoughts of the strange old woman were swept from Samara's mind by the sight of several people in servants' garb lined up in front of the main entrance.

"Are you ready?" Cade asked her softly when their horses stop. She swallowed hard and nodded. She wouldn't let anyone know she was afraid—she knew that servants, unless they were unusually decent people, would seize upon any weakness and use it against her if they could. She would need their help, so it was best if she was confident from the start.

Cade dismounted and came around to help her down, taking her waist in his hands as he gently pulled her from the horse. She was distracted for a moment, thinking of the previous night when his hands had been in other places, and her cheeks got warm. He set her down before he could see her blush. She hoped. If he did see it, he said nothing.

"This is your new mistress, my countess," he announced to the shivering little group. "We were married yesterday. You will do as she says, and show her the respect due her station, and you will make the transition from Brentford to Easton as easy for her as possible. Is that understood?"

There was a chorus of *yes, my lord*s and *welcome, my lady*s. Samara smiled widely, albeit shakily.

"What are your names, please?' she said.

She met the cook, Goodwife Crosby; and the housekeeper, Goodwife Bingham, who wasn't any older than Samara herself, who said, "Margery, if you please, my lady. Goodwife Bingham was my ma." Then there were Margery's sister, Nan, the head laundress; Harry, the bailiff; and Jefferson, the steward, who had once served at Riverview. There were others, Margery told her—chambermaids, grooms, and the like, who were busy preparing for her arrival and were ready to meet her when it was convenient for her. And would she need a body servant?

"No, thank you," Samara responded as she heard the baggage cart and the coach rumble into the courtyard behind them. "I've brought my maid with me from home."

"Let's go inside," Cade suggested, touching the small of her back. "Hayden, help Aunt Madge, would you?" He grinned at Samara, a surprisingly boyish grin, and escorted her into Easton Manor.

She'd been here before, but not since she was a child. It had seemed so large to her then, and gloomy, with its dark corners hung with spiderwebs, half-melted, deformed candles on the walls, and cracked glass windows. It had been the setting for many of the scary stories she'd liked to tell her sisters. She stood in the Great Hall and noticed that the windows were no longer cracked. The floor was strewn with fresh, fragrant rushes, and she didn't feel the prickle, however imagined, of insects running through her hair. That was comforting. Though she'd known she would be living at Easton Manor, it hadn't occurred to her until now how eerie the building had appeared to her childhood self.

A fire crackled cozily in the hearth as Samara continued her inspection. The high board was oiled to a glossy sheen, lined with benches and two carved wooden chairs in the head spots. Other, smaller tables flanked the archway that, Samara supposed, led to the Great Chamber, but their surfaces were bare. So were the walls. There was nothing like the beautiful screen at Hill House, no tapestries on the walls, no coat of arms, and no paint on the wainscoting or even the plaster.

She turned herself in a circle, searching for anything that might strike her as beautiful. The oak paneling on the walls was lovely, but she'd seen it before. The furniture was well-made but had no personality. She gazed around until her eyes met Cade's, and she was mortified to see that he wore a grin on his face.

"I thought I would leave it up to you," he explained.

"What?" she asked innocently, though she knew he'd figured her out.

"Decorations," he replied. "This place was in a shambles when I inherited it, and it took every second until I left to take you to the city to make sure it wouldn't collapse around us. When I came back, I did have a few weeks to decorate, but I thought you might enjoy it far more than I would. And I thought it would help you feel at home if you had some say in the pieces we would display."

A warm sensation grew around her heart as she absorbed his words. Before she could stop herself, she threw herself into his arms. How did he know her so well?

He laughed; beneath her cheek she felt his chest shudder with the action.

"I take it you're happy?" he asked as he put his arms around her.

"Very," she assured him. "I should love to decorate the hall. When can we start?"

"Soon," he promised. "I have other things to show you."

He led her around on a tour of the chambers, many of which she'd never seen before. For all his apologies on the bare state of most of the rooms, she thought they looked wonderful, if boring, compared to the rooms in her memory. Easton Manor had been crumbling since she was a little girl. She was amazed that he had managed to repair it so thoroughly, so quickly.

"I couldn't have without your father's aid," he admitted. "His generosity was a great help, although at the time I didn't want to admit it."

"Why not?" she asked, curious.

"Because the only thing I had of value was the thing that was most important to me," he answered. "Glenwood. It had belonged to my mother, and my father never did gain ownership of it. That's how she was able to will it to me when she died. It was all I had left of her. When your father offered to buy it, I almost turned him down."

"But now you have it back," she said. Her eyes widened as a thought occurred to her. "Is that why you offered for me? Did you know my father would make it part of my dowry?"

Oh, please, no.

"Of course not," he assured her. "I had no idea. I was ecstatic to get it back, don't get me wrong, but I realized that Glenwood is no longer the most valuable thing I have."

She frowned. "It's not?" He must mean Easton.

He shook his head.

"You are," he said.

✸

He went to her again that night, and this time she wasn't afraid—he could tell by the way she reached for him when he appeared in the doorway separating their bedchambers.

An hour after he'd entered her bed, she lay half-sprawled over his chest, her hair a blazing curtain over her bare back, her breathing soft and even. She'd entwined her fingers with his and idly traced the base of his thumb with the tip of hers. The sensation lulled him, and he felt his eyelids growing heavy, but then she spoke.

"Cade?" Her voice was soft.

"Hmm?"

"Who was that woman there this morning, in the village? The one dressed in black?"

Damn. So she'd seen her. Not that Goodwife Hawke was easy to miss, standing there in her black mourning clothes like the witch out of a child's tale. But he'd been hoping to avoid the subject for as long as possible. The last thing Samara needed while she was adjusting to her new life was the threat of the old bat showing up to make that new life miserable.

"That was Lucy Hawke. She used to be the housekeeper here."

"Used to be?"

"I dismissed her when my father died."

✸ 372 ✸

"You dismissed her? Why?"

She didn't need to know the details. "It wasn't going to work," he said simply. "She was very loyal to my father, and not so loyal to me. She couldn't be trusted, so I allowed her to retire to her daughter's home."

"The woman that was standing with her?"

"Mmm-hmm."

"I see." She was silent again, her thumb still tracing circles on his hand. He relaxed. "Why did you not get along with your father?"

He wouldn't get annoyed. It was something she should know, if only to clarify any misconceptions she might have about him thanks to his father and the stories he'd spread after Cade took off. But he didn't particularly want to have this conversation on their first night together in their home.

"Not tonight, Samara." Even he heard the tightness in his voice.

"But—"

"I *said* not tonight." He disentangled his hand from hers and reached down to pull the coverlet up to cover both of them. As he did, he felt her stiffen against him. Damn it. He'd hurt her.

He made an effort to tuck the coverlet around her so that none of her was bared to the chill that hovered in the air even with repaired windows and a merry fire in the corner of the room. She softened a bit at the gesture. He wrapped his arms around her and pulled her close to him again. Strange, how he'd never wanted to spend a full night in bed with a woman but here, on their second night as husband and wife, he couldn't imagine falling asleep without her near.

"You will tell me at some point," she said.

He kissed her hair. "I know."

Chapter Twenty-Eight

CADE WOKE LATE THE NEXT MORNING AND FOUND THAT SAMAra had already managed to slip from the bed without disturbing him. Cade went to his own bedchamber, washed, and dressed in worn breeches and a linen shirt that had been laundered so many times it was softer than any velvet doublet he owned. In the old, simple hand-me-downs from another era, he felt so much more comfortable. He realized he would be completely happy if he never had to wear court finery again.

He checked Samara's sitting room, but she wasn't there. Betty was, however, busily unpacking her mistress's clothing and belongings.

"Good morning, Betty," Cade said. "Where is my wife?"

"Oh! Good morning, my lord." Betty curtsied quickly. "I'm sorry, but I don't know where she went. She's usually not an early riser, Lady Samara—excuse me, Lady Easton—but she was up with the sun this morning. I brought her something to break her fast, and she ate it, but I haven't seen her since."

"That's fine, Betty. I'll find her." He glanced toward the casement window and took note of what a lovely day it was. As usual, the snow that fell the day before hadn't stuck to the ground, but the same snow that had glazed the juniper branches by the church frosted the trees outside and made a pretty picture. He thought he knew where Samara might have gone.

He threw on his cloak and went out to the knot gardens, which had been painstakingly pruned, shaped, and replanted over the summer and throughout the autumn. It was barren now, but if he knew Samara, she would manage to find something beautiful. But there was no sign of her near any of the stone benches, nor was she concealed by any of the tall shrubs. Had she fallen into the pond? Probably not, but he checked anyway. She wasn't there.

Worry gnawed at him. He thought back to the previous night, the way she'd stiffened beneath his arm after he'd snapped at her. She wouldn't have run away, would she? No, she wasn't that childish. And she hadn't been angry enough to demand that he sleep in his own bed. She had to be around here somewhere.

He skirted the perimeter of the manor, occasionally noting what a good job Brentford's men had done repairing the crumbling stone and cracked windows. He remembered how he had dreaded appealing to the other man for help. Funny how it had all been worth it in the end. He was so busy marveling over his good fortune that he didn't see Samara, kneeling in the herb garden in an old green gown and fur-lined cloak, until he almost tripped over her.

"There you are!" he said. Relief colored his words.

She looked up, sheepish, a sheaf of drawings in her arms. The rich, dark fur of her cloak framed her face, rosy with the cold. Her eyes sparkled. "I wasn't drawing," she said. "Not really."

He was puzzled. "I don't mind if you draw," he said. "We discussed that. Remember?"

She shook her head. "A good wife wouldn't," she said. Before he could protest, she stood and showed him what she had been doing.

He squinted. "What is this?"

"I know flowers, but I'm not so good with herbs," she confessed. "That was Kat's area of expertise. But I know it's important, and I want to learn. I sketched the layout of the herb garden, and I was going to ask either Goodwife Crosby or Margery to tell me what goes where. It's winter, but they should at least be able to tell me where to find things in case I need them. For medicines or soaps or whatever else they are used for."

"A good idea," he agreed. "That was wise of you."

She smiled and stuffed her drawings back into their case.

"Were you looking for me long?" she asked as they began to walk back toward the gardens. "I'm sorry. You were in such a deep sleep when I woke that I couldn't bear to disturb you."

"No," he said. "I was coming to apologize to you, for speaking harshly to you last night. Your questions were honest and warranted. I shouldn't have let my personal feelings get in the way."

"I should have known better than to pry," she countered. "I remember well your reaction that day by the lake when I called your father a gentleman. You looked as though I'd slapped you. I have to admit I was making it up. I don't have many memories of your father, but *gentleman* is not the first word I would normally use to describe what I remember. I'm sorry, but it's true."

He grinned ruefully.

"You're right. He wasn't a gentleman. He hated me, and he hated my mother. He fell on hard times after Stephen's mother died, and he was forced to marry my mother for her dowry. She conceived me on their wedding night, I suppose, because the stories say he never touched her after that. I've never been sure why hated me. I imagine it's because Stephen was his pet, and I am everything Stephen was not. And I am not being arrogant. You knew Stephen."

"I did," she agreed, and pulled her cloak more tightly around her.

"Goodwife Hawke and my father were children together. She was the daughter of two household servants," he continued. "None of my father's siblings survived infancy, so I suppose she was like a sister to him. She was even educated with him. Strange, I know, but it allowed them to communicate when my father was away, on the rare occasion she didn't travel with him."

"Was it—were they in love, do you think?" Samara ventured.

Cade shuddered at the thought. "I don't *think* so. I never knew my father to express love for anyone but Stephen, although he did tolerate Goodwife Hawke's arrogance. No, I think he just regarded her as a sister. She even traveled to London with the family the year Stephen was born. She and Stephen's mother both gave birth at Riverview. Her daughter died, unfortunately, but as Stephen's mother also died shortly after birthing him, Goodwife Hawke devoted herself to him. I suppose that's another reason Stephen was so spoiled."

"And your mother?" Samara asked. Her tone was cautious. "You don't have to talk about her if you don't want to. I don't remember her at all. Just as I don't remember you."

"My mother…" Cade allowed his voice to trail off while he gathered his thoughts. Why wouldn't Samara want to know about his mother? She couldn't have memories of her own, being only a child when Lady Brentford had died, but he'd had sixteen years with his. "My mother was an angel. She was my grandfather's only daughter, and he doted on her, though not to the point of spoiling her. My father treated her horribly. He resented having to marry her, and he resented her birthing another son. She even named me after him, John, in hopes he would soften toward us. But it only seemed to make him angrier. He was not averse to beating her over some imagined slight or wrongdoing."

A lump emerged in his throat. He swallowed hard. The last thing he wanted to do was cry in front of her.

"She died when I was sixteen, of a wasting sickness. I saw to her funeral and burial. My father and Stephen couldn't be bothered."

"Is that why you left?" Her voice was soft.

"She was the only reason I'd stayed as long as I did. I wasn't going to leave her behind with him. As soon as her funeral was over I left. I went to Hayden and stayed with him for a few months, and then we both went to London."

"And you changed your name."

He shook his head. "I didn't change it. My full name is John Cade Badgley. My mother's maiden name was Cade. I simply started to use it in an attempt to keep her near me, and distance myself from any vestiges of my father that might have remained in me."

"I like it better," she told him. "You don't seem like a John."

"I'm more like a John than I want to be," he muttered darkly, glancing at his hand, which still bore slight traces of mottled yellow and brown proof of the beating he'd given Linton.

They'd reached the garden. She took his arm and drew him toward one of the stone benches, the first one he'd gone to in search of her. They sat.

"What do you mean?" she asked.

"Come, Samara. You've seen it. The way I grabbed you that day in the palace and dragged you to the alcove. I hurt you."

"You weren't trying to hurt me," she argued. "You were trying to save me from being overheard. You were anxious for me."

He considered that.

"Well, you're right about that, I suppose," he allowed. "But I almost did the same to Lady Beddington, when she was angry that I didn't want her."

A shadow passed over Samara's face. Then she gave a little laugh. "She nearly drove me to violence at one point as well. The only thing that stopped me from kicking her in the shins was Jane Dormer."

"What?" Cade was momentarily distracted from his self-loathing. "What happened?"

"I accidentally stepped on the hem of her skirt, and she called me a clumsy ox."

Cade laughed out loud. He could imagine the scene. Women—on an individual basis, they could be God's greatest gift to man. In groups larger than two, however, they could be downright dangerous.

"Forget about her," he said. He reached out and touched her cheek. "I have."

"And this," she said.

"What?"

"Another reason why you are not like your father," she declared. She placed her hand over his and held it to her face. "Did you ever see your father do this?"

"No," he admitted.

"Would your father have given your mother free rein to decorate the great hall as she saw fit? Or agree to allow her to do some utterly unorthodox thing simply because she loved it, even if it got in the way of her wifely duties?"

He started to smile. "No, he wouldn't."

"There, do you see? You're nothing like him. If you were, I wouldn't be here. At least, not of my own volition."

"Of course, you would." It was time to lighten the atmosphere. "If your only other choice was Lord Pustule."

"Oh!" she gasped. She dropped her drawings to the frost-covered grass and pummeled him with fists no more powerful than a honeybee's wings. He laughed and grabbed at them, stilling her assault.

Her eyes sparkled, and her face was flushed with laughter, in addition to the cold.

She was so beautiful.

"Samara, I—"

Was it his imagination, or did she flinch? His resolve faltered. He shouldn't tell her he loved her. Not when she didn't return the sentiment.

"I'm glad you're happy. At least, you seem happy. You're contented with all this? With marriage to me?" He held his breath, waiting for her answer.

"I am perfect with all this," she replied. "How could I not be? I'm near my family and the part of the world I know. And my husband is kind and patient with my ignorance and oddness and—" she blushed—"handsome. Even if I'd chosen you, I couldn't have done better."

He supposed he should have focused on her compliments rather than the reminder that she'd been forced to choose him for lack of a better option. But he couldn't help it. His heart twisted in his chest, and the ache radiated to the pit of his stomach.

He was stupid to have fallen for her. He'd always been good at keeping women at an arm's distance. How had she managed to get past his defenses?

❀

The days sailed by. Winter melted into spring, and Samara, to her surprise, was only slightly overwhelmed by the duties that greeted her as the air turned warmer. She must have paid more attention than she'd thought, or perhaps the knowledge, though still mind-numbingly tedious to her, was intrinsic. Either way, she found herself tending the herb and vegetable gardens with Goodwife Crosby in the morning, helping make soap and perfume after dinner, and planning menus in the late afternoon. It still bored her almost to tears, but she was rewarded in the evenings, which were spent poring through paintings and tapestries dragged down from the storage room in the east tower and choosing which ones she liked best for the servants to hang in the great hall.

Nights—which were quickly becoming her favorite part of the day—were spent with Cade, first in conversation and then in his arms.

She hadn't expected to enjoy *that* part of marriage as much as she did. She knew the fact that Cade almost always spent the night in her bed caused gossip among the household servants, but not of the malicious variety. Whether they were happy to see their master and his wife get on so well or if they were just excited over the prospect of an heir, she didn't know, but of the tiny bits of gossip she caught while moving about the house, none of it was mean-spirited.

"You've endeared yourself to them," Cade told her one night as they ate supper in her sitting room. "They like how you aren't afraid to ask for their help or opinion on household matters. My father treated his servants so badly that by the time I arrived most of them had resorted to poaching to feed themselves rather than work for him. The servants we have now were probably terrified at the thought of working here. You have reassured them."

She grew pleasantly warm at his words. If only Kat could hear them! How surprised her sister would be!

Oh! That reminded her.

"My father sent a message earlier today," she said. "I had forgotten to tell you. It seems Kat's wedding will be held this July. Wexley and his family will come down from Yorkshire and take her with them when they return."

"Poor Katherine," Cade said. "I have a feeling she'd hate it, but I pity her."

"As do I," Samara agreed. "I'm so glad everything between us was worked out before this. I can't bear the idea of her going to live there, with them, all the while thinking no one here cared about her."

Cade smiled.

"There's another bit of news I've been saving," he said casually. "From the message I received today, it looks as if Catholics in England are safe for the time being. In February Elizabeth's Parliament passed something called the Act of Uniformity, which serves to make her Supreme Governor of the Church while basically uniting the Catholic and Protestant churches."

"Unite them?" Samara asked. She set down her dagger and stared at him. "How is that even possible? And why?"

"To do away with the religious divide that has plagued England for the past thirty years, I would think," he said. "All of the fighting has weakened us considerably. Not that I believe this act will eradicate the animosity completely, for there are zealots on each side, but I think it's a step in the right direction. She has many reasons not to want to alienate Catholics, relations with Spain and France being only two of them."

"So what does it mean?" Would she be now be considered a heretic? Or would she lie and imperil her immortal soul? She didn't think she had it in her to be a martyr.

"Everyone is to go to church once a week or be fined twelve pence. The Book of Common Prayer is to be used, but Communion will use the wording from the book of 1549, and so it is open to interpretation no matter who is reading it. We will not be forced to deny the real presence of Christ in Communion. At least not privately." He took a swig from his goblet. "It would appear that Elizabeth is mostly concerned with *conformity on the outside*. As long as we don't challenge her authority as Supreme Head, or Governor, of the Church, she is willing to look the other way if we are quiet about what we do."

Samara found the explanation confusing, but she didn't have the political experience Cade did. That was all right. She would follow his lead. She didn't think he would endanger her.

She nodded. "God knows what is in my heart, anyway. I don't believe He would look down on us for practicing self-preservation."

"I agree," he said. Then he sneezed. Four times, in quick succession.

"Are you ill?" she asked, her attention diverted. This would be a test. Neither of them had been ill since the wedding. In fact, it had been a surprisingly healthy winter for everyone, both in the household and the village. She had yet to nurse anyone through sickness and wasn't sure she was ready.

"I'm fine," he said, but sneezed again. "I was out of doors all day overseeing the planting. This happens to me sometimes in the spring. I'm not ill, but perhaps it's best if I sleep in my own bed tonight so I don't keep you awake."

"All right." She was disappointed but tried not to show it. She'd be fine without him for one night.

He washed his hands in the bowl of water that had been left on the small table, then dried them with his linen napkin. Standing, he came over to her and kissed her cheek quickly before he spun away and sneezed loudly.

"I promise I'm fine," he said, half-laughing. He shook his head. "A good night's sleep is all I need. I'll see you in the morning."

"All right," she repeated, still concerned but determined not to show worry if he didn't. "Sleep well."

"You too, sweetheart." He kissed her again and was gone, the door separating their chambers shutting behind him.

"Betty," Samara called, hoping her maid could hear her from her tiny chamber adjacent to Samara's. "Are you hungry? There is plenty of food left. And I need you to come and help me undress. I'm going to bed."

Betty emerged from her room, her eyes scanning the remains of their meal.

"Aye, I'm hungry, and thank you," she said. "Let's get you undressed first. Where is his lordship?"

"He claims he's not ill, but he started to sneeze toward the end of supper." Samara turned and let Betty unlace her bodice. "He chose to sleep in his own bed tonight so that he didn't keep me up."

"Thoughtful and considerate, he is." Betty's approval was plain in her voice.

"He is," Samara agreed softly.

Clad now only in her chemise, Samara bound her hair in a braid and moved around the room while Betty devoured what was left of the meal. She poked at the low-burning fire, straightened the gauzy emerald bed hangings, opened and closed her jewelry box for no apparent reason, and arranged her slippers in neat pairs in the chest in which she stored them. Betty took the trenchers back to the kitchens, and Samara was alone.

She missed Cade.

No, you don't, she told herself. You've simply grown used to having him around. One night apart will not kill you. You are not your father.

Funny, how she and Cade spent so much time telling themselves that.

But she should go and see if he was all right. That's what a wife would do. She went to the door and moved to push it open but before she could, a wave of nausea gripped her. She clapped a hand to her mouth and whirled, her eyes scanning the room for the chamber pot.

She couldn't find it right away, but as it turned out, she didn't need it. The nausea passed as quickly as it came over her. But it left her chilled, shaky, and damp with sweat. Was she ill too? It was good, then, that Cade was spending the night away from her. She didn't want to make him sicker than he already was. Though he said he wasn't.

She was suddenly exhausted and had to grip the door frame to keep from collapsing. Yes, she was ill. No doubt about that. She staggered to the large, velvet-covered bed and burrowed beneath the linen sheets piled there. She curled into a ball on her side and promptly fell asleep.

❋

She woke to silence a few hours later. The fire had been reduced to embers, but she wasn't cold. Her stomach felt fine. In fact, she was ravenous.

She swung her legs over and stuffed her feet into the kid slippers she kept beside her bed. She pulled a robe over her chemise and picked up a candlestick. She remembered that Goodwife Crosby had baked several small cakes with the quince preserves left over from the winter's stores. And now that she remembered that, nothing would do but that she have one.

She padded quietly through her chambers and to the top of the staircase, where she met with more silence. She fled down the steps and into the hall, then through the door to the kitchens. She located the cakes, on a platter high on a shelf, took one, and ate it with her hands. Nothing had ever tasted so good. When she was done, she even sucked the smudges of preserves from her fingers. She considered having another but remembered her quick bout of nausea earlier and decided it probably wasn't a good idea. Not if she wanted to be well enough to nurse Cade through whatever illness he denied having.

But she was wide awake. And if she remembered correctly, there was a book on herbal remedies and healing in Easton's library. It could only help her to pick it up and read it. If she could cure him of his illness, it might give her the confidence to do the same for others when need arose. She wiped her hands on one of Goodwife Crosby's drying cloths, picked up her candle, and made her way to the library.

The room was dark and silent. She went to the shelf where she thought she'd seen the book and held up the candle, illuminating the titles on the wood-and-leather-bound tomes.

Plant Remedies and Medicines. There it was. She pulled the book from the shelf, but as she did a page fluttered out, having worked its way free of the binding.

"Oh, no," she muttered, and bent to pick it up. But it wasn't a page from the book—no, it was smaller. A folded sheet of vellum. A letter, perhaps?

A thrill ran over her. How old was this book? Perhaps decades, if not centuries. How exciting would it be if she'd discovered some long-misplaced love letter? She should put it back, but the lure was too great. She set her candle down and unfolded the paper.

Dearest, it read in warbling script. *I write to tell you how I long for you and count the days until I can rest my tired eyes on your sweet face again.*

"Hmm," Samara murmured. A bit overdramatic, but it could be entertaining. She kept reading.

All is well here. Stephen thrives, and John is growing. I watch them together and marvel at the lucky hand Fate has dealt us. For it shall be Stephen who grows up to be the Earl of Easton, not Mary Cade's brat. It is unfortunate that you had to recognize the boy as your own, but we are so lucky to have Stephen. He misses you, too, and sends his affection. But he does not miss you as I do, I who have placed my heart with you for eternal safekeeping. Be well, my love, and come home to me. Yours, as long as life endures, Lucy.

"Lucy?" Samara asked aloud. Who was Lucy? Why did the name sound familiar? Stephen was obvious. As was John, although it wouldn't be if Cade had never told her his real first name. Oh! Lucy was Goodwife Hawke, the old white-haired woman she'd seen the day of her arrival. Cade had told her the woman could read and write. And quite obviously, she *had* been in love with the old earl, despite Cade's belief that it was impossible.

But what did she mean by "Mary Cade's brat"? And why did Goodwife Hawke say it was unfortunate that the old earl had been forced to recognize him?

It clicked before she even had to think too hard about it.

Cade was not the earl's son.

His mother had been unfaithful to her husband, and someone else had fathered Cade.

"Oh, my God," she whispered, and let the letter slip from her fingers and drift to the floor.

What on earth was she going to do? Should she tell him? It might be something of a comfort to him to know that he wasn't the son of the man who had always hated him or the brother of one who had tormented him. But he idolized his mother. What would it do to his perception of her if he knew she'd cuckolded her husband?

And if he was not the third earl's son, that meant—*he was not the fourth earl.*

Samara again felt she might vomit.

She couldn't tell him. She just couldn't. She would burn in hell if she kept this to herself—did the Bible not say that one of the things the Lord hated was a lying tongue?—but she couldn't hurt him like that. She would risk her soul to keep him happy and safe. If he was not the earl, he would have no claim to the land. Without the land, he had nowhere to live. Well, that wasn't really true. He had Glenwood. And as it was rightfully his, it wouldn't revert to the crown as Easton would. But he had worked so hard, sacrificed so much, to rebuild Easton. He couldn't be expelled from it now. And she would do whatever was in her power to see that no one discovered what she had discovered.

Footsteps from the great hall distracted her—a chambermaid or a groom, she hoped. She held her breath, picked up the letter, and clutched it to her chest. When no one entered, she allowed herself a sigh of relief, but she had to escape back to her rooms before anyone found her. She tucked the letter into the book and ran back up the stairs and into her room, which was exactly the way she'd left it, although the sky through her window was just a tiny bit lighter.

She sighed and placed the book on the bed. She would burn the letter. No one need ever know what she had found.

But before she could remove the letter from between the pages of the book, nausea washed over her again. This time she knew she would vomit. She dropped to her knees and dragged the chamber pot—thankfully, it was empty—from beneath the bed and heaved into it, expelling the fruitcake along with everything she'd eaten at supper. She retched until her ribs ached and tears leaked from her eyes. When she was done, she used a trembling hand to shove the chamber pot back beneath the bed and out of her sight. She forced herself to her feet and climbed back into bed, not even removing her robe, since she was chilled again. She closed her eyes.

She would burn the letter in the morning. No one would find it before then.

Chapter Twenty-Nine

CADE WOKE EARLIER THAN USUAL, AND AS PREDICTED, HE FELT fine when he opened his eyes. He wasn't ill. It was something about the spring—something in the air, perhaps—that irritated him. It happened nearly every year.

It was a bit disconcerting to wake up without Samara beside him. He'd grown used to having her there, her warmth a comforting presence, especially when the mornings were cold. He washed and dressed quickly before slowly pushing open the door to her chamber.

She was still in bed, curled into a small ball of red hair and white skin beneath the green coverlet. That was surprising—they usually woke near the same time. It was unusual for her to sleep later than he did. Obviously she needed it today, for whatever reason. He slipped through her bedchamber silently and into her sitting room, closing the door behind him, and down the steps to his library. He needed his ledger, for he had plans to go over the summer planting with Harry Stanton.

He wasn't paying much attention to his steps, and just a few feet from the door to the library he almost slipped and fell on a piece of paper on the floor. Cursing, he bent down and picked it up. What was it? A letter?

He unfolded the vellum, and his eyes scanned the words. The letter was short, but before he could even see who had signed it, the blood roared in his ears and the room spun before his eyes.

Stephen will inherit
Not Mary Cade's brat

Lucky to have Stephen
What did this *mean?*

But the answer was already there. Hadn't he always known, deep down, that he didn't belong? His father wasn't his father. Stephen wasn't his brother. It explained too well why they'd treated him as they had his entire life.

He glanced at the letter again.
Yours, as long as life endures, Lucy.
So Goodwife Hawke *hadn't* been like a sister to the old man.
What was he going to tell Samara?
Samara!

Last night's supper threatened to reappear, but he swallowed hard and the sensation ebbed. She wasn't a countess after all. Not if he wasn't the earl. Could she even still be his wife, if he wasn't who she'd thought he was when she'd married him?

He felt sick right to his bones. He should have seen this coming. Everything had turned out far too well for him. He didn't deserve anything he had. His father—no, John Badgley—had been right. He was nothing. An accident. A bastard. None of this belonged to him.

And his mother—hell, he couldn't even think about her.

He had to get out.

He flew up the back stairs, taking the long way to his bedchamber, found his saddlebag, and stuffed the letter into it, along with a change of clothing. He started for the door but paused. Did he have it in him to look at her one last time? For he knew what he had to do. Samara was the daughter of an earl. She deserved better than the bastard son of God only knew whom and a woman who couldn't keep her skirts down.

Pain curdled his stomach. All these years idolizing her, thinking her the most wonderful woman God had ever put on his earth. And she'd been nothing but a whore. Just like the rest of them. Who knew—perhaps his own wife would be the same someday. Another Lady Beddington, to whom honesty, purity, and fidelity meant nothing.

He wouldn't look. He didn't want to risk waking her. He wanted to be miles away before she realized he was gone.

❀

When she woke, Samara was ill again. She barely had time to throw back the coverlet and fall onto the floor beside the chamber pot before she retched into it. She wouldn't have thought there was anything left in her stomach after last night, but she was wrong. She heaved until her arms, supporting her over the pot, threatened to give out. Eventually there really was nothing left, and she could only gag until her nausea receded.

Samara's arms trembled as she pushed the chamber pot away as gently as she could to avoid sloshing its contents onto the floor. She took a deep breath and climbed back into bed to lie against her pillows. When she wiped her hand across her forehead, it came away damp with a thin sheen of sweat. Her limbs quivered, and she was afraid her legs would not hold her if she tried to get up and cross the room to splash her face with the water in the basin by the window.

Where was Betty? The maid had a special recipe for stomach ailments—horehound and mint leaves steeped in wine that had been heated to boiling. It tasted vile, but the relief it brought was quick and lasting.

Samara decided to risk walking. She sat up and tentatively touched the soles of her feet to the floor. Cautiously she staggered the few feet to the basin. She plunged her hands inside, brought the water to her face, and reveled in the cool relief.

Only for a moment. The nausea came back tenfold, and again she almost didn't make it to the chamber pot.

Betty entered the room as Samara finished vomiting. Her eyes widened in alarm, and she dropped the neatly folded pile of clean chemises in her arms.

"Lady Samara! Are you ill?"

"Yes," Samara groaned. She lifted her head from the pot and looked at her maid. "I cannot seem to stop vomiting. I'm dying, I think."

"Don't be silly." Betty's expression was calmer now. In fact, she seemed to be fighting a smile. *I'm delirious. Surely she can't be* happy *that I feel so wretched?* "I'll brew you some of my special elixir. Here, change your shift—you've sweated clear through that one. I'll be back as soon as I can."

Betty helped Samara to her feet, then picked up the clothing she'd dropped and handed Samara a clean gown. She bustled from the room, humming—*humming?*—and Samara stripped off her damp gown. She pulled the clean one over her head. The soft, dry linen felt wonderful against her clammy skin.

She must have completely emptied her stomach, for it felt a bit better, but she still wanted Betty's tonic if it would keep the nausea from coming back. She climbed back into bed and pulled the coverlet up to her chin.

She dozed. Betty woke her by gently shaking her shoulder and handing her a wooden mug full of the steaming, pungent brew.

And she *was* smiling. No, she was beaming!

"Thank you," Samara said. She took a sip and wrinkled her nose. "Now tell me why my illness has you dancing about like it's Midsummer's Eve and you've just handfasted with the head groom?"

Betty still smiled, but her eyes clouded with confusion.

"You don't…" She didn't finish her sentence.

Samara took another sip of the concoction. "I don't *what?*"

Understanding dawned. Betty sat down on the bed.

"The laundresses were talking," she said. "About how your bed linens have been clean every morning for over two months now."

Samara closed her eyes and prayed for patience. "Well, that is disgusting. Do they think me an infant yet incapable of using a chamber pot?"

Betty smiled. "Lady Samara, if you don't mind me asking, when were your courses last upon you?"

Samara's heart stuttered, then picked up and began to race as she realized what Betty was telling her.

"Not since before the wedding," she breathed. "Oh, Betty, do you think?"

"Yes, I do," Betty confirmed.

Samara handed her the mug and flew from the bed to the looking glass by the window. She gazed at her reflection, but it didn't look any different. She turned to the side and tried to force her stomach out. Nothing. She was as slender as she'd ever been.

"Are you sure?" she asked.

"Give it time," Betty said with a laugh. "Only a few months from now your girlish slenderness will be but a fond memory."

Samara brushed her fingers against her still-flat belly in wonder. She saw nothing, felt nothing, but with the knowledge that a child now grew inside her, the terror of birthing that had plagued her fled on the spring wind that blew outside her window. She was no longer frightened of dying in childbed like her mother. She would gladly give up her life for that of the tiny soul she and Cade had created.

A smile spread over her face.

"Cade will be so happy," she said as her eyes filled with joyous tears. "Do you think he is awake? It's late, he must be."

"Come to think of it, I haven't seen his lordship yet this morning," Betty answered.

"He's probably still abed. I *knew* he was sicker than he let on," Samara said. "Well, if I wake him with this news, he cannot get angry with me."

"That's true." The maid chuckled.

Samara slipped into her robe and went to the door that separated her rooms from Cade's. She pushed it open quietly, preferring to wake him by curling up beside him on the bed rather than by letting the door shriek on its hinges.

But she didn't even have to open the door all the way to see that he wasn't there. The blankets on his bed were rumpled, the pillow dented, but there was no sign of him.

She smiled. He was probably out already with Harry Stanton, as he had been the previous morning. One of the things she loved most about him was his willingness to work alongside his people, not direct them from above and reap the benefits of their hard work.

A tiny flutter—softer than the brush of a butterfly's wing—vibrated against her belly. She gasped. It was too soon, of course, and probably just remnants of her nausea, but it filled her with wonder.

She was with child. She'd be a mother. Cade would be a father.

She had to find him.

"He's already out in the fields," she told Betty, going back into her own room. "Help me dress, and I'll go and find him."

"Can't you wait until he comes back? You shouldn't be on a horse right now," Betty said. "The child will still be there when he comes in for his dinner."

"No. I need to tell him now." Samara had already gone to her linen chest and found an old gown. She pulled it over her head. "My cloak, Betty?"

Betty handed her the garment, but disapproval was written plainly on her face.

"Just wait," she begged Samara. "You don't want to hurt the child, do you?"

Samara paused. No, she very much did not want to hurt her child.

"I suppose I'm going to have to learn to think like a mother now," she said. "All right. I won't go riding out. But I will go to the stables to ask Wat to ride out and find him."

Apparently satisfied, Betty gave Samara her cloak.

She threw it over her shoulders as she ran down the steps, out the kitchen door and down the hill to the stables. It was a beautiful morning, cool and clear with just the remnants of hazy fog suspended over the dew-jeweled grass. But with every step she took she was mindful of the child inside her. She wondered if running would do it any harm, dislodge it somehow. She thought probably not. She hadn't known many pregnant women, but of the ones she *had* known, none of them had spent her entire confinement on her back. Still, she slowed her pace and wasn't even out of breath by the time she reached the stables.

"Wat," she called, banging through the door. "Where are you?"

His mousy brown head, half-covered by a lopsided cap, popped up from one of the stalls.

"Here, milady. What can I do for you?"

"I need you to saddle a horse and ride out to find the earl. I must speak with him. It's urgent."

"Umm," Wat said. He straightened. "His lordship isn't here, milady."

"What?" Of course he wasn't *here*. He was in the fields. "I realize that. That's why I said to go and *find* him. He can't be far. I know he and Harry were to decide what to plant in the summer fields today."

Wat looked increasingly uncomfortable. He tugged on the brim of his hat.

"No, I mean he isn't *here*. Isn't at Easton."

This was frustrating. Wat was a nice boy but certainly not very bright.

"Wat," she said, mustering every drop of patience she could find inside her. "What do you mean, he's not at Easton? Where did he go?"

"Not sure, really. All I know is he tore out of here when the sun weren't hardly up. Saddled Whitehawk and took off. Haven't seen him since. Thought you knew."

"No." Something was happening to her heart. It was sinking into her stomach, or at least it felt like it. Her fingertips tingled, and there was a humming in her ears. "No, I didn't. Thank you, Wat."

Before he could reply, she had taken off running again, this time back up the hill, into the house, up the stairs, and into her bedchamber.

"Betty!" she gasped. "Where is the herbal remedies book?"

The maid looked bewildered. "I don't know what book you mean."

"This one." There it was, still on the table where she'd left it. She picked it up and shook it. *Please. Please.*

The tightly bound pages stayed in place, and nothing fluttered from between them.

"Oh, *no,*" she moaned. "This cannot be happening."

"What is it?"

"I found a letter," she said. She sank into the chair beside the table. "A letter from the former housekeeper to Cade's father, and it said that Cade wasn't his father's legitimate son. I didn't want him to see it. Don't look at me like that, Betty! I have my reasons. I hid it in this book, but it looks like it might have fallen out. Wat said Cade left early this morning and didn't say where he was going. He must have found the letter, Betty. He found it, and now he's gone somewhere, I don't know where." She was having trouble drawing breath.

"Shh," Betty soothed. "Sit down and think about it."

She remained standing. "Hayden's," Samara said. "He must have gone to Hayden. But why did he leave? Surely he was devastated, but why run away?"

"What did the letter say, exactly? Besides the fact that Cade wasn't his father's son?" Samara considered the consequences of telling Betty what she'd learned. Servants gossiped, but would Betty? She'd kept Samara's confidences since she was a small girl. Surely she could be trusted.

"It didn't say anything explicitly, other than that they were lucky to have Stephen and that it was unfortunate Cade's father had been forced to recognize him. Goodwife Hawke called him *Mary Cade's brat.*" She grabbed Betty by her fleshy upper arms. "Betty, you *must* remain silent! This cannot get out. I will go to Goodwife Hawke and find out what she knows. If there is anything that can convince Cade to come back, she will have it." She didn't know why this was such a certainty, but it was. "I am going down to the village to talk to Goodwife Hawke."

❋

"Cade! What are you doing here?"

Hayden jogged from the entrance to Hill House and across the courtyard, surprise evident on his face as he grew nearer.

"Where is Samara? Is she all right?" his cousin asked.

"She's at home. She's fine." Cade slid from Whitehawk's back, his boots making a soft thud as his feet made contact with the cobblestones. "Well, as fine as she can be, considering." The pleasant sting the cold wind left on his cheeks was already fading now that he was no longer in motion. He wanted it back. It was a pain he could deal with.

"What is going on?" Hayden demanded.

Cade reached into his saddlebag and pulled out the letter. He thrust it at Hayden.

"This," he spat.

Hayden took the vellum from his hands and unfolded it. His eyes scanned the words, words that had already burned themselves into Cade's memory as surely as a branding iron marks a bull.

"What is this?" Hayden breathed. He looked up from the letter to meet Cade's eyes.

"Evidently, it is proof that I'm not the son of John Badgley after all. My mother was already pregnant when she married him, or she cuckolded him and conceived me then. I don't know. And it looks as though I never will. Not that it matters. Either way you look at it, I'm not the earl."

"Come inside," Hayden said. "Someone will take care of the horse." He led Cade into Hill House, a place Cade hadn't imagined he would see again so soon after his last visit. He'd fully expected to be spending the spring helping with the planting and sitting before a fire with his wife. Not questioning everything he'd ever known to be true, whether he'd liked it or not.

"Some wine?" Hayden asked when they were safely ensconced in his Great Chamber.

"Please," Cade replied. To hell with his vow not to drown his sorrows in drink. One goblet wouldn't hurt, and it might numb him enough to be able to look at this situation rationally.

He drained the goblet Hayden handed him and held it out for more even as the pleasant and familiar warmth sank to his stomach and spread throughout his limbs. All right, so rationality wasn't likely. But if he drank enough to put him to sleep, then he couldn't think about it, could he?

"Where did you find this letter?" Hayden asked.

"On the floor next to my study." He quaffed the second goblet.

"So someone had it and dropped it." Hayden ran a finger over the vellum. "Who would have something like this? And why would they be carrying it on their person, near your study?"

"I haven't thought that far ahead," Cade replied. "I was slightly more concerned with the fact that I don't know who I am."

"All right," Hayden said. "Fair enough. But think about it now."

"Goodwife Hawke wrote it," Cade said slowly. "I know she learned to read and write with my father when they were children, although I can't say I'm familiar with her penmanship. But it doesn't make any sense to think it was anyone else. Certainly not my own mother. As far as I know, none of the other servants were literate, except the old steward, but I can't think of any reason why *he* would forge a letter from Goodwife Hawke to my father."

"You're right," Hayden said after a moment. "It doesn't make any sense." He put the vellum down on the desk. "I'm sorry, Cade."

"We are not even cousins. Aunt Madge is not my aunt. Do you realize that? Everything I've believed, for my entire life, is false.

Although I have to say it's a bit of a relief to know why the old man hated me my entire life. I can stop asking myself about that, at least." Stinging heat pooled behind Cade's eyes.

"You *are* my family," Hayden said fiercely. "Blood or no blood. You're as much a brother to me as Matthew is. Even more."

Cade ground the palms of his hands into his eyes. He would not weep like a child. He might not have an identity anymore, but he was still a grown man.

"Thank you, Hayden," he said. "I've always felt the same about you, you know. Even when I thought Stephen really was my brother. As far as I'm concerned, you're the only brother I've ever had."

They looked at each other for a moment—Hayden silent because he probably had nothing to say that would make anything better; Cade silent because if he opened his mouth, he thought he might scream.

"I'll have to have my marriage annulled," he said when he had a grip on his emotions again.

Hayden refilled their wine goblets a third time. "On what grounds?"

"I don't know. Fraud? Can I do that? I'm not who she thought I was. Nothing she thought I owned is actually mine. Even Glenwood. Her father returned it to me as part of her dowry. Will I have to give it back?" A sour taste filled his mouth, and it wasn't due to the wine.

"You don't have to think about that right now."

"I have to think about it at some point."

"Wait until tomorrow," Hayden suggested. "Once the shock has worn off, you may be able to think more clearly. And I promise to help you come up with ideas. Eventually Samara will wonder where you've gone, and you'll have to tell her what happened. But you can stay here as long as you like."

He thought of Samara, alone at Easton, wondering where he'd gone and why he'd left without telling her. He imagined her directing the servants and trying to run the entire household without his help. And he pictured her in their big bed, falling asleep night after night without him.

A tear burst forth and rolled, unchecked, down his cheek.

❀

Samara was careful to keep the horse at a middling pace as she rode down into the village, a concerned Harry Stanton at her side. He wasn't unfamiliar with Goodwife Hawke, and he refused to allow Wat to saddle a horse for Samara unless she consented to let him accompany her.

They drew close to the small wattle-and-daub building that was the last in a row of similar dwellings. The middle-aged woman Samara remembered from her first ride through the village stood outside the door, her back to them, sweeping the small dirt path leading to the door with a roughly made broom.

"Excuse me," Samara called.

The woman started and whirled to face them. When she saw Samara she dropped her broom and fell into a curtsey.

"Good morning, Lady Easton," she said.

"Good morning," Samara replied. Harry quickly dismounted and came to help her down. When she had her feet firmly on the ground, she took a step toward the woman, whose eyes regarded her with uncertainty.

"Your name is Joan, correct?"

"Yes, my lady," Joan replied. "Is there something I can do for you?"

Samara took a deep breath. "I'd like to speak with your mother, if she's available. In private."

Joan's eyes turned wary. Samara couldn't blame her; from what Cade had told her there was little love lost between him and Goodwife Hawke. Surely Joan saw her as an extension of Cade and assumed she was here at his bidding.

"I need only a few moments with her," Samara said, softening her tone. "Please. It's very important."

"All right," the woman answered. Not that she could have denied her countess, but still, Samara was glad she hadn't had to force the issue. Having to fight for access to Goodwife Hawke could have easily broken her tenuous grasp on calm.

Joan pushed open the door and stepped aside to allow Samara to enter. She did, taking a moment to let her eyes adjust to the dimness of the small living area. When they did, she spied the old woman in a chair by the hearth, wrapped in a quilt though the early-May day was warm.

"Please sit, Lady Easton. Mother," Joan said. "The Countess of Easton would like to speak with you."

Goodwife Hawke did not respond at first. Instead her cloudy blue gaze grazed Samara from head to toe even as Samara settled herself on a rather uncomfortable stool.

"I see," she said. "Well, I don't know what you think I can do for you. I was forced from my position at the manor. Nothing that happens there is of any matter to me."

"Mother," Joan protested. "You forget yourself."

"It's all right, Joan," Samara said. Something told her she had to tread lightly with the old woman if she wanted to get anywhere. "I know well how it feels to be yanked from everything you know to be real and true. It's very disconcerting."

"Hmph." Goodwife Hawke pulled the quilt more tightly around her shoulders.

"But Goodwife, I do have some questions for you. Nothing that concerns recent matters. It's history that I'm interested in."

Joan, apparently satisfied that her mother was not going to spit on the countess, quietly went back outside. Through the oiled paper window Samara could see her resume her sweeping.

"History, eh?" A spark of interest flared in the woman's eyes. "Now that's something I know."

"I thought you might." Samara pasted a smile on her face and leaned forward. "Goodwife Hawke, who is the earl's father?"

Chapter Thirty

A BEAT PASSED WHILE GOODWIFE HAWKE SEEMED TO ABSORB Samara's words. She blinked, and shrank back into the chair until she was dwarfed by her quilt.

"The old earl was his father, of course," she muttered. "Why would you even ask something like that?"

"Because you see, Goodwife, last night I happened across a letter buried in a book of herbal remedies," Samara answered. Her voice shook only slightly. "It spoke of Stephen and how the former earl was fortunate to have him, and how it was *unfortunate* that he'd been forced to acknowledge Cade—John—as his son. That, to me, suggests that the old earl knew he was not Cade's father." She paused. "The letter was signed by you."

A gusty sigh escaped Goodwife Hawke's wrinkled lips.

"That's what you got from that, is it?" she asked. She shifted in the chair. "Well, I supnpose I can see why. It was a damned tragedy that John had to allow Mary Cade's brat to take everything that should have been Stephen's. If Stephen hadn't died, it never would have happened." Her milky eyes filled with tears.

"Why is that, Goodwife?" Samara's heart thumped. Did she even want to know? Oh, why had she gone searching for that book? This whole mess was her fault! If she hadn't found the letter, Goodwife Hawke would have taken the secret to her grave—and soon.

"Because we planned it that way!" Goodwife Hawke cried. "It was the way it should have been!"

They'd *planned* it? Planned what?

"What did you plan?" Samara demanded.

"Stephen. He should have been John's. It worked out so well—Jane Crawford was a sickly girl. Always had been. We were shocked when she conceived so quickly."

Samara's head was starting to spin. She had to get Goodwife Hawke to start making sense, or she would lose Cade. She felt certain of it. "Could you start from the beginning, please, Goodwife? I'm not sure I follow you."

Goodwife Hawke sighed again, and the fight seemed to go out of her. She slumped in her chair.

"Why not?" she asked, her tone lifeless. "John is dead. Stephen is dead. I'll soon be dead. None of it matters anymore."

Samara waited.

"John and I were in love," Goodwife Hawke said. "My father was a groom in John's father's stables. We were of an age, and we played together as children. We did everything together. I was even schooled with him. His father didn't like that, but John kicked up such a fuss his father gave in." The ghost of a smile distorted her thin, colorless lips. "We fell in love. But of course, we couldn't marry, him bein' the earl and I just the daughter of a groom. So I married Roger, the head groom's son, and John married Jane Crawford, who was picked for him by his father."

Goodwife Hawke paused to take a breath and drink from a cup almost concealed in her gnarled hand by the quilt.

"John didn't want to marry her, but he had to for the earldom. To have a son. Jane conceived within weeks of their wedding. And I conceived a child with Roger at almost the same time. Roger was a good man. Kind. Not too bright, though. He died when he walked behind a horse. Kicked him clear across the stable, the horse did, and crushed his skull."

"I'm so sorry," Samara murmured.

"I felt bad at first. I would have a baby who didn't know its father. But my child wouldn't be the first to have that happen to him. Anyway, about midway through our confinements John was summoned by the king, for a reason I long ago forgot, and he wanted me and Jane to go with him. Jane fought him at first. London is filthy, she said, and the baby could die. But he wouldn't hear it. What

John wanted, he got. And I wanted to go with him, of course. So we packed up and drove to London."

Samara's breath quickened. She sensed that they had reached the real meat of the story.

"We stayed for a few months. Jane complained the whole time. The city air smelled. The food didn't agree with her. It was too noisy for her to sleep. She never stopped! Then she went into labor. She birthed a girl child."

"A what?" Had she missed something? "She had a daughter?"

"Yes," Goodwife Hawke confirmed. "A sickly little thing like her mother. Pretty, but we all knew it wouldn't live. It didn't. It died just days after birth. And Jane followed a week later."

She was so confused. So very, very confused.

"Then who was Stephen's mother?" But even as the words left her mouth, a sick, knowing feeling crept over her.

Goodwife Hawke smiled again. "I went into labor with my own child soon after Jane died. My baby was a healthy, lusty boy."

"Stephen," Samara whispered.

Goodwife Hawke nodded. "It worked out too perfectly. John and I always knew that it should be our child that inherited Easton. My baby's father was dead. John's baby and its mother had died. We switched them. The only ones who knew Jane had birthed a girl were the few people John employed at Riverview. He paid them heftily for their silence and threatened them with bodily harm if they spoke of it. Once Stephen and I could travel, we took the bodies of Jane and her daughter back to Easton for burial. Roger was dead, so he couldn't ask questions, not that he would have thought to anyway. I remarried and had Joan. Stephen grew up never knowing that I was his mother but always believing that John was his father, *as he should have been.*"

"My God," Samara whispered. The deviousness of this woman and the old earl was astounding! "And Cade's mother? She didn't conceive him outside her marriage?"

"Of course not," Goodwife Hawke scoffed. "Mary Cade was the very picture of virtue. The poor thing tried so hard. John only married her for her dowry, because the droughts took his fields and he poured all of his money into replacing them. He wanted nothing to do with her. It was pure bad luck that she conceived on their wedding night, because he never touched her after that. John thought to try and deny the child, but it would have been pointless. From birth the boy looked so much like him, no one would have believed it."

Samara searched her memory for an image of the old earl. When she found one, his hair was thin and gray, his mouth twisted into a permanent sneer and his back stooped. Where in that picture was her heart-stoppingly handsome husband, with his full head of thick dark hair, blinding smile and tall, straight figure?

No matter. She knew the truth now. And soon Cade would too. If…

"Goodwife Hawke?"

"Hmm."

"Would you be willing to commit that to paper and sign it? You see, Cade has left Easton. I'm not sure, but I believe he's with his cousin Hayden. If he thinks he's not the legitimate earl, there's no telling what he might do. Easton belongs to him. He's sacrificed much to retain it and to support its people. The least you can do is reaffirm that. He deserves that much, after the way his father treated him his entire life simply for being born."

Goodwife Hawke glared at her, and for a brief, sickening moment, Samara thought the old woman might deny her.

"I lost my son," she said. "A son I was never able to acknowledge. *He* should have been the earl. And if not for that damned epidemic that stole him, he would have been." Her wrinkled face crumpled, and she let out a heartrending sob. "And John. I lost John. My love. I have no one left."

She was silent but for her sniffling. Then she spoke. "I suppose," she muttered. "Not that I'm sorry. I'm not. John and I both knew that *I* should have borne Easton's fourth earl. We only did what was right. But I have happy memories of Easton. I'd hate to see the Crown take it when I have so little time left."

"Thank you, Goodwife," Samara said. Relief made her weak. "You're doing the right thing." She produced the small box of letter-writing materials she'd stuffed into her saddlebag and took out a sheet of vellum, a quill, and a small bottle of ink. She resisted the urge to tap her impatient feet against the packed-earth floor as the old woman slowly scrawled her confession.

When Goodwife Hawke finished, Samara took the paper from her. She waved it a few times to dry it and packed the quill and ink back into the box before returning them to her bag. Then she stood.

"Thank you," she repeated. "You've done a good thing this day."

"I'm not sorry," Goodwife Hawke reiterated.

"I know you're not," Samara replied. "And for that your soul will probably linger in Purgatory for a fair amount of time. But you've begun to redeem yourself by writing this. And because you did, I promise to pray for you so that you'll find yourself in heaven sooner than you might have otherwise."

"I don't want to be bothered again," Goodwife Hawke said in response. "I want to live out my days in peace, with the few happy memories I've managed to save."

"If it's at all possible, we'll grant you that," Samara said. "Farewell, Goodwife Hawke."

She stepped out into the May sunshine. Joan knelt now in front of the small patch of newly sprouted vegetables. She looked up when Samara's shadow fell over her, and Samara saw that her plain, kind face was tear stained.

"I'm so sorry," she whispered. She got to her feet and brushed her hands on her apron. "I had no idea. I knew she was married before she married my father, but everyone believed the baby girl was *hers*. As a child I visited my dead sister's grave, never knowing that the viscount was my *brother*. I swear, my lady, I never had an inkling. If I had, I would have forced the truth out of her years ago."

"I believe you," Samara said. Her heart twisted for the poor woman. Had she heard Goodwife Hawke's lamentation that she had no one left? Samara hoped not. "Thank you for allowing me access to her. I hope her signed confession will bring the earl back home."

"I'll pray for it," Joan said fervently. She caught Samara's hand up and kissed it. "Thank you, Lady Easton."

Harry Stanton and his horse were a few feet away. The animal grazed lazily while Harry shifted his weight from foot to foot as he watched her approach.

"I think I have what I need," she said when she reached them. "Take me to Hill House, Harry. I'm going to bring the earl home."

❀

"Cade, it's time for supper. Will you join us?"

From his seat before the unlit hearth, where he'd been sprawled for a few hours, Cade looked up at Hayden. Aunt Madge peeped out from behind him.

"Cade, darling," she said. "Come and eat with us."

"No, thank you," he said. "I'll join the servants in the kitchens when it's their turn."

"Damn it!" Hayden exploded. "Cade, I know you're upset. I understand. But you're still family. You're one of us whether different blood flows in your veins or not."

Cade sighed. He had spent the better part of the day wallowing in self-pity and was content to do so for a while longer. But it looked as though Hayden was refusing to allow him that luxury.

"Fine," he said. "But no meat for me. If I'm to be homeless and nameless, I'd best get used to surviving on vegetable pottage. Have you any black bread?"

"Just sit down." Hayden sighed.

"Fine." Cade got to his feet and went over to the dais, where servants were bringing out dishes. He slid onto the bench and clenched his fingers around his napkin. It was either that or his own throat.

He had taken only a few bites of his meal—savoring them, for who knew if he would ever taste beef again?—when a commotion rose from the courtyard. There was the sound of a door banging against the wall and voices, raised and excited, as if in a scuffle.

"What the—" Hayden half-rose from his seat at the head of the table. Then they all heard it.

"Cade!"

Thin and distant, certainly, but there was no mistaking it.

Samara had come to Hill House.

"What is she doing here?" Cade asked. Of course, no one responded. But the beginning of a smile curled the edges of Aunt Madge's lips. Hayden sat down again, apparently satisfied that Hill

❀ 404 ❀

House was not under attack. Cade pushed back from the high board and headed for the entrance hall.

Samara almost collided with him as she flew through the doorway, but he stepped back in time. She took only a second to glance around her and toss her bag to the floor before she raised her eyes to him, then threw her arms around him.

"I knew you'd be here," she said, her voice muffled by his shirt. Her shoulders and chest rose and fell with each heaving breath she took. He was so shocked by her sudden appearance that, without thinking, he wrapped his arms around her and breathed in her scent—outdoorsy, like sun and air, with the faint fragrance of wildflowers clinging to her hair.

"What are you doing here?" he asked. He held her tightly, for again it might be for the last time. "How did you find me? You're not alone, are you?"

"No, my lord earl." Harry Stanton's voice floated in, reaching them mere seconds before the man himself did. "The lady's a hard one to keep up with when she has a mission, but I did. I got her here safe though it near killed me to do it." He bent over, his hands on his knees, his breath coming heavily.

"Thank you, Harry," Cade said. He gave Samara a final squeeze before disentangling himself from her and stepping back. Best to keep his distance, so he could send her away when he told her the horrible news.

"Samara," he said, but she wasn't looking at him. She was digging in her saddlebag. "I have something to tell you."

"No, you don't," she said. She found what she was looking for—a piece of parchment—and stood, waving it at him triumphantly. "I have something to tell *you*."

"Just let me say it," he begged. "Before I lose my courage. I'm not who you thought I was, Samara. I'm not the Earl of Easton. I don't know who I am."

"Cade." She stood before him and placed a finger against his lips. "*I do.*"

Her eyes sparkled and her lips curved in a faint smile. What was she getting at? She couldn't possibly know what he'd discovered, unless—

She had been the one to find the letter.

"You're not illegitimate," she told him. "John Badgley was your father. And I have proof."

"Proof." Never mind; he was at a loss for words. "So it was you who found the letter? How did it end up on the floor by my study?"

She nodded. "I found it. Tucked into a book of herbal remedies. I couldn't sleep, and you were ill, so I decided to look up ways to heal you. But the letter fell out of the book, and I realized what it said—what I *thought*, and apparently *you* thought, it said—and wanted to hide it. I know it was wrong. But I wanted to keep it from you, to avoid all this." She waved her hand around the room. "But when I went to seek you out this morning, Wat told me you had left early and didn't say where you were going. Then I realized the letter was gone and that you must have found it. *Then* I went and got my proof."

Cade was having trouble digesting her rapidly uttered words. Any reply he could have made stuck in his throat. Hayden spoke up instead.

"What proof, Samara?" he asked. "How do you know Cade is the earl?"

"Goodwife Hawke," Samara said. She held the paper out to Cade, shook it a little until he took it between his own fingers. "A confession from her very hand, and signed by her too."

"Goodwife Hawke?" he breathed. "What has she to do with any of this?"

Samara's smile twisted into a grimace. "Everything."

His eyes scanned the parchment, and with every word his heart beat faster. There was a roaring in his ears, and by the time he reached the quivery letters that made up the old housekeeper's signature, his hands shook so badly he was amazed he'd managed to maintain his hold on the thing.

He looked up. Samara's eyes were steady on him.

"This is true?" he asked.

She nodded. "I don't see why she would have made it up."

"Cade, what *is* it?" Aunt Madge begged.

He turned to face them.

"Stephen," he said.

"What about him?" Hayden asked.

"Stephen is the illegitimate one. Not me."

"How is that possible?" Aunt Madge wondered.

"He was born in London. I always knew that. Everyone did," Cade answered. "But apparently so was my *sister*. My real sister. My father's first wife birthed a girl, who died almost immediately. Goodwife Hawke, who was widowed, also pregnant, and there with them in London had a baby boy a few weeks later. Because Stephen's mother—I'm sorry, my father's first wife—because she also died, they decided to switch the children so that Stephen would be raised as the heir."

"But why would they do that?" Hayden demanded.

Cade gestured to the paper. "Because they were in love."

"Who was in love?" Aunt Madge asked. "I'm confused."

"My father and Goodwife Hawke. It's all here, plain as day. They'd been in love since childhood. Couldn't marry, of course, but apparently kept up the affair throughout both of my father's marriages. They seem to have decided that their child was always meant to inherit Easton, so they made it happen. Goodwife Hawke provided the child, and luckily for the old man, Stephen was born soft in the head, so he was able to impose his personality on him. He became *their* child." He shook his head. He'd known his father was cruel. But had the old man also been mad?

Then the realization hit him.

"That's why he hated me," he said. "Because Stephen, the son of the woman he loved and couldn't marry, wasn't his. He knew that I was his rightful heir and if anything happened to Stephen, I would get everything. He resented the fact that I was his legitimate son."

Samara's hand came to rest on his elbow.

"My goodness." Aunt Madge pressed a hand to her heart and sat back down.

Hayden shook his head.

Cade turned to his wife. "How did you get her to confess this?" he asked.

"It was far easier than I thought it would be," she admitted. "I think, after so many years of pretending, she *wanted* to tell someone that she was Stephen's mother. I didn't have to do much to prod her. After a few resentful glares, she was only too happy to tell me her story."

"Amazing," Hayden said. He grinned at Cade. "Are you happy now? You're done wallowing in pity? Sit down then, and have some beef and manchet. Celebrate your legitimacy!"

"Hear, hear!" Aunt Madge crowed, lifting her goblet.

"It's strange," Cade said slowly. "I never thought I'd be happy to have it reiterated that the old bastard is my father. But I am." He glanced at Samara, and the smile on her face nearly blinded him. "I'm delighted to be me."

❋

Later, after a meal spent cheering, toasting—Cade filled his goblet with cider instead of the perry everyone else guzzled—and laughing, and Molly coming out, a half-grown Danaë struggling in her arms, to greet her aunt and uncle, Cade and Samara lay in the master bed, which Hayden had given up to them for the night, and talked quietly.

"I owe you everything," he told her, entwining his fingers in hers. "You have done so much for me, most of which you don't even know. I wouldn't be the person I am right now if not for you."

"Have you forgotten?" She laughed. "The only reason I even found that letter in the first place was because I wanted to read a book on making medicines. Me! Do you think I'd be doing that if I was still at my father's house?"

"Not necessarily. But you'd be doing it if you were married to anybody else." Heat flared beneath his skin as she dropped a kiss on his bare shoulder.

"But I wouldn't *want* to," she murmured against him.

He lay on his back and stared at the carved wooden canopy over his head. Not for the first time that night he wondered if it was possible that his father had loved Goodwife Hawke so deeply that he was willing to give everything over to her child, even though it had none of his blood flowing through its veins. He guessed so, since he had ended up doing exactly that. Still, it was strange to imagine his father loving another person—other than Stephen—so wholly.

He glanced at the half of Samara's face that was visible. Her eyes had fluttered shut.

"I want a child," he told her. He twirled one of her curls around his index finger.

Her eyes opened again. She propped herself up on one elbow and looked at him.

"That's a good thing," she said. "Because in about six months, we will have one."

He stared at her. "You're—"

"Yes! I realized it just this morning. That's why I went looking for you." She gazed at him. "Are you happy?"

"Happy?" he demanded. "Samara, until you came here tonight I thought my entire life as I knew it was over. I thought I was homeless. Penniless. Worst of all, I thought I'd have to give you up. But you gave back everything I thought I'd lost, and on top of it you're giving me a child? Yes, I'm happy. I'm deliriously happy."

"Good." She snuggled against him once more, and he held her close. *Happy* didn't even begin to describe how he felt. He had everything he'd always thought he didn't want, and as it turned out, it was everything he'd ever wanted.

"I love you," he whispered. It didn't matter if she didn't say it back. After what she'd done for him, she deserved to know she was loved.

She lifted herself onto her elbow again and looked at him. Her hair fell into her eyes. She pushed it away with her free hand.

"I didn't want to love you," she confessed. Her cheeks were pink in the low candlelight.

"But?" he teased.

"But I do. I love you." She laughed. "How unfashionable."

"To hell with fashion," he growled. "I'm done with appearances and politics and always doing what everyone else wants me to do. I've lived my entire life that way. I think it's time to do what *I* want. What do you say to that, wife?"

From the look on her face, and the way she seemed to melt when he pulled her over him and kissed her, he knew she agreed.

Author's Note

HISTORY, THEY SAY, IS WRITTEN BY THE VICTORS, AND I IMAGINE that is the main reason I had trouble finding sources on the daily lives of Catholics in post-Reformation England. Many historians seem to forget that under Mary I, there was a counter-reformation in which many (though not all) of the religious customs banned under Edward VI were reinstated. There also didn't seem to be much out there on the short, sad reign of a hated queen—a woman whose life is usually glossed over in favor of those of her more colorful father or sister. However, during the nearly seven years it took me to write this novel, I came across several sources that proved to be treasure troves of information, and that I would recommend to anyone looking for more information on this oft-neglected but important era of English history.

Cressy, David. *Birth, Marriage, and Death: Ritual, Religion, and the Life-Cycle in Tudor and Stuart England.* Oxford: Oxford University Press, 1997.

Porter, Linda. *Mary Tudor: The First Queen.* London: Portrait, 2007.

Sim, Alison. *The Tudor Housewife.* Stroud: Sutton, 1996.

Sim, Alison. *Pleasures and Pastimes in Tudor England.* Stroud: Sutton, 1999.

Whitelock, Anna. *Mary Tudor: Princess, Bastard, Queen.* New York: Random House, 2009.

Acknowledgments

To John, who poured me a glass of grape juice to toast the completion of my rough draft and then took me to England so I could make revisions—among many, many other things, too many to list here. To my parents, who besides being the greatest parents in the world passed down to me a love of books and history: even though I didn't write about the JFK assassination or the US Civil War, I hope you like my book. Even if you don't, I know you're both kind enough to say you did. To my dit, who cheered me on and helped whenever I needed it, whether I was after a name for a Tudor-era pet dog or the determination to meet my daily word goals. I love all of you more than mere words can express.

To Heather, for your unfailing encouragement and willingness to read the rough mess of a novel I gave you. To Robin for your helpful comments and enthusiasm every step of the way. To Rob for having enough faith in me to offer to be my manager before I even had a first draft, and to George for not ratting me out when I was writing at work. You're all awesome.

And finally, to the best, most wonderful, most supportive critique partners—I'm so lucky to have stumbled across the bunch of you. Without you ladies I never would have made it past chapter 6, and on the *very* off-chance I did, I would have ended up with a quite different and much worse story. Carolyn, Kathryne, and Janet—I owe you. Big time.

The Author

BORN IN PHILADELPHIA, COURTNEY J. HALL'S WRITING CAREER began when she figured out how much fun it was to make words rhyme. She has since gone on to publish embarrassingly bad poetry and melodramatic short stories and has written beginnings to at least a half-dozen novels. Since June 2008, her writing has been steadily improving thanks to the Pennwriters Area 6 critique group, of which she is an active member.

Courtney lives with her husband in Media, Pennsylvania. *Some Rise by Sin*, a historical romance that takes place at the tumultuous end of Mary Tudor's reign, is her first novel.

THIS BOOK WAS TYPESET USING GARAMOND, A BODY FONT DATing from the sixteenth century, with headings in Bickham Script Pro to evoke the style of Elizabethan handwriting and Tudor roses derived from Monotype Sorts. The "abstract roses" opposite the title page come from Brian Kent's Faux Snow, a freeware font available via the Internet and permitted for commercial use.

www.ingramcontent.com/pod-product-compliance
Lightning Source LLC
Chambersburg PA
CBHW030817090426
42737CB00009B/760